Seven Logics of Sculpture

Apollonius (attr.), *Belvedere Torso*, 1st century BC, Rome; copy of Greek bronze, c. 2nd century BC

Didier Vermeiren, *Place*, 1994

Ernst van Alphen

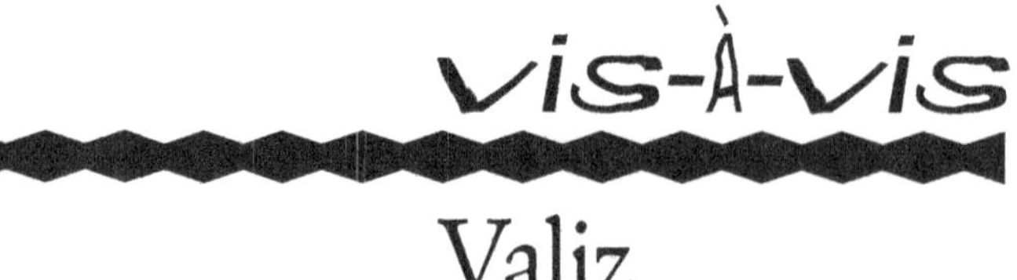

Valiz

Seven Logics of Sculpture

Encountering Objects Through the Senses

Contents

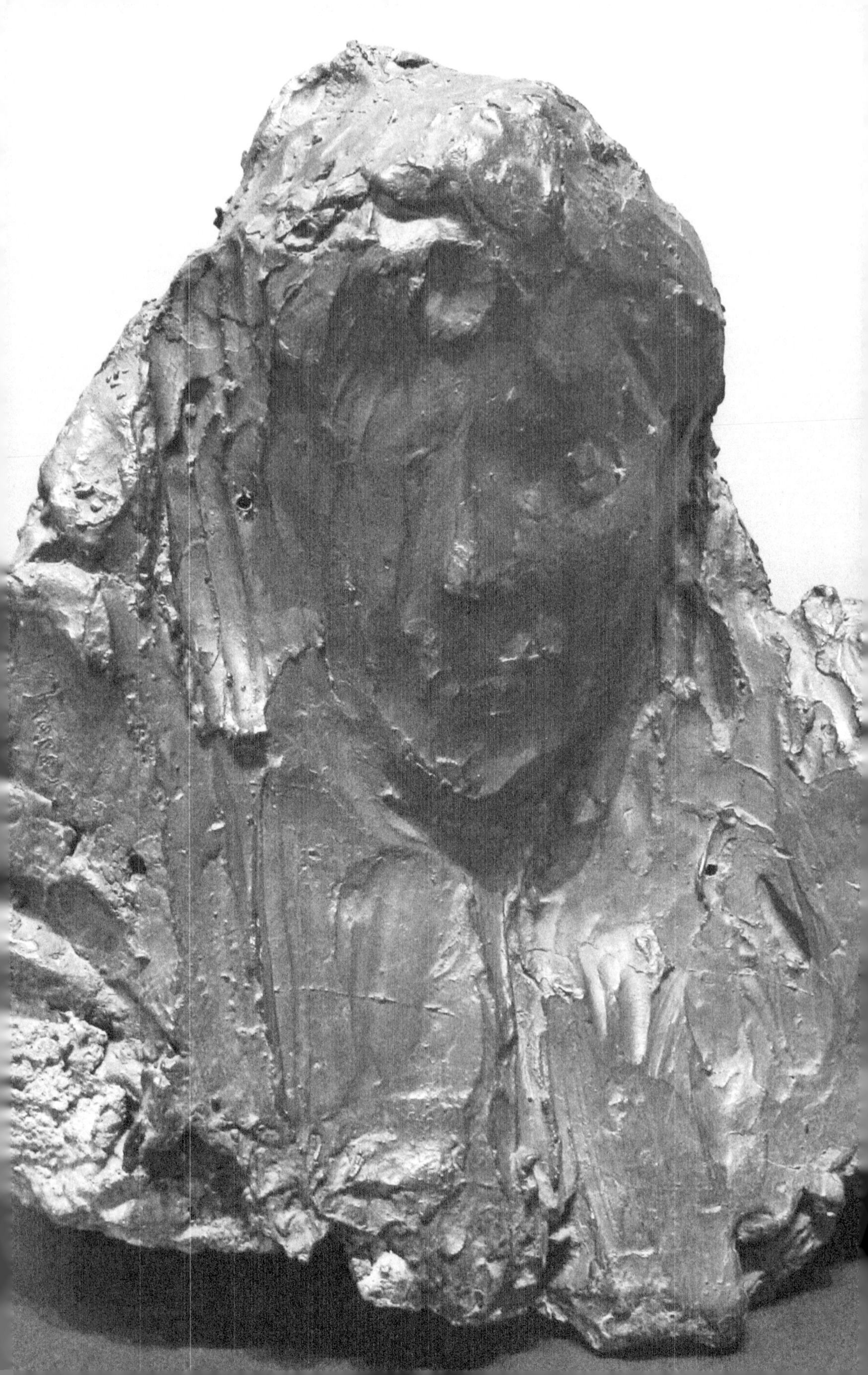

Introduction

Logics of Sculpture

Pygmalion, or the Birth of Sculpture

For centuries, the Greek mythical story of Pygmalion and Galatea has served as an assessment of the nature of sculpture. Let me begin by telling this story, which grants a special role to the sense of touch. The legendary figure Pygmalion, king of Cyprus but also a sculptor, is said to have fallen in love with a statue he had carved of Galatea. It was not just seeing the sculpted body which made him fall in love, but touching it. The story is widely known in its Latin version of Ovid's prose poem in *Metamorphoses*. This is what Ovid writes:

> Often he ran his hands over the work, feeling to see
> whether it was flesh
> or ivory, and would not yet admit that ivory was all it
> was. He kissed the
> statue, and imagined that it kissed him back, spoke to it
> and embraced

Medardo Rosso, *Madame Noblet*, 1897

> it, and thought he felt his fingers sink into the limbs he
> touched, so that
> he was afraid lest a bruise appear where he had pressed
> the flesh.[1]

Pygmalion's relationship to his sculpture is highly physical and verges on the erotic. It is due to this physical and sensorial relationship that the sculpted body of Galatea comes to life, although literally it is in response to Pygmalion's prayers for Venus to let the statue come alive. In the words of Douglas Bauer: 'That the ivory statue melted to life under the loving touch of Pygmalion is surely the most significant feature of his (Ovid's) story and the one on which this entire allegory hinges.'[2]

> When Pygmalion returned home, he made straight for the statue of the girl he loved, leaned over the couch, and kissed her. She seemed warm: he laid his lips on her again, and touched her breast with his hands: at his touch the ivory lost its hardness, and grew soft: his fingers made an imprint on the yielding surface, just as wax of Hymettos melts in the sun and, worked by men's fingers, is fashioned into many different shapes, and made fit for the use by being used.[3]

On the basis of Ovid's story, Victor Stoichita concludes that the figurative sculpted body is transformed into flesh by feeling, touching, caressing, and kissing; in other words, through erotic touch.[4]

To better understand what this mythical story tells us about sculpture, I will bring in another mythical story, also narrated by Ovid in his *Metamorphoses*; namely, the Narcissus story. This myth, however, is not about the nature of sculpture, but the nature and origin of painting. In his

Ovid, *Metamorphoses*, Book I, quoted in Paraskos, 'Bringing into Being', p. 62; Bauer, 'The Function of Pygmalion in the Metamorphoses of Ovid', p. 21.

Bauer, 'The Function of Pygmalion in the Metamorphoses of Ovid', p. 21.

Ovid, *Metamorphoses*, Book I, quoted in Paraskos, 'Bringing into Being', p. 64.

Stoichita, *The Pygmalion Effect*, p. 14.

book *On Painting*, artist and writer Vasari called Narcissus 'the inventor of painting'.

> I say among my friends that Narcissus who was changed into a flower, according to the poets, was the inventor of painting. Since painting is already the flower of every art, the story of Narcissus is most to the point. What else can you call painting, but a similar embracing with art of what is presented on the surface of the water in the fountain?[5]

The idea that Narcissus invented painting is rather surprising given that nowadays we predominantly know of Narcissus through Sigmund Freud's interpretation; the emblematic figure of self-love. But in the Narcissus story touch also plays an important role, albeit a negative one. Ovid's Narcissus story is usually read as a moral tale about the avoidance of touch and the failure to touch. In his short life, he is touched by no one and touches nobody.[6] Narcissus is traditionally seen as the fool who fell in love with himself, but in fact he was cursed by the gods for the specific reason that he refused to accept the physical touch of other people.

> 'Many youths and many maidens sought his love; but, in that slender form was pride so cold that no youth, no maiden touched his heart.' In response to the loving gestures of the nymph Echo, Narcissus retorts: 'Hands off! Embrace me not! May I die before I give you power over me.'[7]

For Narcissus, touch is a force or a form of violence, which is understandable because he was born into the world as the outcome of the violent rape of his mother Liriope by the river-god Cephissus. His self-love was the only alternative for a situation in which the touch of other people was taboo.

5 Leon Battista Alberti, *On Painting* (1435), 64; quoted in Kenaan, 'Touching Sculpture', p. 49.

6 Kenaan, 'Touching Sculpture', p. 47.

7 Kenaan, 'Touching Sculpture', p. 47.

Paraskos, 'Bringing into eing', p. 63.

Ovid, *Metamorphoses*, III, 420.

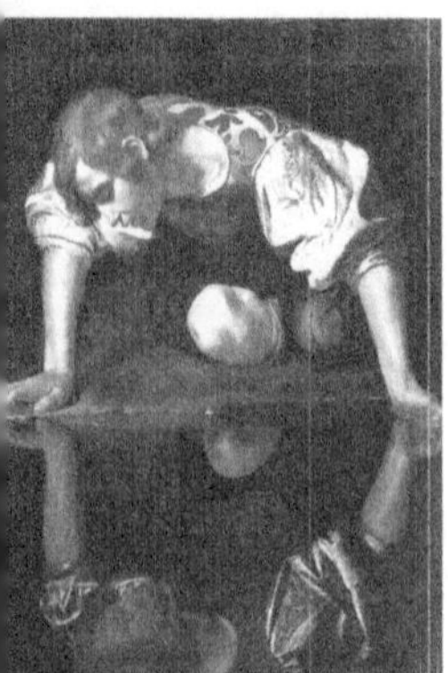
ichelangelo Merisi da aravaggio, *Narcissus*, 1597–1599

Thus, it was not the cause but the effect of his dramatic situation.

In contrast with Narcissus, the Pygmalion story has a happy ending. Pygmalion begins at first as someone 'who is revolted by the daughters of Propoetus who had been punished for insulting Aphrodite by being turned into the first prostitutes'.[8] As a result, Pygmalion will never touch them because he rejects physical love from then on. Whereas Narcissus and Pygmalion begin their lives with a refusal of touch, the latter is saved from this sad destiny by the physicality and tactility of sculpture, which he cannot resist touching.

But how can the refusal of touch and tactility result in the invention of painting? Narcissus is affected by his own image and falls in love with it; that image is his reflection in the water, a mirror image of him. But in between Narcissus and his image, there is a plane. The surface of the water separates the Narcissus who looks and the Narcissus who is looked at. The plane, as well as mirroring, is transparent. The visual drama of Narcissus, his attentive looking, demonstrates the existence of such a plane, which is at once illusionary and real.

> Thus, Narcissus not only surrenders to a visual illusion, not only falls in love with an object that turns out to be an image, but in doing this he also ends up making the dramatic discovery of a concealed region hidden between the object and its reflection. With Narcissus a new kind of human look is born—a deliberate gaze that in its deep sorrow, can see beyond the object-form of what appears: 'his tears ruffled the water, and dimly the image came back from the troubled pool'.[9] What Narcissus sees for the first time is the inner layer of the

> field of visual appearances—a discovery that indeed inaugurates the possibility of painting.[10]

What Narcissus's visual illusion tells us, according to Kenaan, is that the visuality of painting can open up to the viewer only on the condition that the eye forgets the claims of the body. 'The body of the exemplary viewer is thus one that neither moves nor touches. It assumes a given perspective, takes the form of a fixed point of view.'[11] This condition makes illusion possible by separating and thus singling out the pictorial world. It also marks a threshold which our body can never cross.

But as already mentioned, our experience of sculpture is very different with respect to the role of the viewer's body. The viewer is not separated from the pictorial world a painting gives access to, but viewer and sculpture partake of the same world or dimension. This does not mean that sculpture is real instead of imaginative, however. Sculpture plays with the imagination in a different way to painting.

> Whereas illusionistic painting plays with the possibility of simulating depth or objecthood on a flat surface, sculpture plays with the possibility of finding life in formed matter. In other words, while paintings invite us to enter their world, sculptures are experienced through the possibility that they will enter and become active in our world.[12]

It is precisely because sculptures enter and become active in the world of the viewer that the viewer's body does not become separated, taking instead an active role in imaginatively relating to them.

This conceptual distinction between sculpture and painting is especially important for languages like German

10 Kenaan, 'Touching Sculpture', pp. 49–50.

11 Kenaan, 'Touching Sculpture', p. 49.

12 Kenaan, 'Touching Sculpture', p. 54.

and Dutch, in which the same expression is used for images such as painting, drawing, photography, and sculpture, namely *Bild* and *beeld*. Whereas English has the two different words 'image' and 'sculpture', the conflation of the two in one expression suggests that there is also no conceptual distinction between an image and a sculpture. This is a big mistake, one that seriously complicates the appreciation and understanding of sculpture.

Herder, or the Aesthetics of Sculpture

The two mythical stories of Pygmalion and Narcissus offer a perspective on sculpture and, differentially, also on painting which is still relevant today. But one could say that the notions of sculpture and painting at stake in these myths are very dated. Since the beginning of the twentieth century, a sculpture is no longer just a sculpted human body; painting is no longer by definition an illusionary, three-dimensional world. But what is most interesting about these two myths is that they dramatize and plot not only the sculpted or painted object, but also the viewer, their body, and how they relate to these objects. They thematize and embody the kind of look that is conditioned by these objects. Hence, we can still learn from these old mythical tales.

The Pygmalion story makes clear that the sensorial body of the viewer plays a decisive role in the 'aliveness' of sculpture. And only when a sculpture is 'alive' can it 'enter our world' as an imaginative object or being. The tactility of sculptures makes them 'touchable', and only on that condition can they become alive. This mythical narrative is allegorical and we should not take it literally. To give one simple example: we are not supposed to touch sculptures; we are supposed to walk around them and look at them. And sculptures are made of dead matter, whatever material they are made from, and can never come to life. So, what does touch mean, in this respect? And how does it make sculpture alive? To answer those questions, I will first survey the work of German philosopher Johann Gottfried Herder, author of one of the first aesthetic theories completely devoted to sculpture: *Sculpture: Some Observations on Shape and Form from Pygmalion's Creative Dream* (1778).

It is telling that Herder refers to the Pygmalion story in the subtitle of his aesthetics of sculpture. He writes the following in reference to this mythical story:

> A statue must *live*: its flesh must come to life, its face and expression must speak. We must believe that we touch it and feel that it warms our hands.[13]

13 Herder, 'Von der Bildhauerkunst fürs Gefühl', p. 88.

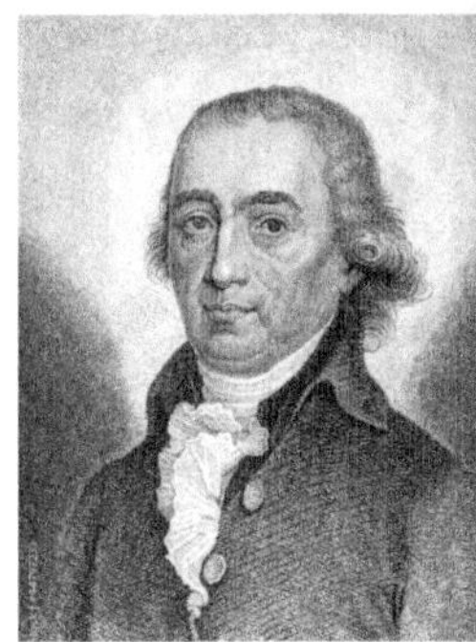

Unknown artist, Johann Gottfried von Herder, 1859

It is the second sentence that is especially important, because it introduces a phenomenological point of view on sculpture: 'We must believe that we touch it and feel that it warms our hands.' So, Galatea does not literally come to life, but she comes to live sensorily through the senses of the beholder: in the eye of the viewer, Pygmalion's Galatea is alive. It also implies that Herder does not understand sculpture in a formal way, in terms of its mass, solidity, volume, and more, but as a belief or illusion activated in the viewer of sculpture. This belief on the side of the viewer seems to imply that sculpture should be realistic, and that only mimesis of the real world, or of human bodies, can create this belief in the viewer. But that is not necessarily the case. As it turns out, in Herder's sculptural aesthetics more importance is placed on a specific mode of looking being activated, a so-called tactile look.

This suggests that Galatea can only come to life when she is endowed with the sense of touch; only then does she

4 On Baumgarten, see Hlobil, 'Alexander Gottlieb Baumgarten'.

5 Gaiger, 'Introduction' to Herder, *Sculpture*, p. 7.

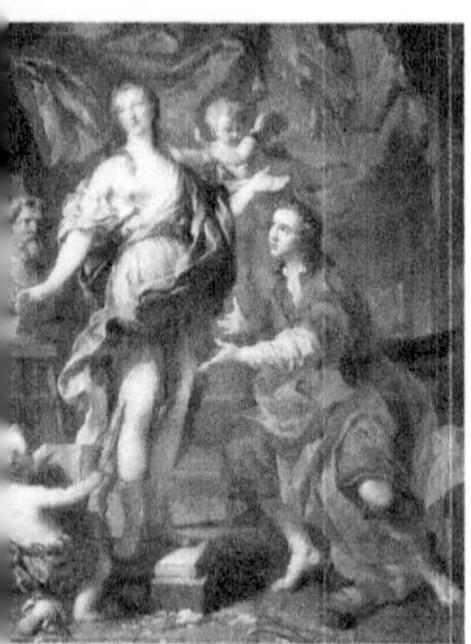

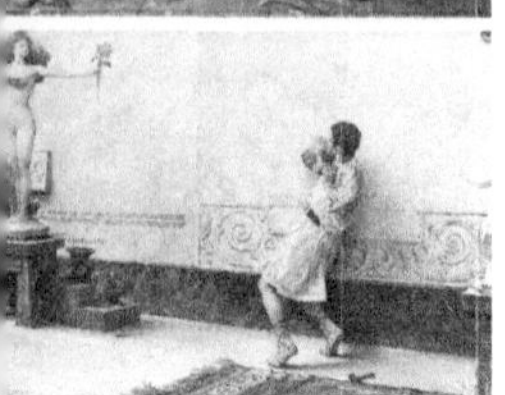

François Lemoyne, *Pygmalion voyant sa statue animée*, 1927; Giulio Bargellini, *Pygmalion*, 1896

become conscious of itself/herself as something different from its/her own representation. And from a phenomenological point of view, it suggests that the viewer should not just touch sculptures (and close their eyes in doing so); the viewer should coordinate the sense of sight with the sense of touch and develop a capacity for *spatial seeing*. It is this spatial seeing that can process visual data in terms of three-dimensional objects.

Herder developed his sculptural aesthetics in response to another German philosopher whom he enormously admired: Alexander Gottlieb Baumgarten. Baumgarten had developed a 'science of sensible knowledge' in his *Aesthetica*.[14] In his time, such a project was highly original and almost a provocation because knowledge gained through the senses was distrusted in the rationalist tradition. Sensible knowledge was seen as unreliable and could not serve as a secure basis for knowledge. Baumgarten still made the conventional distinction between things that are known by the mind (*noeta*) and things that are perceived by the senses (*aistheta*), but he evaluated this distinction in a very different way:

> Where he departs from his predecessors, however, is in suggesting that just as there is a discipline of 'logic' that is concerned with the operations of reason, so there ought to be a new discipline of 'aesthetics' that is concerned with what is learned through the senses. Whereas logic analyzes complex ideas into simple parts, the new science of aesthetics is directed toward the plenitude and complexity of sensations.[15]

The significance of Baumgarten for Herder's thinking was great, but in some respects, the latter radicalizes the former. For instance, when Baumgarten proposed aesthetics as a second domain of inquiry alongside logic, Herder argued that this new 'science' had important consequences for logic itself.

'For Herder, a theory of ideas conceived in abstraction from the operations of the senses must necessarily be deficient.'[16]

Herder had three more specific points of criticism on Baumgarten, which were important for his project of developing an aesthetics of sculpture. First, and in line with his more general criticism just mentioned, for Herder the senses do not provide merely raw data to be worked through by the operations of reason. Rather, they provide our fundamental modes of access to the world, actively disclosing things in a way that merits the closest philosophical attention.[17] Second, according to Herder, Baumgarten conceives the discipline of aesthetics in too general a fashion, for he neglects the specific characteristics of each of the five senses and, as a result, fails to reflect upon the differences between the arts and the media through which they operate. Each of the various art forms such as poetry, painting, sculpture, and music relates in a different way to the five senses and each art calls for its own independent study. For Herder, this criticism opens the possibility to write an independent study on the art of sculpture and to specify a sculptural aesthetic.[18] Herder's third criticism concerns Baumgarten's point that the discipline of aesthetics should also fulfil an educative role. For Herder, however, aesthetics should not provide rules or instructions to artists for what they must do but, conversely, must remain a descriptive discipline.

> Its task is to discover the laws of art and beauty through observation and reflection. Not to direct us toward the right or appropriate way of doing things. [...] Aesthetics should enable us to recover the complex web of experiences that informs our most primitive concepts and to locate the origin of those concepts in the activity of the senses.[19]

16 Gaiger, 'Introduction', p. 8.

17 Gaiger, 'Introduction', p. 9.

18 Using expressions like 'the soul of sculpture', Herder's discourse initially looks rather idealistic. But the soul is defined internally as that which animates and gives life to matter and material presence. And that animation happens in and through the senses. So, due to this unexpected definition of th soul, Herder's aesthetics take distance from idealism and can be seen as a kind of phenomenology *avant la lettre*. See Benjamin, 'To Touch'.

19 Gaiger, 'Introduction', p. 1

Sight without Touch, Touch without Sight

0 Herder, ‘Über die schöne unst des Gefühls’, p. 94.

1 Gaiger, ‘Introduction’, p. 15.

Of great importance to Herder’s project of developing a sculptural aesthetics was Diderot’s *Letter on the Blind for the Use of Those Who Can See* (1749). This essay, in the form of a letter to an anonymous addressee, ‘madam’, contrasts the perceptual and sensory experiences of the blind with the experiences of those who have sight. Diderot concludes that the blind do not know a concept of beauty and cannot make aesthetic judgments. Herder opposes this conclusion vehemently. He takes issue with Diderot’s suggestion that the concept of beauty is restricted to objects of vision alone. He argues, for example, that ‘the blind can take genuine, immediate pleasure in beautiful touch’, and describes the beauty of touch as follows:

> The sense of touch perceives only bodies; the sense of sight only surfaces. What then is beauty for the sense of touch? It is not colours! Nor is it light and shadow. [it is] bodies![20]

Herder reverses Diderot’s central question. He does not ask: What can the blind perceive without the use of sight? But rather: What could the sighted perceive without the use of touch?

> What could we actually see if we had been permanently deprived of the ability to grasp things with our hands and to intervene physically in the world through our own bodies? His [Herder’s] answer to this is: far less than most of us think.[21]

Herder argues that we gain awareness of three-dimensional space through the sense of touch and that concepts such as solidity, mass, volume, and depth cannot be derived from vision alone.[22] Animals such as fish, birds, and horses are creatures without hands; they cannot grasp things or touch them. As a result, they cannot know the world as human beings do.

> Our knowledge of the world, even when we simply look upon it, is fundamentally codetermined by our tactile knowledge of volume and mass, and by the kinesthetic experience of touching and manipulating bodies in the round. Sight on its own can give us access only to surfaces, that is, to images arranged on a plane. Bodies, or three-dimensional forms, are first revealed to us through our sense of touch.[23]

Herder concludes that the privileging of sight above touch has resulted in a neglect of what distinguishes sculpture from painting. Sculpture obeys very different laws and principles of perception, which is why we should not talk about the visual arts in general or subsume sculpture under painting (still common practice in twenty-first-century museums). To conclude, one can see Herder's sculptural aesthetics as an attempt to rehabilitate the sense of touch and to defend its legitimate claims over the sense of sight. The viewer looking at sculpture should coordinate the sense of sight with the sense of touch and acknowledge the crucial role of touch in sight. Sculptural form can only be appreciated when we acknowledge the contribution of tactile knowledge to sight. Herder describes beautifully how tactile knowledge is activated when looking at sculpture:

> The eye that gathers impressions is no longer the eye that sees a depiction on a surface; it becomes a hand, the ray of light becomes a finger and the imagination becomes a form of immediate touching.[24]

22 Gaiger, 'Introduction', p. 15

23 Gaiger, 'Introduction', p. 15

24 Herder, *Viertes Wäldchen*, p. 64.

In the eighteenth century, it became common to distinguish five different arts: poetry, painting, sculpture, music, and architecture. Herder argued that each art has its own aesthetics, because it depends on a different sensorial 'logic'. At first it seems strange, or contradictory, to call this a sensorial logic because rational knowledge was produced by the discipline of logic and sensorial knowledge by aesthetics. But, as explained above, it was Herder who had deconstructed this opposition in his critique of Baumgarten by arguing that the new 'science' of aesthetics had important consequences for the old science of logic itself. Thus, the two sciences are, or should be, in many respects entangled, making it possible to speak of a sensorial logic and a logic of sculpture. The logic of sculpture differs, then, from the sensorial logics of painting, music, poetry, and architecture.

Herder's Relevance for Understanding Contemporary Sculpture

5 Herder, Sculpture, p. 60.

Herder wrote his sculptural aesthetics in the second half of the eighteenth century, when Neoclassicism was the dominant movement and the first signs of Romanticism manifested themselves. He was critical of Neoclassicism, deeming it too normative in its imposition of all kinds of rules on sculpture, and its inspiration not from its own time, but from the past; it sustained the illusion 'that we should live in *another* time, among a *different* people under a *different* sky'.[25] His criticism of the privileging of sight in his time, which the shift from touch to vision entailed, impels him to 'recover the tactile experience that lies at the basis of antique sculpture'. As a result, all the examples discussed in his *Sculpture: Some Observations on Shape and Form from Pygmalion's Creative*

Dream are classical. He discusses works like the *Belvedere Torso*, now in the Vatican Museums, the *Borghese Gladiator* from the Louvre, the famous *Laocoön* sculpture, also in the Vatican Museums, *Castor and Pollux* in the Museo del Prado in Madrid, and many others. He also refers to a great number of classical authors such as Ovid, Homer, Virgil, and Pliny and to authors of later periods, such as Shakespeare and Milton. The framework he imposes on his sculptural aesthetics is general and historical (although utterly Western, as was usual in those days). But as general as this aesthetic was intended to be, it was based on a very specific notion of the human body, namely that the human body is a unity and is complete. His classical examples of sculpture are informed by the Greek concept of *kalokagathia*, meaning the unity of inner and outer perfection, or of beauty and morality. The human body is a perfect unity not only because it is more than an assemblage of body parts and limbs, but also because its outer appearance and inner world of emotions and passions cannot be distinguished.

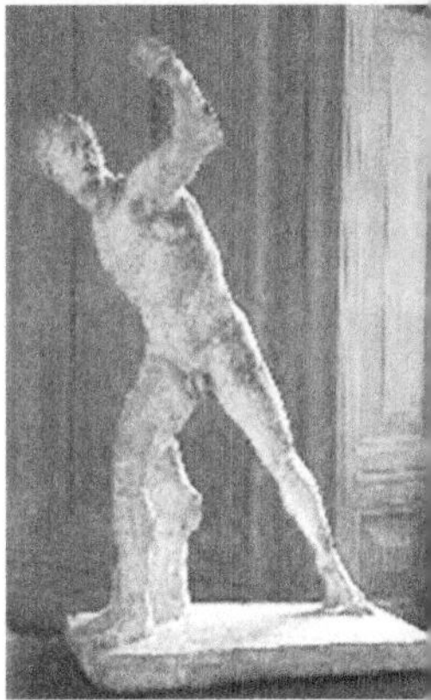

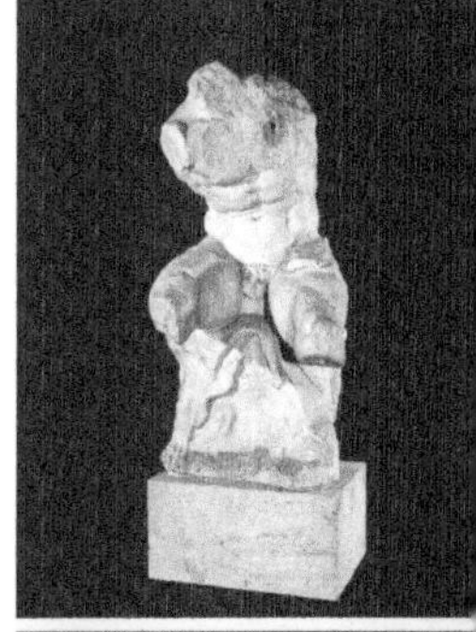

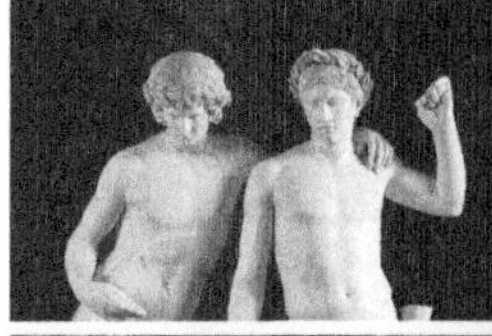

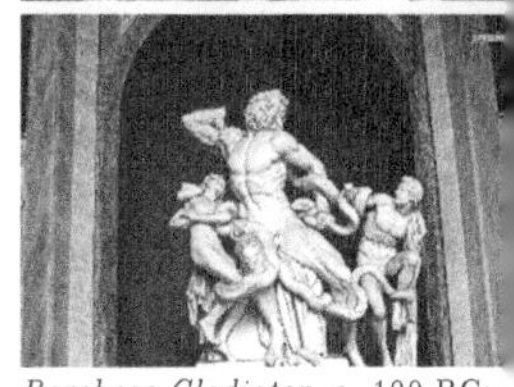

Borghese Gladiator, c. 100 BC; *Belvedere Torso*, 1st century BC; *Castor and Pollux*, 1st century AD; *Laocoön and His Sons*, 40–20 BC

The mimetic ideal of the imitation of beautiful nature (human bodies in the case of sculpture) was challenged at the end of the nineteenth century and the early twentieth century. Figurative sculpture, the only kind of sculpture Herder knew, was no longer the rule. Of course, although artists like Constantin Brancusi and Jean Arp no longer represented the human body, it was still evoked by their abstract forms. But with the rise of Minimalism, even the evocation of the human body was cancelled in the most radical ways. Instead of the sculptural body, and its formal and syntactical characteristics, what became important was the relation between the sculptural object, the space it occupies, and the viewer. This suggests that with the decline of figurative sculpture Herder's aesthetics of sculpture also lost its relevance. For the human

26 Jędrzejczyk, 'The Corporality of Form', p. 39.

27 Gaiger, 'Introduction', p. 27.

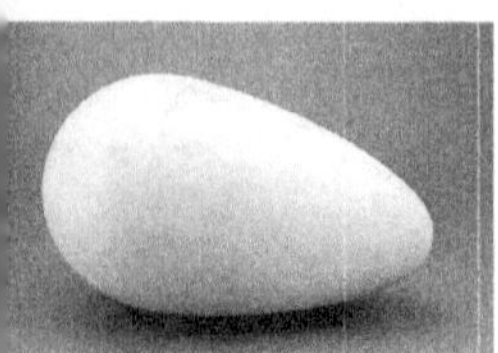

Constantin Brancusi, *Sculpture for the Blind*, c. 1920

body as an emblem of inner and outer perfection is no longer credible. But this conclusion would imply a fundamental misunderstanding of Herder's notion of sculpture. His aesthetics is not determined by his examples of classical sculpture, but by the role of the perceiving body, the viewer's that is. Herder's analysis of the sensorial logic activated in the viewer standing in front of freestanding objects enables an investigation of our affective responses to those objects. Herder's notion of sculpture can be recognized in how Małgorzata Jędrzejczyk defines sculpture when writing about the Polish artist Katarzyna Kobro (whose work I will discuss in the chapter 'Sculpting Space'). Sculpture is:

> A three-dimensional body among other three-dimensional bodies, eliciting a particular kind of response from the onlooker in terms of sensation—including the embodied act of perception, which is rooted in the onlooker's physicality, and in a sense, constitutes itself through the onlooker's corporality.[26]

Throughout this book I will use this notion of sculpture.

One could even argue that Herder's understanding of the sensorial, perceiving body 'offers a remarkable anticipation of some of the ideas that helped to generate these new forms of sculptural practice'.[27] This suggests that Herder's work is as relevant for us in the twenty-first century as it was for the eighteenth century.

An iconic sculpture that thematizes the importance of touch in looking at sculpture is Constantin Brancusi's *Sculpture for the Blind* (c. 1920). The title of the work, of which three versions exist, was given by Brancusi himself and is clearly a reference to Diderot's aforementioned text. The title indicates that he associated the simple, egg-like form with blindness, and subsequently with tactile reception.

The work was not conceived to be felt with the hands. It is not only a simple, perfect form but also a conceptual articulation of the importance of touch in looking at sculpture.

The perceiving body looking at freestanding objects is entangled in these objects; they should be distinguished but not separated. This idea, which is Herder's, guided me in writing the following chapters of this book. It is literally at stake in sculptural works of the Arte Povera movement. One could say that in these cases Herder's aesthetics is an anticipation of the central issue in the following works by Jannis Kounellis, Giuseppe Penone, and Joseph Beuys, who does not really belong to this movement. Their works not only foreground the importance of touch, but also sound and smell.

The work *Untitled* (1968) by Jannis Kounellis consists of four poles covered with wool. The work has no title, which is significant in this case. The artist does not want to represent anything or to convey meaning; he wants to activate a sensorial experience in the viewer. These 'totems' are tactile, visual, and spatial at the same time, but it is their tactility which is truly remarkable—whereas in most sculpture, qualities such as solidity, mass, volume, and depth cannot be derived from vision and depend on the sense of touch, this work radicalizes the general phenomenological characteristic of sculpture. The viewer experiences first of all the woollen body that covers the totems and is inclined to touch it. Kounellis calls his works 'vital figures', their vitality comparable to Pygmalion's sculpture of Galatea, which did not literally come to life, but had a vitality bestowed on her by the sensorial body of Pygmalion.

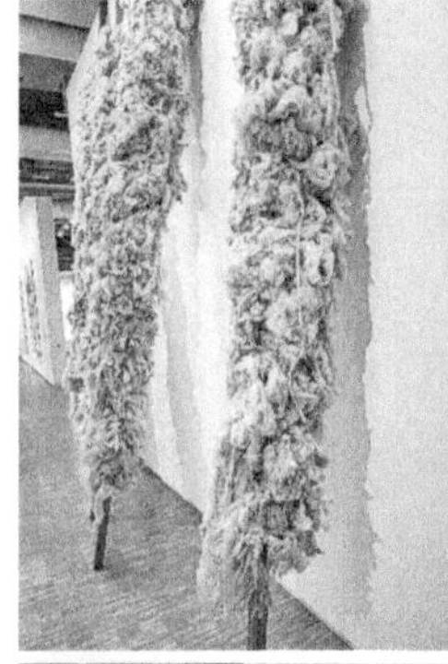

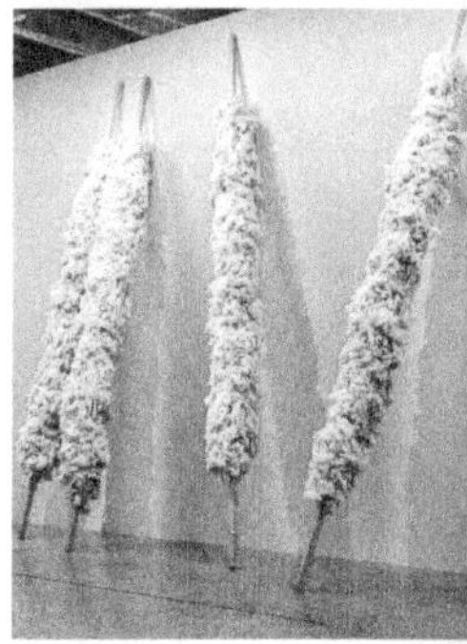

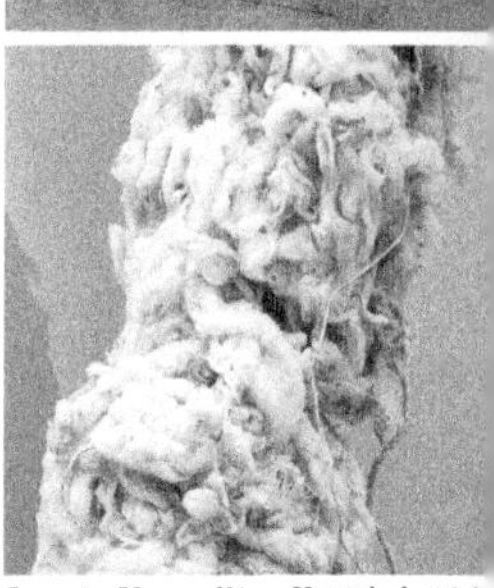

Jannis Kounellis, *Untitled*, 196

The sensorial body of the viewer is in yet other ways the central element of Joseph Beuys's *Plight* (1985) and Giuseppe Penone's *Respirare l'ombra* (1999–2000). For the work *Plight*,

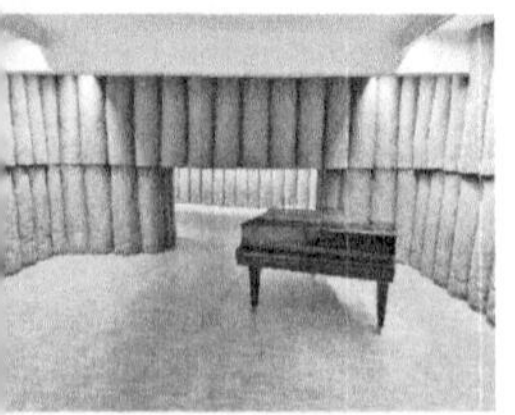
oseph Beuys, *Plight*, 1985

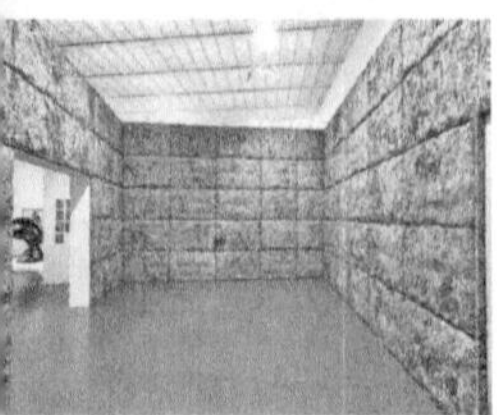

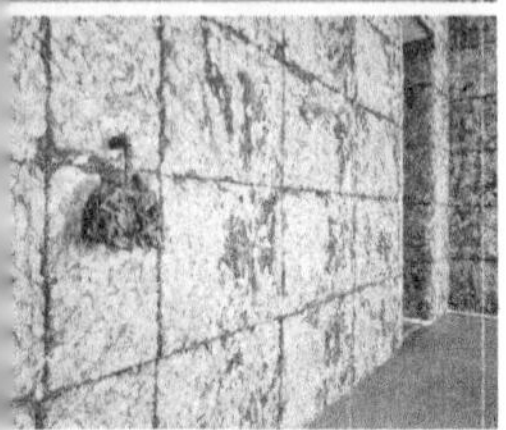
iuseppe Penone, *Respirare ombra*, 1999–2000

Beuys covered the space with roles of felt, with thermal and acoustic insolation an important quality of this material. The acoustic insulation is foregrounded by the closed piano and a blackboard with a musical staff without notes, the thermal insulation by a thermometer (both on top of the piano). When the viewer enters the space not only sight, but all other senses are called upon. Experiences of silence and isolation, but also warmth and protection are activated in the visitor of this space. Penone's *Respirare l'ombra* activates yet another sense, smell. The walls are covered with laurel leaves; against one of the walls hangs a sculpture of lungs, also covered with laurel leaves. The predominant sensorial experience of this sculptural space is smell, yet the other senses are also involved. Life and vitality are evoked by the lungs; human beings but also plants breathe and are alive. But as we have learned from the Pygmalion myth, this aliveness depends on the sensorial body of the viewer.

The three sculptural works discussed do not only activate touch and sight, but also smell and hearing. One could say that they radicalize Herder's notion of sculpture as depending on a viewer who not only sees but touches, not literally but embedded within sight. As extreme examples they make the point of the entanglement of the viewer's sensorial body, the sculptural object, and the space where both are located.

Classical Sculpture, or the Origin of Western Sculpture

To understand the prevalent Western sculptural traditions, those of classical and Neoclassical sculpture, the Greek concept of *kalokagathia* is of crucial importance. As already explained, it means the unity of inner and outer perfection, or the beauty of outer appearance or form, and morality which is an inner quality, located in the mind or psyche. This unity implies that the outer appearance and the inner world of emotions and passions cannot be distinguished.

This notion of the human body provides at the same time a notion of sculpture, because for the Greeks and the Romans sculptures mainly represented the human body. This notion provides the key to how the viewer should look at sculpture and give meaning to it. The meaning of a sculpted body relies on the illusion of a sculpture's inner essence, responsible for the outer appearance. The skeleton or the muscles under the skin determine the look of it. Or from a psychological point of view, the mood, emotion, or passion is expressed on the skin or as exteriority. The meaning of a sculpted body is located in its inner essence but can be read on the surface.

Classical sculpture acquires this outer form as a direct expression of an inner centre or previous meaning, an inner experience or structure. For example, the experience of pain is expressed in a specific physiognomically recognizable appearance of the body. Expression, such as rage, is translated into yet another outward appearance, another gesture or physiognomic expression. The work of German eighteenth-century sculptor Franz Xaver Messerschmidt is probably the most radical or excessive example of sculpture in which the outer form is an expression of an inner experience or personality. Messerschmidt made so-called 'character heads', busts with faces contorted in extreme facial expressions.

In his writings on art and aesthetics, the German thinker Georg Simmel articulates the sculptural duality between outer appearance and inner essence in the more general artistic terms of form versus content. In his essay 'Michelangelo and the Metaphysics of Culture', Simmel argues that the

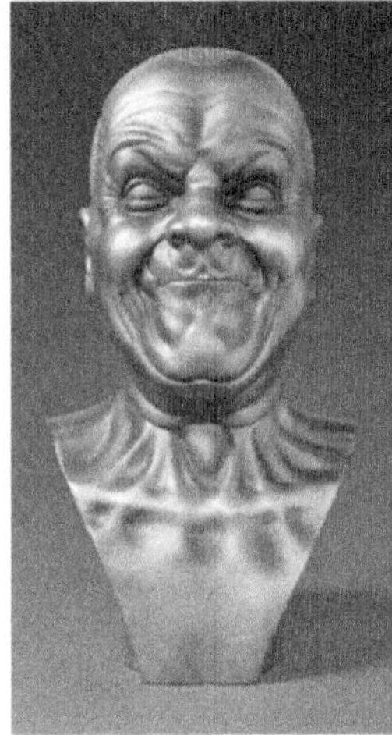

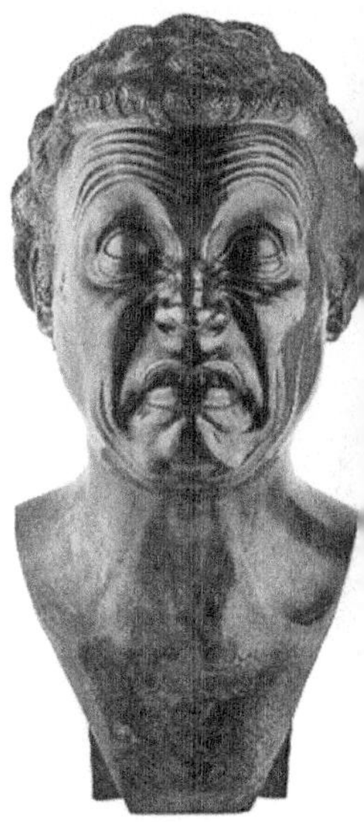

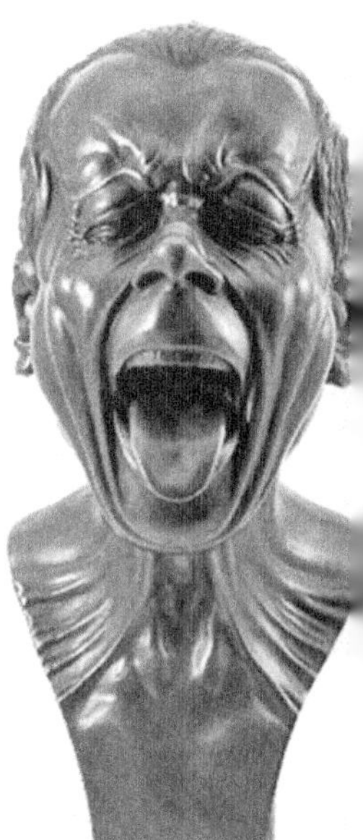

Franz Xaver Messerschmidt, *Character Heads*, 1770–1783

8 Simmel, 'Michelangelo and
ːe Metaphysics of Culture',
. 285.

9 Simmel, 'Michelangelo and
ːe Metaphysics of Culture',
. 287.

dualities defining Michelangelo's sculpture reflect human dualities. Dualities become antagonisms, which in the case of Michelangelo's sculptures are overcome.

> In Michelangelo this occurs in the synthesis of an antagonism more fearsome and portentous than anything else in art history. Physical gravity dragging the body downward now stands over against a countervailing impulse of movement of the soul. Every movement of our limbs shows at any instant the state of this struggle.[28]
>
> [...] gravity seizes upwardly aspiring energy itself and drives down to the deepest seat of all impulses opposing or cancelling it, repressing them from the outset. And yet this burdensome mass, this palpable heaviness, is countered and animated in its innermost being by spiritual impulses struggling for freedom and light.[29]

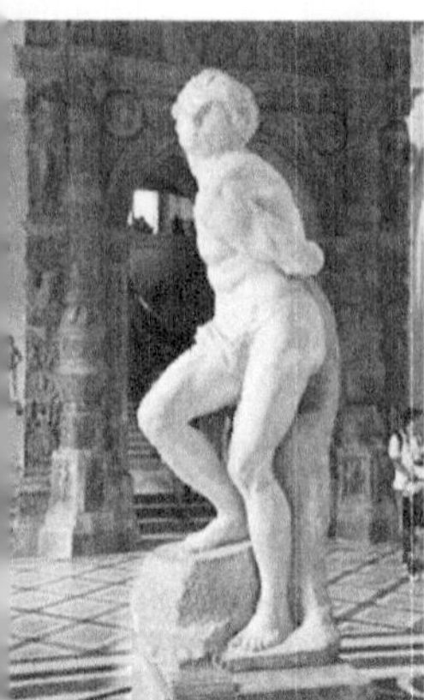

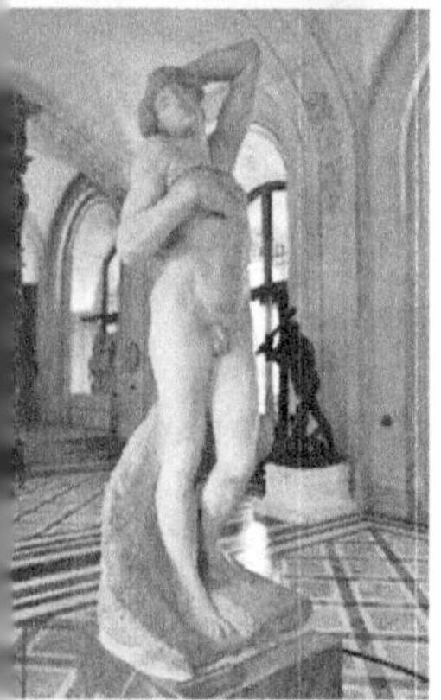

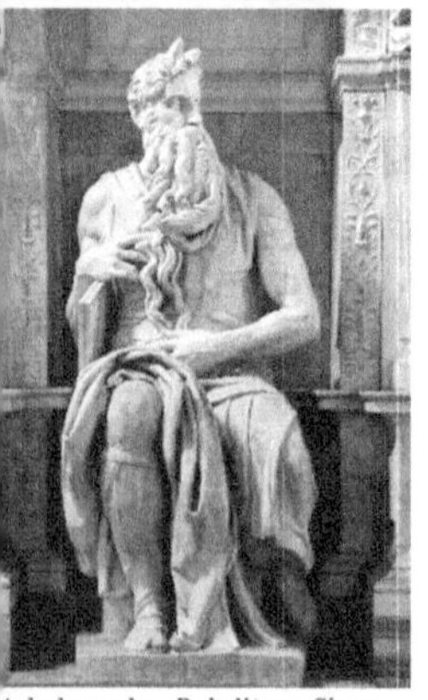

ichelangelo, *Rebellious Slave*,
13; *Dying Slave*, 1513–1516;
oses, 1513–1515

In Simmel's writing, the human struggle is at the same time the struggle between the weight, the gravity of the massive stone out of which the sculpture is made, and its meaning sculpted out of that stone. Two movements determine this struggle: the weight of stone pulls the sculpture downwards, but the movement of the soul (its meaning) goes upwards. It is in the struggle that the sculpture becomes alive.

And according to Herder, this gravity is not seen by the viewer but is felt by the viewer's sensorial body. For Simmel, it is not just the meaning of form, but also of movement, or rather of the form of movement, that distinguishes Michelangelo's sculpture from classical sculpture:

> The fusion of all dualistic elements in an unprecedented perceptual unity of life—unprecedented inasmuch as the ancient world's unity was more a naïve absence of

> differentiation, not deeply conscious of any such deep unreconciled antitheses of existence—finds further expression in the relation between form and movement in Michelangelo's figures. How a figure moves shows its psychic life unfold, and the naturally given form of its substance registers the flux of its psychic impulses. [...] Only in Michelangelo's characters do we feel a unity of the given corporeal form breaking into this particular current gesture as its visible logical consequence, for which only this particular body can be the substrate.[30]

30 Simmel, 'Michelangelo and the Metaphysics of Culture', p. 283.

In Simmel's writing on Michelangelo's figures, the analysis of sculpture and human existence are completely entangled. This entanglement is significant and necessary because it is enabled by a notion of sculpture that relates, in the most intimate and subtle way, outer appearance to inner essence.

This outer appearance and inner essence relation leads to sculpture being 'lonely'. Compared to other artistic media like painting or poetry, 'sculpture is the form best adapted to expressing beings complete in themselves and balanced in all their moments'.

> Yet precisely in the capacity of sculpture to give purest representation to self-sufficient, impeccable, inwardly balanced existence, it becomes engulfed by a cool shadowlike solitude, never lifted by any turn of fortune. This solitude of sculpture in general is of course something very different from any solitude of a represented subject—just as the beauty of a work of art need not owe anything to the beauty of its object.[31]

31 Simmel, 'Michelangelo and the Metaphysics of Culture', p. 284.

Sculpture is self-enclosed and self-sufficient, which has implications for how the viewer relates to it. Although it needs the sensorial body of the viewer to be alive, it exists

32 Simmel, 'Michelangelo and the Metaphysics of Culture', 290.

33 Simmel, 'Michelangelo and the Metaphysics of Culture', 290.

independently. Self-sufficiency cannot be recognized in the more recent artistic medium of installation. Installation art needs the viewer not just sensorially, but as an active subject walking through it.

I have invoked Simmel's writing on Michelangelo's sculptures because it demonstrates so well and so beautifully the logic of sculpture which translates the outer appearance of a sculpture into its supposed inner essence. Let me end this section with one more example of Simmel's writing, his affective reading of Michelangelo's *Rondanini Pietà*. He calls this Michelangelo's most tragic sculpture. It is tragic not because of its subject matter, but because 'we [the viewers] feel neither any dualism of directions of life in their artistic formal cancellation, nor any desperate dualism of finite perceptual image and demand and desire for the infinite'.[32] It is the sculptural embodiment of the *Pietà* as subject matter that fails to offer any redemption or conciliation. The stone does not release any victory. 'The soul, freed from bodily weight, has not run its lap of victory into the transcendent but collapsed at its threshold.'[33] The bodily weight of Christ shows itself as the gravity of stone.

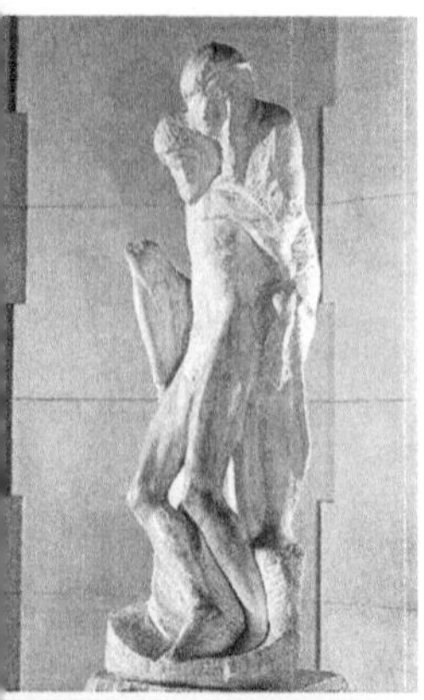

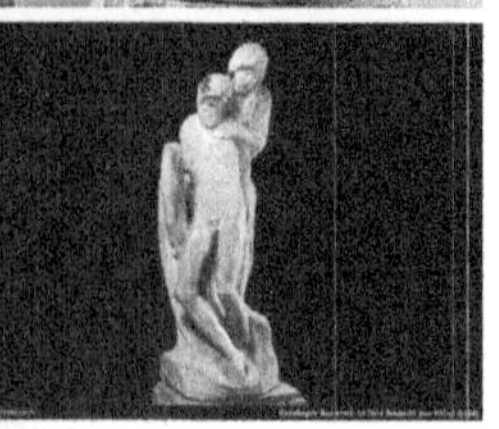

Michelangelo, *Rondanini Pietà*, 1564

Sculpture as Theoretical Object, or Charles Ray

American artist Charles Ray considers his sculpture *Tractor* (2005) a 'philosophical object'. I will use a similar term—namely, Hubert Damisch's term 'theoretical object'. As Hubert Damisch explains in an interview with Bois, a theoretical object:

> obliges you to do theory but also furnishes you with the means of doing it. Thus, if you agree to accept it on

> theoretical terms, it will produce effects around itself ... [and] forces us to ask ourselves what theory is. It is posed in theoretical terms; it produces theory; and it necessitates a reflection on theory.[34]

34 Bois et al., 'A Conversation with Hubert Damisch', 8; Bal, *Of What One Cannot Speak*, p. 13.

35 Bal, *Of What One Cannot Speak*, p. 13.

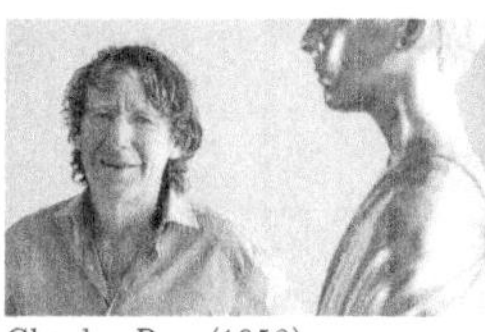
Charles Ray (1953)

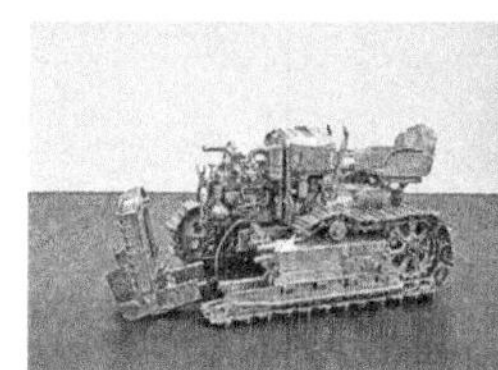
Charles Ray, *Tractor*, 2005

As Mieke Bal wrote:

> Damisch's concept of the theoretical object sometimes seems to suggest these are objects around which theories have been produced. At other times, as in the interview quoted here, he attributes to the artwork the capacity to motivate, entice, and even compel thought.[35]

Charles Ray's *Tractor*—and one could argue all his sculptures—are theoretical objects because they always address essential characteristics of the medium of sculpture. Is *Tractor* an example of Pop imaginary, like for example the sculptures of Jeff Koons are, or does it foreground something fundamental about sculpture? The distinction between outer appearance and inner essence which I have cited so far is provocatively missing when a sculpture is made of a tractor. The whole distinction makes no sense in this case because all elements of this vehicle belong to the same ontology, but by making a sculpture of a tractor Ray alludes to the importance of this distinction in understanding sculpture negatively by negating it radically. Instead, he proposes another kind of relationship as defining sculpture, the part-to-part relationship. For a tractor is built out of different parts which together constitute an object. From this perspective, *Tractor* can be seen as theorizing the logic of assemblage sculpture, to which I will later devote a chapter in this book.

Ray himself uses another distinction that is very similar to the one between outer appearance and inner essence, but his distinction is more outspoken, namely armature and insertion. The outer appearance of a sculpture works like an armour. The beholder is inclined to insert an imaginary dimension into that armour which one has no access to, for instance passions, emotions, or just muscles. Ray's terms are a structural articulation of form in space; not only the space surrounding the sculpture, but especially the space inside.[36] Ray's recent work *Doubting Thomas* (2021) can be seen as an allegory of this inclination of the viewer. Thomas is one of the twelve apostles of Jesus Christ. He doubted the resurrection until the Lord appeared and invited him to touch his wounds and see for himself. The touching of the wound usually takes the form of putting one's finger in it, as in Caravaggio's painting of the subject. Although representations of this biblical story have been frequently made in painting, I do not know of any important ones in sculpture. This is strange, because it can be seen as an allegorical representation of how one relates to sculpture. One must understand and access the inside to believe the credibility of the outside appearance.

Further, Ray has made several works based on mannequins, and although some of his sculptures seem to be inspired by the Classicist tradition, which is realist as well as idealized, one sometimes wonders if Ray's models have not just been mannequins.[37] The difference between an idealized representation and a mannequin is their 'aliveness'. A mannequin can be seen as an abstraction of an idealized representation of a human being; it integrates, and as a result abstracts, common notions of the female or male body, instead of idealized ones. Nobody assumes that mannequins have inside passions, emotions, or whatever essence; they are not enveloping anything. They are just the imaginary skin on which clothes can be draped. Again, mannequins negate the illusion of an imaginary interior world. In this respect, it is also important to explain how Ray makes his sculptural objects.

3 Kumar, 'Holding Space', 33.

7 Ray's sculpture is not only eoretical because it addresses ndamental principles of sculp- re, but also because most of s works relate intertextually iconic works in the Western story of sculpture, from Greek d Roman sculpture to inimalist sculpture. See a ading of Ray's work in terms references to the history of ulpture in Hal Foster's *Objets ilosophiques*.

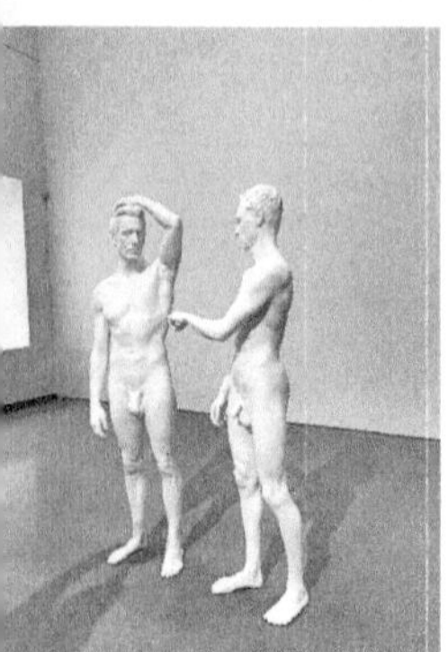

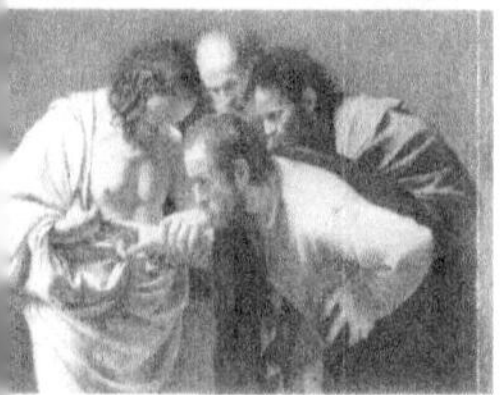

harles Ray, *Doubting Thomas*,)21; Caravaggio, *Doubting of int Thomas*, c. 1600

Although he still uses the traditional technique of modelling clay for proofs, all his other techniques are very new. For his steel sculptures, for instance, first he makes a digital Forton MG scan, and then a metal block is worked upon by a computer-driven machine process. 'Counter to everything we know about metal sculpture, the pieces are not cast, therefore, but carved; consequently they are very heavy.'[38] His works in (painted) fiberglass have an armature in stainless steel defining the total volume. This means that Ray's metal sculptures do not have an interior space of any kind.

Ray's approach to sculpture is never that of the maker but of the beholder. He does not try to assess the many possibilities of making them, but rather how to read or understand sculpture. In his own words:

> Sculpture can be made in many forms from any material. It can be made through the reduction of a solid block or any of a thousand materials modeled, carved, chipped, chiseled, ground, smoothed, painted, or scraped. Chemical and physical processes turn plaster, resins, and epoxies hard. Molds are taken, waxes pulled and invested. Bronze and other metals are melted and poured. Castings are welded or brazed together. Seams are chased. Constructive processes abound. Sculptures are nailed together and, sawn in half, painted, sanded, or ground to take the color off. Iron and steel are forged and milled. Hands are used with machines and techniques that close the gaps of human history. Welded seams and glued edges combine not just surfaces, but vernaculars, too.[39]

Ray ends this long description of the many possibilities of making sculpture with the following sentence:

38 Sénéchal, 'Animals in Silve[r] and Stone', p. 126.

39 Ray, 'How Many Sculptures Can You Fit into a Room?', p. 156.

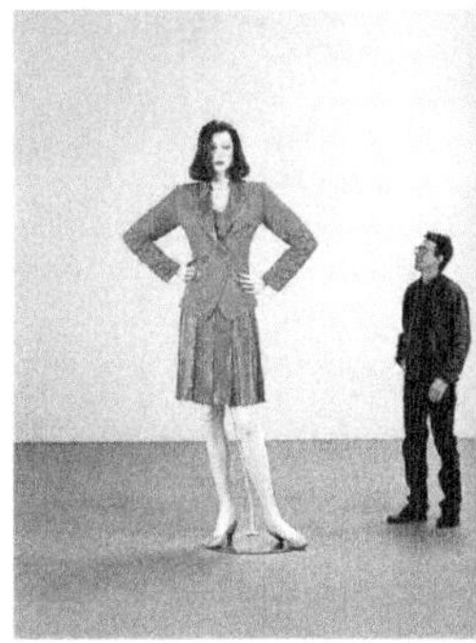

Charles Ray, *Fall '91*, 1992

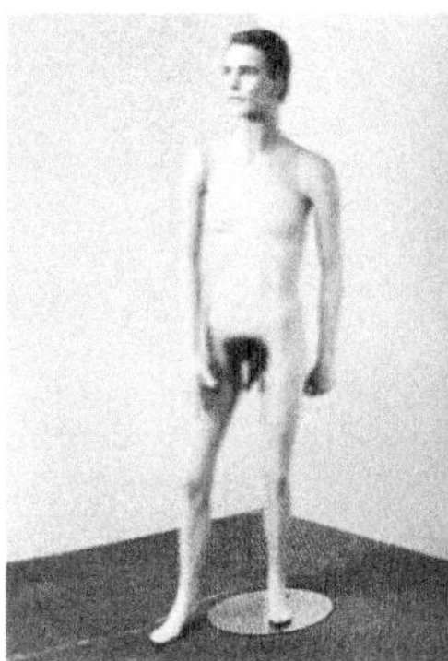

Charles Ray, *Male Mannequin*, 1990

0 Ray, 'How Many Sculptures an You Fit into a Room?', 156.

Sculpture made from the physical world is a language written in three dimensions and read in the fourth dimension of time. But what is the sculptural text, where is it located, and what is its font? Is space the page, and the physical sculpture a kind of font?'[40]

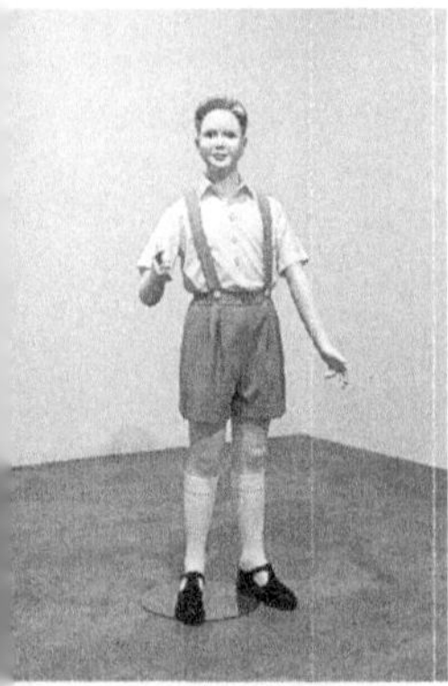

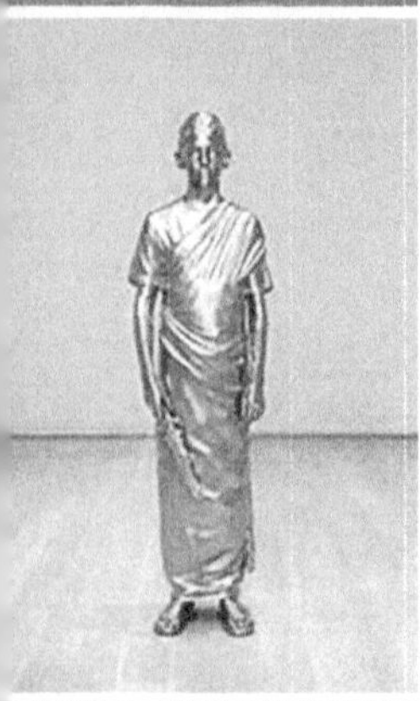

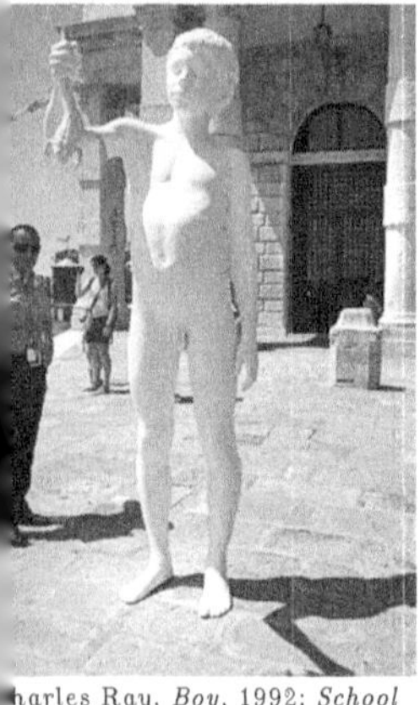

harles Ray, *Boy*, 1992; *School ay*, 2014; *Boy with Frog*, 2009

His transition from making sculpture to reading sculpture is significant because the fourth dimension of time is the one in which one reads sculpture. One must understand the language of sculpture to relate to it, to understand and behold it. Although a maker himself, he makes sculptures as theoretical objects from the perspective of a beholder.

When the language of sculpture must be understood from the perspective of the viewer, it implies that the human body of the beholder is the measure or standard by which we gauge the size and scale of sculptures. Every sculpture is measured by the standards of the human body; it is proportionally smaller or larger in scale. This fundamental principle of how we relate to sculpture is foregrounded in most of Ray's works. Some are life size, while many are larger than that and a few are smaller. For example, *Boy* from 1992 is 182 cm high, a normal height for an adult but not for a young boy. It is clearly a mannequin of a boy. Standing before this work, one is aware of the tallness of this little boy in comparison to how tall one is oneself; for a child this young boy must be a giant. The female mannequin of *Fall '91* is 244 cm high and towers above the viewers who gaze at her. The nineteen-nineties dress-for-success clothing she wears helps to intimidate the viewer. *School Play* from 2014 has an alienating effect on the viewer in a more ambiguous way. This figure is not extremely tall (193 cm) only a little taller than the average viewer. But then it turns out that the figure represents a boy, its title *School Play*. Although the size of

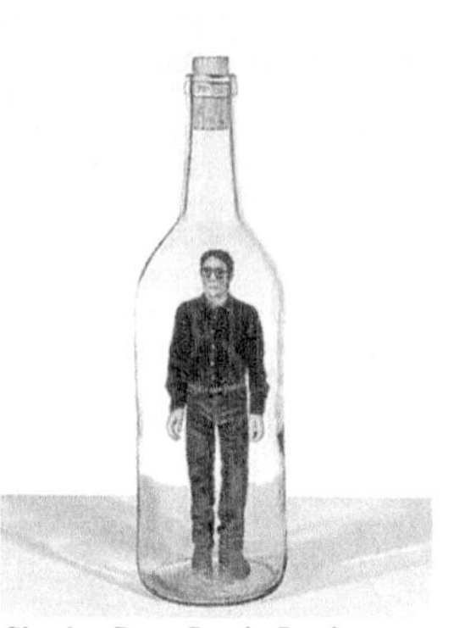

Charles Ray, *Puzzle Bottle*, 1995, glass, painted wood, and cork, 34 cm high

this sculpture is not enormous, its scale is for what it represents.

The most disorienting is Ray's *Family Romance* (1993), showing two parents with two children—the height of all four of them is 135 cm. The children, who are in fact still babies, are taller than life size, whereas the parents are smaller. The strange disorienting effect of being too small as well as too tall of this work comes about in relation to the viewer's body, which is the measure of sculpture's size. Something similar is effectuated by the sculpture *Huck and Jim* from 2014. This work is more than life size, rising up to 283 cm. The two figures represent two characters from the American novel *Adventures by Huckleberry Finn* (1884) by Mark Twain: the main character Huck and one of the many characters he meets, the runaway slave Jim. In this sculpture Ray imagines Huck bending over in the river collecting frog's eggs. Jim holds his hand out to protect him. What strikes the eye, however, is that here the black slave Jim is a white man, perhaps even a male mannequin. The white character Huck looks like a boy, perhaps his son, whom Jim tries to protect with a fatherly gesture. The scale of the two figures is again important—because the character Huck is bending, it is difficult to gauge his real height, but he looks shorter than Jim. This creates the illusion of a father-son relationship, although in the novel the title refers to the relationship as something different. The fact that Jim is bigger than life size and Huck looks smaller helps to create this effect.

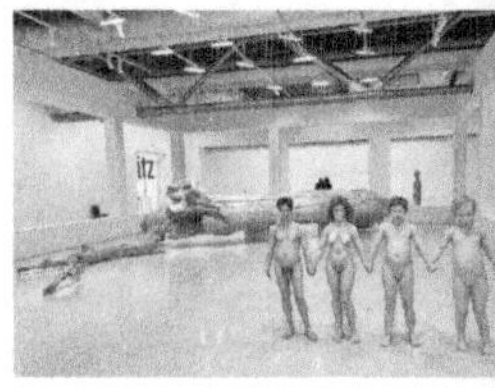

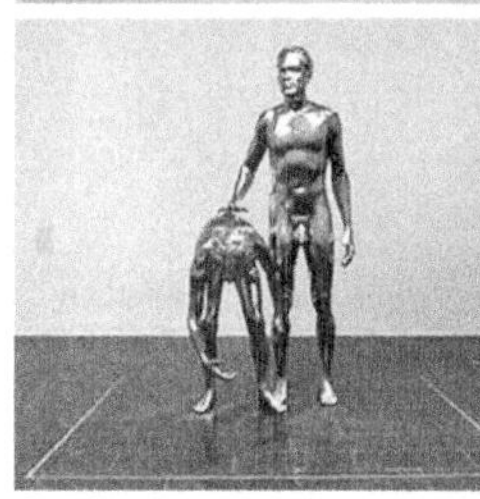

Charles Ray, *Family Romance*, 1993; *Huck and Jim*, 2014

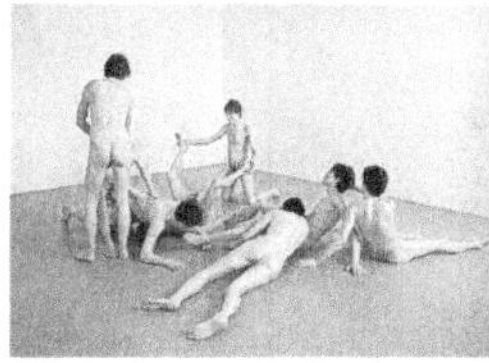

Charles Ray, *Oh! Charley, Charley, Charley...* , 1992

The 1992 work *Oh! Charley, Charley, Charley...* looks at first glance like an orgy. We see seven naked men involved with each other in what seems to be sex. But looking more closely, it turns out that the bodies remain distant from any sexual action, and it turns out that the seven men are the same man: they are all replicas of the artist Charles Ray.

Kumar, 'Holding Space', 31.

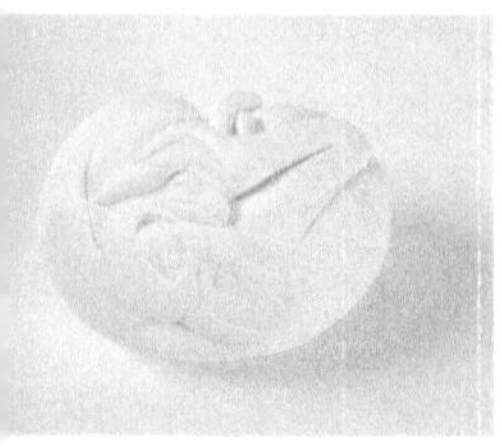

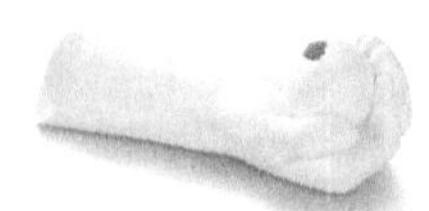

harles Ray, *Handheld Bird*,)06; *Hand Holding Egg*, 2007

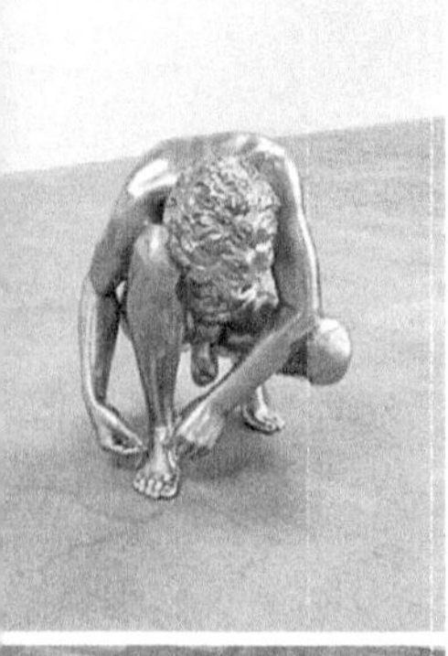

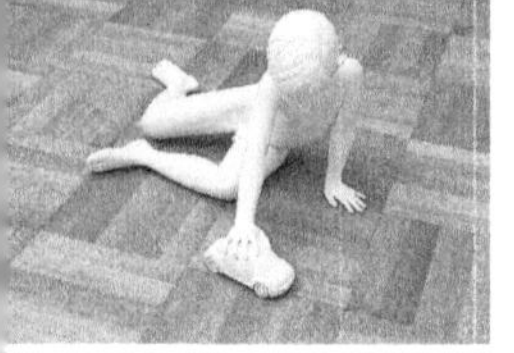

harles Ray, *Shoe Tie*, 2012; he *New Beetle*, 2006

Having been made in the nineteen-nineties, one associates this work at first with artists like Paul McCarthy or Mike Kelley. But Ray's take on sexual desire is not that festive, because it shows that the other whom one desires is ultimately a projection of oneself. Why did Ray use replicas of himself for this work? When we read it as a theoretical object it suggests that all Ray's sculptures are ultimately projections of himself, not because the figures look like him, as in *Oh! Charley, Charley, Charley...*, but because he is himself always the standard by which he measures his works.

Touch plays a crucial role in Ray's sculptural practice, from informing and the conditions of making to mediating the encounter with his work.[41] The materials' tactile characteristics determine the encounter with the viewer in important ways. This does not mean that he prefers soft materials, or a soft look; the hard and cold look of, for instance, stainless steel activates touch negatively. The works *Chicken* (2007), *Handheld Bird* (2006), and *Hand Holding Egg* (2007) are in porcelain and address touch by the fact that they are what Ray calls handheld pieces. Although the porcelain is very hard, it is fragile and has a soft appearance. *Hand Holding Egg* also thematizes touch by showing a scene of a hand holding an egg. *Handheld Bird* is the only one that is explicitly intended to be held as well as seen. Instead of a plinth, the viewer's hand is the base for this work. But many of Ray's other sculptures also foreground touch by showing figures who touch an object: *The New Beetle* (2006), *Shoe Tie* (2012), *Huck and Jim* (2014), and *Boy with Frog* (2009) are good examples.

Krauss, or the Logic of Sculpture

In my discussion of Herder's sculptural aesthetics, I argued why the discipline of aesthetics could also be called logic. At first, this seems strange because rational knowledge is produced by the discipline of logic and sensorial knowledge by aesthetics. But as explained above, it was Herder who deconstructed this opposition in his critique of Baumgarten by arguing that the new science of aesthetics had important consequences for the old science of logic itself. Consequently, the two sciences are, or should be, in many respects entangled, which makes it possible to speak of a sensorial logic, and in the wake of that extension, a logic of sculpture. In the remainder of the present book I will use the term 'logic of sculpture', pluralized into 'logics of sculpture', because I contend that there are several logics of sculpture. This becomes particularly evident at the turn of the twentieth century. Although the logic of sculpture that translates the outer appearance of a sculpture into its supposed inner essence has been prevalent for many centuries, at the beginning of the twentieth century new, alternative logics came about, pushing the logic that was based on the human body into the shadows.

Already in the nineteen-seventies, Rosalind Krauss used the term 'logic' when she wrote about the logic of sculpture. In her book *Passages of Modern Sculpture* (1977) and her article 'Sculpture in the Expanded Field' (1979), she demonstrates, on the basis of sculptures by Carl Andre, Robert Smithson, Richard Long, and Donald Judd, that 'sculpture' is not a universal category, but a historical one.[42] Sculpture has its own internal logic with its own set of rules and assumptions, and although those rules apply to a great number of objects, they allow little change or adaptation. But as she

42 Krauss, *Passages in Modern Sculpture*; Krauss, 'Sculpture in the Expanded Field'.

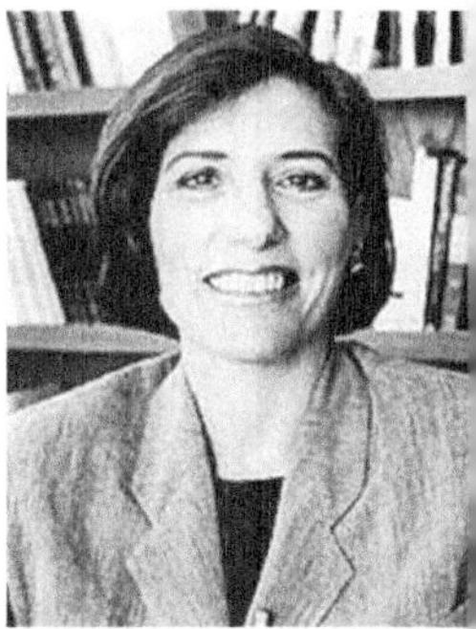

Rosalind Krauss (1941)

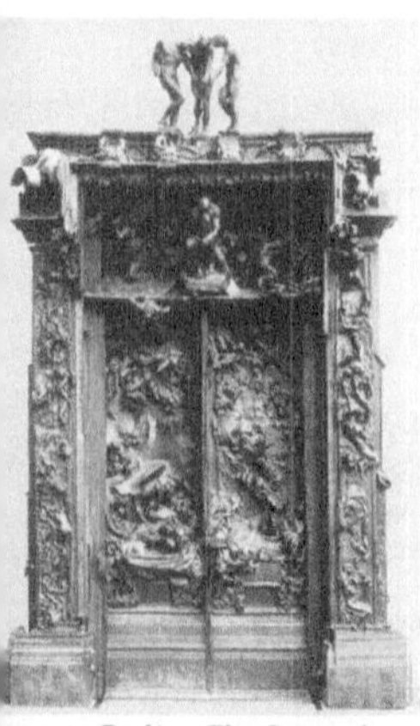

uguste Rodin, *The Gates of ell*, 1917

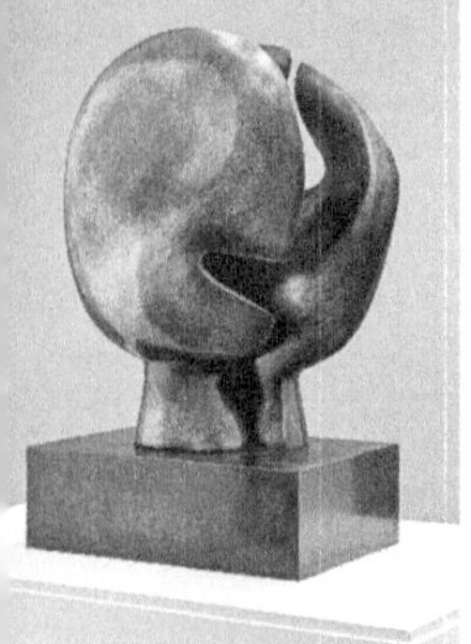

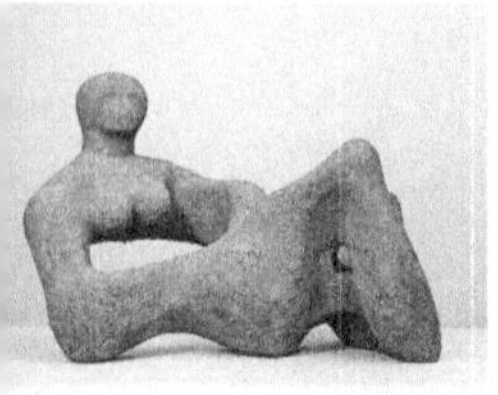

enry Moore, *Moon Head*, 1964; ecumbent *Figure*, 1938

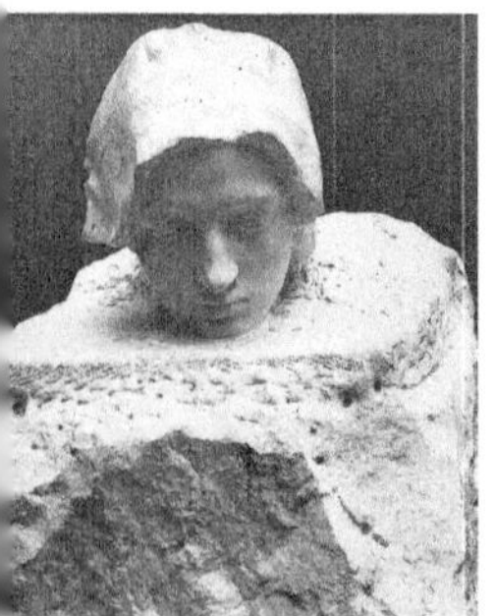

uguste Rodin, *La pensée Portrait of Camille Claudel)*, 95. Photo by Jacques-Ernest ulloz

demonstrates, a logic is not universal but historical. For centuries, the logic of sculpture could not be differentiated from that of the monument, but at the end of the nineteenth century these genres split up. Rodin's *Gates of Hell,* meant as a monument, did not comply with the rules of the commissioned monument. Deviating from the logic of the monument, sculpture is no longer bounded by a specific space or place. Modernist sculpture began to absorb the shelf on which it stood, freeing it from a location. It also shows its own material and/or process, demonstrating sculpture's autonomy. Whereas Rodin's work shows the making, Brancusi's absorbs the shelf or pedestal.

In her book *Passages in Modern Sculpture,* Krauss discusses and describes 'passages' in modern sculpture and how it deviates from classical sculpture. As previously explained, the meaning and effect of classical sculpture relied on the illusion of a sculpture's inner essence, which was responsible for the outer appearance. The skeleton or the muscles under the skin determined the look of a sculpture, and, psychologically, mood was expressed on the skin or exteriority. The meaning of sculpture as body is displaced from inner essence to the surface. The abstract forms of Henry Moore still suggest that the dead materiality obtained its form from an organic, inner essence that has shaped the outer appearance. Only with the Minimalist 'specific objects' of Donald Judd or Carl Andre is the assumption of an inner essence accountable for the outer appearance left behind. Starting from Krauss's idea that sculptural traditions have their own internal logics, I will write a study of different, new logics of sculpture.

The first example of a passage in modern sculpture Krauss discusses is the work of Auguste Rodin. In the case of this sculptor, the absence of a convincing relationship between the internal structure of the body and its outward appearance can be perceived as expressive, but then as an expression of a different kind. The surface of his sculptures gives expression to the process of formation and production. The sculptor's hand is more evident on the surface than the internal structure. So, the body at stake is no longer the metaphorical body represented by the sculpture, but the body of the sculptor left visible on the surface as traces of the sculpture's production.

Krauss has clarified her understanding of Rodin's sculpture by comparing it with Art Nouveau design in architecture and applied arts. In the inkpots and candlesticks of Victor Horta or Henry Van de Velde, the furniture of Hector Guimard or the architecture of Antoni Gaudí, we encounter a style of design which is not at all concerned with the internal structure of an object. A degree of nuance is required here. In some Art Nouveau objects, such as those of Émile Gallé, an internal structure is in fact expressed in a very emphatic and extreme manner, namely in the form of muscles, tendons, or stems. The idea that an object constitutes an organic whole is not abandoned here, but rather accentuated in this intense form. Precisely by way of their extremeness (literalness), these

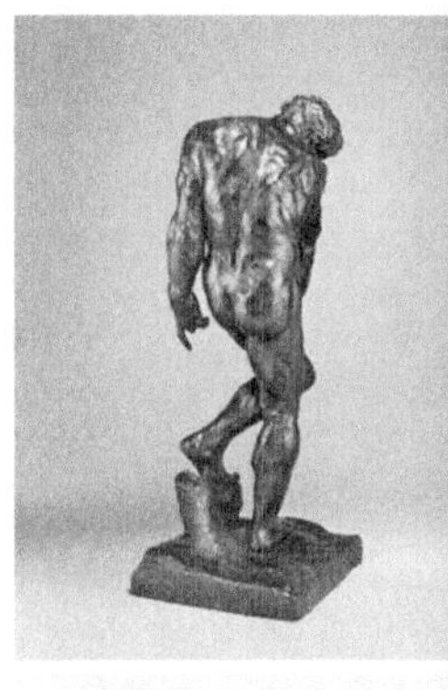

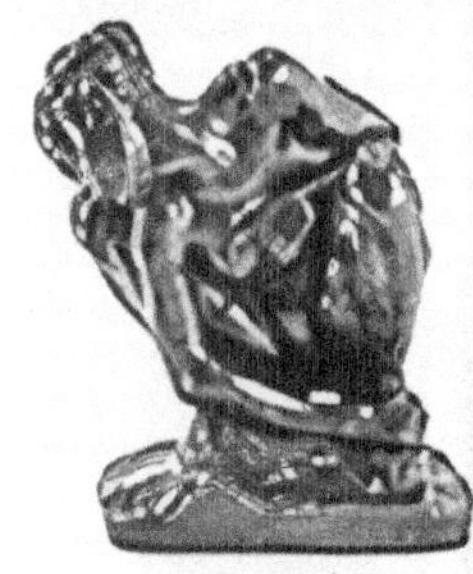

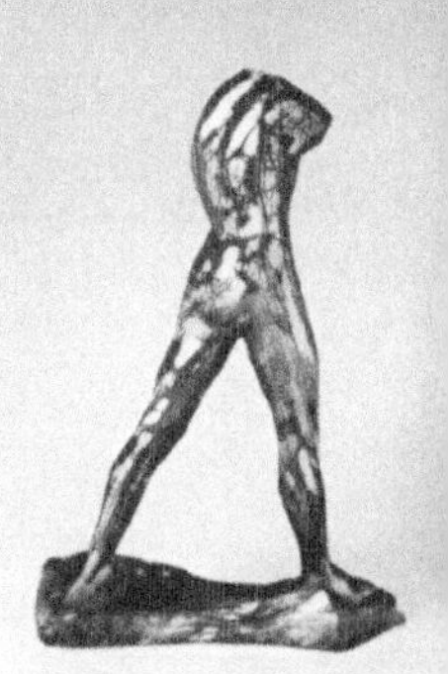

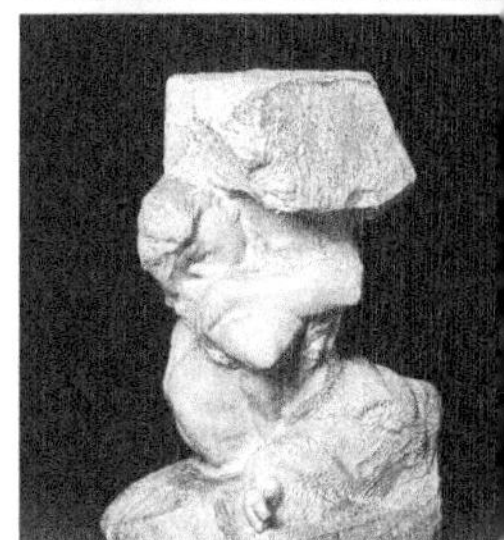

Auguste Rodin, *Adam*, 1880–1881; *Crouching Woman*, 1882; *Walking Man*, 1907; *Fallen Caryatid*, 1894

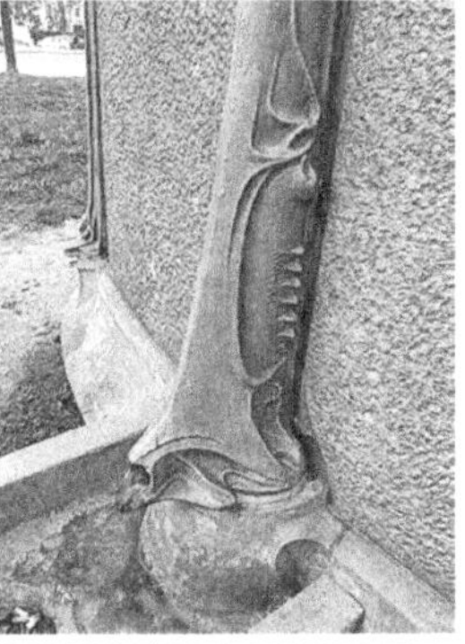

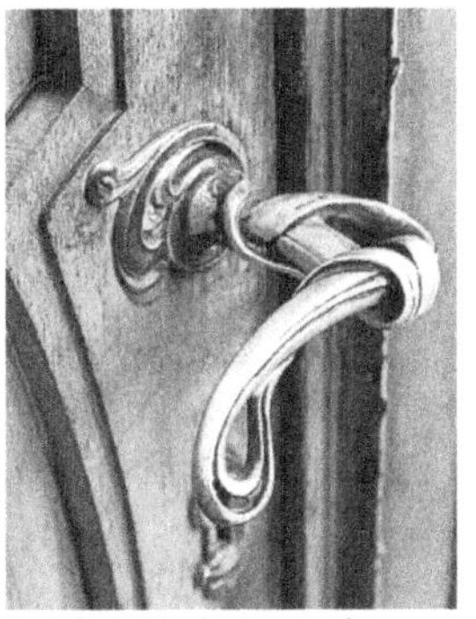

Victor Horta (1861–1947), doorknob

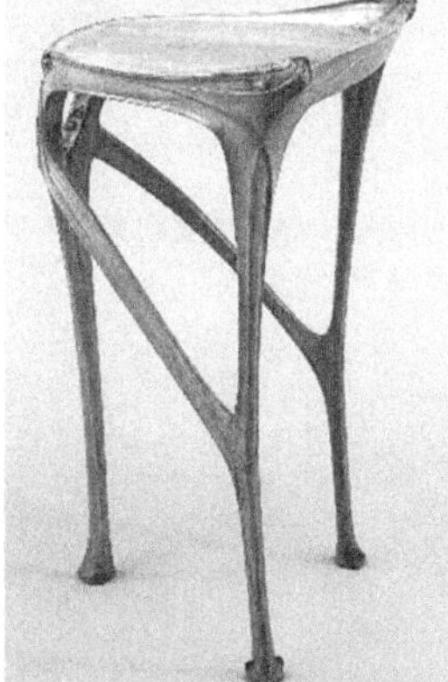

Hector Guimard (1867–1942), downspout and side-table

examples of Art Nouveau confirm the view that the relationship between interior space and outer form is a key aspect of the movement's design or is even a problematic area that is the style's focus. Generally speaking, Art Nouveau presents volume with an undifferentiated sense of interior, concentrating instead on its surface.[43] This means that the surface of Art Nouveau objects, but also that of sculptures by Rodin and Italian sculptor Medardo Rosso, gives rise to the illusion of a formation process carried out externally. There is no longer a relationship between outward appearance and internal structure, but rather between outward appearance and external forces or influences. The kind of design, this logic, suggest that it:

> was shaped by the erosion of water over rock, or by the tracks of waves on sand, or by the ravages of wind; in short, by what we think of as the passage of natural forces over the surface of matter. Shaping those substances from the outside, these forces act with no regard to the intrinsic structure of the material on which they work.[44]

The design of Art Nouveau objects relates polemically to the Neoclassical tradition in which the surface and the appearance of the sculpture are a direct expression of a previous meaning, an inner experience, or a structure.

Minimalist artists such as Donald Judd and Sol LeWitt radicalize this decentring of the body by countering any kind of expressiveness, replacing the 'meaning' of sculpture with the experience of the viewer; that is, the experience of the viewer's body being positioned in relation to the object. Thus, this time it is the viewer's body, in relation to the sculpture or object, that counts. Minimalist sculptors take, one could say, the sculptural aesthetics of Herder to heart.

3 Krauss, *Passages in Modern culpture*, p. 33.

4 Krauss, *Passages in Modern culpture*, p. 33.

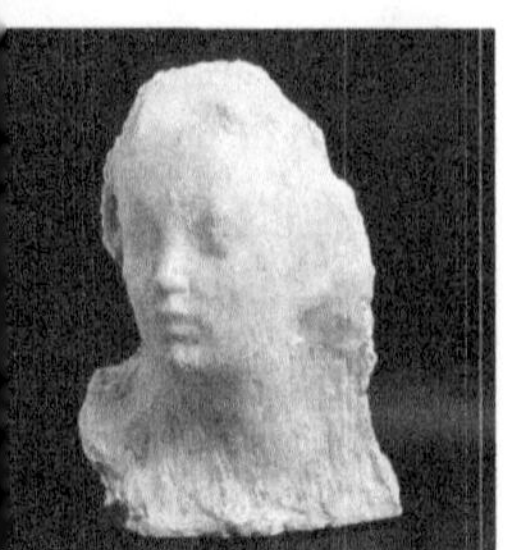

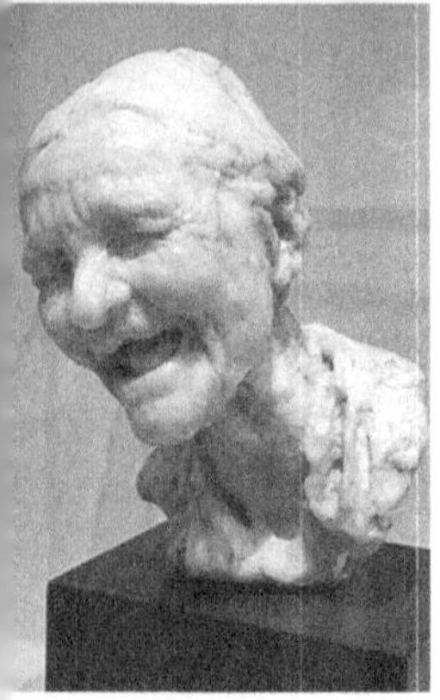

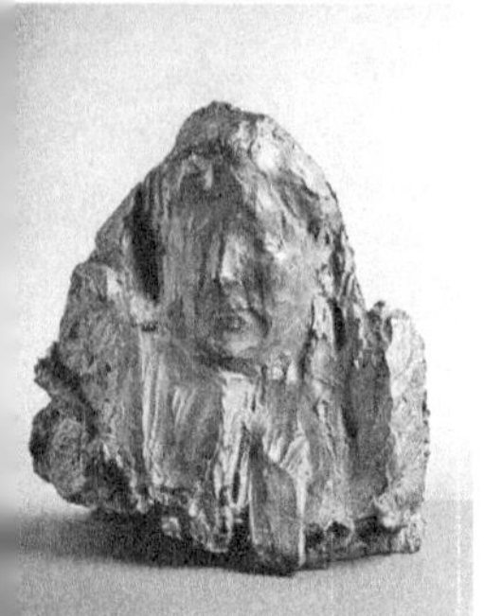

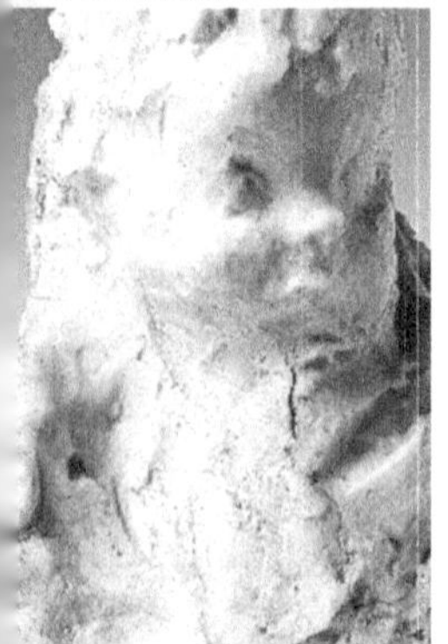

edardo Rosso, *The Sick Boy*; *vecchia*, 1883; *Madame oblet*, 1897; *Child in the Sun*, 92

From these thoughts we can conclude that (Neo)classical sculpture consists of objects that depend on the distinction between an outer appearance and an inner structure or essence that produces the outer appearance. Art Nouveau objects refuse this distinction by presenting objects that are shaped from the outside in, instead of from the inside out. These objects do not depend on the illusion of an inner essence for how they look. That is why they introduce a new sculptural logic.

Trying to assess Minimalist sculpture, Krauss understands the work of Donald Judd as taking distance from the idea that sculpture should be understood in terms of the appearance and meaning of the (human) body. Judd's work implies, then, a radicalization of the thinking of two crucial figures in the early history of modern sculpture: Rodin and Brancusi.

> The art of both men represented a relocation of the point of origin of the body's meaning—form its inner core to its surface—a radical act of decentering that would include the space to which the body appeared and the time of its appearing.[45]

The steps Krauss makes from classical to early modern sculpture to her endpoint in Minimalism are vast. In my project, I want to focus on several logics of sculpture to which she does not pay attention, because her goal was centred more on better understanding the logic of sculpture of Minimalist artists such as Judd and Smithson. She did not aim to write an overview of all the different logics that were being practiced in the twentieth century. Her goal was more modest and more specific.

45 Krauss, *Passages in Modern Sculpture*, p. 279.

46 Curtis, *Sculpture*.

47 Collins, *Sculpture Today*.

Starting from Krauss's idea that sculptural traditions have their own internal logics, that traditions get exhausted, and that new logics come about, I will devote chapters to the following logics of sculpture: 'The Body Undone', 'Scenic Sculpture', 'Sculpting Space', 'Building Blocks', 'Assemblage', 'Architectural Sculpture', and 'The Specific Object'. By distinguishing these different logics of sculpture, I hope to present a study on this medium that is more coherent than other recent efforts to assess modern sculpture. For example, in her recent book Penelope Curtis understands the 'vocabulary' of sculpture on the basis of four 'qualities' or 'functions': horizontal, vertical, open, or closed.[46] In the respective chapters she discusses these qualities through different series of sculptures from different times, from the Middle Ages until the present. Rachel Whiteread's casts of mattresses has horizontality in common with medieval tombs, and relic holders have closedness in common with Damien Hirst's *A Thousand Years* (1990). Curtis's approach is based on the conviction that the four qualities are universal; they are archetypes that can be recognized in sculptures from any period. The principle of the analysis is likeness. By classifying sculpture in this way, not difference but instead similarity with different and earlier traditions is paramount.

Another recent book on sculpture understands the medium of sculpture through a thematic approach, mixed with a materialistic one: Judith Collins's *Sculpture Today* (2007).[47] She devotes chapters to 'the figure', 'the body fragmented', 'memory', 'inspired by nature', 'clothing', 'traditional materials', 'colour, surface, and light', 'gravity' and more. Installation art is not seen as a separate medium, but as a sub-category of sculpture. Here, the problem is that everything three-dimensional is considered to be sculpture.

These examples demonstrate that in art criticism the generic term 'sculpture' is no longer viable, although the same can be argued about painting—the 'death of painting' has been challenged many times in order to show new manifestations and new futures for painting. As far as I know, the death of sculpture has never been declared, but still, in art criticism sculpture has become an obsolete term. And with the important exceptions of Richard Serra and Donald Judd, and Charles Ray, few prolific artists reflect on the various possibilities of the sculptural medium. Instead, when works of art are three-dimensional, the much more general term 'installation' is now in vogue. It suggests that sculpture is old-fashioned, and that if one wants to belong to the present, one makes, or appreciates, 'installation art'.

I contend that the obsoleteness of sculpture, the term and also the practice, is an enormous loss for our understanding of art in general, and of sculpture more specifically. First of all, it is a loss because many artists continue to make works that can only be understood as sculpture. Second, it is a mistake because, to use Krauss's term, the logic of sculpture differs from the logic of installation art. In order to assess many contemporary art practices, one should have a better understanding of the logic of sculpture, or rather: the logics of sculpture.

And on top of this, the difference between the logics of sculpture and the logics of installation should be assessed. Claire Bishop provides a definition of installation art that contradicts my earlier assessment of sculpture on the basis of the Pygmalion myth and Herder's aesthetics:

48 Emphasis in original text; Bishop, *Installation Art*, p. 6.

> Installation art [...] differs from traditional media (sculpture, painting, photography, video) in that it addresses the viewer directly as a literal presence in the space. Rather than imagining the viewer as a pair of disembodied eyes that survey the work from a distance, installation art presupposes an *embodied* viewer whose sense of touch, smell and sound are as heightened as their sense of vision. That insistence on the literal presence of the viewer is arguably the key characteristic of installation art.[48]

According to Bishop, the logic of installation art relies on a different notion of the viewer. For her, whereas both mediums are three-dimensional, sculpture relies on a disembodied viewer and installation art relies on an embodied viewer. However, my starting point in this book is that the embodied viewer distinguishes sculpture from painting, the viewer of which is indeed disembodied. Yet, there is another element in Bishop's definition that clarifies an important difference, namely the idea that the viewer of an installation is addressed 'as a literal presence in the space'. In the case of sculpture, one cannot speak of the literal presence of the viewer in the space. The viewer is not part of the space a sculpture occupies but is facing it all the time when s/he walks around or along it. This means that viewers are yet again a decisive element, not because they are embodied, but because they are positioned differently.

The book you are beginning to read does not present a historical overview of sculpture, which implies that many important sculptures and their makers are not being discussed. This book is analytical rather than historical, although it does discuss many notions of sculpture which are considered to be historical. The most important criterion for discussion was: How does a specific sculptural practice elucidate a specific logic of sculpture? And, of course, many sculptures do not fit neatly within one logic; sometimes one must activate several logics to understand the specific nature of an individual artwork. Ultimately, I hope that this book will renew the importance of sculpture in the cultural domain.

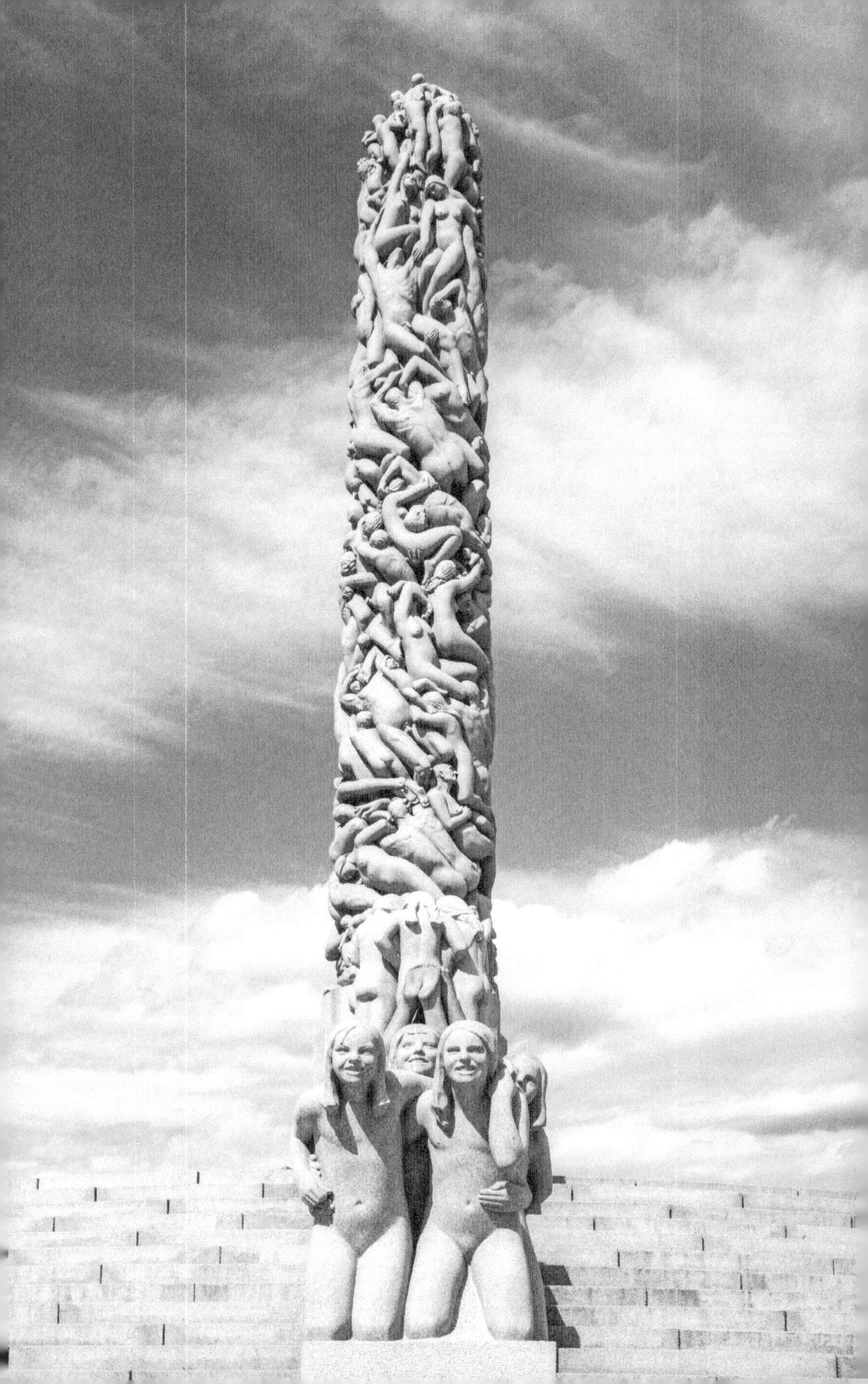

The Body Undone

The Appearance of the Body: Alberto Giacometti

The unity of inner and outer perfection or beauty and morality was an axiom from the classical period until the end of the nineteenth century. The outer appearance of the human body and its inner world of emotions and passions were the two sides of the same coin and could not be seen independently from each other. But Swiss-French artist Alberto Giacometti (among others) no longer believed in this intimate connection between the outer appearance of a sculpted body and the suggestion of an inner dimension that resonates with what the body looks like. In the chapter on the logic of scenic sculpture, I will discuss Giacometti's early work from the Surrealist period. But first, I will try to understand the logic behind the later so-called tall, elongated figures which made him world-famous.

For Giacometti, the inside and outside of a sculpture are disconnected:

> [...] if I copy exactly the surface of a head in sculpture,

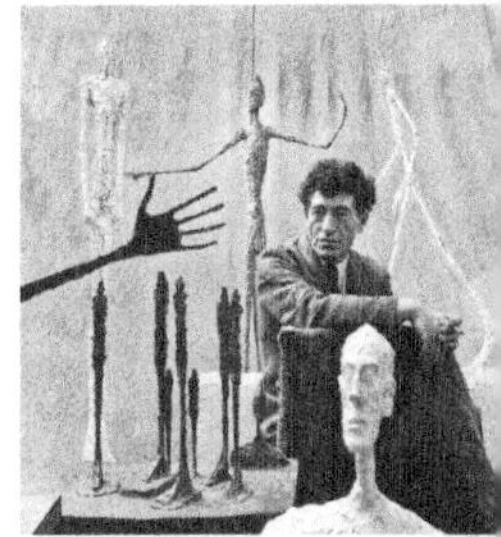

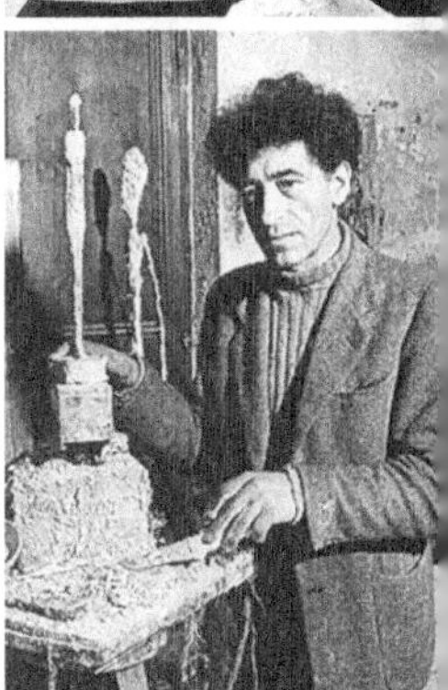

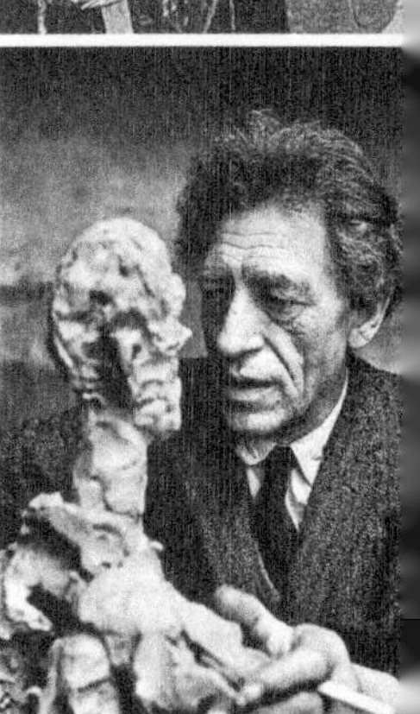

Alberto Giacometti (1901–196

Gustav Vigeland, *Monolith*, 1919

Sylvester, 'Interview', p. 130.

Sylvester, 'Interview', p. 130.

what has it got inside it? A great mass of dead clay! In a living head, the inside is as organic as the surface, isn't it? So, a head that looks real, a head by Houdon, for instance, is in fact like a bridge, in that the surface looks like a head but you have the feeling that the inside is empty, if it's in terracotta. And if it's in stone, that's a lump of stone. But the fact that it's empty or a lump of stone already makes it false because it isn't at all like that, since there isn't a millimeter inside your skull that isn't organic. Therefore, in a certain sense, heads that are narrow have just enough clay to hold them together: the inside is absolutely necessary. It's necessary more like a living head than if it were a copy of the outside.[1]

Giacometti's narrow heads and figures have just enough clay inside to hold them together; they are no longer 'false', deceptive sculptures because they do not rely any longer on the suggestion of an inside that relates organically to the outer appearance. For him, it implies that the artist should just focus on what the body looks like, its appearance:

> Whereas with a sculpture by Maillol—I do not say this to criticize Maillol—but, with a life-size sculpture by Maillol, if it takes four men with machines to move it, isn't that enough to make it false to start with? The problem is to find the real through external appearances.[2]

This exclusive focus on the external appearance implies a phenomenological point of view, especially that of Herder. For the external appearance of a sculpted body is always in the eye of the beholder, not in that of the sculpted subject. It is important to emphasize that for Giacometti it is not just the external appearance of the human body that is 'real'; it concerns, at the same time, the external appearance of the

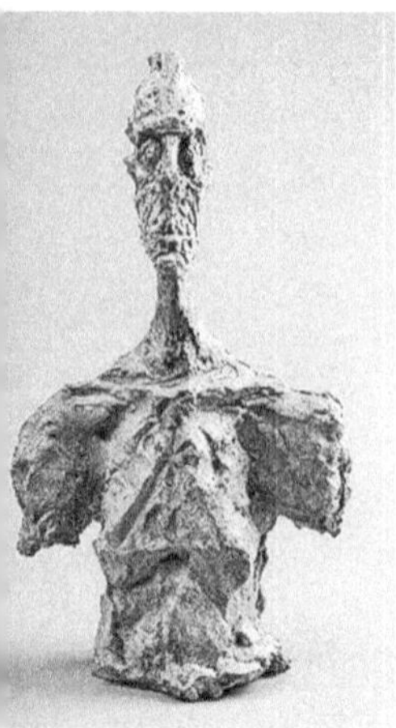

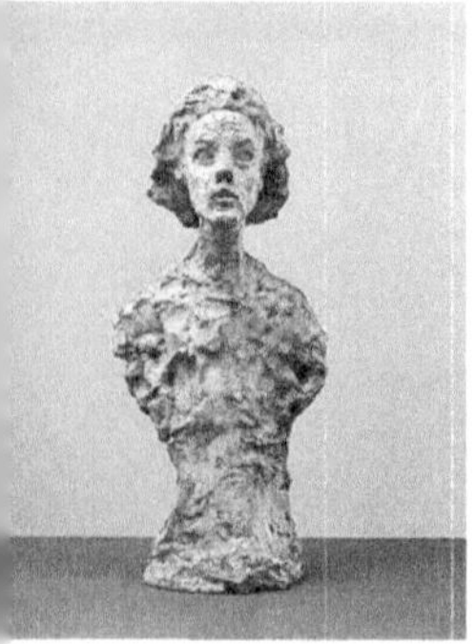

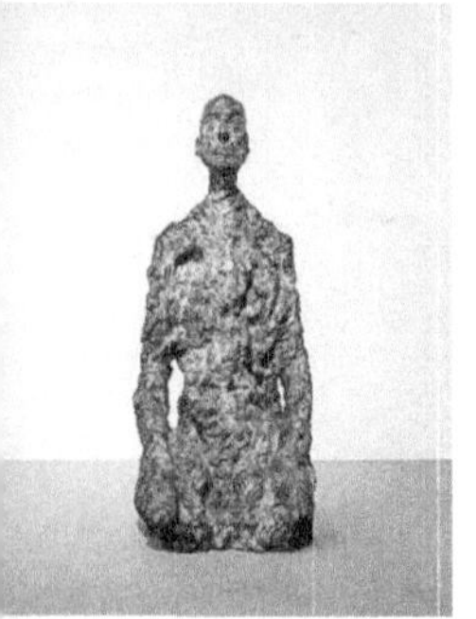

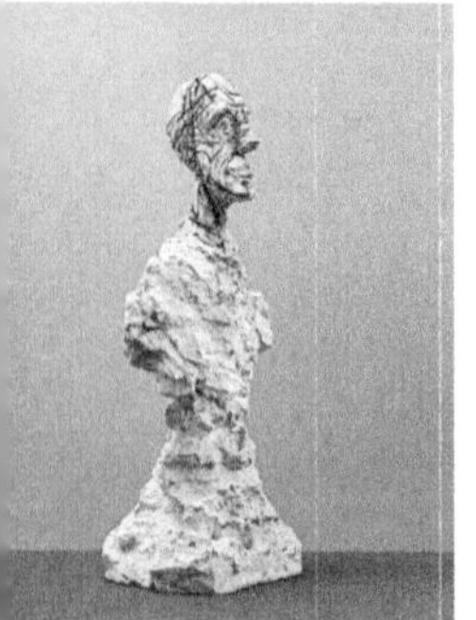

berto Giacometti, *Bust of ego*, 1956; *Bust of Annette II*, 1962; *Lotar III*, 1965; *Bust Diego*, 1964–65

sculpture in which 'the real' should be discovered. Answering a question about the attraction of painted sculptures, he answers:

> Because sculpture too has suddenly become an illusion. It's no longer an object in bronze or stone, a beautiful material one wants to touch; it has become a questionable or very equivocal object, really, because if it's painted with the colors one chooses, those which are nearest to what one sees, let's say, then the material is of no further interest, it no longer counts. So, you can't really touch it anymore. It actually becomes a sort of appearance itself.[3]

3 Sylvester, 'Interview', p. 128

For Giacometti, the appearance of the human body as well as the sculpted body, and in this case also the painted, sculpted body, defines the logic of sculpture. It is no longer the relation between an inner dimension and an outer appearance that provides meaning to sculpture and its affective impact, but rather the relationship between different appearances.

The starting point for the sculptor should be what one sees, not what one knows. Giacometti's description of Rodin's working process is revealing in this respect. I will quote him at length because he gives a beautiful analysis of the Western sculptural tradition, deeming it overly conceptual and not visual enough.

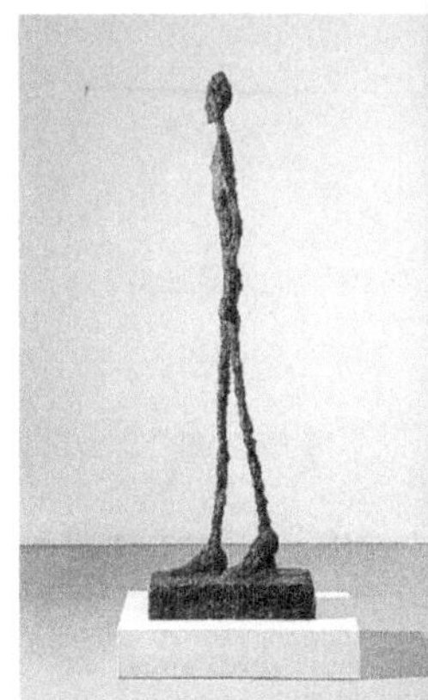

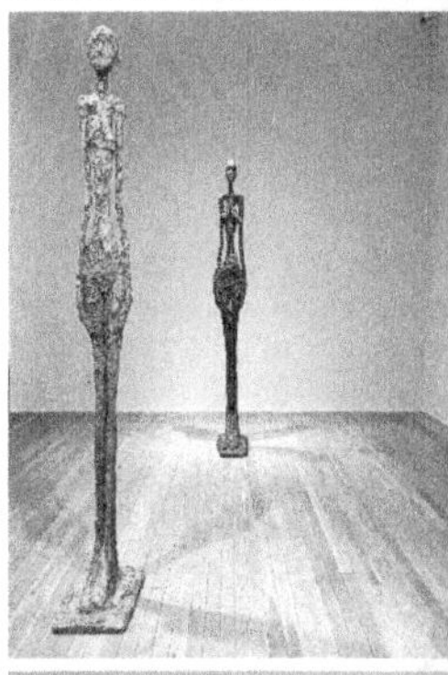

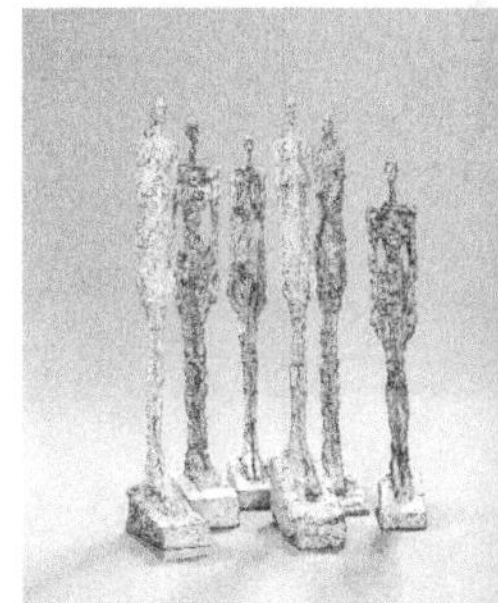

Alberto Giacometti, *L'homme qui marche*, 1960; *Grande femme debout I*, 1960; *Femmes de Venice*, 1956

> Even Rodin still took measurements when he was making his busts. He didn't model a head as he actually saw it in space, at a certain distance, as I see you now with a certain distance between us. He really wanted to make a parallel in clay, the exact equivalent of the head's volume in space. So basically it wasn't visual but conceptual. He knew it was round before he began: that's to say, he

Sylvester, 'Interview', p. 125.

started from the conventional idea of a head that has prevailed in all European sculpture since the time of the Greeks, and made a volume in space unlike anything he actually saw, because in the ordinary way it would never occur to me to get up and walk around you. If I didn't know that your skull had a certain depth, I wouldn't be able to guess it. [...] I think we have for so long automatically accepted the received idea of what a sculpted head should look like that we have made ourselves completely incapable of seeing a head as we really see it.[4]

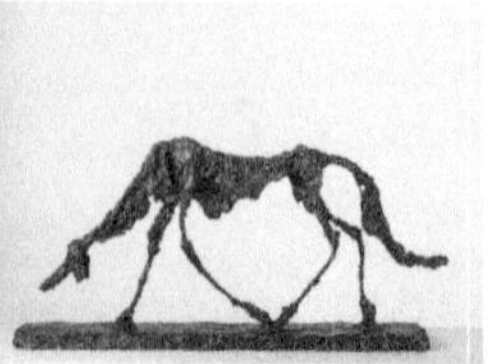

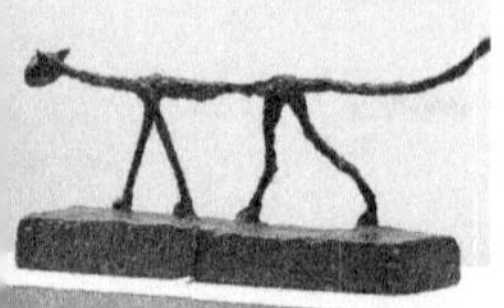

lberto Giacometti, *The Dog*,)51; *The Cat*, 1954

By focusing radically on the appearance one sees, Giacometti does not only hollow out the body, deprive it of its inner space. He also introduces a new logic of sculpture. By undoing the intimate link between the outer and inner perfection of the body, he proposes a logic that relates to the body negatively. He undoes the body's inner essence, physical or emotional, and replaces that inner dimension with its outer appearance.

An important consequence of the role of the body's appearance is that distance to the body comes into play. And distance determines the scale. The body appears differently depending on the distance from it. Looking at a human body means looking from some distance, and that means that a sculpted body is by definition smaller than life size. 'Large sculpture is only small sculpture blown up', Giacometti claims.

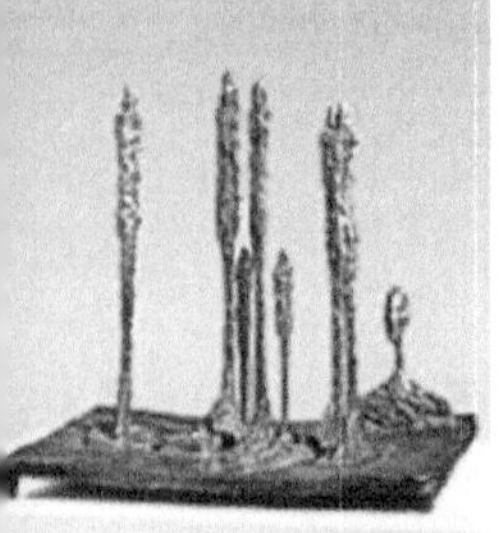

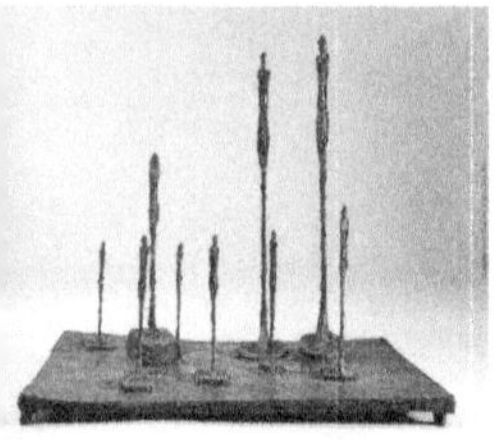

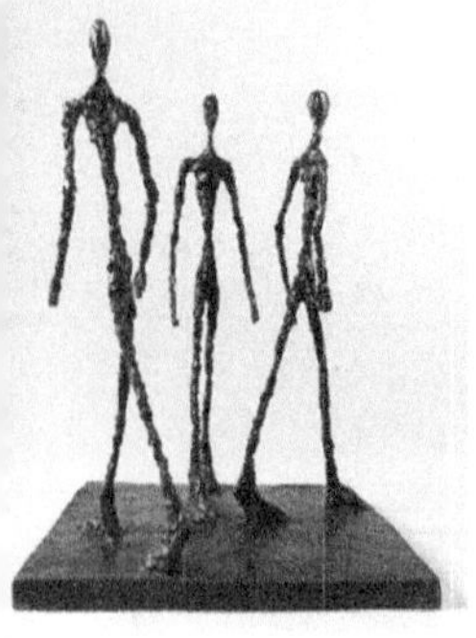

lberto Giacometti, *The Forest*, 50; *The Glade*, 1950; *Three en Walking*

Sometimes, in a café, I watch the people going by on the opposite pavement and I see them very small, like tiny little statuettes, which I find marvelous. But it's *impossible* for me to imagine that they are life size; at that distance they simply become appearances. If they come nearer, they become a different person. But if they come

> too close, say two meters away, then I simply don't see them anymore. They're no longer life size, they have usurped your whole visual field and you see them as a blur.[5]

5 Sylvester, 'Interview', p. 127

6 Sylvester, 'Interview', p. 127

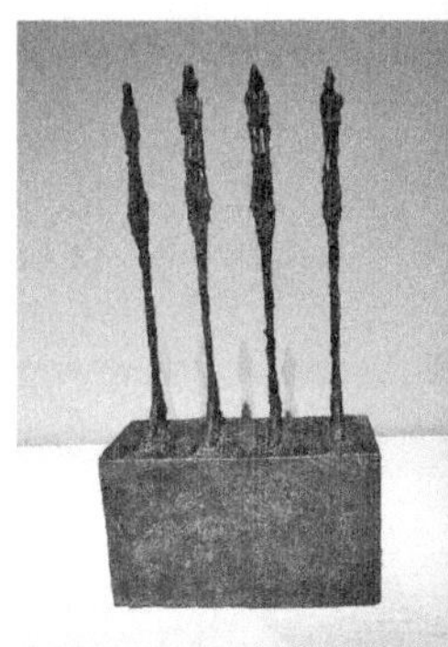

Alberto Giacometti, *Four Women on a Plinth*, 1950

Distance and size are explicitly at stake and foregrounded in Giacometti's groups of figures, such as *The Forest* (1950) and *Three Men Walking* (1948). The size of the figures varies; the tallest placed in the front, those which are smaller at the back. The figures in *Four Women on a Plinth* are more or less the same size, but they stand next to each other. The work *The Glade* contradicts this distance-based organization because some taller figures are placed at the back. But the figures collected on this small piece of land were probably not seen at the same time; they were brought together and seen from different distances.

Giacometti ends his discussion of the distance towards human bodies as follows:

> Everything is only appearance, isn't it? And if the person comes nearer, I stop looking at her, but she almost stops existing, too. Or else one's emotions become involved: I want to touch her, don't I. Looking has lost all interest.[6]

Like Herder, he demonstrates how touch can be activated by sight. In Herder's case, however, the sense of touch is embedded within sight, while for Giacometti sight is overruled by touch. Whereas vision is only possible from a certain distance to the body or object one looks at, when this distance decreases the sense of touch takes over.

Sight and touch do not cooperate in Giacometti's account; they are presented as rivals. This is somewhat paradoxical for a sculptor—it almost looks as if Giacometti fights against touch in order to keep the distance through which the appearance of the human body can come about. He approaches sculpture as a painter, and his undoing of the conventional sculptural logic comes with a prize: the sensorial participation of the viewer's body is reduced to sight only.

Multiplication, Doubling, and Pairing: Louise Bourgeois

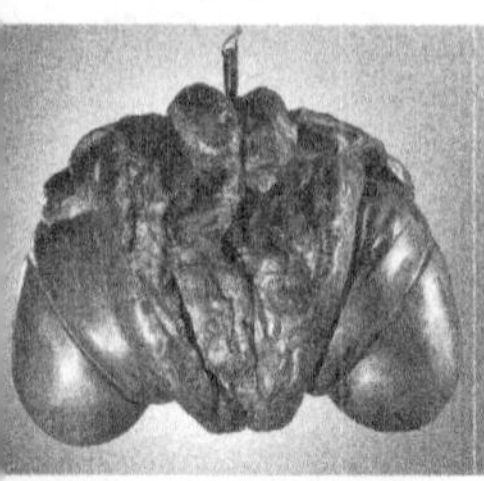

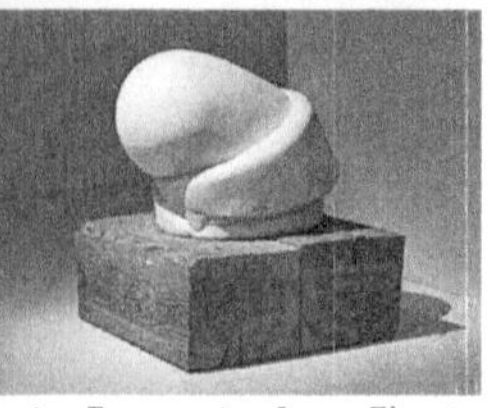

ouise Bourgeois, *Janus Fleuri*,)68; *Sleep II*, 1967

In Louise Bourgeois's sculpture *Janus Fleuri* (1968), the male and female genitals have coalesced. In this hanging sculpture we see the symmetrical doubling of the glans of a penis; this penis sticks out of huge lips reminiscent of a vulva. For this work, Bourgeois used two casts from another work of hers: *Sleep II* (1967). How to understand these same-sexed genitals? What kind of body is it and with what kind of sculptural logic does it comply?

These same-sexed genitals certainly do not rely on the idea of the perfect body. According to that idea, the body is gendered and we can distinguish the male body from the female body. Of course, the reality of the human body is more complex than this simple, binary opposition, but the perfection of the human body is conceptual rather than real. This conceptual idea leaves no room for ambiguities. When the appearance of this body part cannot be called 'perfect', its resonance with inner perfection is also short-circuited. What kind of male or female passions or emotions are reflected in this grotesque object? Bourgeois herself has said the following about these doubled genitals:

> It is symmetrical, like the human body, and it has the scale of those various parts of the human body to which it may, perhaps, refer: a double facial mask, two breasts, two knees. Its hung position indicates passivity, but its

> low-slung mass expresses resistance and duration. It is perhaps a self-portrait—one of many.[7]

From beginning to end, Bourgeois uses modalities that undermine the idea of a perfect, unambiguous body. 'Perhaps' it should be seen as resonating her own passion or inner world as a woman artist or sculptor, but that is not sure either. Nevertheless, the traditional sculptural logic based on the perfection of the human body is subversively undermined in this work by means of doubling and pairing 'opposite' human bodies to each other.

Bourgeois's ironic work *Fillette* (1968) transforms the supreme phallic object, a big erect penis, into just a penis. First of all, this is done through the title *Fillette*, meaning little girl.[8] Second, by hanging the penis on a hook, as if it were a slaughtered ox, the phallus is shown after the act of castration. Robert Mapplethorpe's well-known photograph of a smiling Louise Bourgeois carrying the 'little girl' under her arm foregrounds Bourgeois's ironic appropriation of the mythical question of who owns the phallus and who does not? In 1999, she made a so-called 'sweeter version' of *Fillette*. The difference between the two versions makes it retrospectively clear that the oldest, non-sweet version is not just a big penis. This hanging sculpture shows a phallic figure which is again ambiguous because it is an enormous penis as well as a vulva; or is it just an uncut penis? The penis is 'dressed' by a vagina and sticks out of it. The non-sweet version of *Fillette*, in particular, is much rougher or unformed than the sweeter one; it is more like a vagina than an erect, uncut penis. This reading is confirmed by a later work of hers.

In *La Maladie de l'Amour* we see, first of all, a suspended fabric object that reminds us of pieces of meat

7 Louise Bourgeois, quoted in Krohn, 'Doubling and Pairing', p. 55.

8 For a brilliant reading of these Bourgeois works in relation to her so-called cells and spiders, see: Bal, *Louise Bourgeois' Spider*.

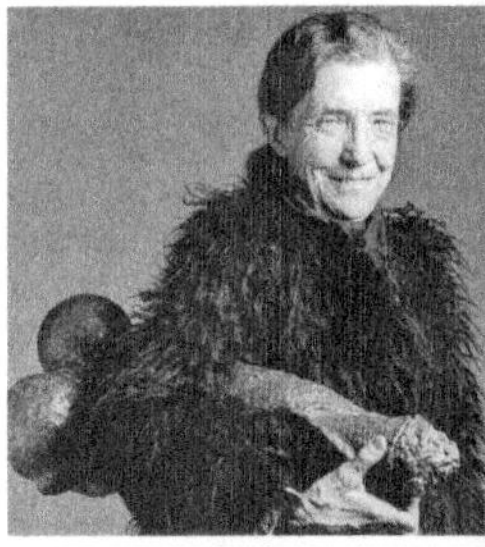

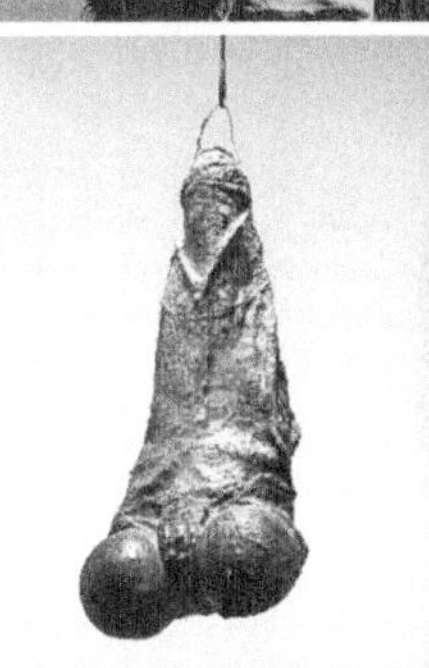

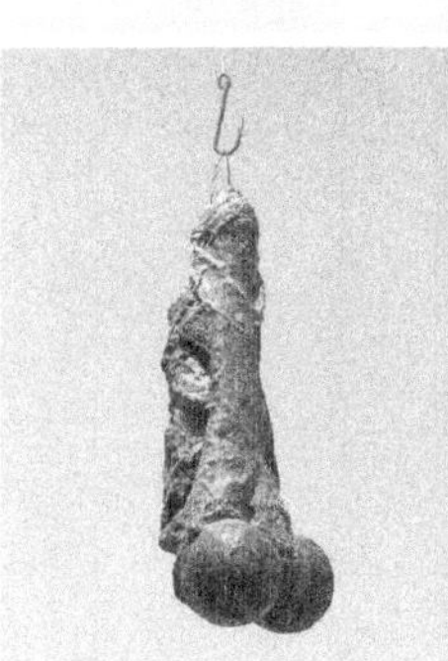

Robert Mapplethorpe, *Portrait of Louise Bourgeois Carrying H Fillette*; *Fillette*, 1968 (the version which is not sweet)

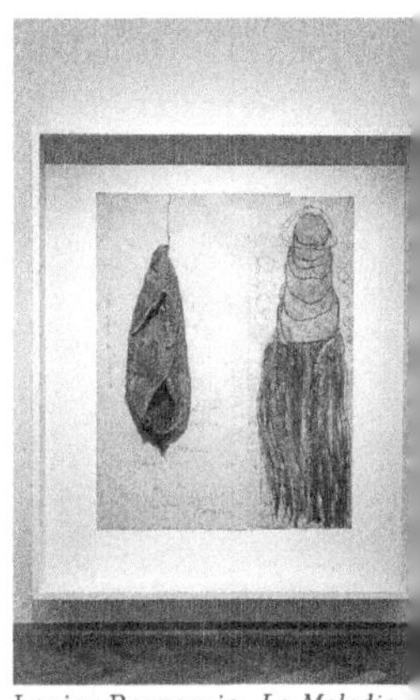

Louise Bourgeois, *La Maladie l'Amour*, 2008

Louise Bourgeois, quoted by rohn, 'Histoire de l'oeil', 103.

) Krohn, 'Histoire de l'oeil', 103.

hanging in the butcher's shop. Next to the hanging fabric is a phallus-like figure that comes out of flesh. Bourgeois said herself about this work that: '*La Maladie de l'Amour* is a state of addiction, to be obsessed by someone.'[9] According to Silke Krohn, the drawing on the right side shows 'the pure desires of the flesh that compel the phallus upward'.[10] Bourgeois has made other works based on the same devices and resulting in a sculptural logic that undoes the traditional notion of the body. Her work *Tits* (1967/1982) condenses the whole female body in two doubled breasts. Tits usually come in two and they are juxtaposed on the body, but here they are coupled and not attached to the body; instead, they form the body, in perfect symmetry. *Tits* suggests a perfect fetish and the result of male fear of castration; anxiety for his object of desire, the female body, displaces all attraction to one single body part, women's feet, or the high heels on which these feet stand. But as a fetish, Bourgeois's *Tits* is more radical, because the breasts do not displace the female body with one body part, or fragment it. Rather, the female body is condensed into two coupled tits. From the Freudian perspective of castration anxiety, this is the perfect female body, because in this condensation the wholeness of the female body has given rise to a new body, instead of displacing the body to one body part. The bronze has been polished beautifully and perfectly. So, as an object it cannot be more perfect.

When the sculpture *Tits* is seen from an anxious male perspective, the perfect female body, the sculptural logic that bases itself on the perfection of the human body, male or female, is undone. But this undoing differs from the way Giacometti performed it. The perfect female body does not in Bourgeois's case ironically resonate the inner world or inner passions of the female subject; instead, it is the result of the male beholder of that body. This female body will never say something or do something; it is exclusively there to be touched.

The series of works titled The Couple literally present a 'pair' of human beings. Yet Bourgeois's spiral bodies are not sexual bodies differentiating male and female, even though the term 'couple' conventionally refers to a relationship between a man and a woman. The two bodies in this series are doubles of each other, rather than a couple, although these spiral bodies as doubles is not so clear, either.

In Bourgeois's work, the spiral is a recurrent motif. She is fascinated by it because it is a form of 'disorientation': 'To me the spiral is a form of arranging chaos. The spiral is completely continuous, predictable or infinite. It is a form of disorientation.'[11] In the case of the series of works The Couple, disorientation concerns, first of all, the sexual nature of their bodies. According to Bourgeois, human subjects need references to live in an orderly way, but the difference between man and woman has disappeared in *The Couple*. In the 2002 version, the two bodies can still be distinguished, but in that of 2007–2009 they are completely entangled. Does this mean an idealization of the 'couple' as being 'one'? Or is it a critical reflection on it, resulting in a loss of self? The last option seems to be more plausible. Whatever the case, it is disorienting in all respects and offers the viewer no clear reference, or bodies, that they need in order 'to live in an orderly way'. The passion resonated or reflected in these spiral bodies is not a crystal-clear emotion, but a troubled and disorientating one.

Bourgeois's sculpture *Nature Study* is based on the famous classical sculpture of the goddess of fertility, *Ephesian Artemis*, of which the exact date is unknown. This goddess of fertility has many breasts, although some have argued that the breasts are in fact bull's testicles. Whatever they are, the exuberant body clearly signifies an excess of fertility. Like the

11 Louise Bourgeois, in Gorovoy and Tabatabai Asbaghi, *Blue Days and Pink Days*, p. 170

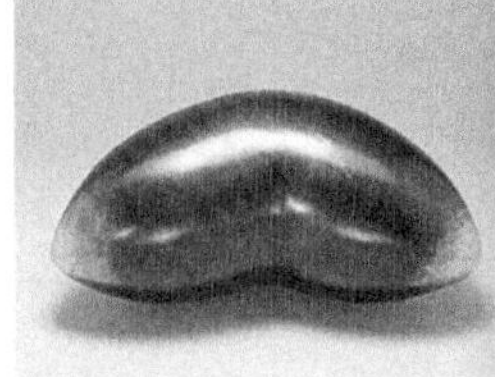

Louise Bourgeois, *Tits*, 1967/1982

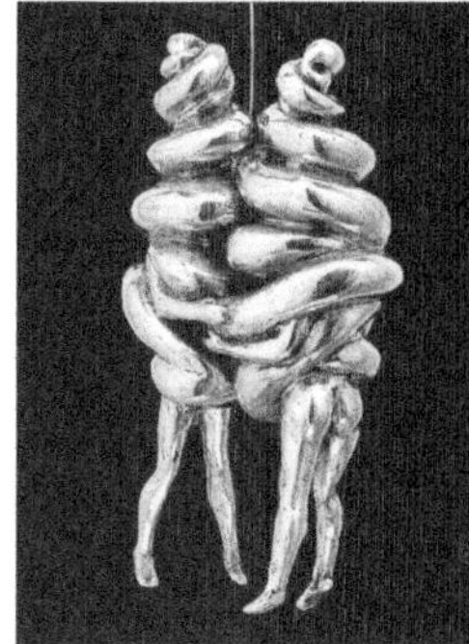

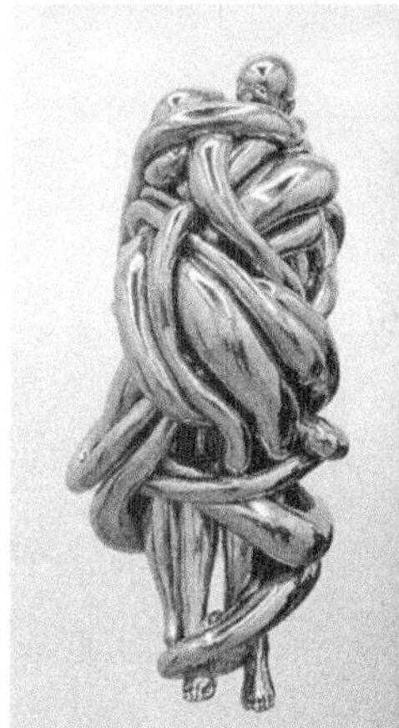

Louise Bourgeois, *The Couple*, 2002; *The Couple*, 2007–2009

2 Bourgeois, quoted in Krohn, 'Diana van Efeze', p. 89.

3 Krohn, 'Diana van Efeze', 89.

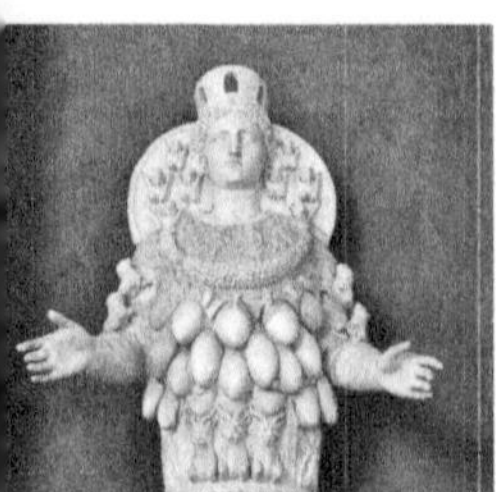
phesian Artemis, date unknown

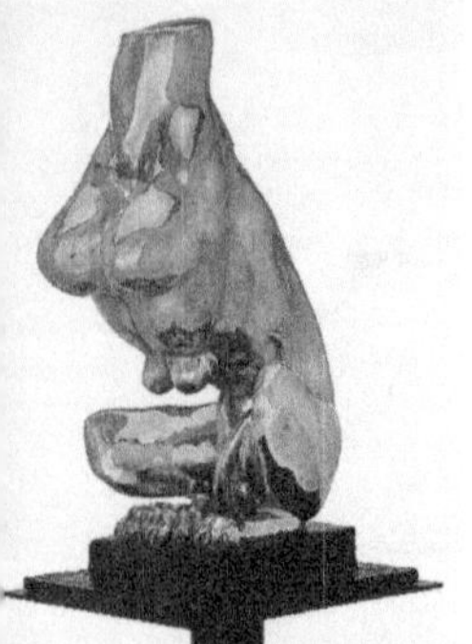

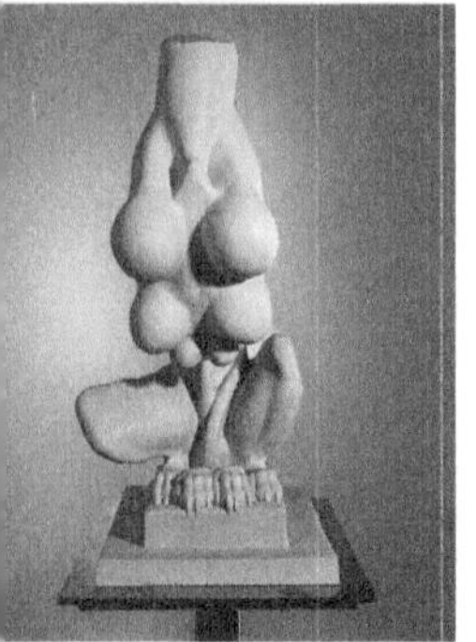

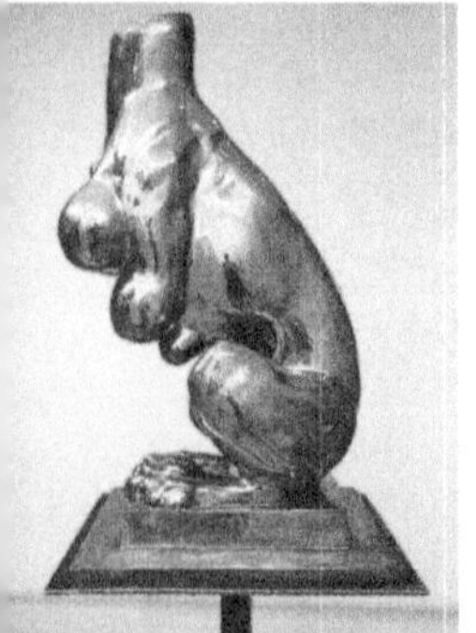
ouise Bourgeois, *Nature Study*, 984/2001, different versions in fferent materials

fertility goddess, Bourgeois's *Nature Study* also presents a multiplication of breasts.

The sculpture *Nature Study* has many breasts, but is headless and has a long phallus-like tail and a sphinx-like pose. The fact that it is ambiguous and undecidable if the protuberant body parts are breasts or testicles, or phallic breasts, is exactly the point. This ambiguity turns the figure into a phallic woman. According to the artist, the work is a self-portrait:

> *Nature Study* is a self-portrait. The multiple breasts represent the fact that I had to protect my husband and three sons. The breasts are the nurturing mother which hover over the phallus.[12]

Phallic breasts were also the main element of the costumes she made for the performance *The Banquet/A Fashion Show of Body Parts* (1978). In the upper part the round objects look more like breasts, in the lower part, more like phalluses. 'With the intention of ridiculing the symbolic power of the phallic she had male art historians and art critics appear in these costumes.'[13]

When it is ridiculing the symbolic power of the phallus that Bourgeois intends to achieve with her multiplications of breasts and phalluses, she ridicules, by the same gesture, the sculptural logic of the perfect male and female body in relation to their inner essence. The symbolic power of the phallus in these works is not the inner meaning of the male body. The female body is endowed with this symbolism in the same way, which undoes the male authority and ownership of this power. A new sculptural logic is being performed in these

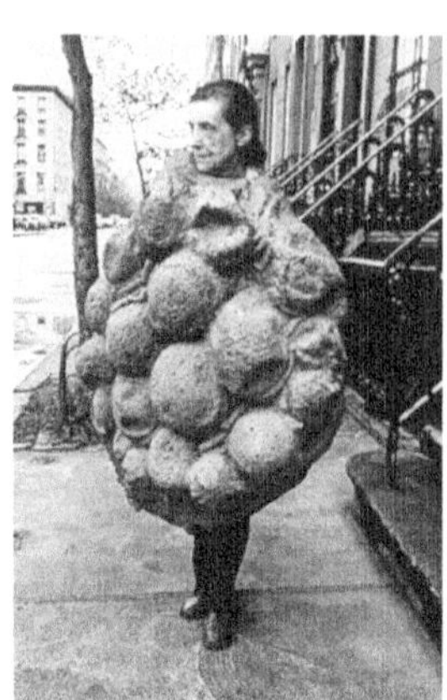
Louise Bourgeois (1911–2010) in one of the costumes of *The Banquet/A Fashion Show of Body Parts*, 1978

works by Bourgeois, one which undoes the body, and which for the signification of bodies and body parts, relies on cultural and symbolic processes, instead of on inner passions or essence.

14 Louise Bourgeois, quoted in Zacharias, 'Dolly and Prosthesis', p. 37.

Besides the multiplication, doubling, and pairing of the body, Bourgeois uses another device to undo the perfect body, namely its extension by means of a prosthesis. In her sculpture *Henriette* (1985) we see a hanging leg, extended below the knee with an artificial leg or prosthesis. Another untitled work from 2005 features a pink textile figure without arms but with a wooden leg.

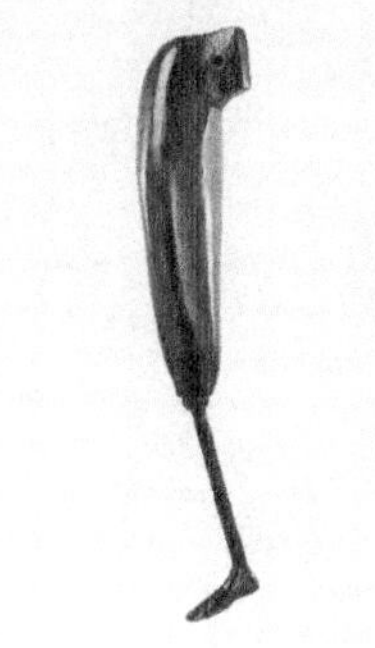

Louise Bourgeois, *Henriette*, 1985

The meaning of body extensions in Bourgeois's work is ambivalent: although they refer to a handicap, the prostheses suggest a regained power, and although this power is far from phallic, it pretends to be. This power is not symbolic, but artificial, which also helps. Bourgeois herself said the following about this sculpture:

> It applies to my sister, who had a stiff knee; she had, in effect, a wooden leg. This bothers me very much, because her demeanor when she walked was very special.[14]

Her sister's demeanour is not negative, but rather 'special'. It is fairly obvious that when the body needs extensions, it does not rely on the logic of the perfect human body. And extensions negate the suggestion of innerness as such.

Formless Bodies: Louise Bourgeois and Hans Hovy

In the twentieth century an important strategy to undo the body is by '*l'informe*', by showing bodies as 'formless'. It was French writer-philosopher Georges Bataille who had introduced this concept in the journal *Documents 7* in order to

15 Bataille, 'Informe'.

16 Krauss, 'Portrait of the Artist as Fillette', p. 28.

counter the academic and philosophical ambition to define and fixate the meaning of everything.[15] The role of the *informe* in twentieth-century art has been authoritatively discussed by Rosalind Krauss and Yve-Alain Bois in their book *Formless: A User's Guide* (1997). They propose a taxonomy distinguishing different devices that result in the formless: pulse, horizontality, base materialism, and entropy. Discussing the work of Bourgeois, Krauss defines the formless as a

> transgression of the formal logic which depends on the distinction of categorial oppositions...like inside/outside, figure/ground, male/female, living/dead. It is the transgression of these distinctions, the dangerous imagination of their collapse, that produces the *informe*.[16]

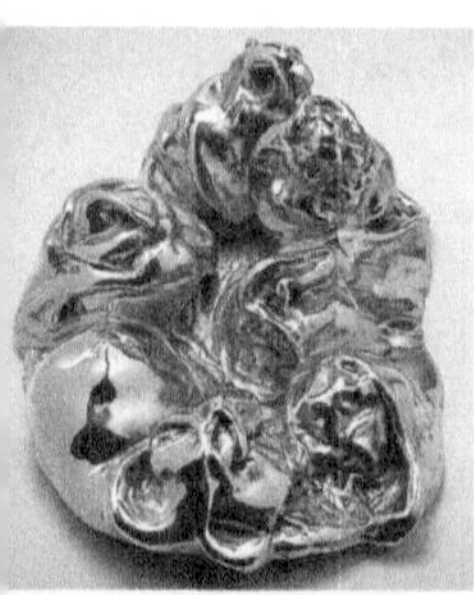

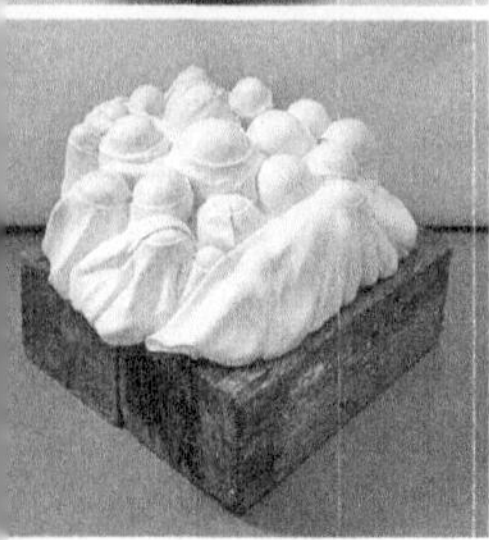

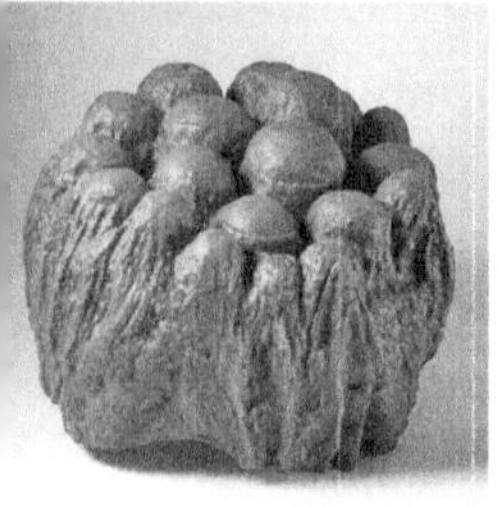

Louise Bourgeois, *End of Softness*, 1967; *Cumul I*, 1968; *Avenza*, 1984

Good examples of the formless in the works of Bourgeois are what she calls her 'sexual landscapes', officially titled *Soft Landscapes*. The sculpture *End of Softness* is shiny, made out of bronze, and as such far from soft. In these works, she explores the human body in different materials such as plaster, bronze, and marble. In contrast with Giacometti, who represented the human body as appearance, in the eye of the beholder that is, Bourgeois represents the human body from within, from her self-experience. This inner physical experience of the body does not result in clearly defined, perfect forms bur rather in a dissolution of form (as in *End of Softness*), or the multiplication of forms (for instance in *Cumul I*). When we consider Bourgeois's works from the perspective of the formless, her already-discussed *Fillette* is also a good example.

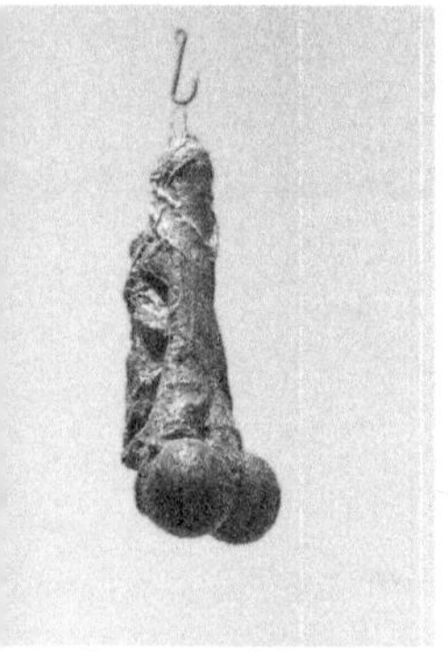

Louise Bourgeois, *Fillette*, 1968

Although at first sight a phallus is clearly not formless at all, when we start to see the erect penis as well as a vulva in the work the sculpture begins to lose its defined form. The part in which we recognize a vagina is especially formless, whereas the balls and glans of the penis are more formed, relatively. The title *Fillette*, or little girl, seems to be ironic, but when we consider it is a physical self-experience it is not ironic at all. The female desire of the flesh compels the phallus upward inside her; she is not subjected by this desire or big penis, but it makes her own body phallic.

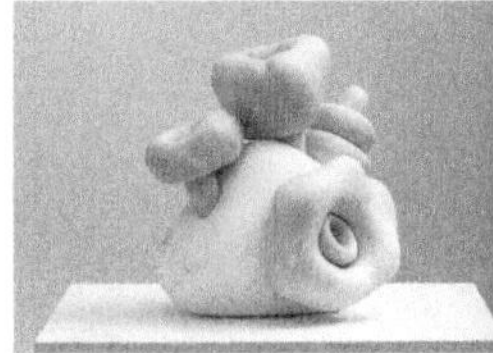

Hans Hovy, *Pure Love*, 2008/2010/2013

The sculpture of Dutch artist Hans Hovy differs, at first sight, significantly from that of Bourgeois, yet it is also comparable, especially when it concerns the formless. His works are suggestive in showing a profusion of male and female genitalia and sexual positions and acts. But it is difficult to disentangle them, to understand which body part is which and what belongs to whom. It is also important that his works do not contain clear-cut, literal representations of body parts; they are just suggestive, implying that as body parts they only exist in the eye of the beholder.

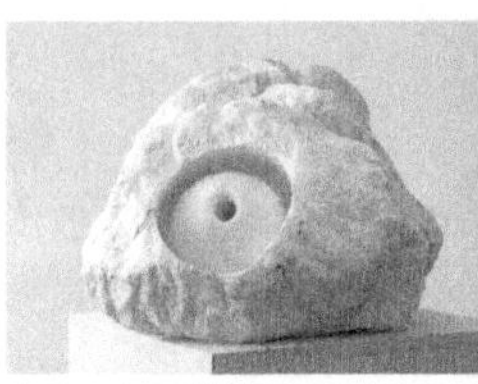

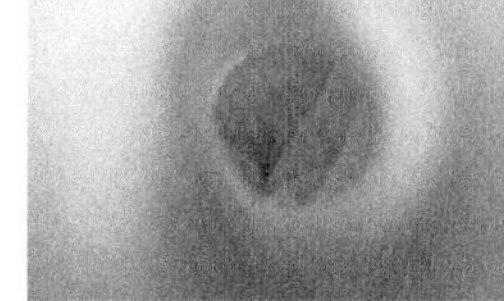

Hans Hovy, *Heavenly Light*, 2015/2016/2017; *Heavenly Light*, 2015/2016/2017, inside

At first glance, Hovy's works bring to mind certain sculptures Bourgeois made in the nineteen-sixties, particularly *Homage to Bernini* (1967), *Janus in Leather Jacket* (1968), *Janus Fleuri* (1968), *Fillette* (1968), and *Cumul I* (1969). Her *Homage to Bernini* literalizes the inner, bodily experiences in question in the most famous sculptures of the virtuoso sculptor Gian Lorenzo Bernini—white marble masterpieces with great erotic resonances. The *Ecstasy of Saint Teresa* (1647–1652) and *Blessed Ludovica Albertoni* (1671–1674) most emphatically show bodily, sexual ecstasy, whatever the religious or mythical pretext of the stories. The blessed Ludovica touches her breast in rapture, which is demonstrated by her open mouth. Bernini's sculpture of Saint Sebastian also resonates with sexual meanings. Of course, the depiction of this male saint has been part of a long tradition in which his body pierced by arrows has been taken as a

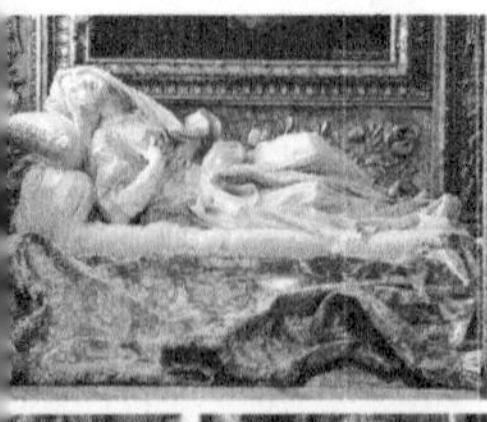

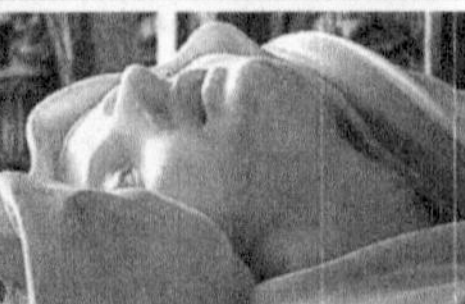

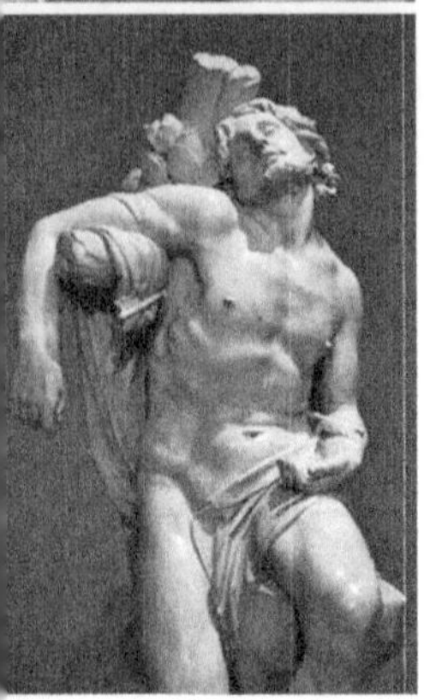

ian Lorenzo Bernini, *The* *cstasy of Blessed Ludovica* *bertoni*, 1674; *Saint Sebastian*, 17

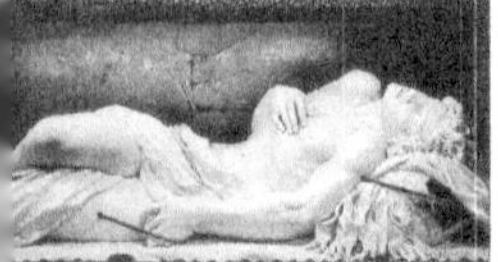

ntonio Giorgetti, *Martyrdom* *Saint Sebastian*, 1671–1672

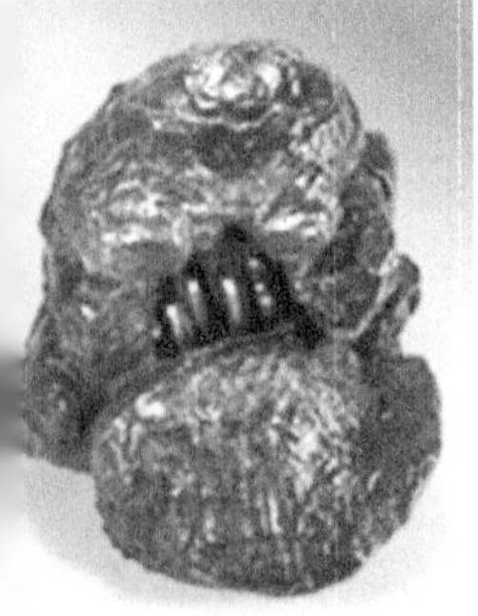

ouise Bourgeois, *Homage to* *rnini*, 1967

pretext for representing, and looking at, a beautiful male body. In the case of Bernini's sculptures, it is, however, not just the viewer who enjoys these bodies, but also the sculpted figures themselves. The Saint Sebastian by Bernini's assistant, Antonio Giorgetti, is another case in which the death of Saint Sebastian is ambiguous, suggesting the 'small death' of ejaculation instead of his physical death. But Bernini's sculptures, radical as they are, are classical or traditional in terms of the logic of sculpture we can recognize in them: an inner experience or passion translates itself onto the outer appearance of the body and is responsible for the figure's meaning.

Bourgeois's bronze homage to this canonical sculptor displaces the erotic affect and meaning of Bernini's sculptures from the skin of the figures to the inner space of an abstract volume. Whereas (Neo)classical sculpture depends for its outer appearance on an inner 'essence' or feeling that becomes visible on the skin and outer appearance, Bourgeois shows an inner, bodily space that is not responsible for the outer appearance of the bronze object. Bernini's inner, bodily experience expressed on the skin by gestures becomes in Bourgeois's work a literal inner space, like a secret world in the body. This inner space can also be recognized in many of Hovy's sculptures and can also be seen as a reconfiguration of the body. No longer an inner essence or feeling that becomes visible as outer appearance, but an exploration of the body as having inner spaces, literally. Eroticism does not only manifest itself on the skin, but also in the inner worlds of the body.

Although the inner spaces of the body are conventionally seen as being characteristic of the female body, male bodies also have them. It is remarkable that Bourgeois's *Homage to Bernini* is ambiguous in not specifying this bodily object as male or female. This is also the case in her white marble sculpture *Cumul I*. The bulging round objects are very suggestive, connoting both male and female body parts. The same can be said of her work from 1984 titled *Blind Man's Buff*; although the title of this work suggests otherwise, its appearance is far from convincingly male. This ambiguous formlessness is also typical of Hovy's work; despite his works showing inner spaces and protruding, phallic forms, it is too easy to see them as referring to the female and male body. And if we read the protruding forms as little penises, then it is clearly not signifying a phallic masculinity.

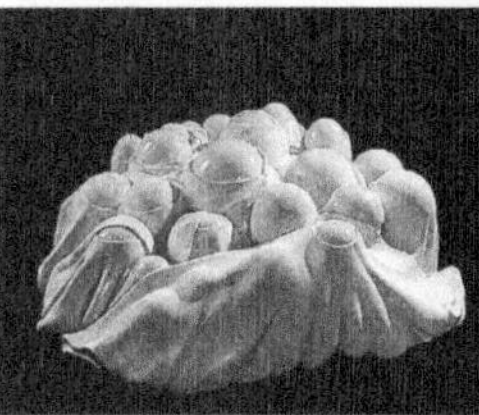

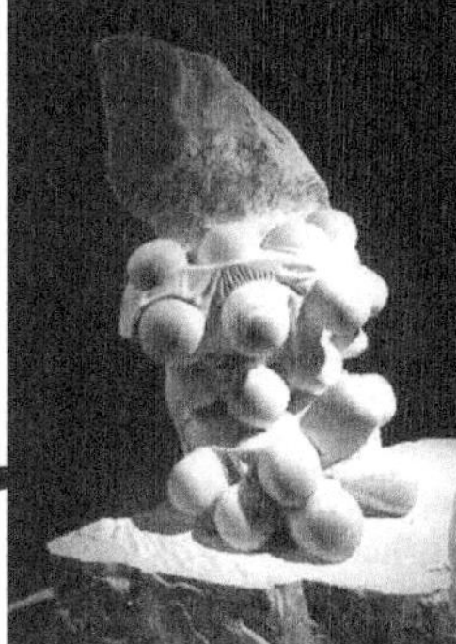

Louise Bourgeois, *Cumul I*, 1968; *Blind Man's Buff*, 1984

The Sculpture of Polymorphous Sexuality: Hans Hovy

The relationship between interior and exterior which, according to Krauss, defines classical sculpture has not entirely vanished from Hovy's work, however. It simply manifests itself in a different way; that is to say, no longer as opposites of each other but in relatedness to each other. All of the forms are 'in the making', which means that an inner space can become an outwardly protruding bulge. Inner and outer are not stable; they seem to merge with each other. This accounts for the many sexual associations inevitably evoked not only in Hovy's but also in Giacometti's Surrealist works, which I will discuss in the next chapter. As I will argue then, Giacometti's works symbolically conjure up, in particular, scenes from a marriage, while Hovy brings this about on the basis of similarity by allowing forms iconically to resemble bulges and cavities. But neither of these forms are fixed, as they seem capable of merging effortlessly with each other.

The form of sexuality that is being evoked here can, in imitation of Sigmund Freud, be called polymorphous in the most literal sense. It concerns forms which, no matter how diverse, can merge effortlessly with each other. Among the

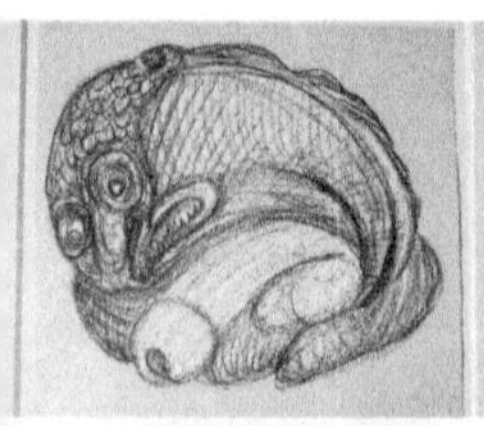

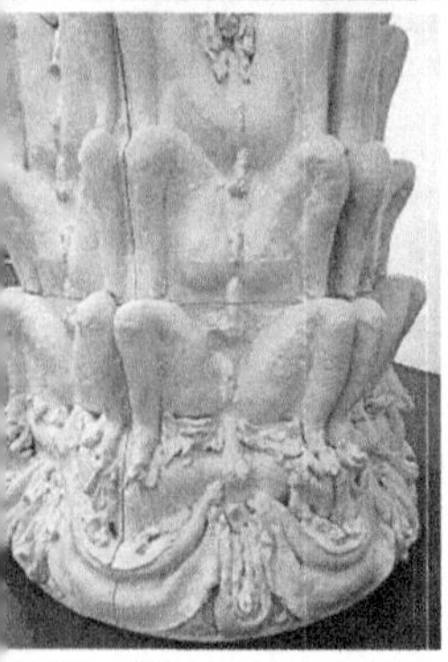

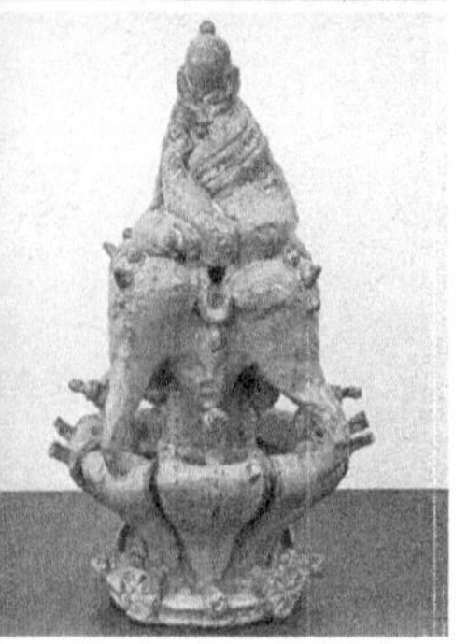

mar Trenkwalder, *Untitled; VZ 0206-S 2008*, 2008; *WVZ 1*, 2016

consequences of this is the fluidity of all associations; in other words, there are no fixed meanings to be ascribed. Male, female, top, or bottom, all fixed positions and roles are inverted or interchangeable. The many inner spaces shown in Hovy's works are no longer typically female, nor can the protrusions be considered typically male. Both bodies and platforms have inner spaces and bulges. But what does that say about sculpture? This is a rephrasing of sculptural logic, and for that reason is the pinnacle of sculpture, by a master of the art. The works thus adhere to their promise, specifically their titles: *Sculptissimo* and *Masterpiece.*

For a better understanding of the type of sculptural logic this concerns, it may be helpful to introduce a third player into the domain of sculpture: the Austrian draftsman and ceramicist Elmar Trenkwalder. On initial consideration, his sculptural work appears unrelated to that of Giacometti and Hovy since he makes no use of platforms, not even pedestals. His works are sooner architectonic constructions, completely covered with ornamentation and comparable to Indian stupas. Even so, I should like to argue that his architectonic structures are comparable to platforms, because they too constitute a stage for elaborately ornamental scenes. Another significant similarity with respect to Hovy's practice is that Trenkwalder's work, too, is sexual, even more explicitly than that of Hovy. In the baroque ornamentation of his drawings and sculptures we can discern vulvas, penises, and anuses everywhere.

Due to the profusion of male and female genitalia and sexual positions and acts in his work, we also begin to wonder with this artist whether it might be a somewhat childlike obsession with sex or if there might be more going on. The critic Frédéric Bodet takes the view that this is no childlike obsession but rather the manifestation of a specific outlook with regard to form. He argues that Trenkwalder's ornamental forms are no longer determined by an inner essence or an expression from the inside out, but by an interaction with the surroundings. Sex is consequently not a provocative, childlike motif, but instead the illustration of how the forms of (sexual) 'bodies' are determined by the interaction with their surroundings. A clear example of that principle of design is one of Trenkwalder's drawings of a penis which, in a semi-erect state, gives shape to the monster-like creature that surrounds it. These two creatures are not stable in terms of form, but one form evokes the other.

With such a concept of form, sexuality is no longer only a metaphor for life but for sculpture as well. It implies a radically different notion of sculptural form than that of the classical tradition. Bodet substantiates this with the following statement that sex is not a theme being represented by Trenkwalder, but that the suggestion of it stems from a specific view as to how sculptural form comes about:

> Plant forms and decorative patterns drawn from sinuous and exacerbated baroque lines become sexual in his work in the same way. Their germinating growth and their symmetrical movements compete in glorious impression of a monumental 'erection', whatever the actual dimensions of the sculpture might be.[17]

The work of Trenkwalder helps us to gain a better understanding of the scenic sculpture by Giacometti and Hovy. With Trenkwalder, too, we repeatedly see a dramatic tension among multiple ornamental elements, but the form of those elements changes due to such tension. This treatment of form translates into sexual 'bodies', because these epitomize such a notion of form in the most natural and literal way. In any case, female ones do, but male genitals, especially, are not

17 Bodet, 'Details to the Point of Dizziness'.

18 Bois and Krauss, *Formless*.

19 Freud, *The Future of an Illusion: Civilization and its Discontents and Other Works*, 82.

20 Freud, *The Future of an Illusion: Civilization and its Discontents and Other Works*, 83.

very stable in terms of form. This polymorphous sexuality shows that the battlefields or playing fields which the platforms comprise do not involve, as in football, established teams of players opposing each other. The sculptural form adjusts itself during the interaction among the elements, thus causing forms to be turned inside out and to become the opposite of what they initially were. Sculptural form consequently has no inner essence which explains or causes its outward appearance; it comes about in the dramatic tension for which the platforms offer or constitute an arena as demarcated spaces.

The question is whether this notion of form can be equated with notions pertaining to formlessness, which have been employed and explored in the work of many artists during the twentieth century.[18] As the antithesis of form, formlessness can best be understood as a negation of the beauty of form, as has been theorized in aesthetics. For harmonious form is supposedly considered 'pure'. As such, it comes as no surprise that Freud said little about the beauty of form in his writings on psychoanalysis. The text in which Freud nevertheless commented most directly on the subject of beauty is *Civilization and its Discontents* where he makes the following observations that cause beauty to become something paradoxical: 'Beauty has no obvious use; nor is there any clear cultural necessity for it. Yet civilization could not do without it.'[19] Several pages later he states the following:

> 'Beauty' and 'charm' are originally attributes of the sexual object. It is worth remarking that the genitals themselves, the sight of which is always exciting, are nevertheless hardly judged to be beautiful; the quality of beauty seems, instead, to attach to certain secondary sexual characteristics.[20]

Here Freud grapples with a potential relationship between a receptiveness to the beauty of form, aesthetic emotion, and sexual excitement. The two emotions both seem closely related and mutually exclusive. The history of Western art appears to have confirmed Freud's remarks—the representation of genitals in painting or sculpture has almost always been considered indecent. If a painting is to be considered 'beautiful', the representation of genitals should be avoided as much as possible. In his *Three Essays on the Theory of Sexuality,* Freud makes a remark about the relationship between art and genitals which also sheds light on the relationship between the (broader) notion of beauty and sexual excitement:

> The progressive concealment of the body which goes along with civilization keeps sexual curiosity awake. This curiosity seeks to complete the sexual object by revealing its hidden parts. It can, however, be diverted ('sublimated') in the direction of art, if its interest can be shifted away from the genitals on to the shape of the body as a whole.[21]

In his masterful study *Le jugement de Pâris,* Hubert Damisch writes that the quality beauty cannot be applicable to genitalia, because beauty is understood in terms of form, while genitals sooner belong to the domain of the unformed (*l'informe*).[22]

But this is not to say that one (the genitals) is a substitute for the other (the unformed). The psychoanalytic concept of sublimation forces us, actually, to justify the fact that the command of the unformed continues to play a role as a kind of undercurrent within the domain of form, and therefore of beauty. Even though this view of the formlessness of genitals ascribes an aesthetic role to them, it does so at the expense of

21 Freud, *The Future of an Illusion: Civilization and its Discontents and Other Works,* p. 148.

22 Damisch, *Le jugement de Pâris.*

3 Translation of fragments om a handwritten page, 1960, ondation Giacometti Archives, aris, reprinted in Giacometti, *crits.*

their form and the beauty associated with this. It is merely due to their instability of form and thus lack of beauty that they make sublimation obligatory and therefore, nonetheless, indirectly yield beauty.

The polymorphous sexuality of works by Trenkwalder and Hovy makes no use of the counterpart to form, formlessness, but rather multiformity. The lack of stability in form signifies in their work not a negation of form, but a continual transformation of form; in short, multiformity. This multiformity is the result of the dramatic interaction among multiple elements. That dramatic interaction can occur, or come about, only within a sculptural logic which provides the opportunity for this by means of a stage. Both Hovy's platforms and Trenkwalder's architectonic 'stupas' offer that. When such a dramatic interaction is staged, the sculptural form adjusts itself during the interaction among the elements, thus causing forms to transform and become polymorphous. This is not a loss of form, but rather the acquisition of form.

The Skin of Sculpture: Alina Szapocznikow

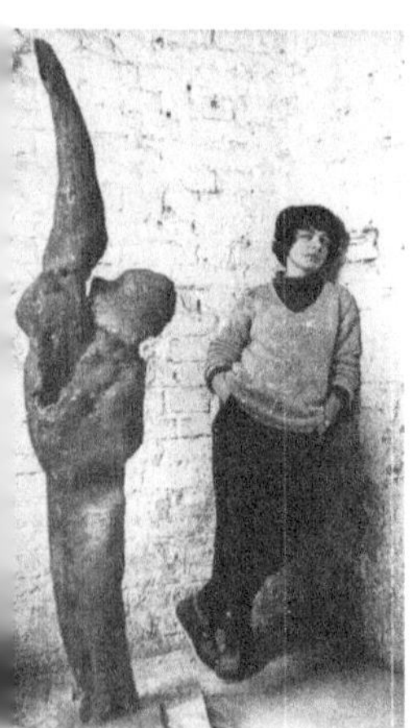

lina Szapocznikow (1926–1973)

In the following two sections I will focus on two sculptors whose works pivot on the skin, on sculpted skin and on, or through, the skin of sculpture: Polish artist Alina Szapocznikow and Belgian artist Johan Tahon. Alberto Giacometti described the relationship between the surface of his own sculptures and their meaning, or what they reveal, as follows:

> The figures are nothing more than a continuous movement from the interior, from the exterior, they are consistently shifting, they have no true consistency [...] ever changing in form and never quite graspable.[23]

The lack of consistency in the relationship between interior and exterior Giacometti describes in his own work is even more radically at stake in the work of Alina Szapocznikow. Most of her practice shows the hinge between interior and exterior, the skin. Although this study is about logics of sculpture and not about the life of sculptors, in this case it is relevant to provide some background information on Szapocznikow's life. Born in 1926 to a Jewish family in Poland, she survived the Holocaust after she had been imprisoned in the Pabianice and Łódź ghettos and in the Auschwitz, Bergen-Belsen, and Theresienstadt Nazi concentration camps. In 1951, when living in Paris, where she received her artistic training, she was diagnosed with tuberculosis, which at the time was not yet treatable, and in 1968 with breast cancer. After this last diagnosis, much of her work revolved around the traumas she endured throughout her life, death, and her bodily existence. Many of these works consist of nothing else other than bodies reduced to skin. Through casts of the human body, she preserved the impermanence of the body as a source of pain and trauma. In 1968, when cancer was diagnosed in her body, she started to make her so-called 'tumour sculptures' using resin, gauze, crumpled newspapers, and photographs, all of which carried a strong sense of melancholy.

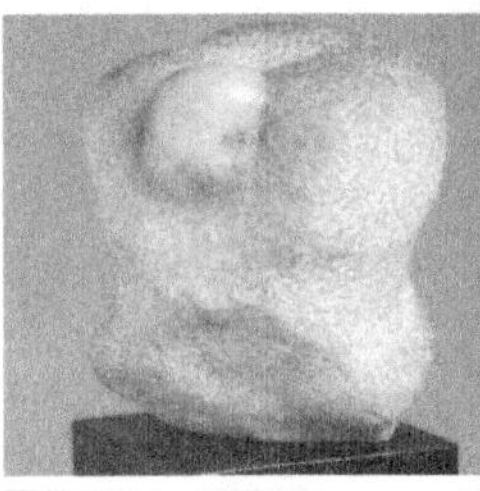

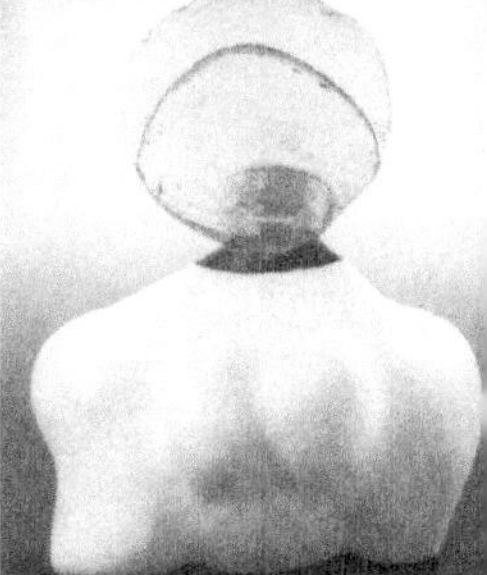

Alina Szapocznikow, *Pink Torso*, 1966–1967; *Self-Portrait I*, 196

Szapocznikow's sculptures from the nineteen-sixties give thematic emphasis to the relationship between internal structure and outward appearance. This occurs in two ways. On the one hand, this relationship is demonstratively ignored. An Example is *Biological Sculpture* (1963). The smoothness of the swelling seems to be the result of processes or labour coming from the outside, wind, water, or the hand of the sculptor. The swellings seem less the result of an inner tension or force. The swelling in *Pink Torso* (1966–1967) is a

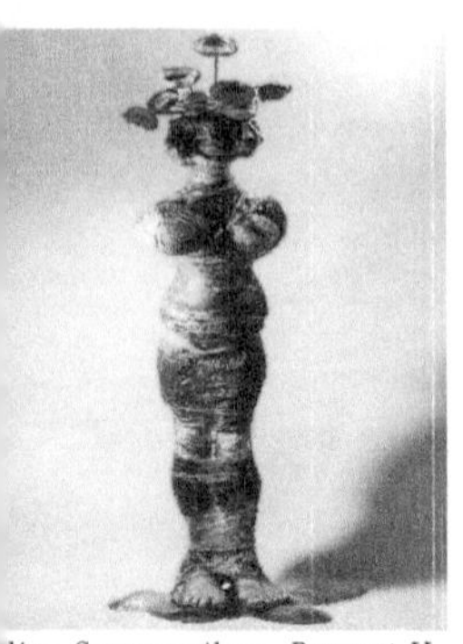
łina Szapocznikow, *Bouquet II*, 1966

growth from the inside, a kind of tumour, when we look at it, as the title suggests, realistically as a torso. But the human form or torso is not the first thing that catches the eye. It is the contrast between the smoothness of the swelling and the belaboured surface of the rest of the volume that stands out. In the belaboured surface one can see the traces of the chisel, the tool in the artist's hand. Different treatments of the sculptural skin are contrasted here. The same can be said of the lower marble part of *Self-Portrait I* (1966). Following the title, the two smooth swellings must be breasts, but such a figurative reading is at the same time challenged by the central location of the two swellings. The image of sculpted skin is then exchanged for an eye for the different treatments of this skin. We see the care with which the skin has been smoothened and the violent gestures which have caused the rougher surface. In both cases, the sculptural skin cannot be explained by an inner structure or feeling, but by a belabouring of it from the outside.

The notion of skin, sculptural as well as sculpted, is foregrounded in yet other ways in two sculptures from 1966 and 1967. In *Bouquet 2* and *Weightless (Homage to Kosmarowa)*, a human figure has been wrapped in layers of cloth as if it were a mummy. An artificial skin has been added to the human skin. In this case, the outer experience is completely motivated by the inner structure it covers: the human body. At the same time, this relation between inner structure and outer appearance is the opposite of organic. The mummification is an added skin which imprisons the inner form artificially and violently. All inner feelings and expressions are imprisoned in *Weightless (Homage to Kosmarowa)*. And in *Bouquet II*, a multiplication of breasts and mouths seems to be intimately related to the closing off, the lopping and cutting off, of the rest of the body. The bouquet of mouths and the breast seem like a desperate cry for contact and expression as a response to the closing off of the rest of the body.

The few works by Alina Szapocznikow discussed so far make clear that the sculptural skin of her works does not function as a mediator of inner structure or inner feeling. At the same time, the notion of skin is not only foregrounded as a formal aspect of sculpture as a medium, but is also a thematic issue at the level of representation. To better understand the importance of the sculptural skin and of sculpted skin in her work, I will first consider different functions of skin. Szapocznikow's works imply a notion of skin that differs from the common one. It is grounded in a phenomenological and psychoanalytical view of skin, although not limited to such a view. French psychoanalyst Didier Anzieu explains this view in his book *The Skin Ego: A Psychoanalytic Approach of the Self* (1989). According to Anzieu, the skin serves the purposes of containment, protection, and communication:

> The primary function of the skin is as the sac which contains and retains inside it the goodness and fullness accumulating there through feeding, care, the bathing in words. Its second function is as the interface which marks the boundary with the outside and keeps that outside out; it is the barrier which protects against penetration by the aggression and greed emanating from others, whether people or objects. Finally, the third function—which the skin shares with the mouth and which it performs at least as often—is as a site and a primary means of communication with others, of establishing signifying relations; it is moreover, an 'inscribing surface' for the marks left by those others.[24]

24 Anzieu, *The Skin Ego*, p. 40

25 Anzieu, *The Skin Ego*, p. 40.

Anzieu is not speaking of the physical properties of the skin but of the metaphorical qualities of flesh. His concept of 'skin ego' articulates this beautifully. 'By "Skin Ego"', Anzieu explains,

> I mean a mental image of which the Ego of the child makes use during the early phases of its development to represent itself as an Ego containing psychic contents, on the basis of its experience of the surface of the body.[25]

The skin's functions of containment, protection, and communication are the result of a dual process of interiorization. Two spatial aspects of the skin need to be internalized. First of all, the interface between the bodies of the child and the mothering figure (what Anzieu calls the 'psychic envelope'), and second, the mothering environment itself with all its verbal, visual, and emotional properties. Anzieu articulates this concept of skin ego and this dual interface by means of the somewhat surprising combination of words: 'The goodness and fullness accumulating there through feeding, care, the bathing in words.'

Of course, this view of a psychoanalyst cannot be unproblematically brought to bear on works of art. But to the extent that it also represents a philosophical conception, it can be put into dialogue with art. I contend that Szapocznikow's work engages a dialogue with this rich conception of skin. The artist's work 'on the skin' seems to challenge the skin's functions of containment and protection. Her works function as visual puns that raise numerous issues of life, touch, and sensation. As a consequence, she also challenges the common notion of the skin's metaphorical meaning of ego. Her works utterly lack the wholeness such a meaning implies. Thus, while endorsing, or absorbing, Anzieu's extension of the skin into the environment, she declines the totalizing wholeness that retreats into the skin as a boundary of the human individual.

Instead, in her work skin is presented as highly communicative. The third function of skin that Anzieu distinguishes seems to be all-pervasive in Szapocznikow's work. Let me repeat his formulation of this function:

> The third function—which the skin shares with the mouth and which it performs at least as often—is as a site and a primary means of communication with others, of establishing signifying relations; it is moreover, an 'inscribing surface' for the marks left by those others.

Her works open out to the world. The skin of her pieces does not mark a boundary. Rather, it is a zone of contact where spaces and beings can entangle. In Anzieu's terms, this can be understood as 'the common skin fantasy'. Anzieu characterizes this fantasy of human relationships as problematic because it is not taking place between autonomous individuals, but as mutual symbiotic dependency. Szapocznikow, however, enacts the common skin fantasy as attractive and seductive, rather than problematic. In the following discussion of some of her other works I will describe the attractions of this fantasy of 'a skin we share' and in which sense this fantasy is a form of idealization.

Most noticeably, it is striking that the first function Anzieu ascribes to the skin is increasingly absent in Szapocznikow's work. Her sculpted skins and sculptural skin are not like the 'sac which contains and retains inside it the goodness and fullness accumulating there through feeding, care, and the bathing in words'. Her work *The Bachelor's Ashtray I* is a good example of how the skin sac fails in containing and retaining inside. It is an example that can be read as an allegory of how, in which sense, skin, sculpted as well as

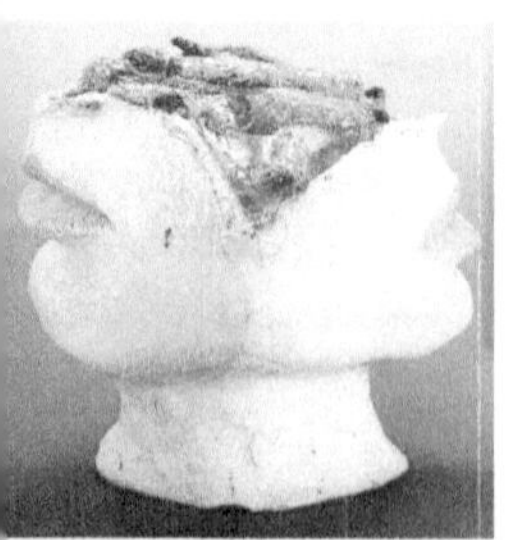

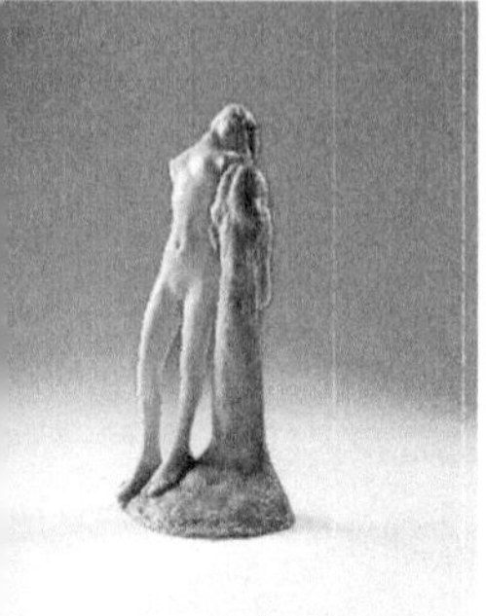

:ina Szapocznikow, *The achelor's Ashtray I*, 1972; *ad White Fiancée*, 1971

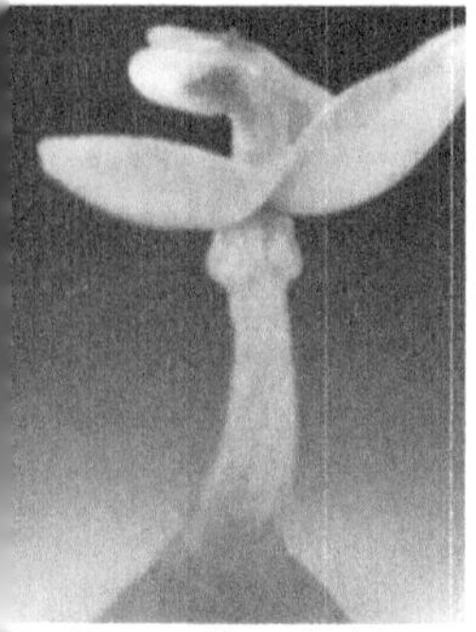

ina Szapocznikow, *Sculpture-amp VI*, 1970

sculptural, fails in its primary function. This double head/container is open at the top and the cigarette stubs flow over the edge. The usual openings, the mouths, are closed, but the cranium is lifted and open. This container does not retain within but is an open whole that can be filled from the outside.

Furthermore, the skin's secondary function according to Anzieu is of little relevance in Szapocznikow's work. Skin is no 'interface which marks the boundary with the inside and keeps that outside out'; it is not 'a barrier which protects against penetration by the aggression and greed emanating from others, whether people or objects'. An example of this failure that is again allegorical is *Mad White Fiancée*. The allegorical narrative suggested by this sculpture shows an enormous penis, announcing its penetration of the female body. She looks as if she is fainting, but whether out of sheer pleasure or fright remains ambiguous. The issue, however, is how the penetration of the body is explicitly and provocatively foregrounded. Another example is *Sculpture-Lamp VI* (1970), where the moment of penetration is represented in the act. Moreover, many of her works show fragments of the body, especially mouths, which are multiplied. The proliferation of these body parts or bodily fragments seems to demonstrate the utter openness of the body and the failure of the skin to function as a boundary between the body and the outside.

Containment and protection are radically undermined by Szapocznikow's treatment of the sculptural and sculpted skin. Yet Anzieu's definition of communication is peculiar: although it compares this function of skin with the mouth and not with the ears, he explains it as an inscribing surface for the marks left by others. Communication is not seen as an exchange but as a one-way process initiated by others from the outside.

Another recurrent motif in Szapocznikow's sculpture is the belly. Presented as a bodily fragment, instead of a body in its own right (like Bourgeois's *Tits*), these bellies are not tight or swollen, but consistently folded. The skin of the belly has folds through which it creates its own inner spaces. The inner space suggested is not behind the outer skin. The space within the fold is an inner space, but in fact it is inner and outer at the same time. There is interiority, but that interiority is located not behind the skin, but on its surface; it is a kind of 'virtual' interiority. The distinction between inner and outer does not really hold here. The skin touches skin, but that skin is not someone else's skin. The sharing of skin that takes place here is like touching one's own skin. The folded belly is like an auto-erotogenic zone. But the open spaces within the folds are not really open the way mouths can be, or vaginas. They are impenetrable inner spaces. When opened up, or penetrated, the fold dissolves and inner space transforms into outer space, as in *Belly Cushions* (1968) and *Big Bellies* (1968). Here the fantasy of the common skin is realized within the subject, not in relation to other subjects.

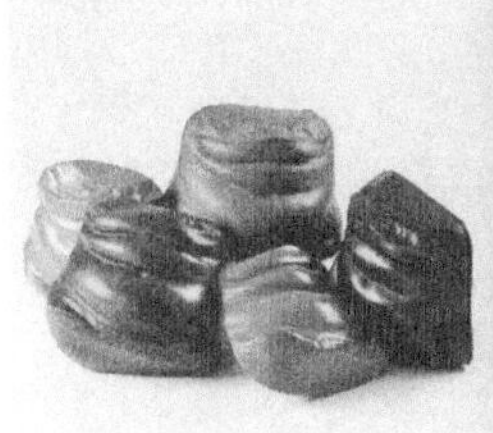

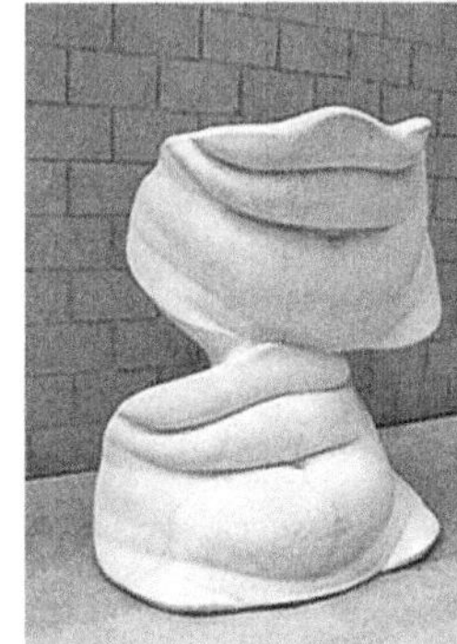

Alina Szapocznikow, *Belly Cushions*, 1968; *Big Bellies*, 1968

The folded belly is and is not like the other recurring motif in Szapocznikow's sculpture, the mouth. They are the same insofar as they are both pieces of unfolded skin. And according to Lacan, the erotogenic zones of the body always consist of folded skin that functions as an opening to the body, as a boundary of inside and outside, of inner and outer. Not only the mouth, but also the eyelids, the vagina, the anus, and the penis are such erotogenic folds or openings. Most of these folds occur in Szapocznikow's work as bodily fragments, instead of as autonomous body parts. The difference between the folded bellies and these other folds is, of course, that the belly is not a real opening of the body. The interiority of the belly is only suggested by its being folded. At the same

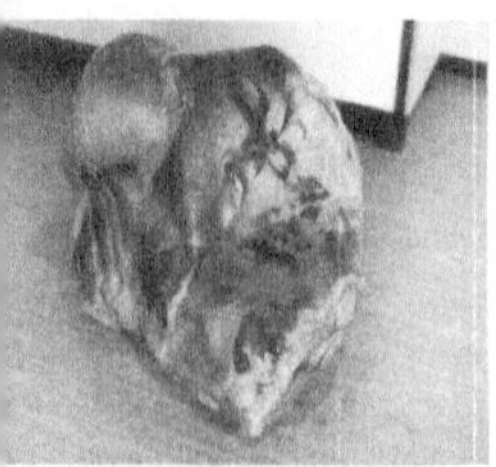

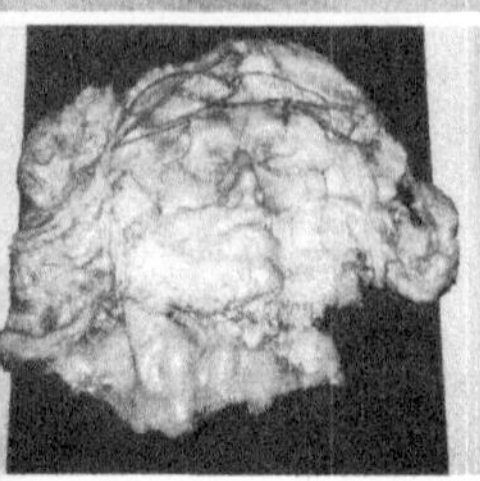

[Al]ina Szapocznikow, *Big Tumor* [II], 1969; *Herbarium IV*, 1972

time, this difference can also be turned into another similarity: it draws attention to the fact that the mouths in Szapocznikow's works are consistently closed and refuse to be an opening to the body. The skin as interface and as a means of communication, of which the mouth is emblematic, is contested in her work.

But the skin is not only a means of communication; it is also a site of communication. It is not the subject herself who is the communication subject, but the other who uses the subject's skin as an 'inscribable' surface. The work *Big Tumor II* (1969) can be seen as an inscribing surface or skin, with photographic imprints left on the sculptural skin. Like the veil of Veronica showing the imprint of Christ's sweating and bleeding face, this appearance shows someone else's outer appearance. The common skin or the 'skin we share' results here in a conflation or appearance at the site of skin as inscribing surface. It is impossible to disentangle these appearances and decide which one is whose.

Other works by Szapocznikow seem to exist of nothing else but skin. They look like flayed skin—the flaying of the human body is an important motif in several mythologies. First of all, the satyr Marsyas was flayed by the God Apollo because of hubris. Marsyas was an expert player on the double-piped, double-reed instrument known as the aulos. He challenged Apollo to a contest of music and lost both the contest and his life when Apollo punished him by flaying his body. In Aztec mythology it was the God Xipe Totec or Xipetotec ('Our Lord the Flayed One') who was flayed. He was a life-death-rebirth deity, a god of agriculture, vegetation, and the seasons. In Szapocznikow's skin sculptures, the face and other body parts like feet and hands can be recognized, but they no longer function as the hinge between inner emotions and outer appearances, nor as a site of communication.

And because the skin does not contain anything any more, the function of protection has also dissolved. Anzieu describes how the skin ego can develop either in a narcissistic direction or in a masochistic one. When it develops in the narcissistic direction, the fantasy of the common skin is transformed into a secondary fantasy of a skin reinforced and invulnerable. The skin becomes like a shield. When the common-skin fantasy develops in a masochistic direction, the fantasized skin is seen as damaged, torn off, and yes, flayed.

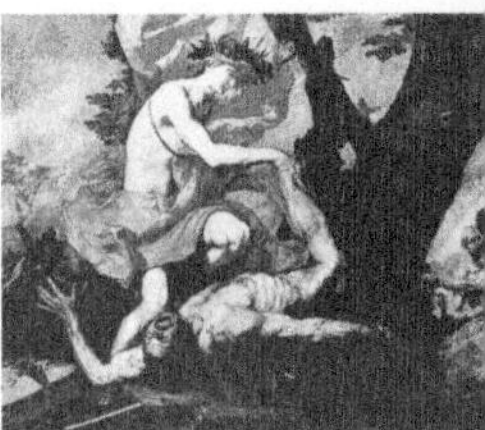

José de Ribera, Apollo flaying Marsyas in *Apollo and Marsyas*, 1637

It is clear that in Szapocznikow's work it is not the skin as shield but the skin as flayed that provides a more specific conception of the common skin fantasy. The sculptures she made in 1972 consist of representations of flayed skin in the most literal sense. The sculptural skin is now utterly flat, not suggesting any volume or interior space, whether brought into being by internal passions or structures or external forces. These skins no longer contain anything, and they have clearly failed to protect because they are damaged and torn off. In *Self-Portrait, Herbarium* (1971), we see the flayed skin of the head, the body, the legs, and the feet attached to a flat surface. The gradual splitting of the skin's three main functions—containment, protection, and communication—seems to have come to a radical closure in this flayed condition.

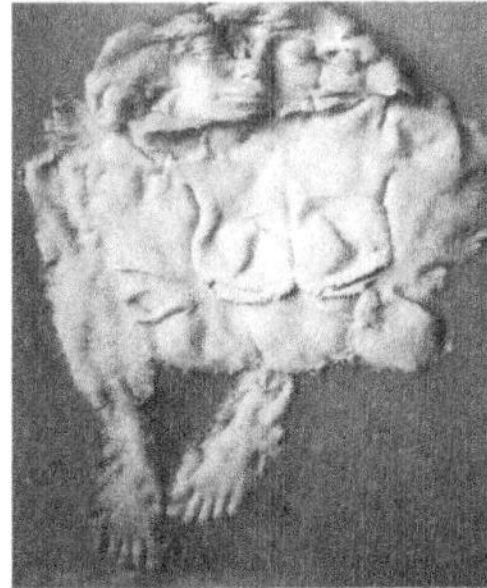

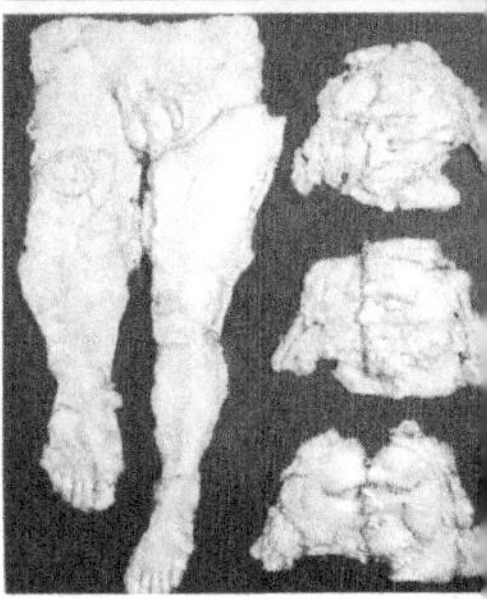

Alina Szapocznikow, *Herbarium III*, 1972; *Herbarium XIII*, 1972

Not only psychologically but also as sculpture, they fail to do what they are expected to do. The three-dimensionality of sculpture has shrunk into the almost flatness of relief. There is a temporal, narrative aspect to this. The sculptural body is only suggested as trace, not as volume. This trace is not only referring backwards as something left behind, but it is also a projection forwards. The sculptures of Szapocznikow that consist of sheer skin operate as trace, not spatially but temporally; they do not refer to inner structures or passion or outer forces. They offer traces that can be read as narrative—

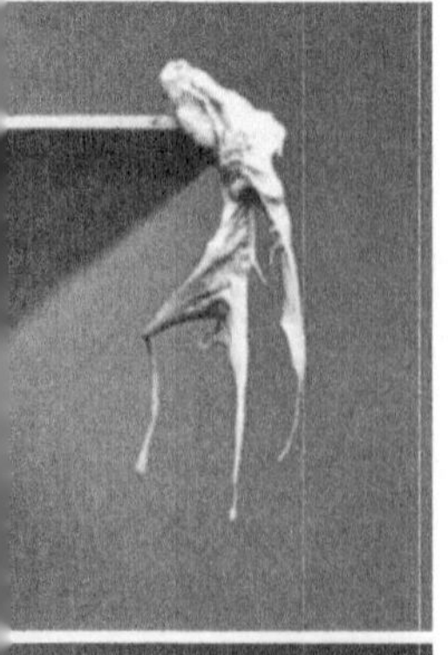
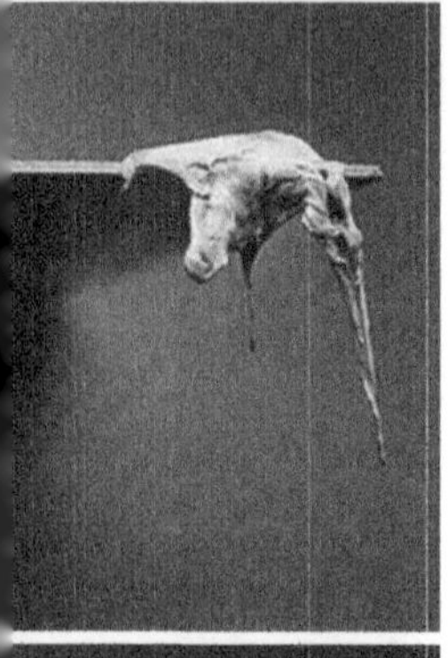
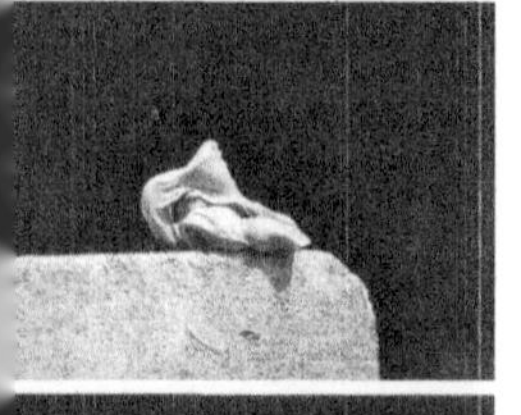
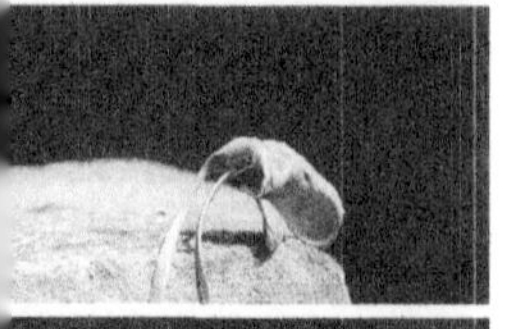
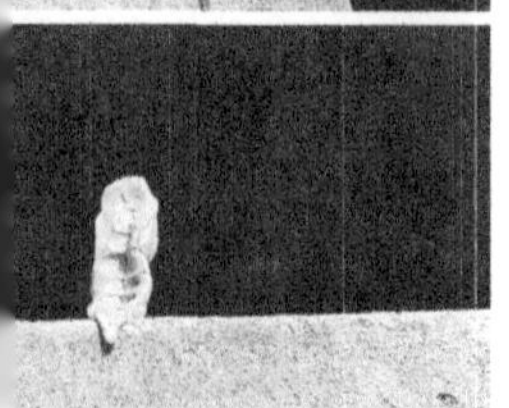
ina Szapocznikow, *Photo-ulptures*, 1971

not only the well-known myth of the flaying of Marsyas by Apollo provides a framework for doing that, but also the life of Szapocznikow herself.

The series of flayed-skin sculptures seems to be a radical masochistic closure of a sculptural project that gradually takes apart the conventional functions of sculpted skin and of sculptural skin. A masochism that no longer contains any pleasure seems to be Szapocznikow's endgame, and the sensuality of the body clearly belongs to the past of these flayed skins. But this is not Szapocznikow's final word on the subject, either. For, in contrast to this fading away of any possible sensuality, the series of twenty *Photo-Sculptures* (1971), made just before the flayed skin series, shows something utterly skin-like as sensual. The tiny sculptures she photographed consist of nothing other than chewing gum. They are radically formless and do not represent anything. No inner-outer relationship is evoked. These chewing-gum sculptures are not bodies or objects; they are sheer skin. But sheer skin is a paradox, because now it has become a body as such, without the outer protection of any skin.

When all remnants of the psychological functions of skin are eliminated, these photo-sculptures seem to suggest this skin-only can shine again, not for a subject it clothes, but as interface to a visual transaction. Thus, a sculptural skin has something to offer beyond psychology. Now it has become a trace that only projects itself forwards, outwards. There is no body left behind; only a visual act resulting in sensual abstract form to hope for.

Slashing Skin: Johan Tahon

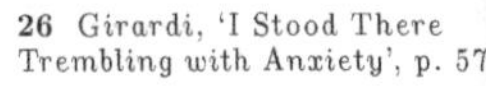

Belgian artist Johan Tahon makes his ceramic sculptures as follows: after making rough forms in plasticine, a synthetic clay, these forms become a mould. The forms are then cast in clay. They are subsequently reassembled to create a volume or 'body'. Often at this stage, perforations are made into the clay. After that the object undergoes further treatment: it is perforated once more, cut, and recomposed. This process of creation is at the same time a deformation of the original composition. The composition continues with and after the first firing, because then glaze is added to it, only partly covering the head, body, or vessel. The glaze is like a skin 'challenging its buffeted envelope'.[26] Although mainly consisting of ceramic, sometimes wood or plaster are added to the composed bodies.

These bodies clearly do not form a unity; they are composed, their skin is perforated, and they consist of several segments. They are slashed, cut, and recomposed. It looks as if these bodies wear stigmata, like 'repeated attacks that define the mapping of the body'. They look wounded. As a result, they are melancholic and introspective, and the viewer is in the position of being a witness, instead of a spectator.[27]

Tahon does not use the term body or figure for his sculptures—for him they are objects. Although we recognize heads or human bodies in these objects, they are not representations of heads or human bodies. They can best be called transitional objects, in the sense of Melanie Klein, with symbolic and social functions. They are like totems or fetishes, suggesting that their meaning does not reside in what they represent, but in the function they have for who makes or beholds them. These objects do not refer back to what they represent,

26 Girardi, 'I Stood There Trembling with Anxiety', p. 57.

27 Girardi, 'I Stood There Trembling with Anxiety', p. 62

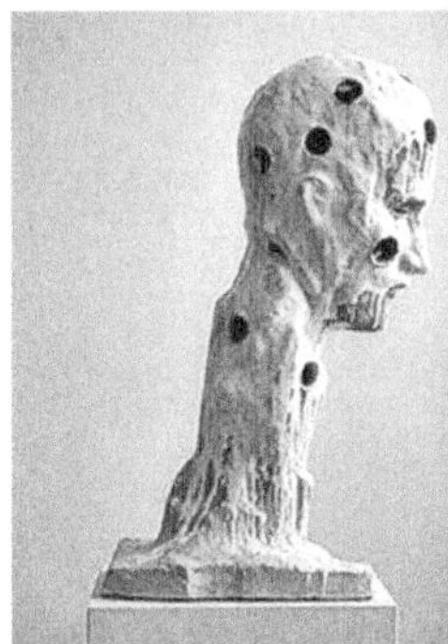

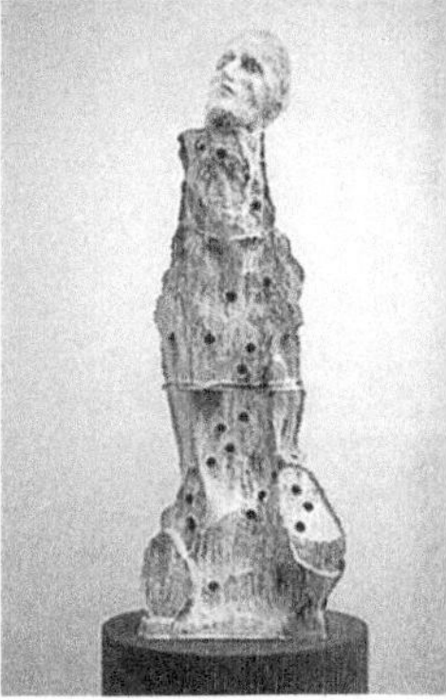

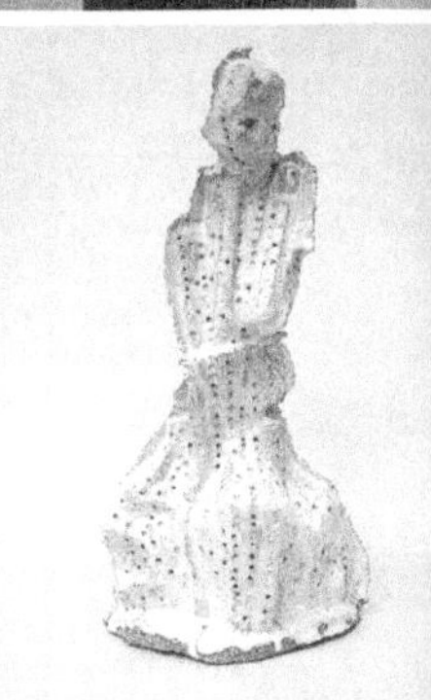

Johan Tahon, *Manresa*, 2014–2015; *Glacier*, 2017–2018; *Pierced Scream*, 2015

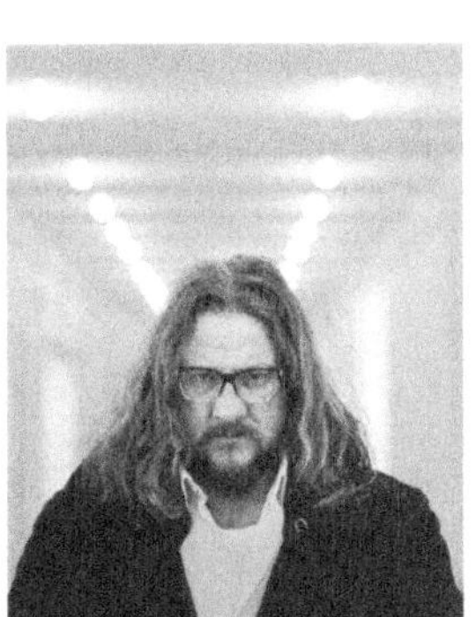

Johan Tahon (1965)

28 Girardi, 'I Stood There Trembling with Anxiety', p. 62.

29 Genet, 'The Studio of Alberto Giacometti'.

but they are new objects entering our world. The hand of Tahon is visible everywhere: 'Their eyes are like the imprints of the sculptor's fingers, sometimes even intensified by a gash, always bare, reminding us of the clay, the underlying material.'[28] The way I have described Tahon's sculptures clarifies that their logic differs radically from the notion of bodily perfection that underlies (Neo)classical sculpture. They resist against being bodies, and instead are objects made out of clay and partly covered by glaze. Yet they have an inner dimension evoked by the materiality of these objects and the way these objects have been treated. A statement by Jean Genet, talking about the sculpture of Giacometti, fittingly describes this evocation of meaning or an inner dimension:

> Beauty has no other origin than a wound, unique, different for each person, hidden or visible, that everyone keeps in himself, that he preserves and to which he withdraws when he wants to leave the world for a temporary but profound solitude.[29]

What is striking about Genet's remark regarding a wound underlying all beauty is that it can be read as a statement about both the artist, and his or her inspiration to make art, and about the viewer. In our art-critical tradition, it is common to read a remark like this as an explanation of the motivation of the work of art and concerning the artist, not the viewer. But Genet's remark is ambiguous and can also be understood as applying to the beholder who bestows beauty on an artwork or recognizes it within. The introspective, introvert figures of Tahon, wounded and slashed as they are, do not relate then to inner emotions or passions of a represented figure, but to those of the beholder. That means that a completely different sculptural logic is at work here than the conventional one.

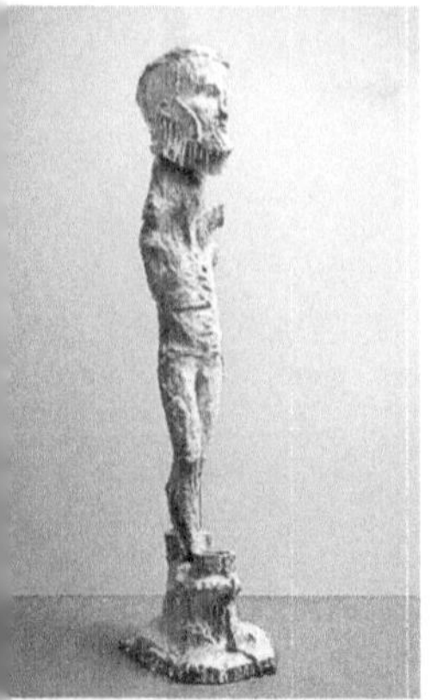

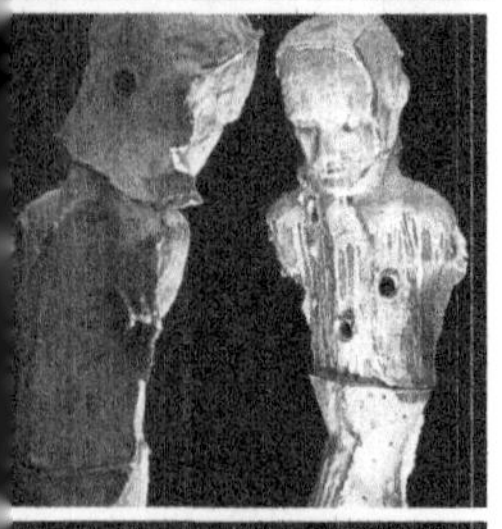

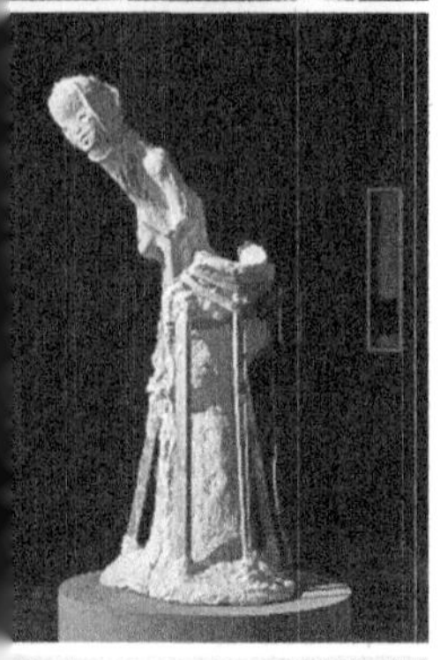

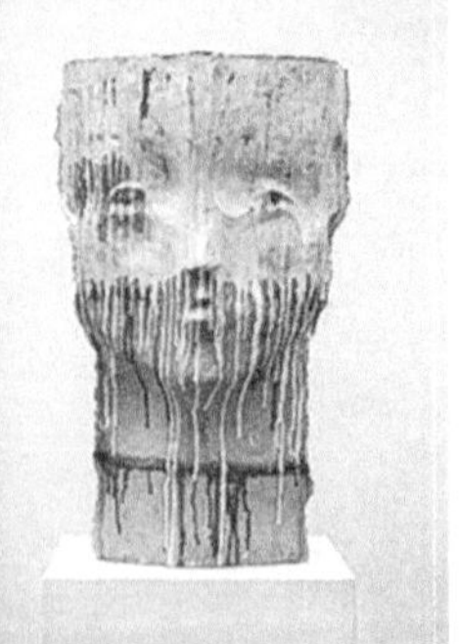

…an Tahon, *Polmen*, 2015; …o *Glacier Monks*, 2019; …*les*, 2016–2017; *Grigory*, 2012

Tahon's main artistic inspiration is Norwegian artist Edvard Munch. Although Munch only made a few sculptures, what he and Tahon have in common is that they are not focused on what their works represent, but on what they bring about performatively. They are concerned with how their works resonate or vibrate. Girardi calls what these two artists share 'a primal form of Expressionism'; it is primal because it does not concern the artist's expression but an expression of the world in which the beholder also partakes.[30] Munch described this mode of Expressionism as follows: 'Vibrations, animated by a tactile force, traversing the natural environment, penetrating all substances (including the sensory barrier of the body).'[31]

The penetration of all substances, performed but also experienced as a tactile force, seems to be almost literally at stake in Tahon's sculptural logic. This explains why the mode of production of Tahon and Munch is in fact very similar. Although mostly working in different media, they both subject their work to special treatments which rather than form or shape, deform. Munch left his paintings outside in all weathers so that the paint and the surface of the painting was animated and penetrated by natural forces, the finishing touch to his work. Tahon belabours the original objects by perforating them, by cutting and recomposing them. It is only after these deformations of 'perfect' bodies that the totemistic quality can come about.

30 Girardi, 'I Stood There Trembling with Anxiety', p. 61.

31 Edvard Munch, quoted by Girardi, 'I Stood There Trembling with Anxiety', p. 61; also, the title of Girardi's article is a quote from Munch.

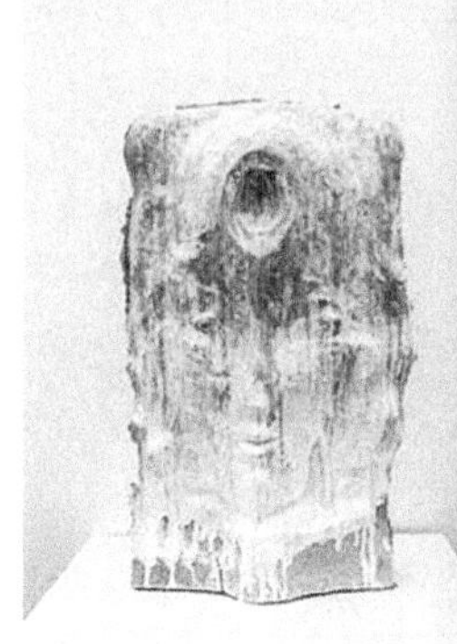

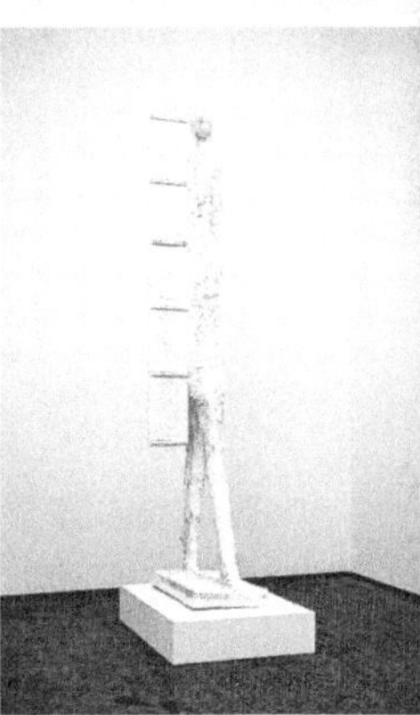

Johan Tahon, *Circumpolar*, 2017; *Fin*, 2004–2014

Layered Skin: Eva Hesse

When American artist Eva Hesse began to show her work in the nineteen-sixties, it was seen as viably different from the 'readymade, industrial surfaces of Minimalism', which

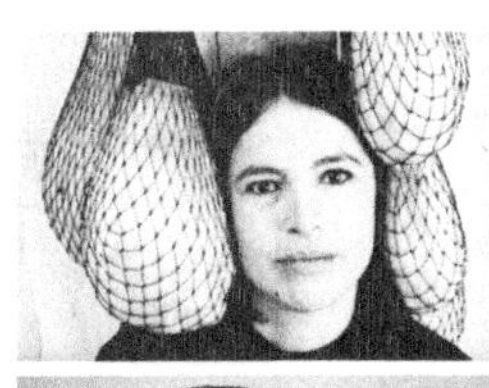

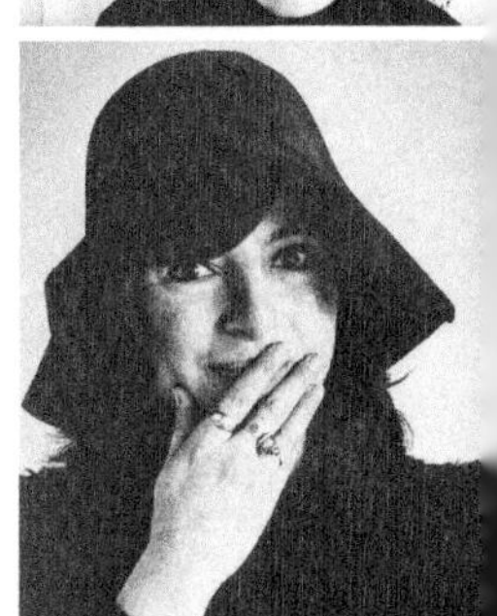

Eva Hesse (1936–1970)

2 Lippard, 'Eccentric bstraction'; quoted in Fer, 'he Work of Salvage', p. 87.

3 Fer, 'The Work of Salvage', 87.

4 Fer, 'The Work of Salvage', 87.

5 Fer, 'The Work of Salvage', 87.

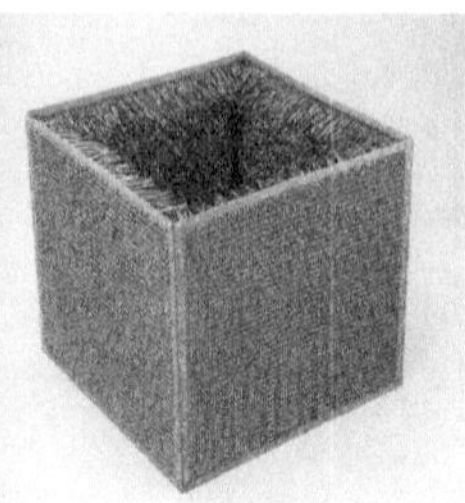

va Hesse, *Accession II*, 968–1969

was one of most important artistic movements of the time. When critic Lucy Lippard reviewed the show 'Eccentric Abstraction', featuring the work of Eva Hesse, Bruce Nauman, and Louise Bourgeois, she wrote that their work was an alternative to 'dead-set Minimalism'.[32] But as the title of the show indicates, these works were abstract, so how do they relate to the body, or to the body undone? According to Lippard, all the artists in this show embraced the bodily, the sensual, and the tactile,

> like a return of the repressed—doubly repressed in actuality by both a Minimalist rhetoric and the modernist optical paradigm of disembodied and disinterested aesthetic experience that it had sought to replace.[33]

The way Hesse's works address the viewer, also the works that are more or less flat, do so like sculpture does. It grasps the viewer principally in terms of touch; not literally, but by touch activated within the sense of sight. The encounter with her artworks activates 'bodily empathies', resulting in a kind of bodily experience 'that was heightened by an awareness of surfaces that were particularly familiar in terms of touch'.[34] As Briony Fer argues, this awareness went further than invoking the material and formal properties of the work as a mode of recognition of something skinlike.[35] The bodily nature of (Neo)classical sculpture seems to have been transferred from the sculptural object to the viewer. How can this be?

First of all, because although Hesse used industrially manufactured components, like steel, rope, or latex, she modified and belaboured them by hand. For instance, the perforated steel box for *Accession II* was itself industrially made, but it was obsessively threaded by hand with thousands of plastic tubes. Hesse always has an intense physical involvement with the industrial materials she uses, but her latex works also emphatically show that they are made, belaboured, by hand. Bill Barrette has argued that Hesse's works in latex move from casting (a traditional sculptural technique) to coating. This coating could only have been done by hand.[36] This activity of coating, of adding one layer to the next, results in a very specific surface, or skin. This is very clear, for instance, in the works *Sans I, II,* and *III,* and also in the well-known *Untitled* work (1970), now in the Centre Pompidou. Hesse 'painted' the latex in layers, so she obtained the thickness she wanted. As she said herself: 'It builds up and if I need thickness it is one layer over the other.' This working method challenges the notion of skin, and as a result the notion of the body. Her objects have a layered skin, which does not comply with the idea of the perfect human body and its inner-outer relationship.

Briony Fer assesses Hesse's undoing of the human body by quoting from Melville's *Moby Dick*:

> 'The question is, what and where is the skin of the whale?' So asked Melville in *Moby Dick* at the very moment when the great, slain body of the whale is cut into, the very moment, that is, when things, one might think, would come clear. Instead, the closer inspection of its vast bodily expanse the less certain his sense of what was the containing surface sealing the body. In the face of such a scene, there is no doubt that laws of inside and outside are ruthlessly abandoned: looking closely only made things fall apart, not come together. [...] At stake in the encounter is an utter dereliction of surface, which can only be reconfigured as a series of layers.[37]

The blubber which envelopes the whale challenges familiar notions of the body and its boundaries. The body that

36 Bill Barrette, quoted in Fer, 'The Work of Salvage', p. 88.

37 Fer, 'The Work of Salvage', p. 79.

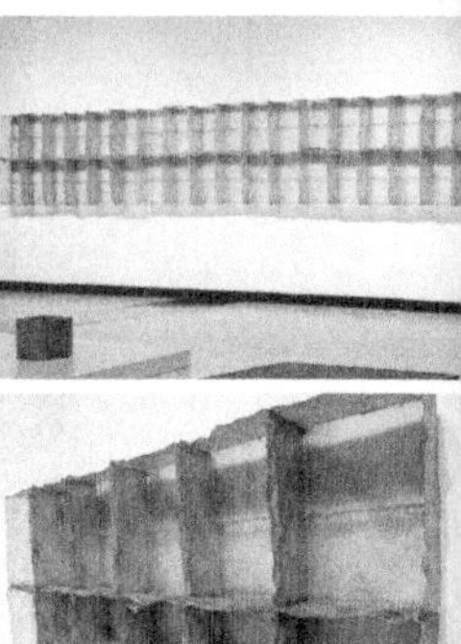

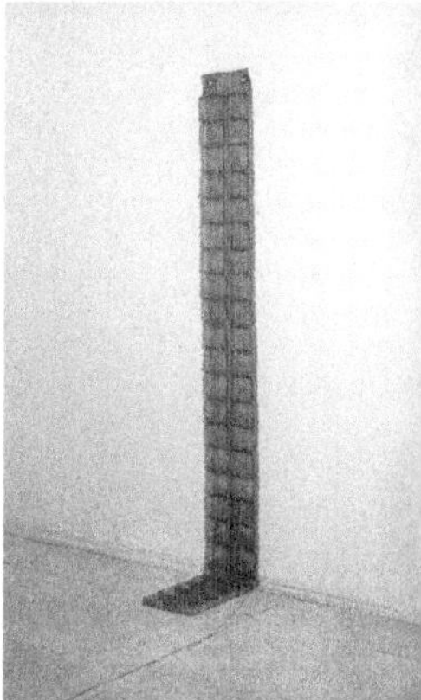

Eva Hesse, *Sans II*, 1968; *Sans III*, 1969

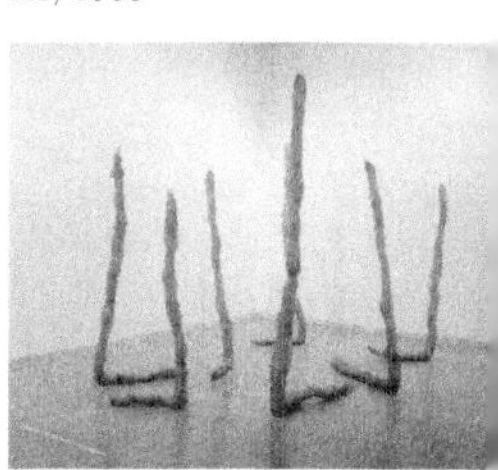

Eva Hesse, *Untitled*, 1970

8 Fer, 'The Work of Salvage', 79.

9 Fer, 'The Work of Salvage', 93.

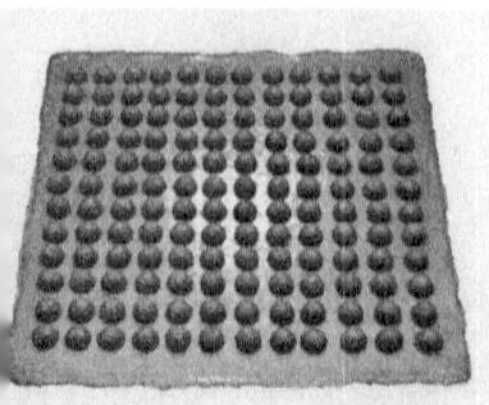

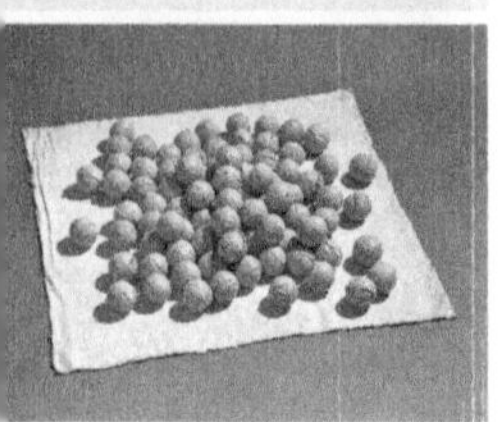

va Hesse, *Schema*, 1967–1968; *equel*, 1967–1968

Melville describes is all material. Fer frames Hesse's sculpture with Melville's question and concludes that her work is 'constantly thwarting a ready iconography of the body in favor of effects that palpably ground it an irreducible and extreme materiality'.[38] So, Hesse's work does much more than just evoke powerful bodily associations—in contrast with Minimalism's hard, industrial surfaces. As Fer argues, Hesse reconfigures the body through a double action: first by disintegrating the body and second by lacing the disintegrating body together again. In doing so, she creates order in chaos, and the repulsive becomes beautiful. But there is a third action: the surface or skin is inscribed by signs of rupture. Altogether, it results in a notion of skin that is no longer the boundary of the body, but a skin that is layered and is a body in itself.

This reconfiguration of the body and its skin is at the same time a reconfiguration of the senses.

> [...] rather than simply recover touch, what was at stake for Hesse was a radical reconfiguration of the relations between touch, sight, and the material nature of the object as psychologically and culturally fraught.[39]

This layered, multi-sensorial body is no longer a perfect unity between its inner dimension and its outer appearance, but demonstrates a double process: it consists of a 'constellation that binds as it severs, undoes as it combines'.

This double process of binding and severing is clearly visible in works like *Schema* (1967–1968) and *Sequel* (1967–1968). *Schema* consists of 144 small bodies; more precisely, latex hemispheres placed, but not fixed, on a latex mat. The hemispheres were not made in a mould, but were created by painting several layers of latex onto half a rubber ball. The latex mat was made in the same way, by painting layers of latex. Of course, this method leaves all kind of imperfections and irregularities. It is clearly handmade instead of industrially made. Although the half rubber balls inside were cast, the layered skin that covers them, and is visible, is coated. The coating binds and severs at the same time.

The work *Sequel* is made in a similar way but is structured as a pile, not as a grid. And it does not present hemispheres but little latex balls. The different ordering of the two works can be understood as regularity versus randomness. The random ordering of *Sequel* increases the imperfections and irregularities of the layering coating process. The perfect, Minimalist ordering of the coated hemispheres in *Schema* is further and completely undone in *Sequel*.

Senses Deceived: Jeannette Christensen

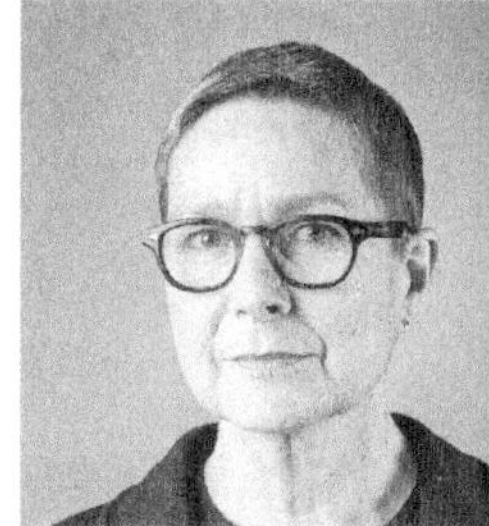
Jeannette Christensen (1958)

In sculpture, the human body is the measure of all things. Not only because in the (Neo)classical tradition the favourite subject was the human body, but because it is also the standard by which we gauge the proportions of sculpture. Every sculpture is measured by the standards of the human body, and is proportionally smaller or larger in scale than the human body. But it is the scale of the human body that enables the viewer's body to gauge proportions, the sensorial dimension of the human body that enables the viewer to gauge the materiality of sculpture.

Like the work of Eva Hesse, the sculptures of Norwegian artist Jeannette Christensen also grasp the viewer by activating different senses, not just sight, but also touch. But the haptic look that gauges the materiality of her works is usually deceived. The matter they are made of is not what it looks like. As a result, it is not the sculpted body that is

[40] See Bal, *Fragments of* [M]*atter*, p. 66.

undone in her work, but the viewer's body, which cannot rely any more on bodily orientation by the senses.

The materiality of her work *Sculpture* (1995) confuses; it is obvious that it is made from silk or something silk-like, but its appearance suggests something else. The work was first made for a window in the department store Steen & Strøm, in Oslo. It consists of a white silk slip dress, a delicate woman's undergarment with a soft shiny surface. From time to time, a fan connected with a timer fills the slip with air, making it stand up, stretching it out. After a while, the stream of air becomes weaker and the sculpture weakens and collapses. When filled with air, the sculpted body is hard like stone and the softness of the silk skin is countered by the suggestion of opposite qualities.[40] And of course, the tactility of *Sculpture* is gendered: when it is soft, it refers to the female body and when it is hard and solid, it suggests the male body.

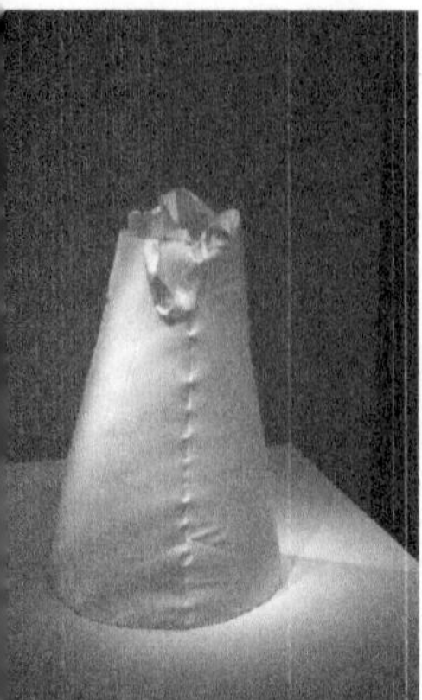

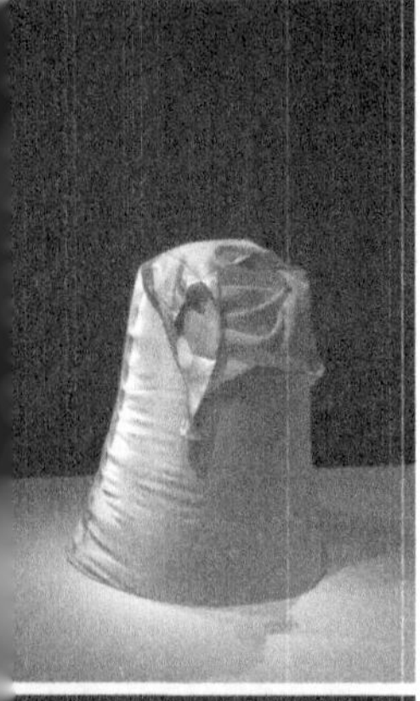

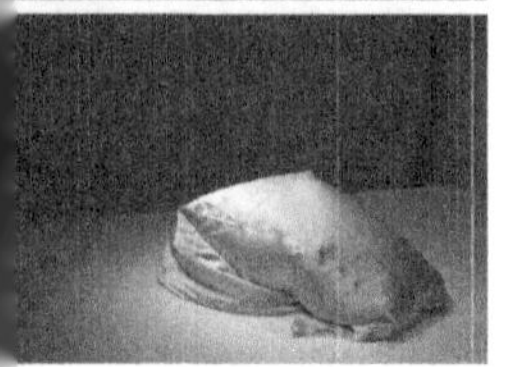

[H]annette Christensen, [Sc]*ulpture*, 1995

The works *The Birth of Liquid Desire* and *White Lies* deceive the senses in yet another way by making use of different materials that are the opposite of soft, materials that are hard and solid. They can both be seen as a reversal of the famous work by Salvador Dalí, *The Persistence of Memory* (1931). In that Surrealist painting we see solid, metal watches melting, soft like butter. The work seems to say that memory is far from persistent or solid and will dissolve. In *The Birth of Liquid Desire,* we see spilled water dripping over the edge of a table, forming a puddle on the ground. But it is only appearance because it turns out to be a solid body of glass. Whereas we are used to sculpture that demonstrates an intimate relation between an inner dimension and outer appearance, in Christensen's work this relation is radically absent. As a result, the viewer's senses are being misled. The same kind of deceit is realized in the ceramic work *White Lies* (1998). What appears to be spilled milk dripping over the edge of a table turns out to be a ceramic object, as hard and solid as stone.

Another work that misleads the viewer's senses is *The Birth of Liquid Anxieties* (2001); as the title already suggests, the sculpted objects only appear to be liquid, but are in fact solid and hard. But most importantly in this case is the context for which this work was made and in which it was shown: The Vigeland Museum in Oslo. The Norwegian sculptor Gustav Vigeland is in many respects the most important Neoclassical artist in the world. In his era, he was so successful that the city of Oslo gave him the opportunity to create a park in which he could show his work. Further, at the edge of the park they built a studio for him, which could at the same time become a museum after he had died. It is in this museum that Christensen held a show in 2001, of which *The Birth of Liquid Anxieties* was also part. In the room next to where *The Birth of Liquid Anxieties* was shown, Vigeland's *Six Giants Holding a Vessel of Water or Carrying the Burdens of Life* could be seen. Christensen's and Vigeland's work is a combination, or rather a clash, of two different logics of sculpture. Vigeland's impressive sculptures are utterly Neoclassical, which means that the logic they rely upon is based on an intimate relation between outer appearance and inner essence. In the case of the *Six Giants*, that inner essence is the muscles under their skin from which their impressive power stems. But in many sculptures in Vigeland Park, next to the museum, the inner essence is not physical but psychological: passions, emotions, and feelings explain the appearance of the sculpted bodies.

Christensen's *Liquid Anxieties* break with this logic completely; there is no inner/outer relation and when one tries to understand it, it is deceptive. The puddles that look like water are made of black granite. Their form and

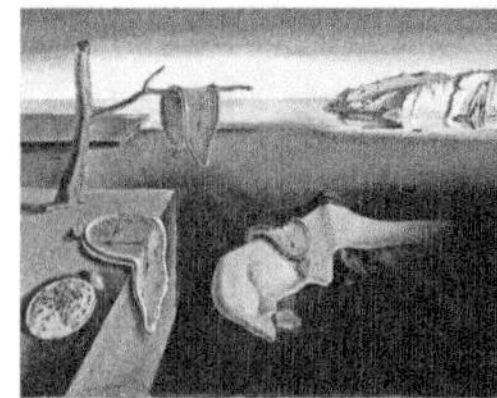

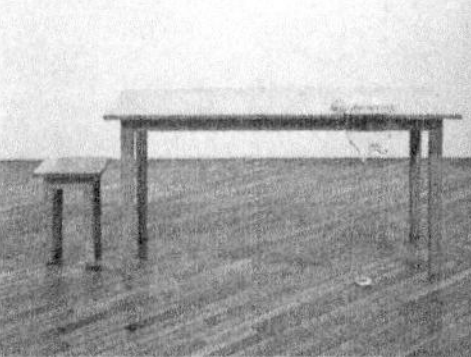

Salvador Dalí, *The Persistence of Memory*, 1931; Jeannette Christensen, *The Birth of Liqu[id] Desire*, 2001

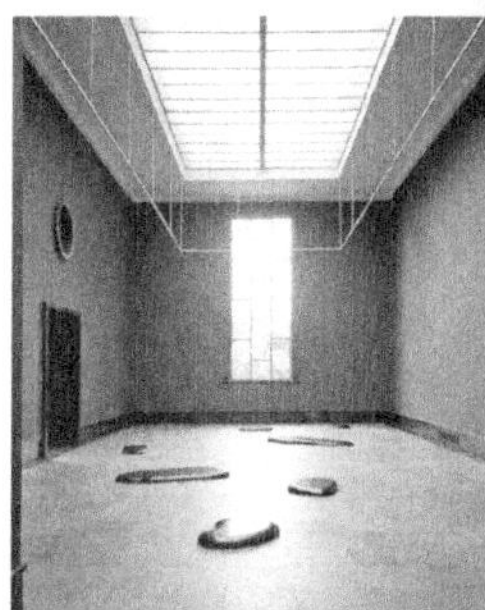

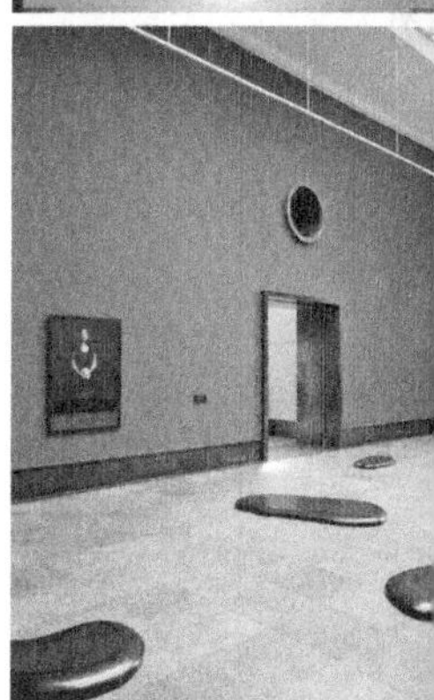

Jeannette Christensen, *The Birth of Liquid Anxieties*, 2001

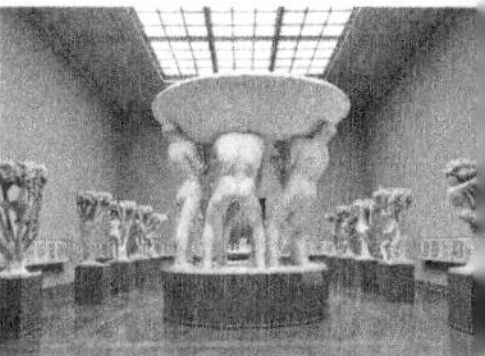

Gustav Vigeland, *Six Giants Holding a Vessel of Water or Carrying the Burdens of Life*, model, 1906

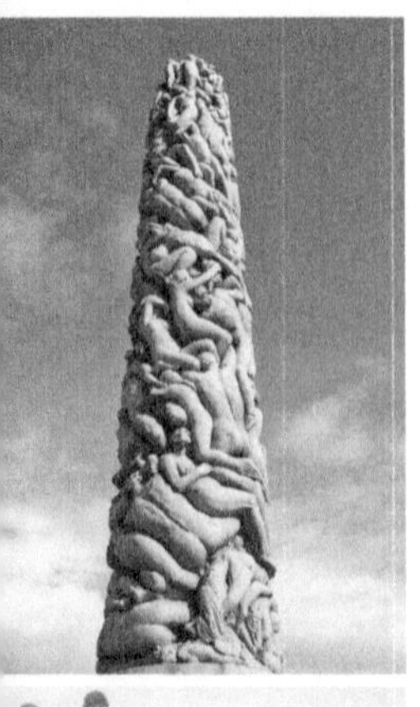

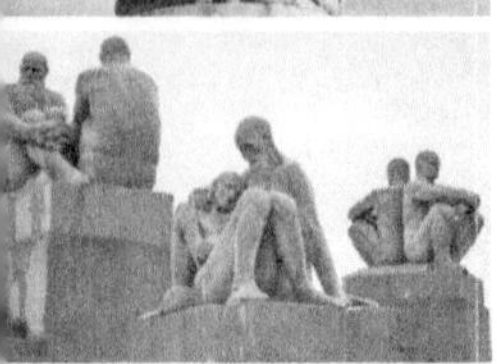

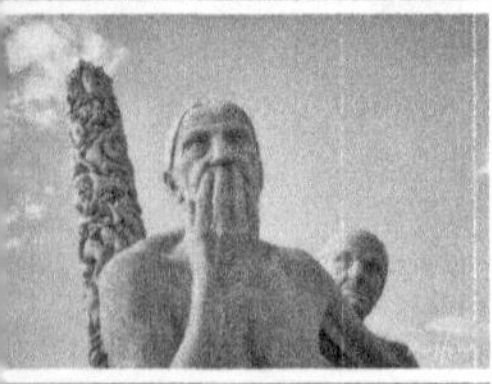

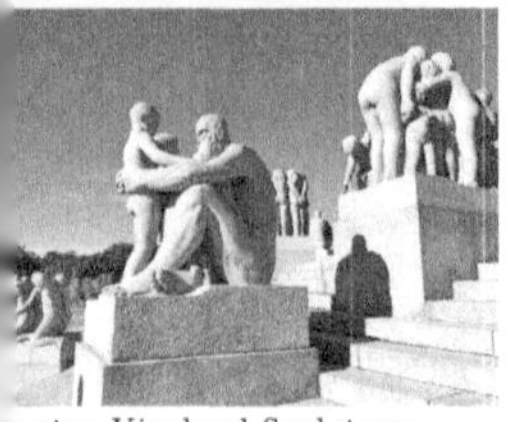

ustav Vigeland Sculpture
ırk, Oslo, with *Monolith*, 1919,
ıd part of its 121 figures
ound it

substance seem to be liquid, but the opposite is the case as they are stone-hard. The materiality of these sculptures does not translate into their outer appearance. Whereas the buttocks of the six giants are tight and beautifully shaped by the illusion of muscles underneath the skin, the liquid appearance of the puddles cannot be explained, nor does it have an origin: they deceive.

The materiality of sculpture is challenged in yet another way by Christensen's *Gelatine Benches*. Although she has made several works with gelatine, let's focus on the metal benches, covered with red or transparent gelatine. At first glance, the gelatine has a material quality that can be compared to glass: it is transparent, or, if coloured, semi-transparent. But the glass puddle in *Liquid Desire* looks hard and solid like stone. The gelatine benches are not hard but make the impression of being soft. The hard solidness of glass also implies a temporal dimension: it will remain like this forever, if not broken. The gelatine with which the benches were covered are materially not solid at all; its substance changes, falls apart, dissolves. One of the main characteristics of the conventional logic of sculpture is challenged by these gelatine works. Just to give an example, in the case of benches with red gelatine, the colour red disintegrates and separates into yellow and red—when we consider these sculptures as human bodies, one can say into urine and blood.

For centuries, the logic of sculpture was synonymous with the logic of the monument. This means that sculpture was meant for eternity; it consolidates time and temporal change into a solid volume or body. Christensen questions this sculptural logic by making sculptures out of material that has a solid shape but is soft rather than hard. And temporality is not clotted: time goes on with frightening results. Mould starts to grow on them and the constituent elements of gelatine fall apart or dissolve. Puddles of liquid, real liquid this time, arise on the floor, underneath the benches. In the gelatine work *Horizontal Vertical* (1993), she combines red gelatine with marble: red gelatine ladders are placed on small pieces of white Carrara marble, the most classical but also prestigious sculptural material one can think of. This combination of materials suggests that the work is a theoretical object, a statement about sculpture, similar to the work Christensen titled *Sculpture*. Like *Sculpture, Horizontal Vertical* foregrounds the issue of the solid and hard nature of traditional sculpture by contrasting it with soft silk or in the case of the last work, gelatine. But *Sculpture* introduces another element that belongs to the traditional sculptural logic. The fact that the human body is the standard for that logic also implies that sculptures are conventionally vertical, standing objects. The ladders in *Horizontal Vertical* are horizontal, laying, not standing, on a bed of white marble.

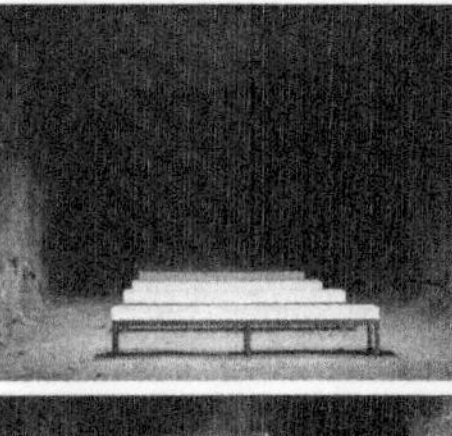

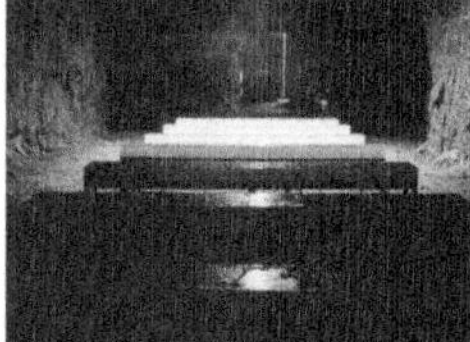

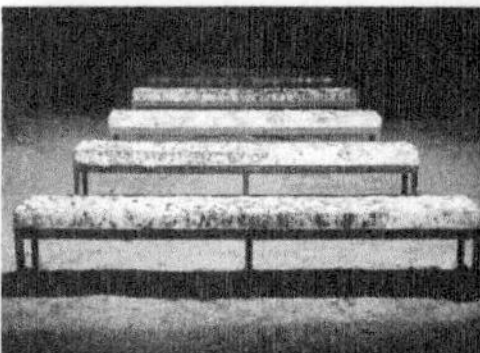

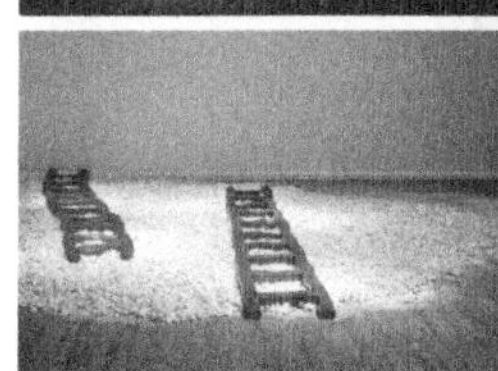

Jeannette Christensen, *Every Day is a Miracle* [Gelatine Benches], 1995; *Horizontal Vertical*, 1993

The last work by Christensen I will discuss does not undo the body only materially, but also in terms of size. *Philosopher's Stone* (2004) consists of two elements: a small school desk for children used as a pedestal for a very big stone. The stone is almost like a cube but not completely: the planes are polished unevenly and the corners are rounded, which begins to suggest a globe instead of a cube. Although this object is unambiguously made of stone, its surface looks rather soft because of its tactility and rounded edges.

When the human body is the standard for the traditional sculptural logic, one may wonder which body is at stake in *Philosopher's Stone*? There is no sculpted human body, so it should then be the viewer's body. But in this case, the image of a child's body is suggested by the small children's desk on which the stone is placed. When we take the viewer's body as the standard, the stone is rather big, but when a

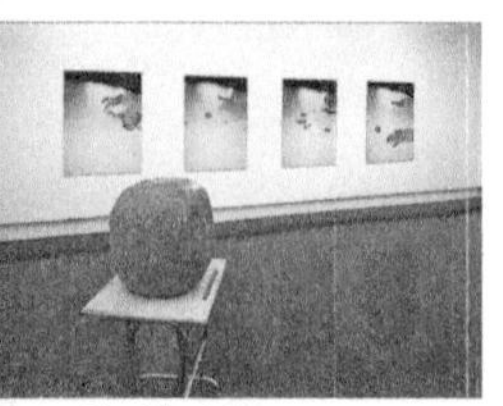
eannette Christensen, *hilosopher's Stone*, 2004

child's body is proposed as the standard the stone is enormous. And indeed, that is the impression it makes.

Different as they are, all sculptural practices discussed in this chapter have in common the fact that they undo the conventional sculptural logic according to which the external appearance of a sculptural object can be understood by the illusion of an inner dimension that is responsible for the appearance of the sculpture. That inner dimension can be physical like muscles or bone structure, but also emotional, like passions or feelings. This logic based on a causal relation between inner dimension and outer appearance is usually at work in how we signify the appearance of the human body. But because in the (Neo)classical discussion sculpted bodies are usually human bodies, the signification of human bodies is also at work in the signification of conventional sculpture, (Neo)classical that is. This explains why all the cases discussed focus on different elements of the human body in order to undo this logic, not only by focusing on body parts, but also by activating the self-awareness of the viewer's body.

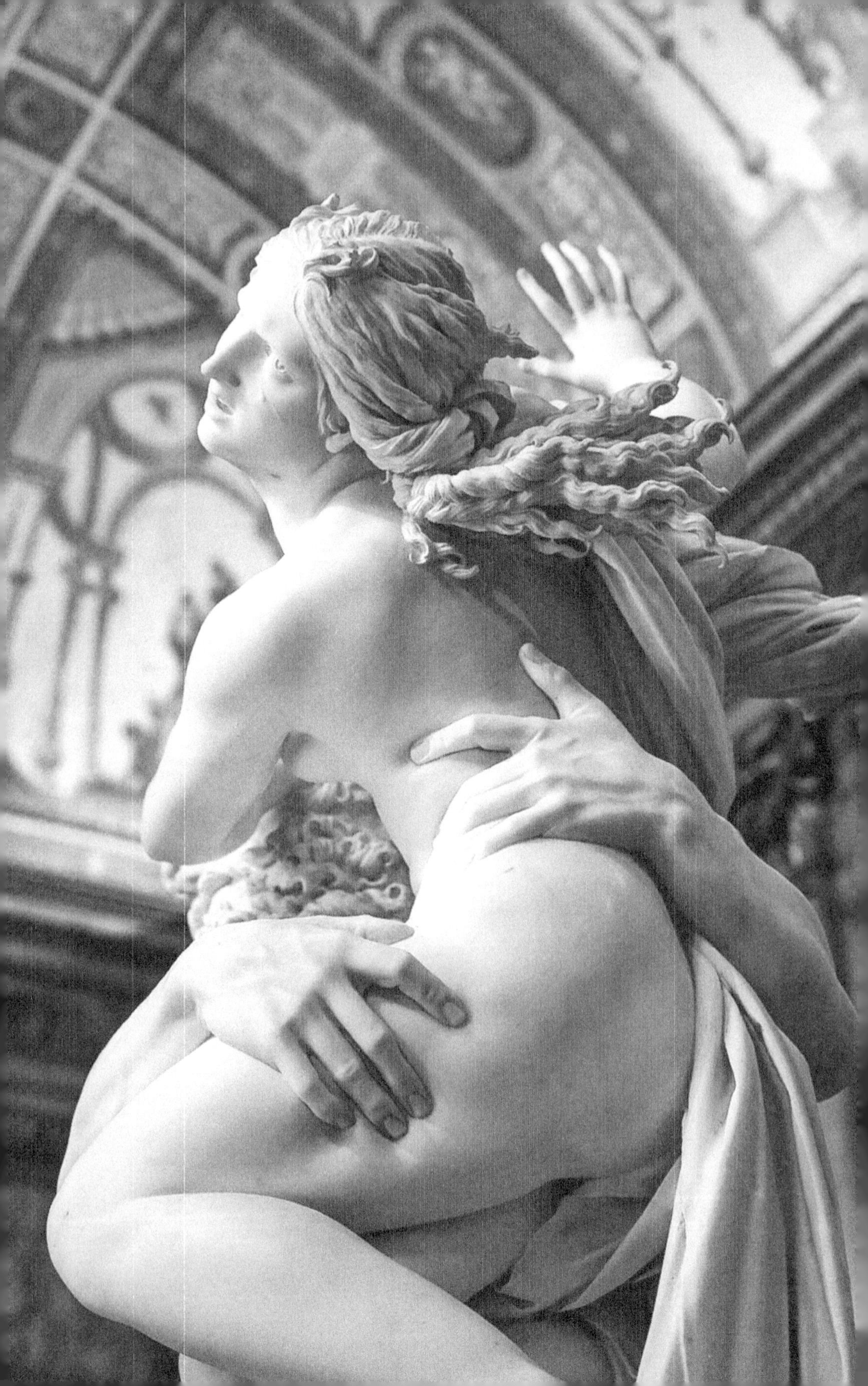

Scenic Sculpture

The Entanglement of the Logic of Inner Necessity with the Logic of Scenic Sculpture: Auguste Rodin and Gian Lorenzo Bernini

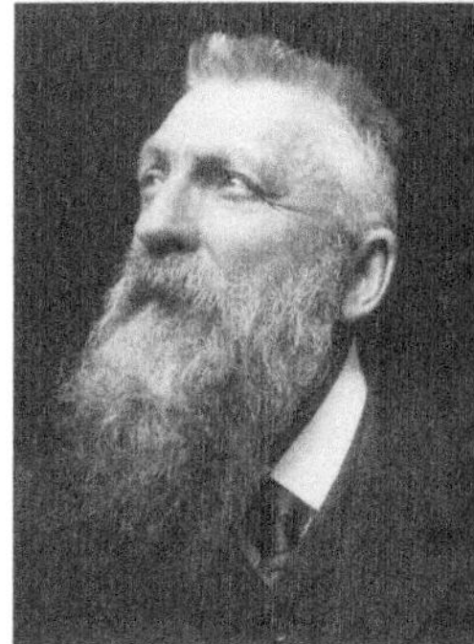
Auguste Rodin (1840–1917)

Auguste Rodin's *The Gates of Hell* and his *The Burghers of Calais* transgressed the conventional logic of sculpture in several ways. Firstly, they did so by no longer complying with the logic of the monument—for centuries, sculpture could not be distinguished from the logic of the monument, but at the end of the nineteenth century that logic began to show cracks. While the patrons of Rodin's *The Gates of Hell* and *The Burghers of Calais* had commissioned monuments, the works he realized no longer complied with the rules that applied to that genre. For, contrary to what can be seen today in Calais, Rodin's intention was to place the six citizens of Calais on a kind of low platform at a height of about twenty-five centimetres. As such, the sculpted citizens of Calais would 'mingle' with the current citizens of this city, a staging that was not consistent with the function of commemoration or tribute presumed in the logic of the monument. A high

Gian Lorenzo Bernini, *Rape of Proserpina*, 1621–1622

Krauss, *Passages in Modern* :ulpture, pp. 251–53.

pedestal was required for that. Abandoning the logic of the monument means that sculpture is no longer tied to a space or place, and the absorption of the plinth into the sculpture, as occurred sometime later in the work of Brancusi, also contributed to that.

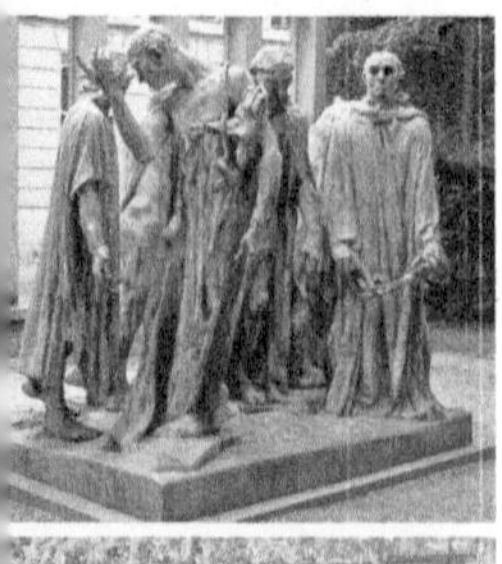

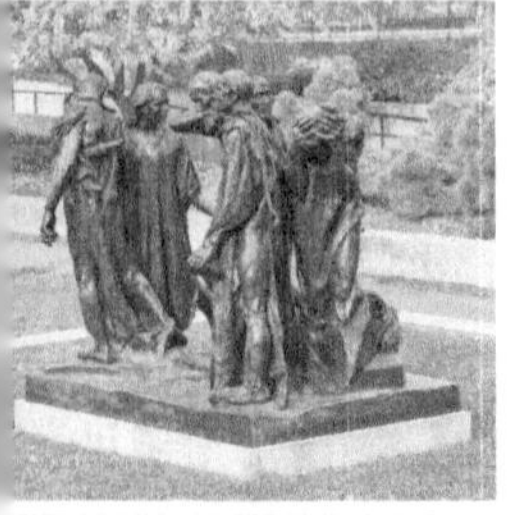

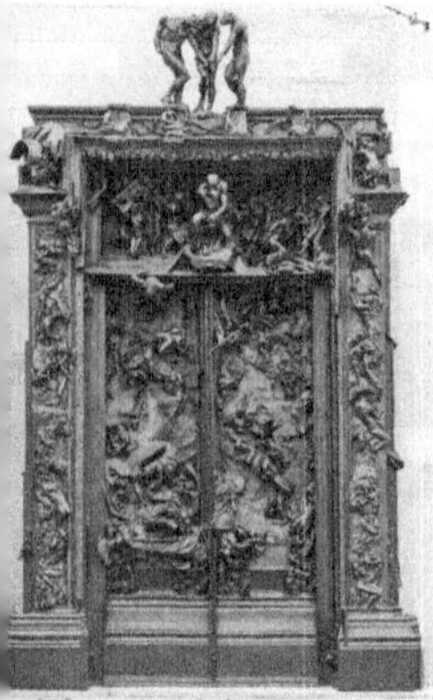

uguste Rodin, *The Burghers of* :alais, 1884–1895; *The Gates of* :ell, 1885–1917

Yet there is more to these two works of Rodin that complicates the conventional logic. *The Burghers of Calais* is a portrayal of human bodies, and the illusion of an inner core continues to exist. All figures emphatically show feelings and passions that explain their outer appearance. There is still a mode of composition based on the idea of an *inner* necessity, in the words of Rosalind E. Krauss: 'The idea that the explanation for a particular configuration of forms or textures on the surface of an object is to be looked for at its center.'[1] But *The Burghers of Calais* was made by Rodin to commemorate a specific event during the Hundred Years' War, when the French port Calais on the Channel surrendered to the English after an eleven-month siege. The sculpture shows one specific scene from this narrative. In 1346, the English King Edward III offered to spare the people of the city if six of its leaders surrendered themselves to him. He demanded that they walk out wearing nooses around their necks and carrying the city keys. Rodin represented the six leaders at the moment of their surrender walking with the nooses around their necks and carrying the keys. This means that 'the configuration of forms and textures' is not only explained by an inner necessity, but also by a narrative necessity. The desperation expressed by the six figures is caused by this history and is represented by showing one specific scene.

Of course, that the medium of sculpture is used to represent scenes from a narrative is not new. Even a sculpture showing a man throwing a discus can be said to be narrative, although the history this scene represents is somewhat tiny for just a sports event. But one of the most famous Greek sculptures, *Laocoön and his Sons,* shows a much more elaborate scene of a mythical story. Although there are several accounts of it, one of the most renowned is by Virgil. According to that interpretation, Laocoön was a priest of Poseidon who was killed with both his sons after attempting to expose the ruse of the Trojan Horse by striking it with a spear. Like Rodin's *The Burghers of Calais,* the *Laocoön Group* combines two different logics, the conventional logic based on inner necessity and one that I will now call 'scenic'. In the history of sculpture, it is usually the conventional logic of inner necessity that prevails; the narrative dimension serves as the background explaining the feelings or passions that cause the appearance of the sculpted figures.

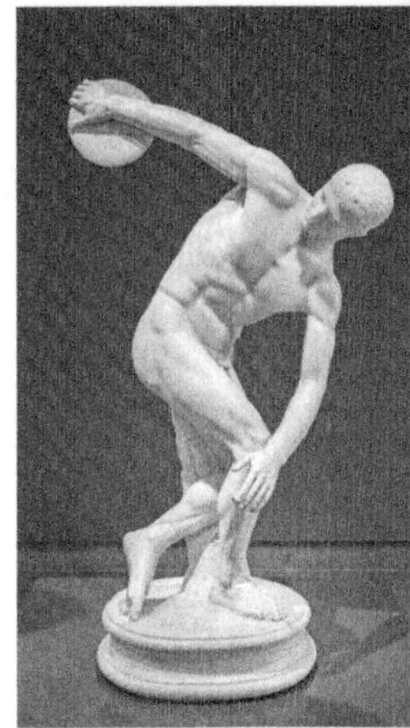

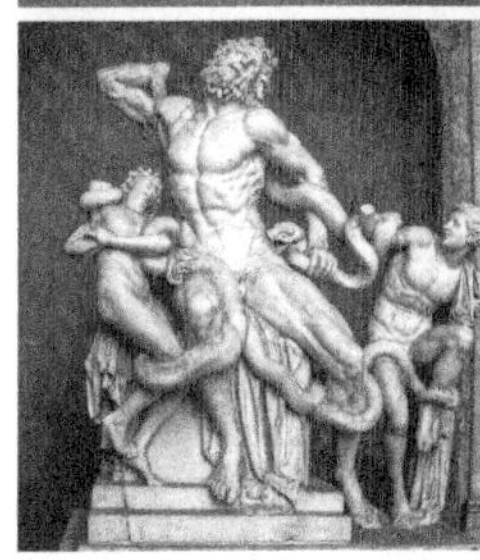

Discus Thrower, Roman copy o[f] Greek original, 2nd C AD; *Laocoön and his Sons*, Greece, 200 BC

The narrative scene shown in *Laocoön and his Sons* is known as the prototypical icon of human agony in Western art. What is remarkable about this expression of agony is that unlike the agony depicted in Christian art showing Christ's passion or that of martyrs, this suffering has no redemptive power or reward. The suffering of Laocoön and his sons is absolute and is chiefly shown through the contorted expressions of the faces.

As iconic as *Laocoön and his Sons* is, some of Gian Lorenzo Bernini's sculptures, particularly his *Rape of Proserpina* (1621–1622), *The Ecstasy of Saint Teresa* (1647), and *Blessed Ludovica Albertoni* (1674), are also very special in this narrative sense. These three works by Bernini all combine the logic of inner necessity with the logic of scenic sculpture. The feeling of terror is expressed on Persephone's face, through tears and the contorted pose and gestures of her body. But the imprint of the rapist Pluto's hand in the skin of Proserpina is not a mark of inner necessity; it can only be explained by the event and the act of rape of which this

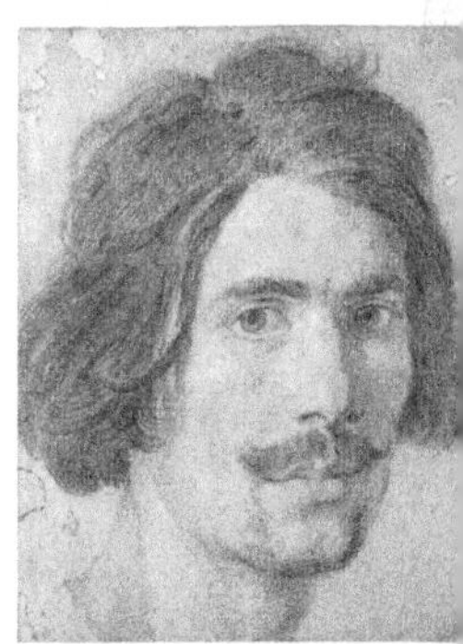

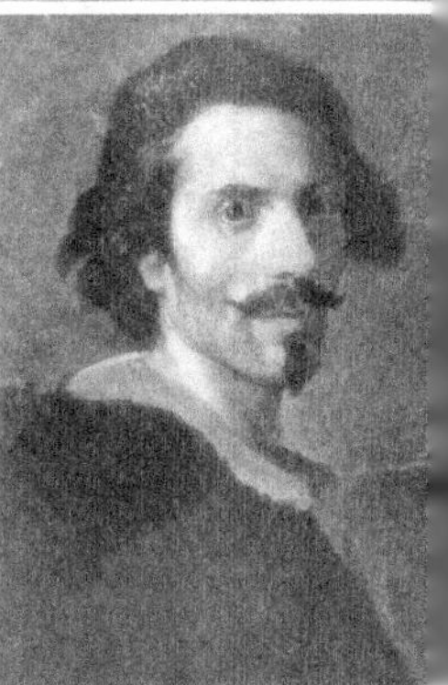

Two self-portraits of Gian Lorenzo Bernini (1598–1680)

The Life of Teresa of Jesus, hapter XXIX, Part 17.

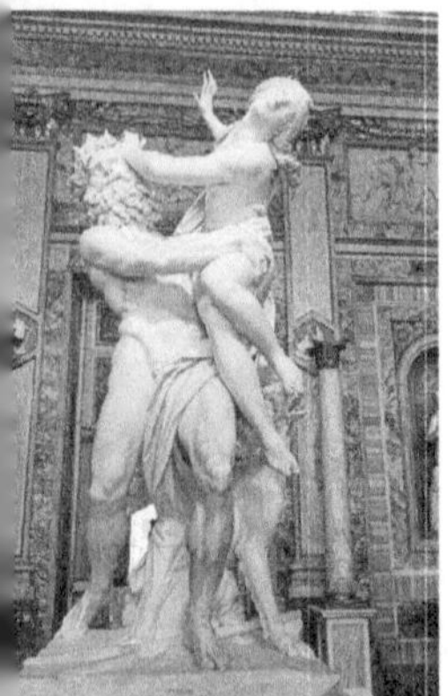

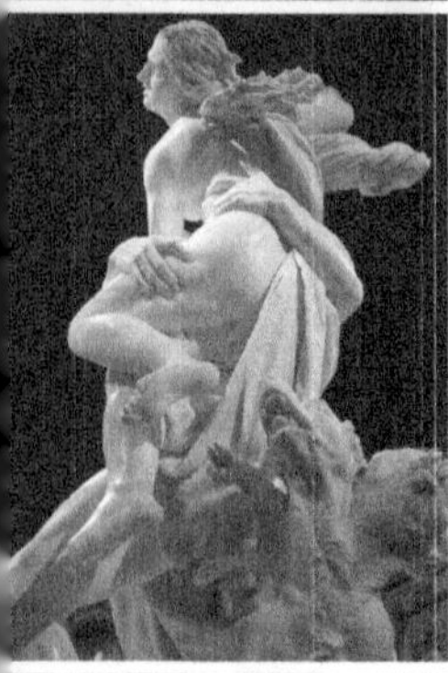

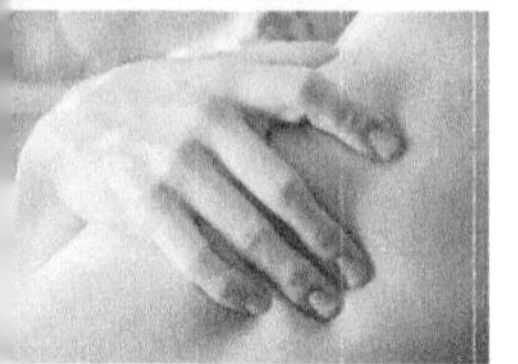

ian Lorenzo Bernini, *Rape of roserpina*, 1621–1622

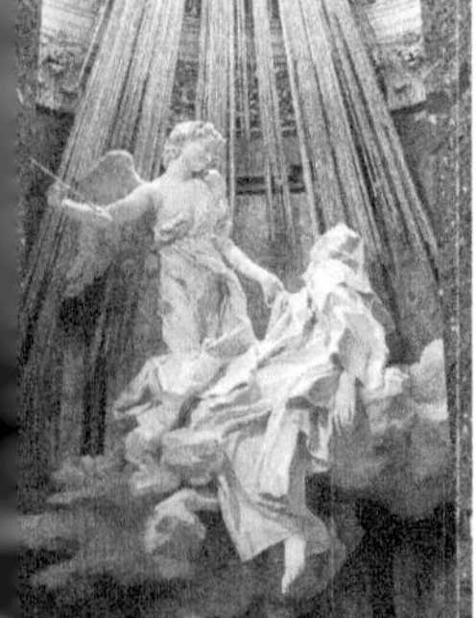

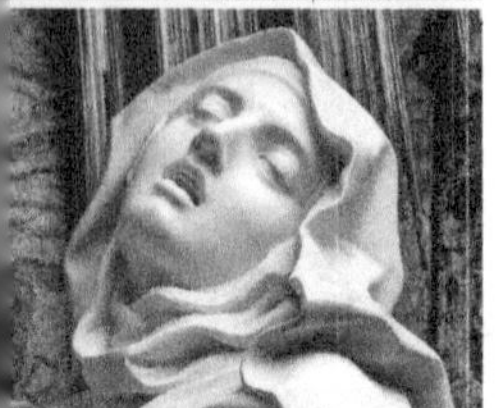

an Lorenzo Bernini, *The stasy of Saint Teresa*, 1647

sculpture shows only one scene. This detail of Bernini's work foregrounds the importance of recognizing the logic of scenic sculpture.

Looking at Bernini's *The Ecstasy of Saint Teresa,* we notice that the entanglement of the two sculptural logics manifests itself in yet another way. The sculpture shows Teresa of Ávila, a Spanish mystic who founded the Carmelites order. But the passion she expresses is ambivalent. The pretext of her appearance is as follows:

> I saw in his [an angel's] hand a long spear of gold, and at the iron's point there seemed to be a little fire. He appeared to me to be thrusting it at times into my heart, and to pierce my very entrails; when he drew it out, he seemed to draw them out also, and to leave me all on fire with a great love of God. The pain was so great that it made me moan; and yet so surpassing was the sweetness of this excessive pain, that I could not wish to be rid of it. The soul is satisfied now with nothing less than God. The pain is not bodily, but spiritual, though the body has its share in it. It is a caressing of love so sweet which now takes place between the soul and God, that I pray God of His goodness to make him experience it who may think that I am lying.[2]

According to Saint Teresa's own account, the expression of her ecstasy can be explained by her spiritual pain. Another narrative event proposes itself in this sculpture, because the scene is more pleasurable than painful: the narrative of sexual pleasure. The pretext of spiritual ecstasy is overrun in this Bernini work by sexuality, the context or explanation of her pleasure not explicitly provided, but ambiguously providing only one scene.

Bernini's *Blessed Ludovica Albertoni* does something similar. What we see is extreme inner passion in her appearance. But again, what is the cause of this passion, or more specifically, her ecstasy? The sculpture is a funerary monument for the Roman noblewoman Ludovica Albertoni. What we see represented is the following, according to Wikipedia and based on art-historical sources:

> The figure of Ludovica Albertoni is presented on a mattress at the moment of mystical communion with God. The folds of her habit reflect her state of turmoil, and her head is thrown back onto an embroidered pillow supported by a headrest. Beneath her figure is a deeply crumpled sculpted cloth above a red-marble sarcophagus, where Ludovica is interred. The panel behind her is carved with stylized pomegranates; flaming hearts adorn the base of the windows. She is surrounded by putti, and waiting to rise to the Holy Spirit.[3]

3 'Blessed Ludovica of Jesus', Wikipedia.

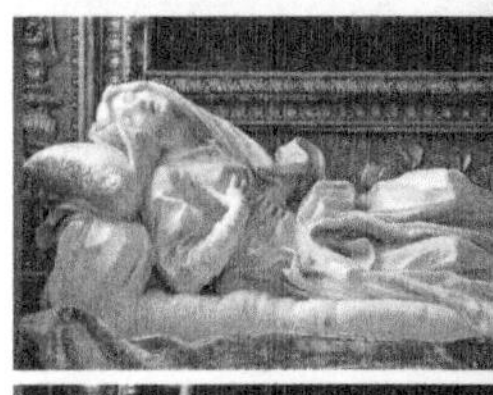

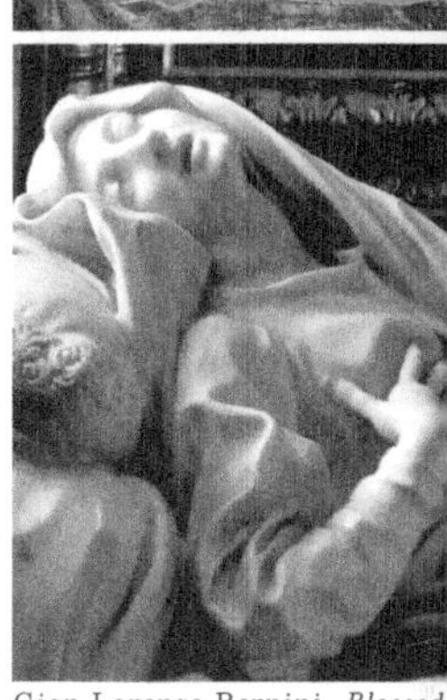

Gian Lorenzo Bernini, *Blessed Ludovica Albertoni*, 1674

Her mystical communion to God and the Holy Spirit is spiritual, not bodily, yet why she should touch her breast, an erotogenic body part, instead of her heart is not clear. Again, and even more forceful than in *The Ecstasy of Saint Teresa,* another narrative imposes itself. Not one of a mystical communion with God, but one of sexual pleasure. The rapture of Ludovica Albertoni is ambiguous, that is sure. But as I have argued thus far, the viewer plays a crucial role in how we relate to sculpture. This implies that the pretext of these Bernini sculptures should not restrict the viewer's response. As spiritual as the narratives of these pretexts may be, the embodied responses of viewers can be different. It is this embodied response on which the medium of sculpture depends, not its pretexts.

The Platform as Theatrical Stage: Alberto Giacometti

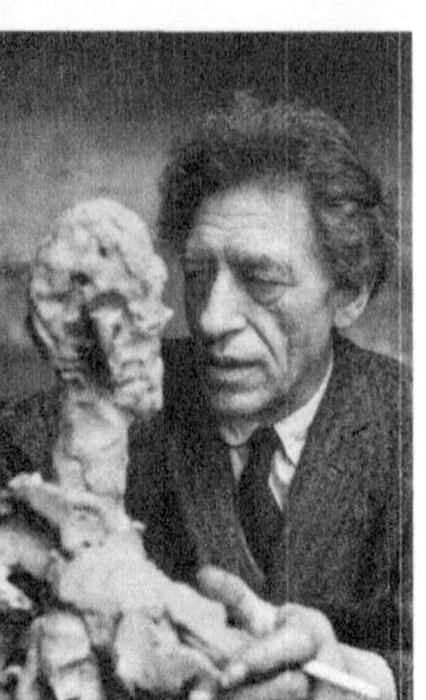
lberto Giacometti (1901–1966)

The works discussed so far in this chapter combine two different sculptural logics: the logic of inner necessity with the logic of scenic sculpture. Although usually the logic of inner necessity is predominant and the logic of scenic sculpture only serves as a background to motivate this inner necessity, in twentieth-century sculpture scenic sculpture became autonomous and did not have to rely on its co-sculptural logic of inner necessity. The early Surrealist sculptures of Swiss artist Alberto Giacometti exemplify this then-new logic very well.

In his work, it is what we can best call a platform that serves as a base for a theatrical moment. On these platforms several objects are placed, and it is the dynamic between these objects on a platform that determines and defines the logic of scenic sculpture. The import of such sculpture should not be sought in an intrinsic essence, but instead in the dramatic tension among the objects inhabiting the scene. And for the sake of clarity: the logic of the scenic platform should not be confused with that of installation. Dramatic interaction on a platform is of an emphatically theatrical nature; this takes place on a stage. Despite the fact that installations are also three-dimensional and, therefore, possibly related to sculpture, the multiple elements that comprise an installation give rise not to a dramatic tension, but rather to a tension that seems to have come about by chance or discovery. The difference is the podium on which the dramatic scenes are staged. They are not part of installations.

In the famous letter Giacometti wrote to Pierre Matisse in 1948, he explicitly distances himself from the sculptural tradition based on a human or abstract body:

> Figures were never for me a compact mass but like a transparent construction. Again, after making all kinds of attempts, I made cages with open construction inside, executed in wood by a carpenter. There was a third element in reality that concerned me: movement. Despite all my efforts, it was impossible for me then to endure a sculpture that gave an illusion of movement, a leg advancing, a raised arm, a head looking sideways. I could only create such movement if it was real and actual, I also wanted to give the sensation of motion that could be induced. Several objects which move in relation to one another.[4]

With his ambition to portray the inducement of motion, Giacometti seems to indicate a transition from sculpture based on the compact mass of bodies to a type of sculpture consisting of a scene involving multiple objects or figures. And the inducement should not be represented but rather happen in the sculpture itself. It is, after all, the dynamics among the figures or elements which prompt the movement. In the words of Matti Megged:

> Giacometti's stage has its own life, its own reality. On this stage, a sense of space-atmosphere surrounds the objects (both human and inanimate), penetrates them, becomes independent yet related to the world outside, through the field of vision that is created between the objects and the observer. In these surrealistic sculptures, one feels the element of dramatic action: the relations between the objects themselves, confined on the stage that the artist created for them, indicate potential movement, struggle, change, although as sculptures they are, of course, static and immobile.[5]

4 Giacometti, '(Première) Lettre à Pierre Matisse', in *Alberto Giacometti 1901–1966*, p. 71; 'Letter to Pierre Matisse' in *Alberto Giacometti*, p. 20.

5 Megged, *Dialogue in the Void*, p. 21.

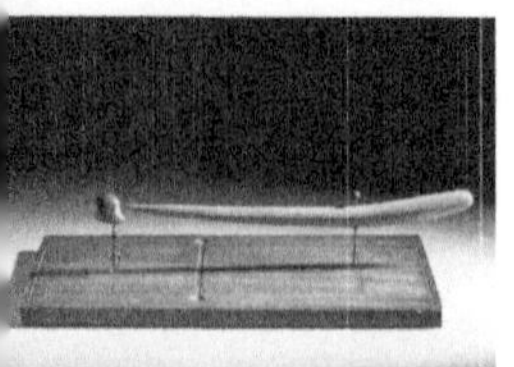

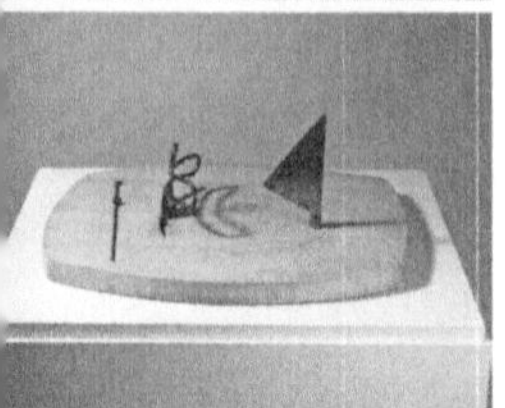

lberto Giacometti, *Pointe à* ɔeil, 1932; *Homme, femme et* ɪfant, 1932

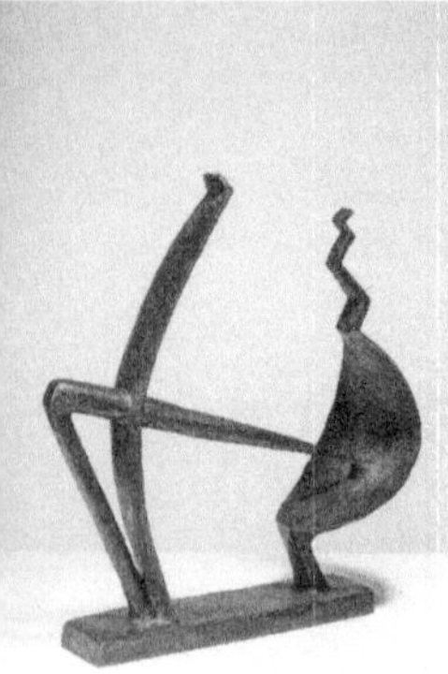

lberto Giacometti, *Homme femme*, 1928–1929

Because the stage assumes various forms in Giacometti's work, I shall discuss a variety of works from different periods. Only then does it become clear that he assertively attempted to develop a new sculptural logic of scenic sculpture. His *Homme et femme* from 1928–1929 is plainly comprised of two objects that relate to each other in a dramatic context. The title and the symbolic forms leave nothing for us to guess. It is about penetration by a man, recognizable by way of the phallic form, in the middle of a woman's broad pelvis. This is no longer a body (abstract or otherwise) on a pedestal, but a scene of multiple objects on a platform which functions not as an anchoring of the scene, but as the location at which the scene takes place. With his *Homme, femme et enfant* from 1932, one can no longer speak of a platform which still has ambiguity; here, three objects have simply been placed on a base consisting of a platform. The three objects on this stage are again obviously symbolic. A phallic triangle is directed at the wide hips of the female figure, while a little ball is supposed to represent the child. The triangle resembles, more than anything, a sharp weapon. The most singular thing here, however, is the platform that functions as a location for the theatrical scene between the man, woman, and child. The male figure is situated inside a carved-out circle, the arena where the encounter between the man and woman will take place. The female figure is in a kind of slot, as though she can dodge to the right or left when attacked. The child remains in the background and is protected by the position of the mother. This marital scene is by no means romanticized—it is an image of violent conflict.

Giacometti's *Pointe à l'oeil* from 1932 consists of a wooden platform into which three lines have been gouged. The lines suggest a division on a playing field or battlefield. On one side, a head has been placed on a metal pin, and on the other a long phallic form has been placed on top of the same type of pin and directed at the eye of the head. Although this scene is not necessarily from a marriage, it is indeed violent. The playing field takes on gruesome forms. Once again, the platform on which this scene has been situated is more than a base to which the objects have been attached. It is the landscape in which the dramatic events unfold. The platform of *Circuit* (1931) offers more room to events that aren't necessarily violent; here the platform is sooner a playing field than a battlefield. Gouged out of the wood are a small cavity and a circular track, and there is a little ball that can be rolled around this track. Giacometti's *On ne joue plus* from 1932 clearly suggests that playing fields can become battlefields. Carved out of the marble slab are a great number of round cavities, with three of them functioning as graves that can be covered. The title can be seen as a variation on the conclusive *rien ne va plus*, which forbids players of roulette from placing further bets.

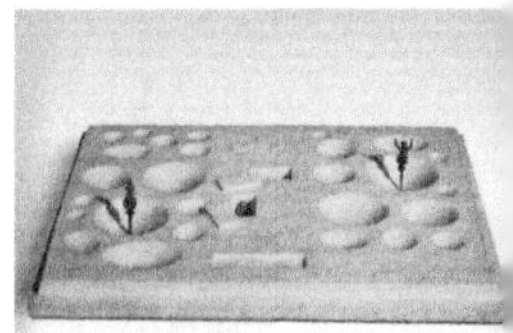

Alberto Giacometti, *On ne joue plus*, 1932

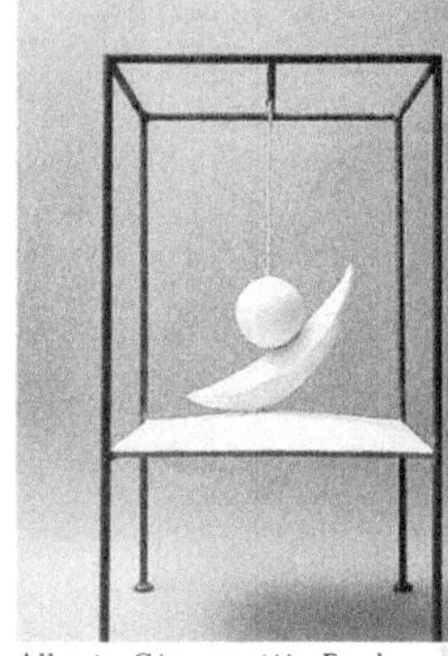

Alberto Giacometti, *Boule suspendue*, 1930–1931

The platforms in Giacometti's work that provide a basis for dramatic scenes function as a defining context. In a few instances, he also used frameworks that assumed more three-dimensional forms: what was referred to as the 'box'. It was these works in particular that the painter Francis Bacon admired, adopting similar structures in many of his paintings. Giacometti's most famous work from this Surrealist period makes use of such a cage- or box-like space. *Boule suspendue* from 1931–1932 is situated inside the ribs of an open cage; a ball and a moon- or banana-shaped form are suspended within this three-dimensional structure. This variation on the platform also offers room for a dramatic scene between two elements, and sexual overtones are again evident. Whether this is a playing field or a battlefield remains ambiguous.

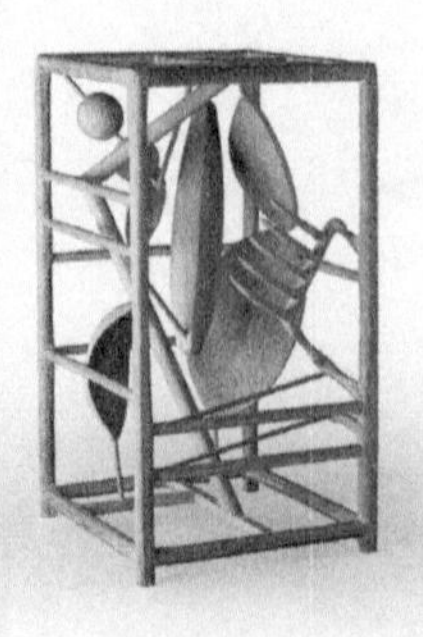

lberto Giacometti, *La cage*, 931–1932

While similar to *Boule suspendue*, *La cage* (1931–1932) is much more complex. A great number of abstract objects have been placed inside a cage construction—once more, the sexual connotations of the work are obvious. Of a more ambiguous nature are the five large teeth that can be regarded either as phallic objects or as a *vagina dentata*. Whether this happens to be a phallic man or a phallic woman, the cage functions more as a battlefield than as a playing field.

When Giacometti begins, during the second half of the nineteen-forties, to produce the elongated figures that made him so famous, he initially continues to make frequent use of platforms. In addition to this, he uses cages around his figures and pedestals on which to place them. In every case, the platforms and pedestals are emphatically part of the work, rather than being a functional base on which it is placed. As such, the platform or pedestal itself is exhibited, and the viewer must think about what its function is. *Quatre figurines sur base* from 1950, for instance, makes use of a tall, elongated pedestal, which in turn has been placed on a bronze table. In this case, no dramatic or narrative tension whatsoever exists among the four female figures on the pedestal. They make up a row or a series which cannot be regarded as a scene.

When Giacometti places his figures not on a pedestal but on a platform, the works are plainly dramatic or narrative. This is suggested as much by the scenic compositions as the titles. Even though only one figure appears on the platform of *Homme traversant une place* (1949), it can indeed be called a scene, since the man is walking. *Place II (quatre hommes et*

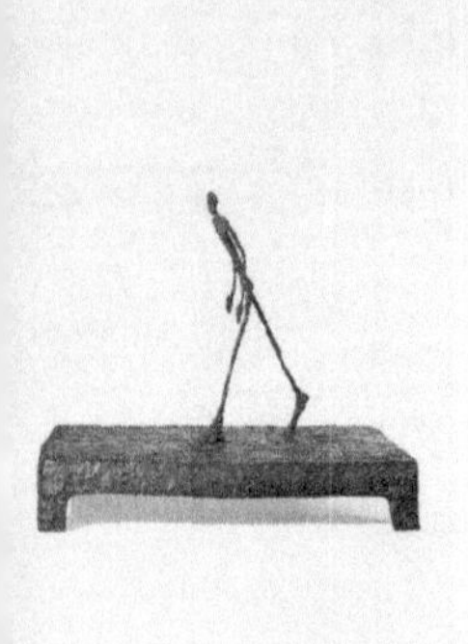

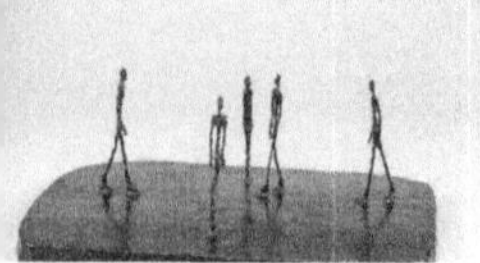

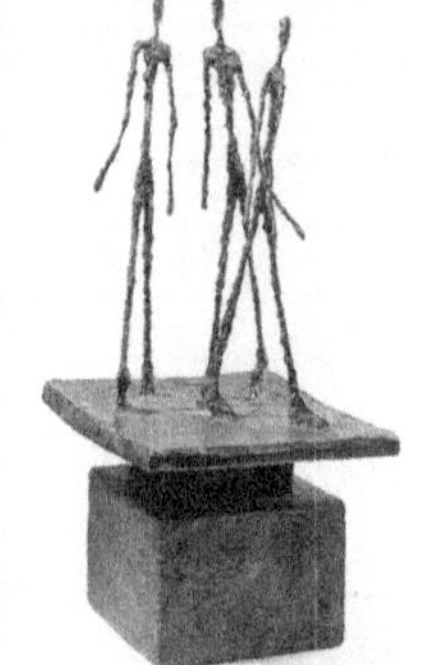

lberto Giacometti, *Homme aversant une place*, 1949; *Place (quatre hommes et une femme)*, 48; *Trois hommes qui archent*, 1948

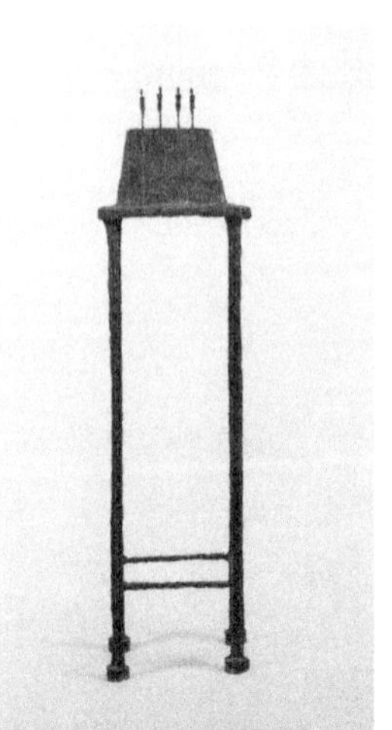

Alberto Giacometti, *Quatre figurines sur base*, 1950

une femme) comprises a scene of multiple figures criss-crossing or meeting each other on a plaza.

The platform on which a figure is standing can, as such, sometimes suggest a dramatic situation. *Le chariot* from 1950 shows a female figure on a cart or chariot. The wheels of the carriage are, in turn, placed on blocks resembling pedestals. The figure is standing still in a forced posture. Initially this makes it difficult to regard this sculpture as scenic, but when we consider the fact that the platform consists of a carriage, we can look upon the figure's posture as a narrative scene, and also due to her arms, which she holds slightly away from her body. The scene consists of the female figure attempting, in a forced manner, to keep her balance, given her base is far from stable. This work, too, makes it clear that Giacometti didn't grapple with the modern artist's familiar question as to what his work should be placed on, but that the stage on which the sculpture appears has become part of the work.

This certainly becomes evident in the work *Trois hommes qui marchent* (1948), which shows three men on a platform which has, in turn, again been placed on a pedestal. Because of that the platform is not a neutral base but a demarcated space which is itself exhibited, thus causing the nature of this space to be questioned by the work.

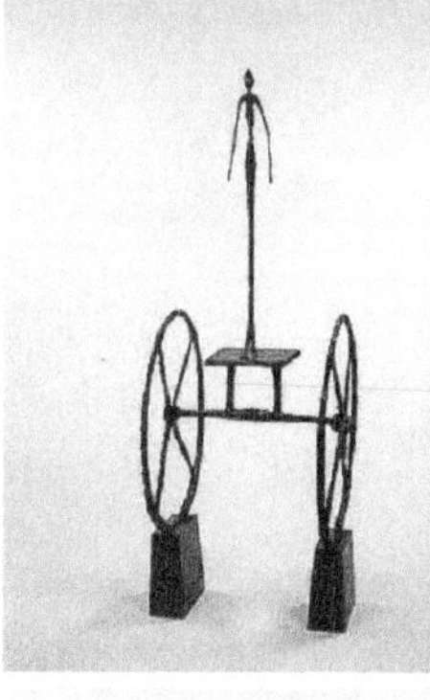

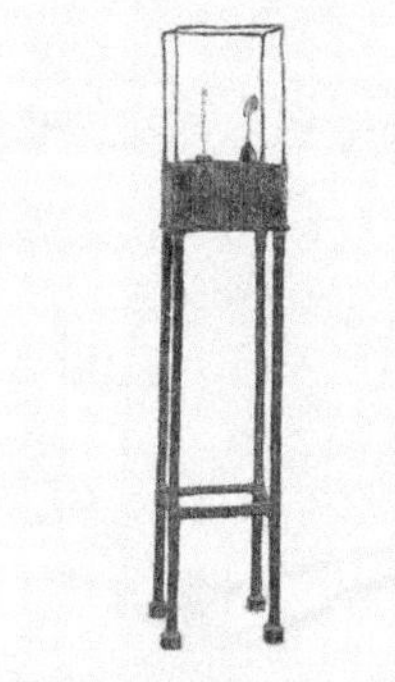

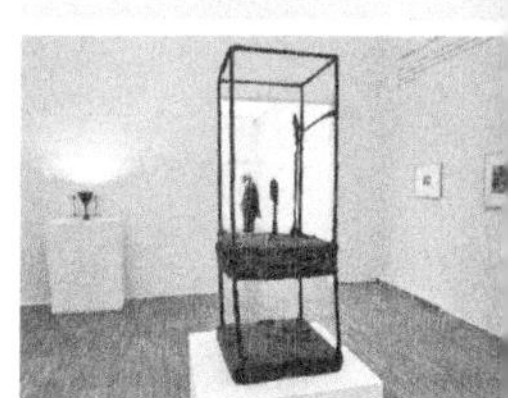

Alberto Giacometti, *Le chariot* 1950; *La cage*, 1953; *La cage*, 1950

The Narrative of Pure Form: Barbara Hepworth

The work of Giacometti discussed in the last section presents abstracted human figures or symbolic forms alluding to human figures on platforms. The sculptures of British artist Barbara Hepworth also activate the dynamics of several bodies, usually presented on a platform. But Hepworth's bodies never literally allude to the human body, with a more general

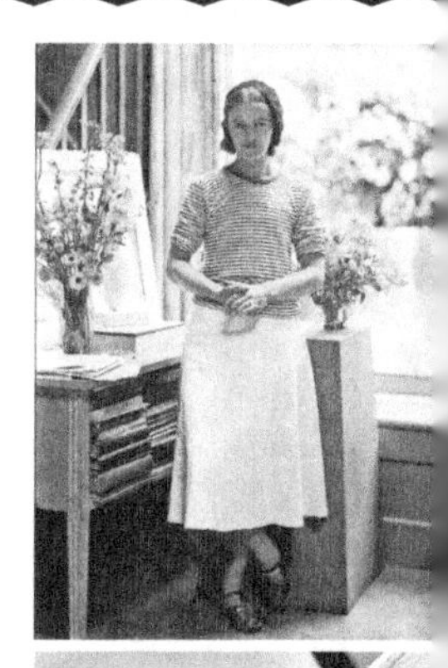

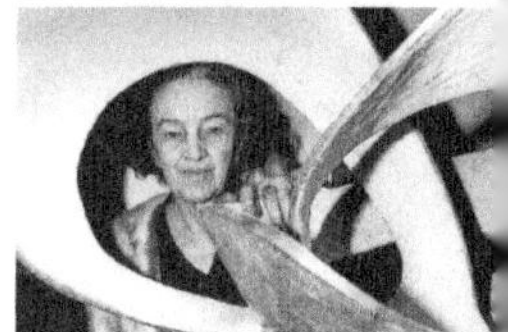

Barbara Hepworth (1903–1975)

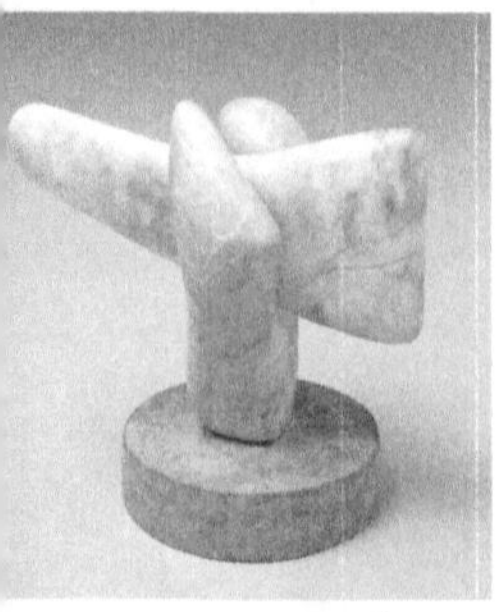

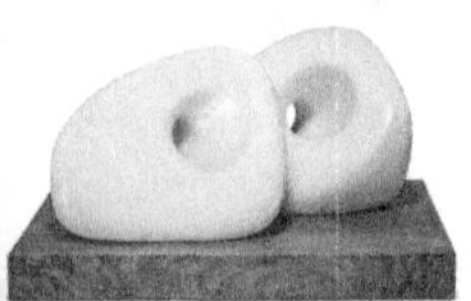

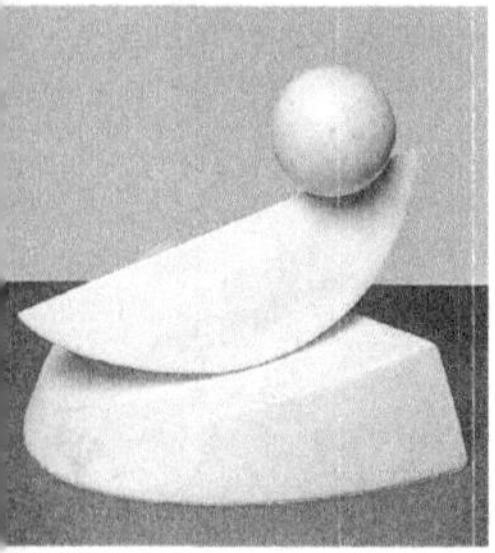

arbara Hepworth, *Two Forms,* 933; *Two Forms Pierced,* 1961–962; *Two Segments and a* phere, 1935–1936

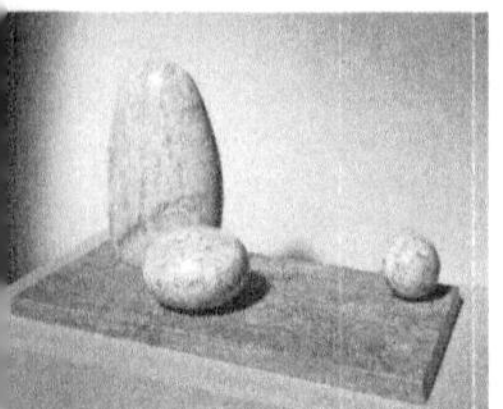

arbara Hepworth, *Three Forms* Carving in Grey Alabaster), 1935

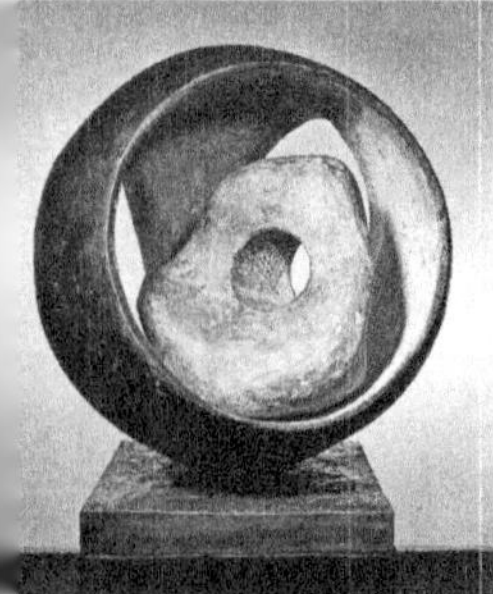

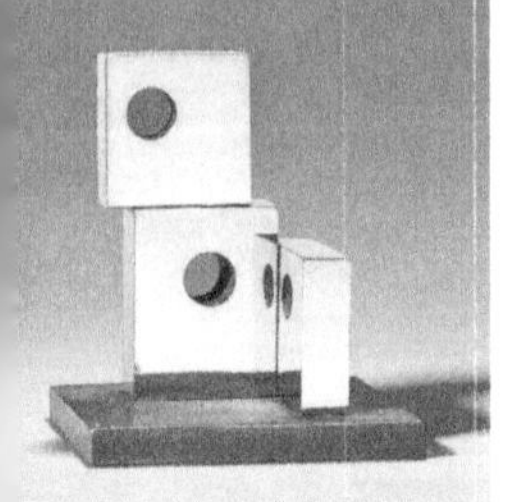

notion of bodies evoked. The dynamic within her sculptural works is a dynamic between forms.

Hepworth was keenly interested in art movements from the European continent, especially Abstraction. With her husband Ben Nicholson (an abstract painter) she travelled to France, where they visited the studios of Pablo Picasso, Constantin Brancusi, and Jean Arp. Together with Henry Moore, they were the first Modernists in sculpture in the United Kingdom. In 1933, she co-founded the Unit One art movement, which pursued the goal of uniting Surrealism and Abstraction in British art.

Despite making different forms, it was pierced forms that became her trademark. Her works consisting of a single form or two forms have such forms placed on a small plate that can still be seen as a plinth or pedestal. But when three forms are placed in relation to each other, the plate on which they are located can more aptly be called a platform. The transformation of plinth to platform introduces the notion of a theatrical stage where the dynamics between forms determines the sculptural logic. The titles of most of her early works are utterly factual and descriptive, for instance *Two Forms, Two Forms Pierced, Two Forms and a Hemisphere.* These titles do not indicate any dynamic between the forms they describe. But later on, she begins to add, between brackets, metaphorical significations to the factual description, for example 'Family Group', 'Extra Eye', and 'Love'. The abstract forms then become anthropomorphic. It is usually not the forms as such that enable such an anthropomorphic reading, but the dynamic between them.

Hepworth's work is often compared to that of Henry Moore because they were both trailblazers of Modernist sculpture in the United Kingdom. But Moore's works usually still rely on the logic of inner necessity; although abstracted,

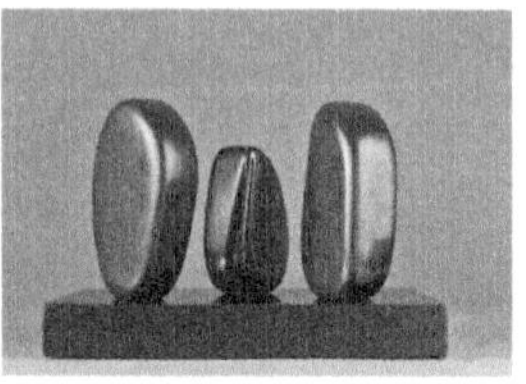

Barbara Hepworth, *Sphere with Inner Form,* 1963; *Three Forms (Extra Eye),* 1969; *Three Forms (Family Group),* 1965

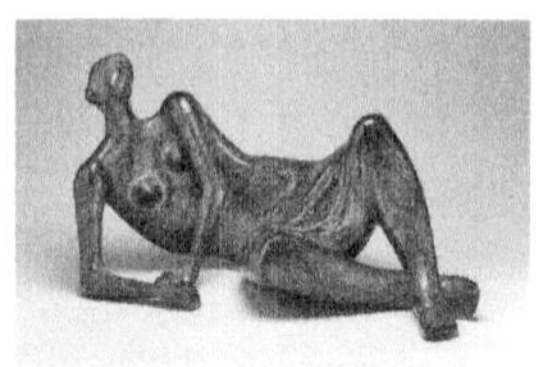

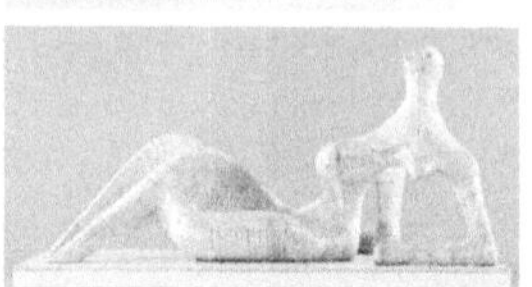

Henry Moore, *Reclining Figure,* 1954–1955; Henry Moore, *Reclining Figure,* 1951

one can still recognize human bodies in themes and most of them have titles like 'Reclining Figure'. Hepworth's work is in that respect more radical, because her abstract forms completely deny the logic of inner necessity. Instead, the logic of scenic sculpture has taken over.

From Battlegrounds to Playing Fields: Hans Hovy

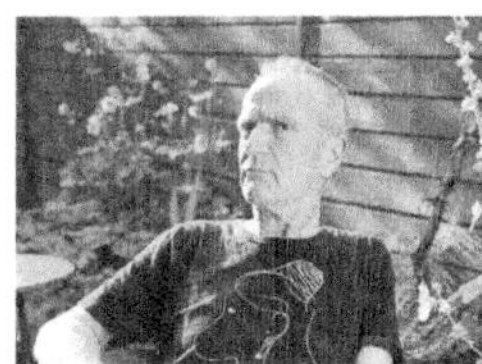

Hans Hovy (1953)

The works of Dutch artist Hans Hovy give the platforms on which his sculptural forms are placed a new meaning. In the chapter *The Body Undone,* I already discussed works by Hovy that challenged the conventional notion of the human body: I will now pay attention to the platforms on which most of his works are placed. His series of pieces from 1995 and 1996, Cast Iron Ordinaire and Cast Iron Deluxe, do not consist of a human or abstract body placed on a pedestal.

Although there is indeed a ground or a base, it sooner takes the shape of a stage, a platform, or a playing field. When we depart from the idea of a playing field, then multiple objects or players continue to be placed on the field. Created in the platform are recesses or grooves in which the objects can be placed. The players on the field seem to adopt no fixed positions; they seem to be movable, and this gives rise to different dynamics among the objects. While the platforms and the objects on them are abstract, they do evoke a narrative dimension. This is where something happens—scenes come about due to the way in which the objects relate to each other.

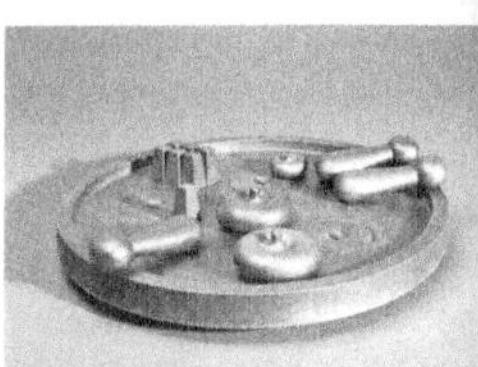

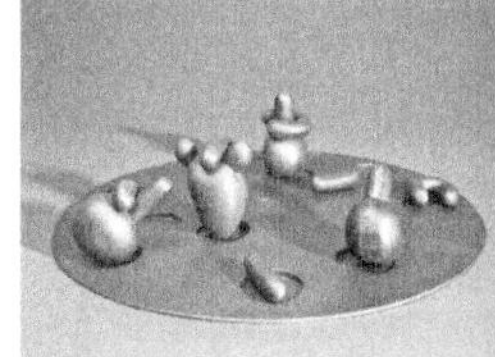

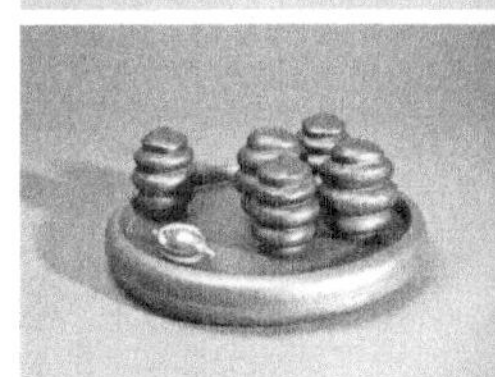

Hans Hovy, *Playground*, 1995–1996; *Sausages Hanging*, 1995–1996; *The Fatties Playing*, 1995–1996

Hovy is certainly not alone in creating such sculpture; he is part of a tradition which crops up on the fringes of dominant sculptural traditions.

Hovy's series Cast Iron Ordinaire and Cast Iron Delux are, along with the work of Giacometti, part of a sculptural tradition that has remained outside Krauss's field of vision. Their scenes on platforms assume continually different forms and utilize continually different possibilities of this sculptural logic. The collection of rules that make up this logic is not absolutely determined; it can be employed in various ways. That is already evident merely in diverse works from different periods of Giacometti's practice that I have discussed. But the exploration and development of this distinct sculptural logic also becomes visible in the work of Hovy. He has clearly been inspired by the scenic sculpture of Giacometti, but implements the principle of scenes on a platform or stage even more emphatically and literally than Giacometti did.

During the early nineteen-nineties, Hovy produced a series of works in which the platform emphatically assumes the form of a playing field. These resemble the tables often used for card playing, but in this case made from a combination of high-quality types of wood, such as maple and ebony, or from cheaper material such as plywood. Two objects from this series, *Lengthwise* (1992–1993) and *Cross-Cut* (1992–1993), consist of tables that have been constructed in two colours and two types of wood. One half comprises black ebony, the other half white maple, a dichotomy suggesting the two halves of a football field or a tennis court. The doughnut-like curves and phallus-like shapes that have been placed on these playing fields are, however, difficult to understand from the perspective of these games. They sooner suggest a game of a more sexual nature.

Other playing tables from this series, not divided into two halves, seem to relate to different types of games. *Untitled* (1993), situated in the middle of a table, has a funnel-like form which opens beneath it, as if this were a kind of snooker table where the ball must be aimed to go into the pocket. The objects on the table, however, are not balls; one object is sausage-shaped (phallic), another looks like some kind of dropping, and a third is shaped like a diabolo. Time and again, the forms of the objects have anthropomorphous, or more specifically, erotic dimensions.

The works with the titles *Sodom* (2006), *Gomorra* (2006), and *The World of Sodom and Gomorra* (2009–2012) constitute further variations on the logic of the scenic platform. These works are made of white alabaster and pink soapstone, materials and their colours fraught with meaning; their sensuality inevitably gives rise to erotic connotations. The white alabaster platforms are, this time, not a neutral ground. In terms of form, they can scarcely be distinguished from the objects that have been placed on or in them. The platform is much more than a location at which the scene occurs; it has itself become involved in the dramatic scene. With its inner spaces the platform offers room for phallic protrusions. The platforms not only have surfaces, but also inner spaces that can be penetrated by the objects that dominate the scene in terms of number. Here, the distinction between playing field and players that move about on it ceases, in fact, to exist. The platform no longer seems to be a stable ground, but is itself in motion and undergoing transformation.

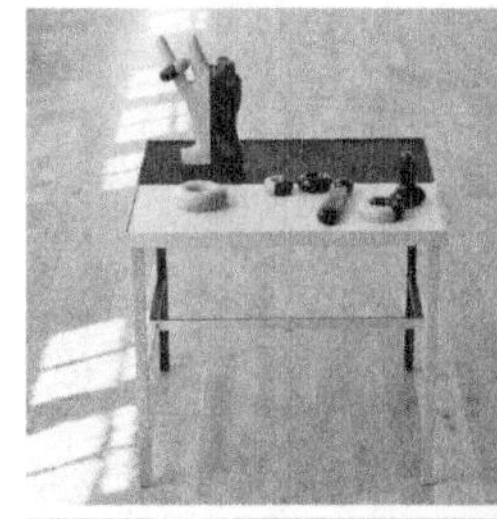

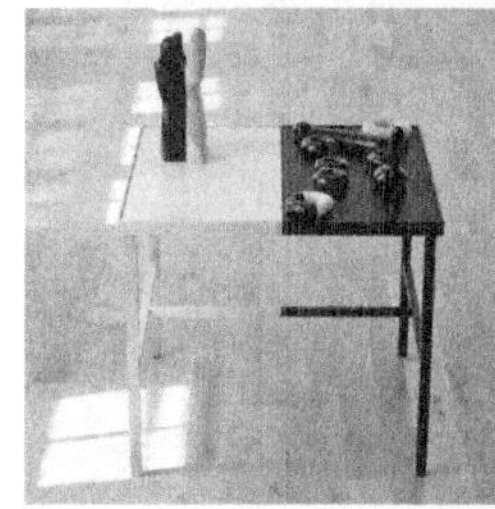

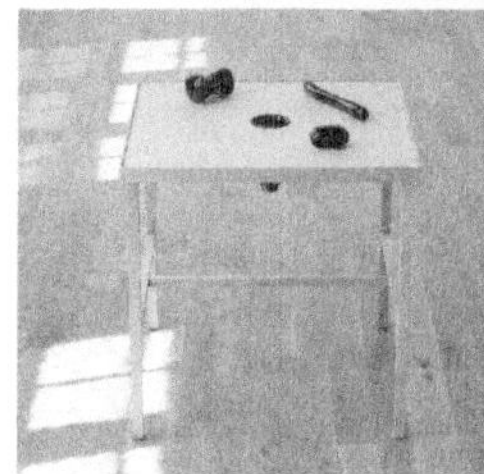

Hans Hovy, *Lengthwise*, 1992–1993; *Cross-Cut*, 1992–1993; *Untitled*, 1993

While the Surrealist-erotic platform scenes of Giacometti assume the gruesome forms of a battlefield, those of Hovy are chiefly playful and light-hearted, despite the ironic designation *The World of Sodom and Gomorra*. With Hovy, the scenes are about innocent and naive children who unsuspectingly, and without any awareness of the implications of sexuality, stick their penises or fingers in every orifice or present their vulvas, mouths, or anus to anyone who asks. In an age dominated by #MeToo conflicts, this portrayal of

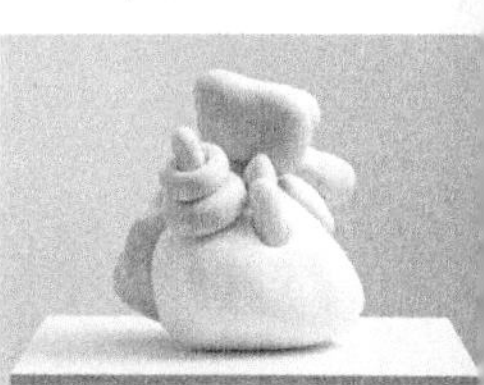

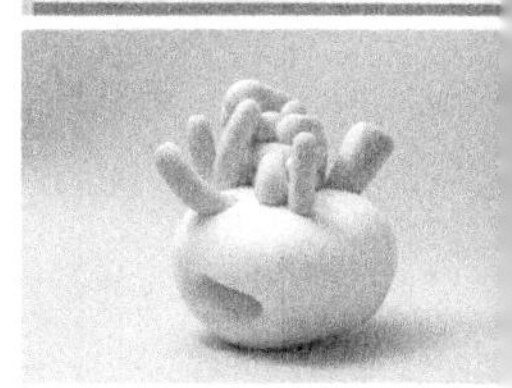

Hans Hovy, *Big Sodom*, 2007/2008/2013/2020; *The World of Sodom and Gomorra*, 2009–201

sexuality is not only literal and emphatic, but also liberating. For sexuality is not only dead seriousness.

Sexuality is evoked by Giacometti and Hovy in very different ways. Giacometti works mainly on a symbolic level: he makes use of objects that symbolize the phallus or the woman, as a wide pelvis does. Due to that symbolic dimension, his Surrealistic universe is a mythological universe. Hovy, on the other hand, suggests sexuality on the basis of form and matter. He does not represent sexuality directly, but suggests it indirectly, giving rise to this association with the aid of, among other things, an affective transmission of form and material. The sensuality of soapstone and alabaster, and his workmanship in this, are the qualities that set the affective transmission in motion. And even though many of his objects are phallic, they are not as such due to the symbolization or representation of the phallus. This is partly suggested by a very vague similarity. They are phallic because they display a similarity: in terms of Peircian semiotics, they are icons rather than symbols. But this suggestive, iconic likeness is affectively heightened by way of colour and material.

Hovy's Arcadian depiction of sexuality should not be regarded as a naive idealization. The scenic depiction of sexuality as a battlefield is, as with Giacometti, more common, and for that reason Hovy's playing fields are more provocative. Or perhaps we should say that Hovy's depiction of sexuality is provocative precisely because it seems a naive idealization. For ever since Adam and Eve were banished from paradise, sexuality lost its innocence once and for all. Nonetheless, some of Hovy's sexual playing fields have titles such as *Total Innocence* or *Small, Little, Lovely*. The distinction between good and evil seems, with these works and their titles, to be denied or ignored. Whereas Adam and Eve become aware of their sexuality outside of paradise and cover themselves in shame, Hovy's works seem to express no sense of shame whatsoever. This is more a matter of uninhibited surrender.

Hovy's works *Small, Little, Lovely I* and *II* introduce scenic dynamics to the nth degree. With Giacometti, we already saw his emphatic focus on scenic dynamics by placing the platform, in turn, on a pedestal. In *Small, Little Lovely I* a spherical white alabaster platform is standing on a flat bronze platform. Standing on the latter are also, aside from the first platform containing objects, two bronze objects. These objects relate not only to each other, but to the other platform as well. Such a stratified dynamic can be seen as a voyeuristic situation: the black figures observe what takes place on the other platform.

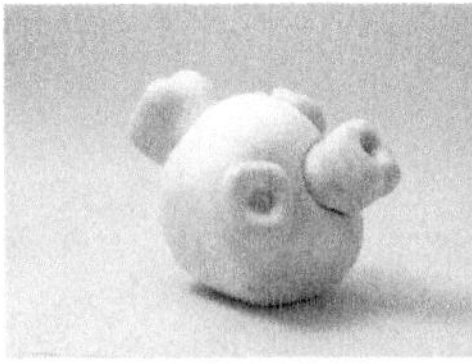

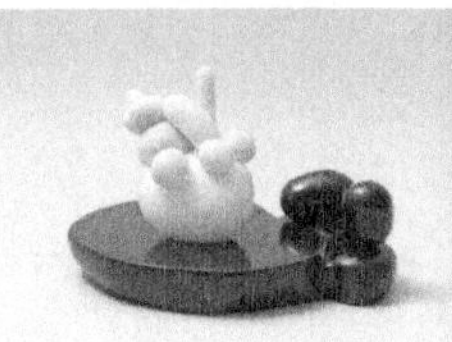

Hans Hovy, *Total Innocence*, 2007–2013; *Small, Little, Lovely I*, 2010–2012

In recent works such as *Sculptissimo* and *Masterpiece*, Hovy reflects on the scenic platform in yet another way. We already saw previously that the platform in his work does not necessarily consist of a flat location; it can also involve hills, bulges, and ball-like shapes. The platform in recent work consists of unpolished rock masses. Placed on these unformed rocks are figures or objects, each containing a letter. The titles of the works, *Sculptissimo* and *Masterpiece*, are displayed on the rocky platforms—the rock masses occupy far more space than the more neutral base of the platforms. Nevertheless, these continue to be bases for objects, although it is unclear as to whether those objects still collectively comprise a scene. They are less emphatic players on a playing field, or warriors on a battlefield. The rock masses are no longer subordinate to the scenes for which they offer room. The integration of the pedestal into the sculpture had already taken place earlier, when the modern sculptural logic emerged, particularly in the work of Brancusi. Here something similar seems to occur, not with the pedestal but with

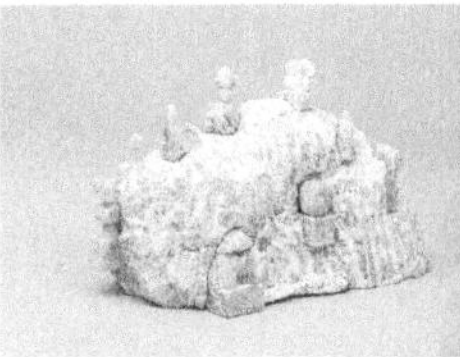

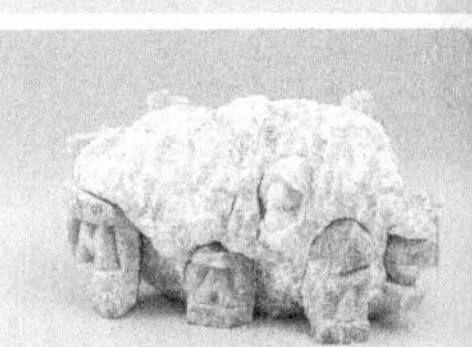

Hans Hovy, *Sculptissimo*, 2014; *Masterpiece*, 2015

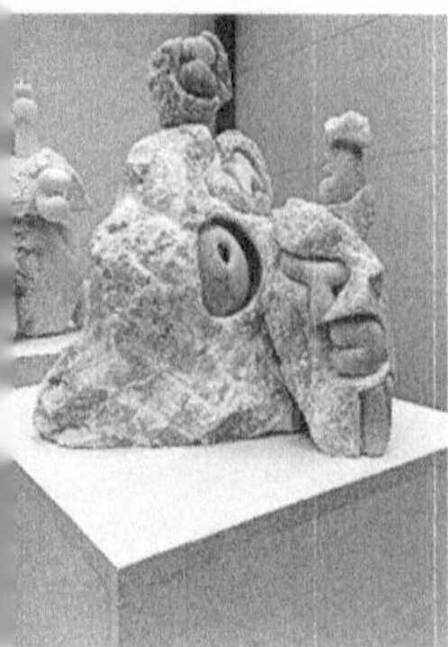

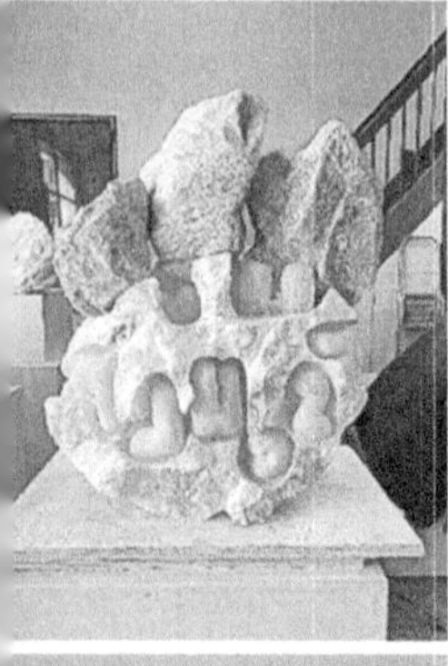

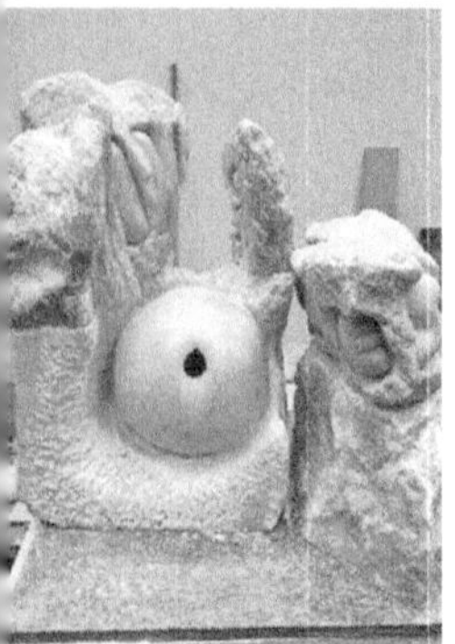

ans Hovy, *Sketch*, 2015–2017; *ing of Sculpture 1*, 2017–2018; *ing of Sculpture II (Memories of ew Gardens)*, 2017–2019

the platform. The dramatic tension is of a different nature as it arises among different elements. The scene now assumes a different form: rather than the usual dramatic tension among various elements on a stage, there is now tension mainly between the elements and the rock-like platform. The platform gains the upper hand and begins to demand more attention.

The elements that have been placed on the rock masses are of a very different nature than before. Instead of phallic shapes, bulges, or curves that evoke sexuality in an iconic manner, we now see, apart from opened spherical forms, letters in particular. Even though many of those letters once again suggest phallic forms, at the same time they symbolically signify the letter for which they stand.

Not all of the objects that collectively give rise to dramatic tension have been placed on the rock masses—with increasing frequency, they are situated in or inside the rock, as if in caverns. The classical tension between the sculpture's outward appearance and an inner essence which 'causes' or 'accounts for' the outward appearance has been turned inside out here. The object, which formerly consisted of a body (be it abstract or otherwise) and which was placed on a pedestal, now constitutes the inner world of a rocky platform.

The podium or platform manifests itself in yet another way in the wearable and unwearable rings Hovy has been making since 2010. These rings are usually placed on small ebony or white alabaster platforms. They suggest or foreground the idea of the podium in a new manner. The part of the ring that contains the hole through which one should stick one's finger already functions as a platform on which the ring can stand, but this functional part looks more like a pedestal instead of a platform. The platforms on which the rings stand suggest that we should also read the hand or body that is supposed to wear the rings as platforms, as bodily platforms, that is. The body is thus not just the carrier of clothing and jewellery, but more like a podium on which scenes can be staged.

The logic of scenic sculpture discussed in this chapter was for centuries combined with the logic of inner necessity. In the history of sculpture, it is usually the conventional logic of inner necessity that prevails. The narrative dimension serves then as the background that explains the feelings or passions that cause the appearance of the sculpted figures. But in the twentieth century with artists like Alberto Giacometti and Barbara Hepworth, scenic sculpture became autonomous, resulting in sculptures of which the meaning and impact is solely affected by the dynamics between several bodies, usually placed on a platform instead of a plinth. The platform as theatrical stage emphasizes the importance of the dynamics between elements, due to which sculpture attains a narrative dimension.

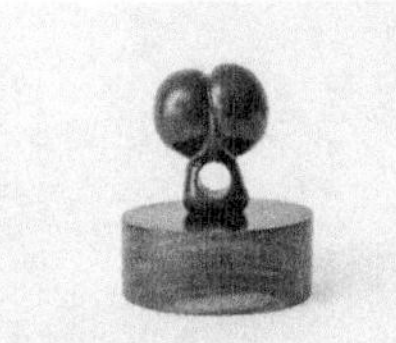

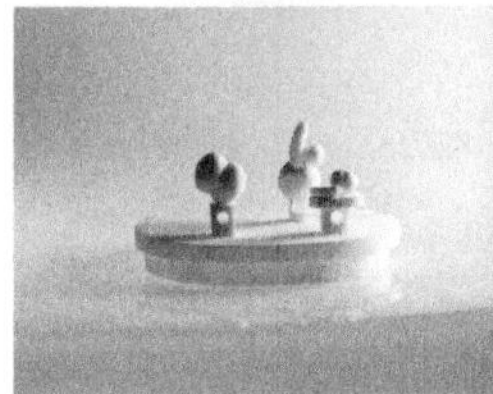

Hans Hovy, *Blossoming & Fruity*, 2014; *Three Unwearable*, 2018

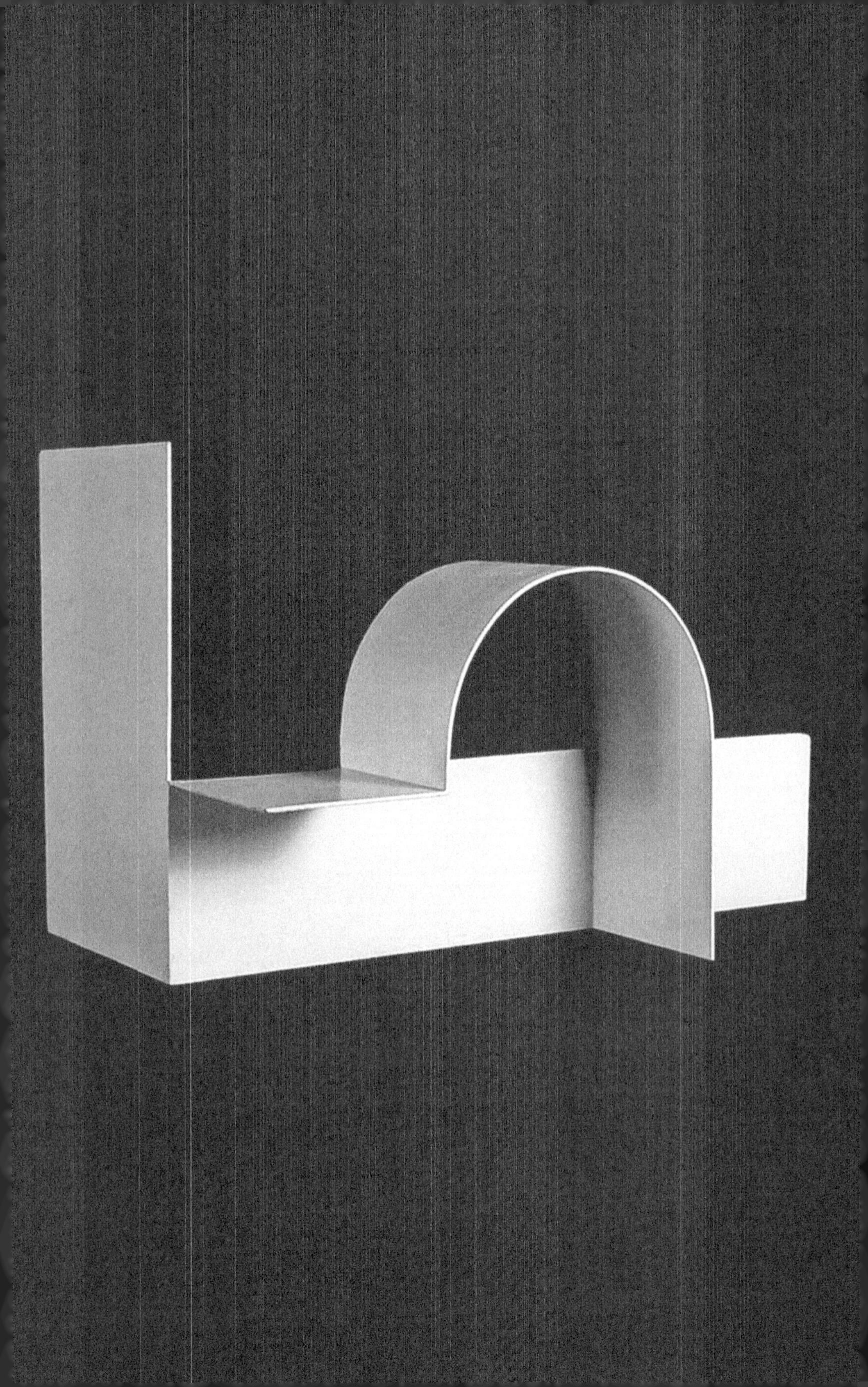

Sculpting Space

Unifying Sculpture with Space: Katarzyna Kobro

The sculpting of space is a logic of sculpture one associates first of all with Polish Constructivist artist Katarzyna Kobro, who famously wrote in 1929 that: 'Sculpture is the shaping of space. A sculpture enters space and space enters it in turn.'[1] In the text 'Composition of Space', which she wrote with her partner Wladysław Strzemiński, who was, first and foremost, a painter, they distinguish painting from sculpture in spatial terms:

> The painting has natural limits that are determined by the dimensions of the canvas. It cannot go beyond its natural limits. This is why the construction of the painting takes its limits as a point of departure... A sculpture, on the other hand, does not have such natural limits, defined a priori. Hence the natural law must be for a sculpture not to enclose itself within a volume, but to unite with the totality of space, with the infinite space. The union of the sculpture with space, the saturation

1 Hastings, 'The Power of Inclusion in Donald Judd's Art p. 54.

Katarzyna Kobro, *Space Composition 3*, 1928

of space by the sculpture, the fusion of sculpture in space and its links with it constitute the organic law of sculpture.[2]

According to Kobro, the most fundamental problem in the entire history of sculpture is:

> [...] the relationship between the space contained within the sculpture and the space situated outside the sculpture. Aside from this fundamental problem, the following issues are relatively secondary: the static or dynamic character of the sculpture, the predominance of line or of volume, the use or nonuse of color, the handling in lights and shadows or in masses. From the solution given to this principal problem will stem both the type of sculpture and the solutions found for the secondary questions.[3]

Kobro and Strzemiński were Russian but lived and worked in the nineteen-twenties and nineteen-thirties in Łódź, Poland. Although part of the Russian European avant-garde, they developed their own theory, which they called *Unism*. This theory is focused on the medium-specificity of painting, sculpture, architecture, and typography, and should be seen as part of the aesthetic tradition that is more interested in the specificity of different media than in what they have in common. Their theory should be seen in relation to Lessing's famous *Laocoon,* and the more recent text by Clement Greenberg, 'Towards a New Laocoon'. But in contrast with Lessing and Greenberg, their theory is not formalist and has a strong utopian element in it. They blamed formalism for being bourgeois and asocial. In the words of Strzemiński: 'The artist's goal is not to express his individuality, but to work collectively toward the creation of objective values whose measure is form.'[4]

Strzemiński and Kobro, 'The omposition of Space', p. 86. ll quotations in this chapter re translated into English by ve-Alain Bois from the French anslation by Baudin from the olish originals.

Strzemiński and Kobro, 'The omposition of Space', p. 85.

Strzemiński, 'Modern Art in oland', p. 78.

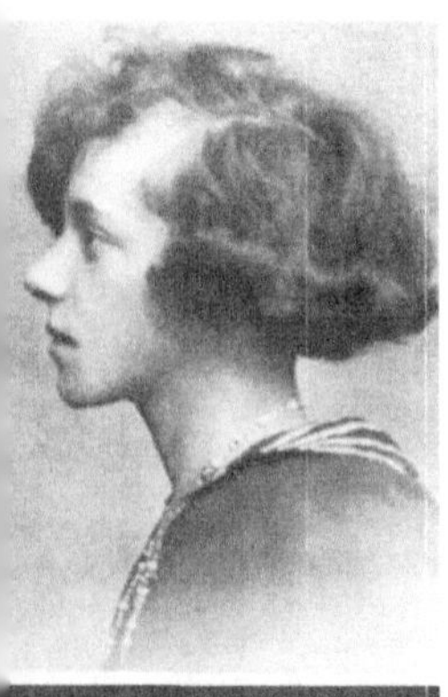

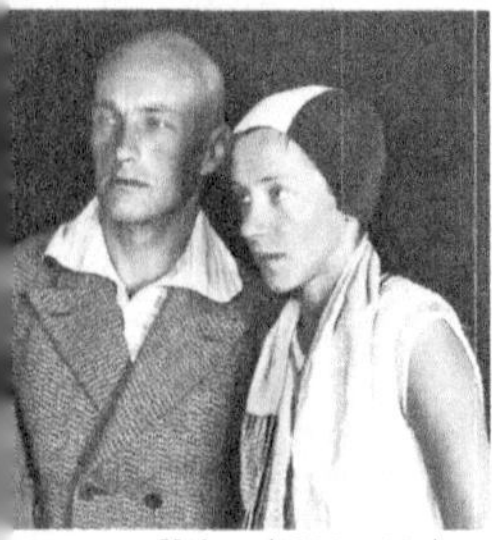

atarzyna Kobro (1898–1951); ght above with her partner ladysław Strzemiński.

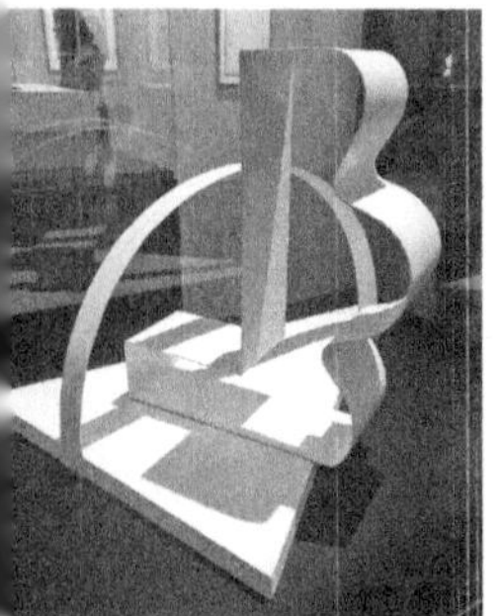

atarzyna Kobro, *Space ulpture*, 1925, reconstructed 1967

One of these objective values was space; as a result, sculpture is defined by spatial relationships. As Strzemiński asserts:

> Unist sculpture does not make sculptures. It sculpts space, condensing it within the limits of its sculptural zone. The Unist sculpture, aiming for an organic unity between sculpture and space, posits that sculptural form is not an end in itself, but only the expression of spatial relationships.[5]

Thus, the main aim of 'Unism' is a union of man with space. According to Kobro and Strzemiński, space is homogeneous and infinite, in a state of constant equilibrium.[6] But every figure introduced into that space is opposed to the homogeneity of the surrounding space. It is a sculptural challenge to make objects that are not foreign to the space of which they are part: 'Sculpture should not be a foreign body in space or a center that seizes a space; its construction has to agree with the fundamental laws of space.'[7] According to Yve-Alain Bois, the notion of space Kobro and Strzemiński adhered to was philosophically phenomenological, albeit implicitly. For, it is only the eye of the beholder which can experience and understand these spatial relationships.[8]

The logic of sculpting space opposes the conventional logic of the commemorative monument. This logic distinguishes sculpture from the ongoing passive contemplation that cuts him off from the concerns of daily life.[9] Kobro's and Strzemiński's concern is, however, the space of our daily experience:

> The union of man and space is the action of man in that space. We come to know space through our actions. The vectors traced by the actions of man in space are: the

5 Strzemiński, 'Modern Art in Poland', p. 149.

6 Bois, 'Kobro and Strzemińsk[i] Revisited'.

7 Strzemiński and Kobro, 'The Composition of Space', quoted in Bois, 'Kobro and Strzemińsk[i] Revisited', p. 8.

8 Bois, 'Kobro and Strzemińsk[i] Revisited', p. 10.

9 Krauss's analysis of the 'log[ic] of the monument' can be found in the chapter 'Sculpture in the Expanded Field' of her book *Th[e] Originality of the Avant-Garde and Other Modernist Myths*, pp. 279–80.

) Strzemiński and Kobro, ;omposition of Space', p. 104.

1 See Sloboda, 'The Movement ' Space-Time', p. 20.

2 Jędrzejczyk, 'The orporality of Form', p. 38.

3 Jędrzejczyk, 'The orporality of Form', p. 41.

> vertical station of man and every object, the horizontal of the environment that he encounters on both sides, and the depth, before him, of forward movement.[10]

Their emphasis on the union of man and space explains how Kobro's *Spatial Compositions* must be seen as models of a future society that enable the viewer to imagine a harmonious society.[11] It is the duality of sculpture that enables it to function as a model for society:

> On the one hand a 'signifying' object, relating to something other than itself; and on the other, a three-dimensional 'actual' body, crossing the threshold of the aesthetic register and moving into the realm of other material bodies.[12]

Kobro's work stems from the conviction that:

> [H]uman surroundings and the rhythm of life can be shaped by art forms which carry within themselves the potential to influence human perception of the world, and the way human *being-in-the-world* is organized.[13]

On the basis of their notion of sculpted space, they also develop a complex typology of culture that helps us to understand the history of sculpture from antiquity onwards. Yve-Alain Bois describes some of the 'types' in such a way that the different dialectic between sculptural object and space becomes clear: Egyptian sculpture: a volume-sculpture which does not raise the issue of exterior space; gothic sculpture, which reaches a union with that portion of exterior space contained within the limits of architecture; baroque sculpture, finally, where 'the limit of form is the limit of the zone of influence of its dynamic forms', and which reaches a union with that portion of exterior space contained within this 'limiting limit'.[14] As Bois writes, the terminology they use is rather odd ('limiting limit'), but it does demonstrate well how these two theoreticians of Unism situate the logic of sculpting space, as materialized in the sculptures of Kobro, in an evolutionist development of sculpture. Her sculptures are the end point of increasingly successful efforts to create a union between man and space.

Strzemiński's and Kobro's text 'Composition of Space' is probably the most elaborate and consistent theory of sculpture from the twentieth century. And Kobro's works demonstrate very convincingly what they argue in this text. Her Constructivist sculptures consisting of iron plates combined into open, three-dimensional structures clearly refute the idea that sculptures are solid bodies or objects. And they refute the idea that space is just the context or environment in which the sculpture is located, implying that it is of less importance than the viewer's centre of attention: the solid object. According to Kobro, artists should discard the solid: 'A solid is a lie about the essence of the sculpture. It closes up the sculpture and separates it from space.'[15] In Kobro's sculptures, the interrelationship between space and structure is completely equal: they shape each other, it seems, and there is no hierarchical distinction between the two.

As a result of the destructive forces of the Second World War, only fifteen of Kobro's sculptures survive. They are almost all in the Muzeum Sztuki in the Polish city of Łódź. The six earliest sculptures, which she made before 1925, are not the result of the theory of Unism, but of Suprematism and Russian Constructivism. The later ones all consist of open planes, curved or orthogonal; it is the intersection of these planes, in particular, that renders space visible. Kobro employs two strategies to prevent her sculptures from being

14 Bois, 'Strzemiński and Kobro', p. 146; he quotes from Strzemiński and Kobro, 'Composition of Space', p. 97.

15 Kobro, 'Sculpture and Solid', p. 19.

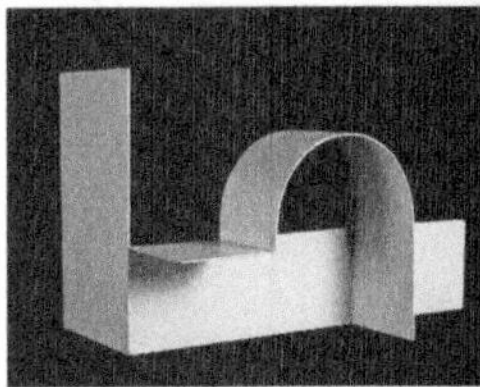

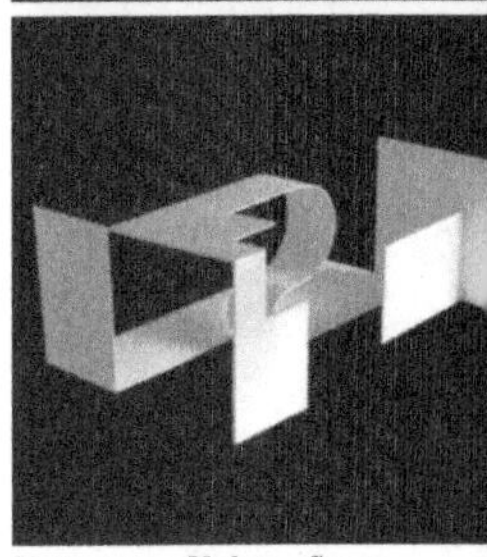

Katarzyna Kobro, *Space Composition 3*, 1928; Katarzyna Kobro, *Space Composition 5*, 1929–1930

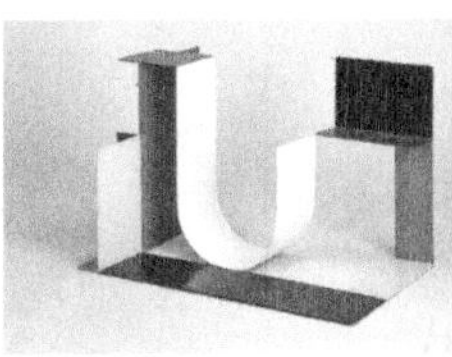

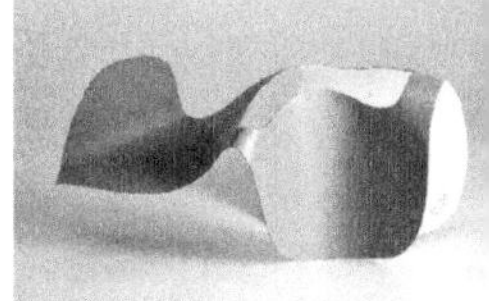

Katarzyna Kobro, *Space Composition 4*, 1929; *Space Composition 9*, c. 1933

16 Bois, 'Strzemiński and Kobro', p. 149.

17 Strzemiński and Kobro, 'Composition of Space', p. 115.

18 Bois, 'Strzemiński and Kobro', p. 151.

seen as objects in space. First of all, she pleads for polychromy in order to resist optical unity. This unity would separate the sculpture from space. The use of several contrasting colours causes the sculpture to explode in space: 'Not only are two sides of a single plane painted in different colors, but each color is also distributed non-contiguously in the three dimensions of depth, width, and height.'[16] Although Kobro argues at length for polychromy, some of her works are monochromatic—painted pink, for instance.

Her second method to prevent a separation between sculptural object and space is the emphatic mobilization of time. A sculptural object should not allow itself to be seen in one glance. Aesthetic experience implies and requires duration. For instance, when we stand before a sculpture 'depth is always hidden from us'. 'When the spectator moves, certain forms present themselves, others hide; the perception of these forms changes constantly.'[17] In the words of Bois:

> As we circulate around her best sculptures, what was negative (empty) becomes positive (full), what was line becomes plane or point, what was straight becomes curved, what was wide becomes narrow. An entire stream-of-consciousness novel would be necessary to describe the transformations that occur as we circulate around the two works mentioned above.[18]

According to Bois, the sculptural theory of Unism is one of the subtlest and most convincing consolidations of Modernism. But although they resisted the idea of composition, the artists held on to the idea of 'unity' and the 'law of organicity'. Although they tried to escape from metaphysics by engaging the viewer's experience of space and creating a dynamic between sculptural object and space, their belief in the unity of the artwork undermined this ambition.

At first, Kobro's notion of sculpture can be recognized in that of the American artist Charles Ray, whose work I discussed previously in the Introduction to this book. He says, for example: 'A sculpture's primary medium is space. A sculpture does not simply sit in space or occupy space; it's made of space.'[19] Nevertheless, his works usually consist of solid volumes, instead of structures that are entangled with space, as in the case of Kobro. His emphasis on the importance of space and space as the medium of sculpture often results in very outspoken ideas about how his works, and in which combination, should be installed in space: 'I have fought for space and the peace and quiet that comes with sculptural elbow room.'[20]

19 Ray, 'How many Sculptures Can You Fit in a Room?', p. 150.

20 Ray, 'How many Sculptures Can You Fit in a Room?', p. 150.

Cutting Space: Carl Andre

The technique of sculpture is conventionally defined as either the removal of matter through carving or as the addition of matter through modelling. In the twentieth century, new techniques were developed such as 'making use of readymades' or 'assembling forms and shapes', resulting in an assemblage. For Carl Andre, sculpture consists of cutting. In a text by David Bourdon, the artist is quoted as follows:

> 'Up to a certain time I was cutting into things. Then I realized that the thing I was cutting was the cut. Rather than cut into the material, I now use the material as a cut in space.'[21]

21 Bourdon, 'The Razed Sites of Carl Andre', p. 15.

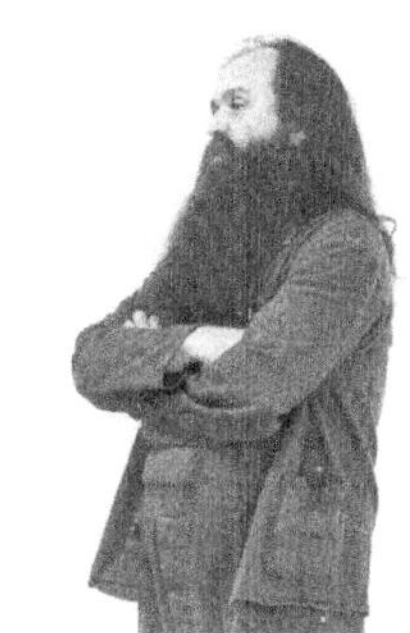

Carl Andre (1935)

The verb 'to cut' has connotations that differ radically from 'to carve':

> 'Carving' tends to invoke a notion of handheld blades piercing the surface of stone or wood; it implies a distinct

2 Rider, *Carl Andre*, p. 53.
3 Rider, *Carl Andre*, p. 53.

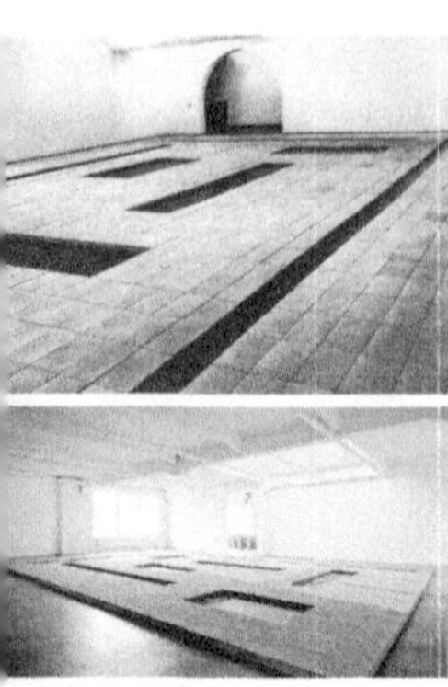
arl Andre, *Cuts*, 1967

> sympathy for traditional standards of craftmanship. 'Cutting', on the other hand, does not. It indicates no level of expertise on the part of the cutter: after all, machines do it just as effectively. Cuts, moreover, can be performed on literally anything—from a pack of cards to the roughest of diamonds.[22]

The technique of cutting implies a different notion of subjectivity: not that of the talented artist or craftsman, but a mechanical de-individualized one. Andre is not cutting a specific material, a substance, however; his phrase 'cut in space' suggests that his works make changes to the environment that surrounds them. Space is then something supplied and shaped by the sculpture.

> Suddenly the emptiness around a work appears more intense, itself an almost palpable presence. In turn this would generate very rich and prolific conversations about what actually constituted the sculptural object. Did sculpture have to be a solid object anymore?[23]

His work *Cuts* can be seen as a literal example of work in which emptiness makes and constitutes the sculpture. The arrangement of concrete capstones does not cover the whole floor but has 'empty' spaces in it. These empty spaces are 'cut' in the floor piece, the arrangement of stones. But a work like *Bloody Angle* from 1985, displayed in the Stedelijk Museum in Amsterdam, can be considered sculpting space in the sense already described and theorized by Kobro. This work consists of identical blocks of wood, twenty lying flat on the floor and nineteen standing upright; it looks as if the arrangement can endlessly repeat itself. More important, however, is that this arrangement of wooden blocks also demarcates and shapes the space that surrounds it. The dynamic between solid shapes and empty space makes the work into what it is. Of course, one could argue that any sculpture shapes the space that surrounds it. But these works of Andre and Kobro exploit, emphasize, and foreground this implicit sculptural element intensely.

Andre also used a very significant aphorism to define the objecthood of sculpture. This phrase defines sculpture in terms of the space it occupies and demarcates instead of objecthood: 'A thing is a hole in a thing it is not.' Robert Smithson was so fascinated by Andre's phrase that he used it as the title for one of his essays.[24] And when Andre had an exhibition in 1966 in the Tibor Gallery in New York, its director John Myers explained to Dan Graham, who had expressed his interest in this work, that he saw it as: 'Our sculptures are holes in the space of the room.'[25]

24 Smithson, 'A Thing is a Hole in a Thing It Is Not'.

25 John Myers, quoted in Rider, *Carl Andre*, p. 53.

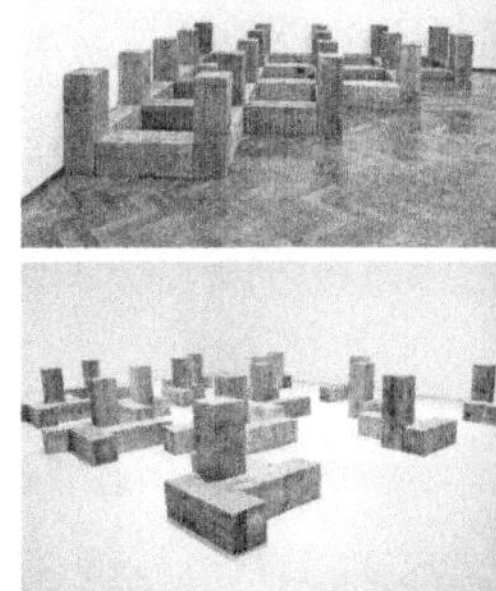

Carl Andre, *Bloody Angle*, 198…

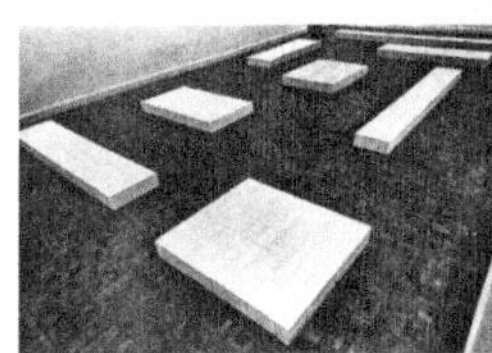

Carl Andre, *Equivalents I–VIII*, 1966

Myers's claim, clearly inspired by Andre's aphorism, displaces the emphasis from the objecthood of sculpture to the space it occupies and surrounds. The works Equivalents are the negative of *Cuts*; there are no empty holes in an arrangement of bricks, but solid arrangements of bricks in the empty gallery space. Still, these solids are described as 'holes' in the space where they are positioned. Solid objecthood is radically bracketed.

According to David Bourdon, the show 'Equivalents' in the Tibor Gallery could be seen as an argument for transcendentalism. It looked like an abstracted Japanese rock garden, conducive to contemplation. Andre had transformed the room, 'itself a Golden Rectangle', into 'an archipelago of Euclidean isles'. But according to Andre, his show was not related in any shape or form to transcendentalism:

> My work is atheistic, materialistic and communistic. It's atheistic because it's without transcendent form, without

3 Carl Andre, quoted in ourdon, 'The Razed Sites of arl Andre'.

> spiritual or intellectual quality. Materialistic because it's made out of its own materials without pretension to other materials. And communistic because the form is equally accessible to all men.[26]

The material and form Andre talks about are not only the stone bricks out of which these works are made, but also the air in which viewers as well as stones dwell.

Gathering Space: Richard Serra

Quoted in the Preface by al Foster in Serra and Foster, *onversations about Sculpture*, 5.

Hal Foster in Serra and oster, *Conversations about culpture*, p. 5.

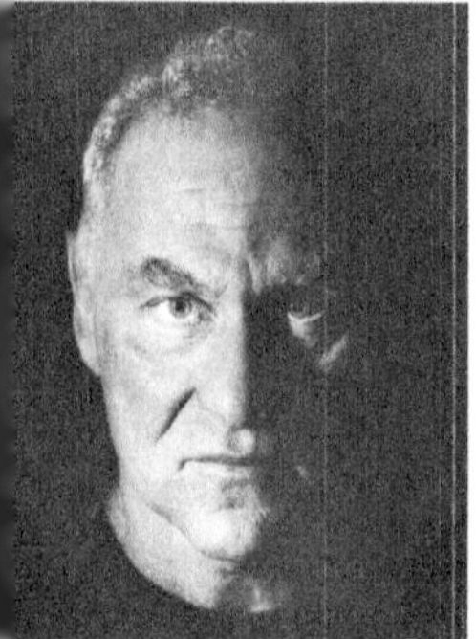

chard Serra (1938)

Although widely bracketed under Minimalism, the American sculptor Richard Serra's approach to sculpture differs radically from, for instance, Carl Andre or Donald Judd. Serra has a phenomenological approach to the world and pursues an embodied experience for the viewer in the space in which the artist, as well as her work, are located. He refrains from framing his works as pictures that can be seen in one glance. In his own words: 'Most minimalists are stuck with gestalt readings. They don't truly open the space; for the most part their constructions remain objects.'[27] His intent to open the space with his works aptly demonstrates that he does not define sculpture in terms of its objecthood but as a form of sculpting space. This sculpted space is not something abstract or general but is always experienced in the present by a viewer. Hal Foster formulates the first and last criterion of Serra for the understanding of his work as: 'How does the work engage us, and how do we engage it, right here, right now.'[28]

Space is more than just the context of the work. That becomes clear when Serra elaborates the notion of context:

> One of the limitations of Minimalism was that it didn't deal with context. The perception of a Minimalist object

is mostly limited to a gestalt reading in a room: you read one side and then fill in the others in your head. That doesn't take in the consideration of time in relation to place, the whole subject-object relationship. The object is content to present itself in its own specificity. Like Smithson, Hesse, and Nauman, I wanted to find a way around that limitation.[29]

Serra's 'consideration of time in relation to space, the whole subject-object relationship' results in work that articulates the space in which it is located and that engages the viewer who walks in time through that space. One could also say that he dissolves sculpture into space.[30]

One could wonder if this articulation of space is the same as making a work that is site-specific, like, for example, Robert Smithson did with his earthwork *Spiral Jetty* (1970) in the Great Salt Lake in Utah. In other words, is a sculptural place the same as a site-specific work? Although many of Serra's works are made in response to, or in relation to, a specific landscape or architectural construction or situation, the term 'specific' takes on another meaning to the one it has in the phrase 'site-specific'. He uses the term 'gathering volumes' for the way he relates to the space in which his work is going to be experienced.

> Urban sites are much more difficult. You have more contingencies with more attributes, and you must push back with your own sculptural invention against a host of narratives, many of which are ideological. You have to gather the volumes that are already there, the circulation patterns, whatever, in fact all that goes into how the site is defined and perceived. I want to reclaim the site for sculpture.[31]

29 Foster in Serra and Foster, *Conversations about Sculpture*, p. 52.

30 Foster in Serra and Foster, *Conversations about Sculpture*, p. 57.

31 Richard Serra in Serra and Foster, *Conversations about Sculpture*, p. 66.

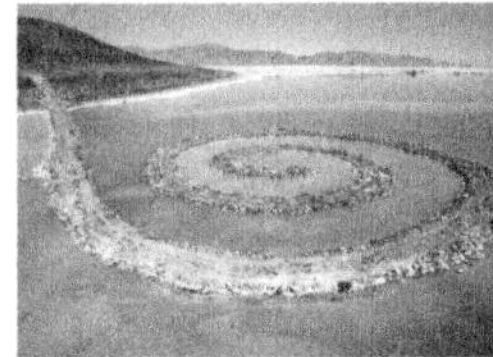

Robert Smithson, *Spiral Jetty*, 1970

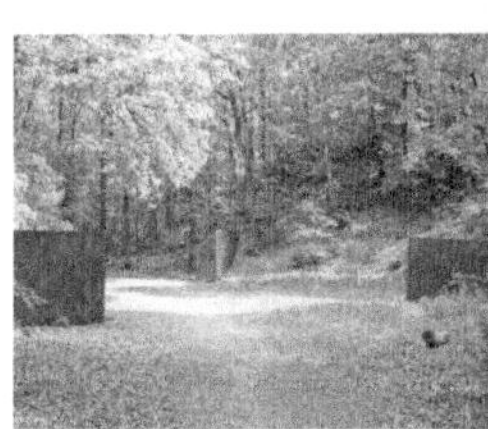

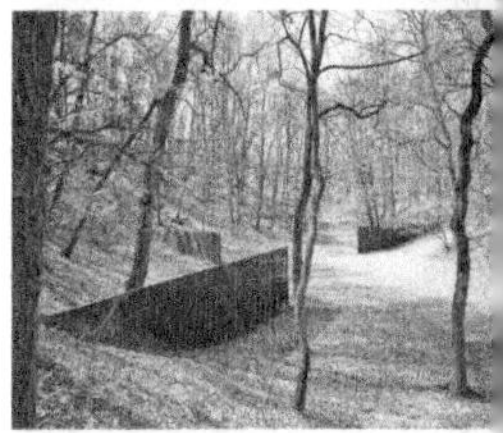

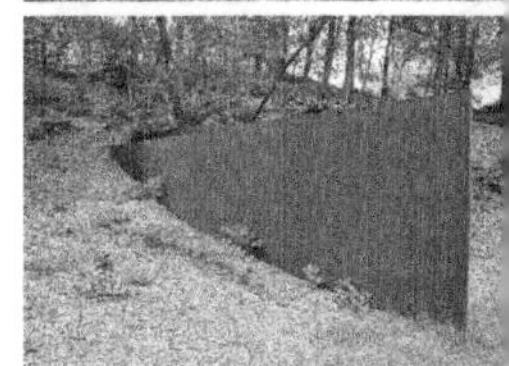

Richard Serra, *Spin Out (For Bob Smithson)*, 1972–1973

2 Hal Foster in Serra and oster, *Conversations about culpture*, p. 66.

3 Richard Serra, in Serra and oster, *Conversations about culpture*, p. 77.

Reclaiming a site for sculpture is rather different from site-specificity. The sculpture comes first but the relation to the site is seriously taken into consideration. The reclamation of a site takes place by 'gathering the volumes that are already there'. In response to Serra, Foster elaborates on the notion of 'gathering space' as the way a piece picks up on aspects of its surroundings and pulls them into itself as part of its content.[32] Another important difference between gathering space and site-specificity is that sites for site-specific works are usually chosen by the artist, whereas in Serra's case the sites are usually given to him.

Serra contrasts 'gathering' with 'framing'. The gathering of space and volumes is the primary act because that act is where a sculptural work begins. Framing, however, is secondary and it leads to image-making.[33] And of course, not only paintings and drawings are images; when a sculpture can be read as gestalt, the result is also an image instead of a spatial experience in time. After the gathering of space has resulted in a work, this work specifies the place, 'you can make it relevant, when you'd otherwise pass it by'. Again, to specify a place is not the same as site-specificity. The former artistic practice consists of a verb, the latter a noun. This implies that to specify a place concerns an experience (the viewer's), whereas site-specificity concerns the work as object.

Serra has made several series of works, for example constructions with flat plates, ellipses and spirals, and more recently also passageways. The spatial experience in the viewer's time is always a crucial element, but in different ways in the respective series. The constructions of flat plates, like the tower construction *Sight Point* (1972–1975), located outside the Stedelijk Museum in Amsterdam, are sculptures the viewer can peep into between the plates, and walk around. A similar work belonging to the same series is *7* (2011), located outside The Museum of Islamic Art in Doha, Qatar. It consists of seven plates and has three triangular openings onto the space on the ground and one opening at the top that frames the sky. But this series began with *One To Prop (House of Cards)* (1969), now in the Museum of Modern Art in New York. What is radically new in terms of sculptural logic in this work, and the series it belongs to, is that it is no longer a solid body or volume but consists of several elements that put pressure on each other, a pressure of opposition. As Serra has explained, other Minimalist artists were especially interested in Brancusi's *Endless Column* (1918), whereas he was more concerned with Brancusi's *The Kiss* (1907–1908) and *The Gate of the Kiss* (1938).[34] The so-called 'House of Cards' series is part of the same sculptural logic as Brancusi's *The Kiss*, because, in the words of Krauss, it creates a 'phenomenological fissure, in which the unity of the body's Gestalt is radically opened and differentiated'.[35] Of course, in Serra's works one cannot speak any more of bodies or the body's gestalt, but the opening up and differentiating of elements in a pressure of opposition is also at stake. This makes his fascination with Brancusi's *The Kiss* completely understandable.

The viewer's body is of importance in yet another way in the work *Circuit* (1972). Krauss's description of the work is very much to the point, so I will quote her at length:

> The implication of the viewer's body in the action of the work is unavoidable, since the only place to experience the sculpture is at its center—as one stands in the three-foot opening in the midst of the jut of four plates—each eight by twenty-four feet—pushing diagonally from the four corners of a room to stop just short of its midpoint. In that centre the viewer must turn 360 degrees in

34 Serra and Bach, 'Interview

35 Krauss, 'Richard Serra', p. 109.

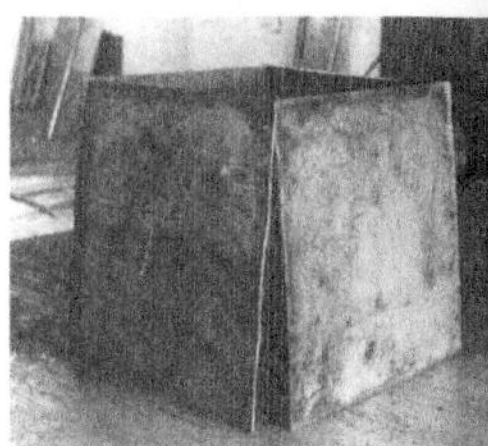

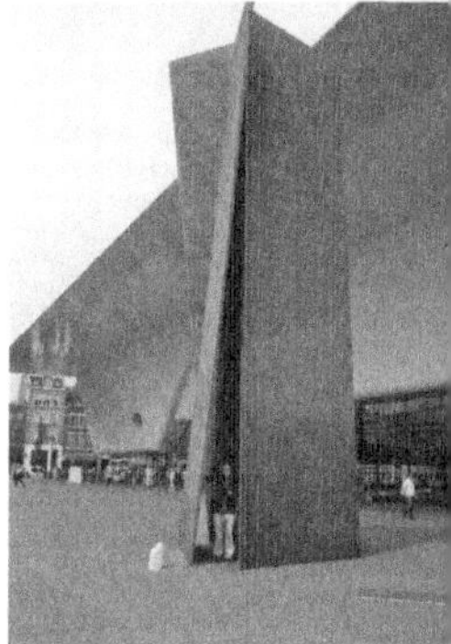

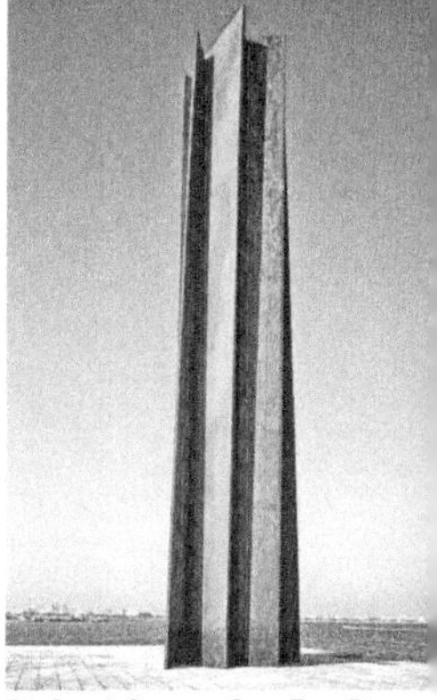

Richard Serra, *One Ton Prop (House of Cards)*, 1969; *Sight Point*, 1972–1975; *7*, 2011

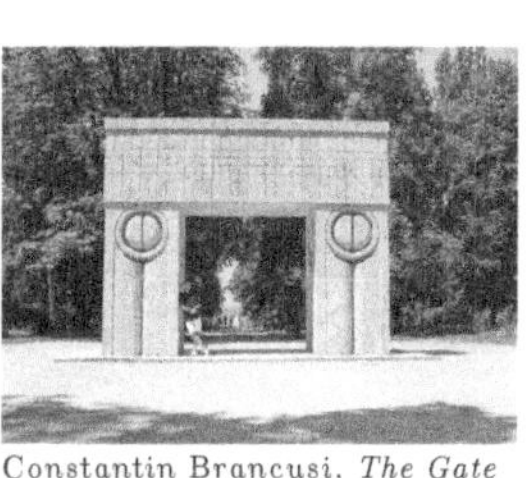

Constantin Brancusi, *The Gate of the Kiss*, 1938

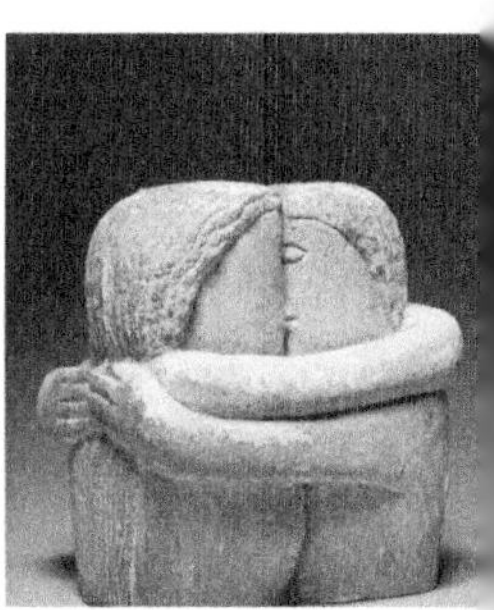

Constantin Brancusi, *The Kiss*, 1907–1908

36 Krauss, 'Richard Serra', p. 120–21.

37 Serra and Béar, 'Sight Point '71–'75/ Delineator '74–'76', 61.

> order to see the work, and the wholeness of his body becomes the guarantor of the reconstructible wholeness of the room's continuity beyond the cellular segmentation of the separate quadrants or "shots" into which the plates cut the architectural space.[36]

Circuit is a prime example of how Serra articulates space by an arrangement of flat plates. By entering the room, the viewer enters the sculpture at the same time. This work is a truly sculptural place.

The series of ellipses and spirals direct the viewer through the works, whereas the passageways give the viewer a choice, often more than one. The passageway *Inside Out* (2011), for example, has four entrances that can also be used as exits; the viewer can choose between multiple directions. The same can be said of the piece *Junction* (2011) given the viewer arrives at an interval, a point of deciding where to go next. The ellipse *Open Ended* (2007–2008) has just one entrance and one exit. The viewer is directed through the work and has no choice.

So far, I have emphasized several times that the viewer's experience is a crucial element in Serra's works. His sculptural logic transgresses the logic of objecthood. But I have not yet explicated the nature of this experience. The experience is first of all visual and optical, but the opticality of experience is imbricated with physical experience. The weight and materiality of the steel plates grasps the viewer's throat, whereas visually it only catches the eye. This is most radically the case in his piece *Delineator* (1974–1975). In Serra's own words:

> It's not opting for opticality as its content. It has more to do with a field force that's being generated, so that the space is discerned physically rather than optically.[37]

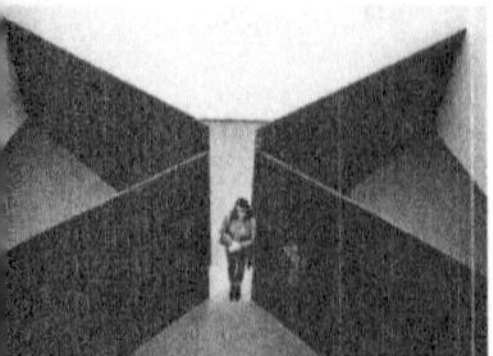

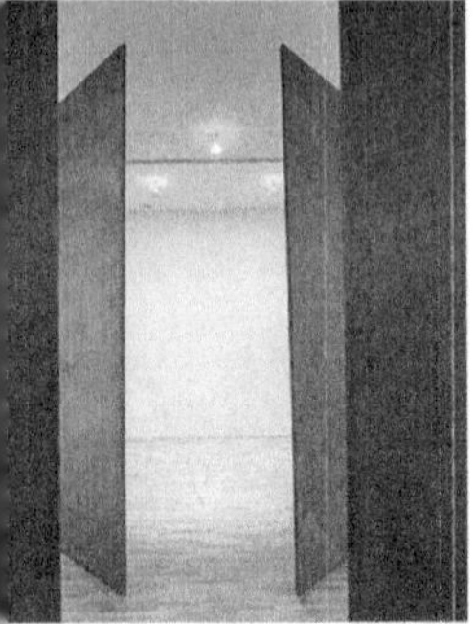

Richard Serra, *Circuit*, 1972

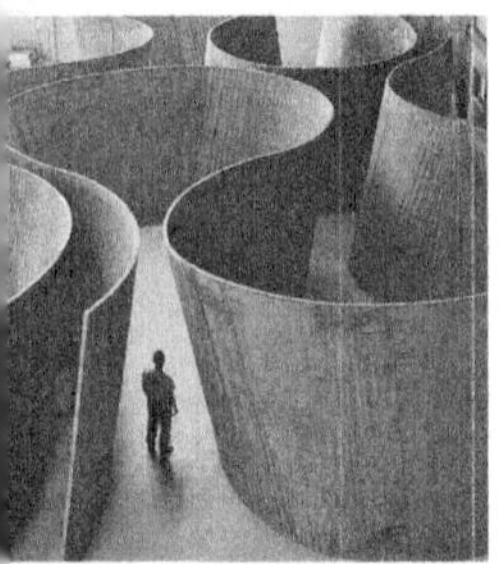

Richard Serra, *Inside Out*, 2011

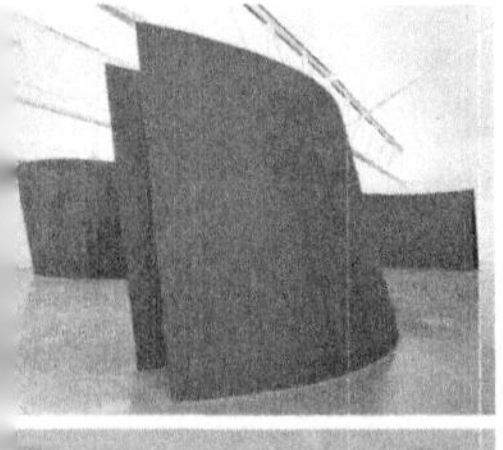

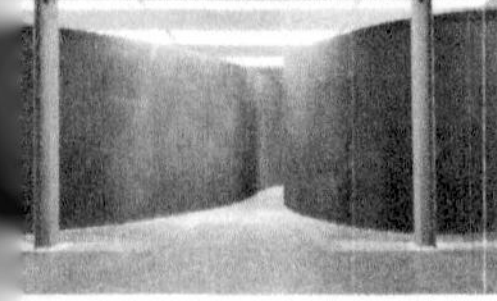

Richard Serra, *Junction*, 2011

This field force is generated by two very large flat plates, one on the floor, the other against the ceiling of the room. The embodied experience of the viewer makes one hold one's breath. To imagine the sheer weight of the plate above one's head is frightening. Although the piece is, in this respect, more radical than Serra's other works because the viewer experiences the work not in front or around but above him/her, the embodied experience of the materiality of these works is always at stake. Serra's work is never transcendental, but always radically physical. In this respect, Krauss connects *Delineator* from 1974–1975 with earlier works:

> This concern with the body as the ground of the sculptural experience is partially comparable to the way the abstract conditions of the body were modelled by *One Ton Prop (House of Cards)* or by *Stacked Steel Slabs*: The body as a will toward erectness, as the seeking of containment through balance. [...] Indeed throughout the decade of the 1970s Serra conceived of the sculptural project as a problem in the domain of perception—perception, that is, grounded in a living, moving, reacting body.[38]

One important element of Serra's work, and as a result of the embodied viewer's experience, still has to be discussed: namely, how it relates to the monument and the monumental. Although 'monumental' is the adjective of 'monument', its associations and meanings are rather different. Serra resists the idea that his works are monuments or monumental:

> My large-scale pieces are often referred to as being monumental and oppressive. Neither in form nor in content do they relate to the history of monuments. They do not memorialize any person, place or event. They relate solely as sculpture.[39]

38 Krauss, 'Richard Serra', p. 124.

39 Serra, *Writings/Interviews*, p. 170.

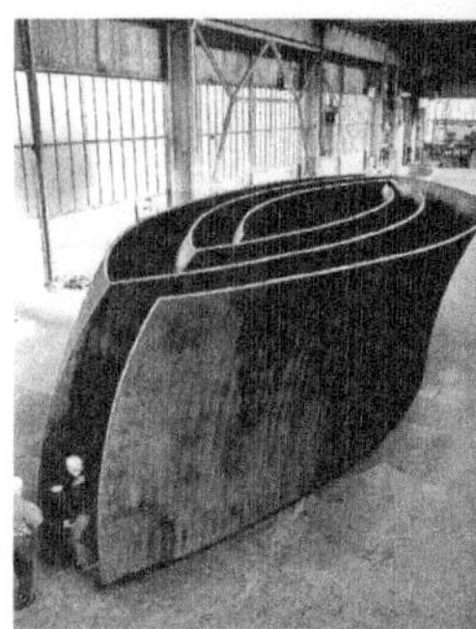

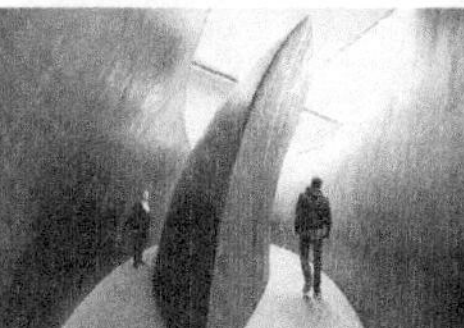

Richard Serra, *Open Ended*, 2007–2008

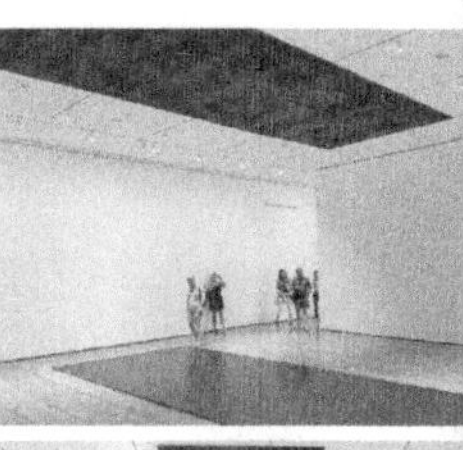

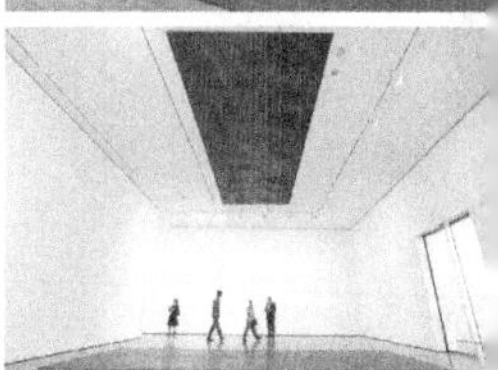

Richard Serra, *Delineator*, 1974–1975

Of course, they usually range from big to enormous, but the negative associations of monumental are related to ideological persuasion and oppressive scale. I do not think that Serra's 'enormous' pieces are oppressive; instead, they engender an intense bodily experience that is not oppressive or intimidating but more physical than the usual visual experience. When we use monumental as 'enormous' without the negative associations, it becomes possible to appreciate sculptures of a big scale.

Serra resists the idea of the monument for his work because of Tony Smith's verdict that anything bigger than six feet—the size of his cube *Die* (1962)—is a monument.[40] If we went along with Tony Smith's opinion, all of Serra's works would be monuments. But Foster proposes a more productive notion of the monument, the one suggested by Krauss:

> In her influential essay 'Sculpture in the Expanded Field' (1979) Rosalind Krauss argued that traditional sculpture in the West was bound up with the logic of the monument; that is, it was situated in a particular place, and its figurative language spoke symbolically of that place—of a person, a community, an event, a history. Further, she argued that modernist sculpture broke with that logic as it became abstract, autonomous, and siteless. Her paragon here is Brancusi.[41]

Serra can live with this notion of the monument for his works, because they usually belong to a particular place, like monuments do. He agrees with the idea that his works are 'monuments without monumentality. That sounds okay.'[42] But Serra forgets the second part of Krauss's notion of the sculptural logic of the monument, namely that they speak symbolically of that place. That is never the case in Serra's work. They do not speak symbolically but through the

) Richard Serra, in Serra and oster, *Conversations about culpture*, p. 165.

1 Hal Foster, in Serra and oster, *Conversations about culpture*, p. 166.

2 Richard Serra, in Serra and oster, *Conversations about culpture*, p. 166.

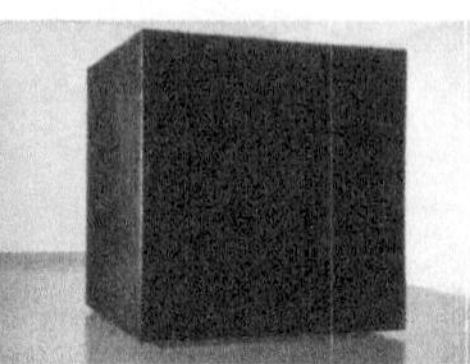

ony Smith, *Die*, 1962

embodied experience of the viewer. In my opinion, it is more appropriate to say that Serra's works are monumental without being monuments.

43 Serra, 'Donald Judd, 1928–1994', p. 177; quoted in Weiss, 'Sense of Site', p. 188.

44 Judd, '21 February 1993', *Writings*, p. 811.

Containing Surrounding Space: Donald Judd

Although Donald Judd wanted his work to be categorized as sculpture, since he made 'objects', or rather 'specific objects', his reflections on the relation between object and space is nothing other than a reflection on how objects, or sculptures that is, sculpt space. This was first of all understood by Richard Serra, who wrote on the occasion of Judd's death in 1994 that Judd was 'one of the first to deal with the contained interior space and the surrounding space simultaneously by emphasizing the continuity from the inside out'. He also wrote that his large works in plywood, steel, and concrete established a 'public space, an expansive, a vastness derived from openness but not contained by a closed solution'.[43] Discussing the relation between art and space, Judd distinguished a sequence of types, 'from that which can be placed on any flat surface, floor or wall or ceiling, or on the ground, with no intention of space other than that implied by the work, a work which articulates part of a room or some area outdoors'. Although his own works clearly belong to the second category that articulates space, even 'the smallest, simplest work creates space around it, since there is so much space within'.[44]

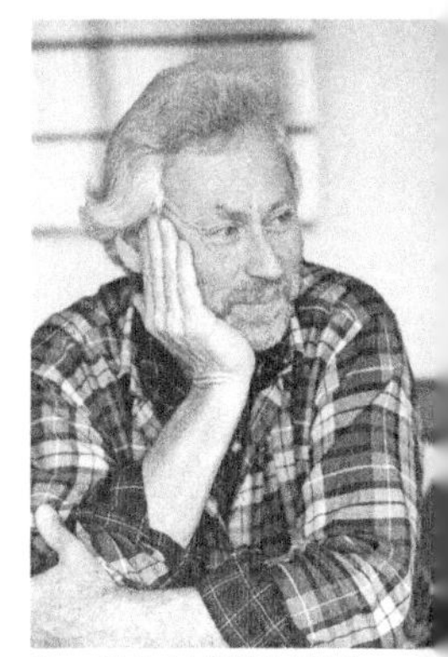

Donald Judd (1928–1994)

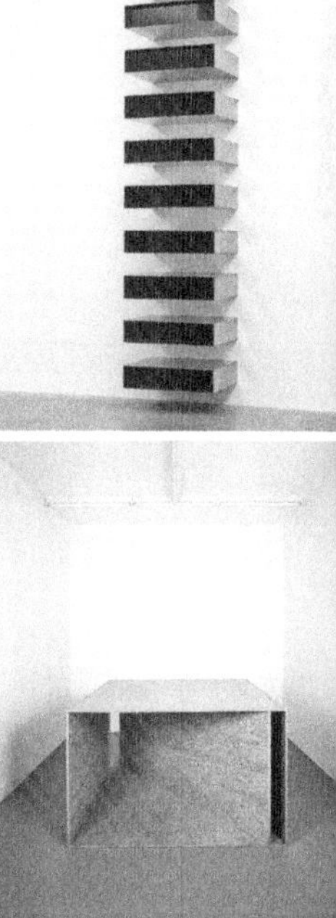

Donald Judd, *Untitled*, 1980; *Untitled (Bottrop Piece)*, 1974–1976

Judd's absorption of space into the notion of the object was, according to him, 'new in art'; in other words, this was his contribution to art. He was probably not aware of Kobro's very similar art practice in the first half of the twentieth century. He distinguished his objects from conventional

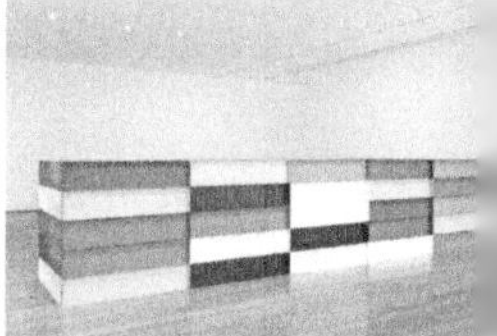

Donald Judd, *Untitled*, 1991

45 Judd, '21 February 1993', 812.

sculpture, which he describes as totems or monoliths: with conventional statuary 'the space around the sculpture is only somewhere from which to look towards the continuous solids'. In Judd's works, however, space is actively engaged and activated:

> I found that if I placed a work on a wall in relation to a corner or to both corners, or similarly on the floor, or outdoors near a change in the surface of the ground, that by adjusting the distance in the space in between became much more clear than before, definite like the work. [...] If the space in one or two directions can become clear, it's logical to desire the space in all directions to become clear. This usually requires more than a unit or it requires a space built around a unit or it requires a great deal of space. This is so of some large indoor works and of most large outdoor ones.[45]

An important shared characteristic in Judd's, Andre's, and even Kobro's sculptures is that they can be looked at as gestalts. Although they are three-dimensional, viewers will have an impression of the whole structure by standing in front of it, on the basis of their visual memory of similar objects. As with classical sculpture, it is not absolutely necessary to walk around it, because by means of visual deduction one can have an idea of how the sculptural object looks from other sides. This visual processing as gestalt is in most cases impossible with Serra's works: the viewer has to look actively and walk through and around them in order to see how they sculpt space.

Drawing Virtual Space: Fred Sandback

In what way do the delicate line constructions in different colours of string by American artist Fred Sandback belong to the logic of sculpting space? The constructions are not site-specific to the rooms in which they are actualized. They might be re-actualized in other spaces or in different ways in the same space. In his notes and interviews, Sandback stresses the fact that his line constructions are ideas and that they are factual, meaning that the ideas are not expressed or demonstrated by means of the line constructions. 'There isn't an idea which transcends the actuality of the pieces. The actuality is the idea', he asserts.[46] There is also nothing illusionistic about them; they do not represent anything. Sandback studied philosophy and sculpture at Yale University. This background may explain his assessment of his artistic practice as a mode of thinking. For him, philosophies are also line constructions, bringing lines of thought together.

When his pieces are not demonstrations of an idea, it means that there is no underlying order which manifests itself in his work. The actuality of his line constructions invites the viewer to think. 'They are not instances of a system or order larger than itself, in contrast to Constructivist line, which takes natural science as its model'.[47] The actuality of Sandback's ideas also implies that his work 'has absolutely nothing to do with Conceptual Art or something you conceive'.[48] According to John Rajchman, the actuality is the idea and the idea is just the sculptural fact, like the script for a spatial game of thought.[49]

The diagrammatic plans of the script rearrange the space in which they occur, 'freeing it from the usual organization, inviting a fleeting sense of co-participation in another vital

46 Sandback, 'Notes', p. 88.

47 Sandback, 'Untitled', p. 95.

48 Sandback, 'Pedestrian Sculptures', p. 102.

49 Rajchman, 'Fred Sandback Line of Thought', p. 11.

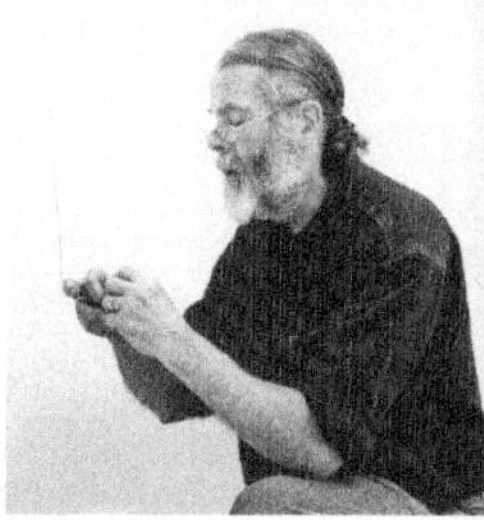

Fred Sandback (1943–2003)

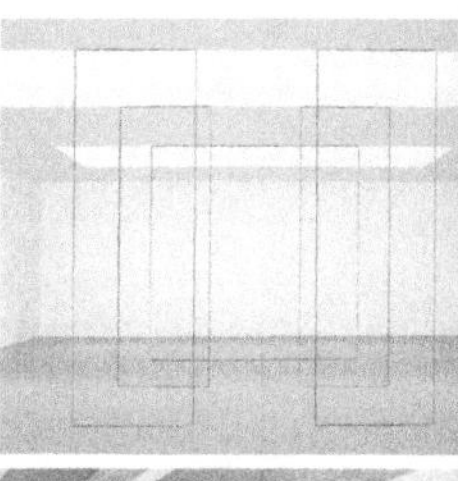

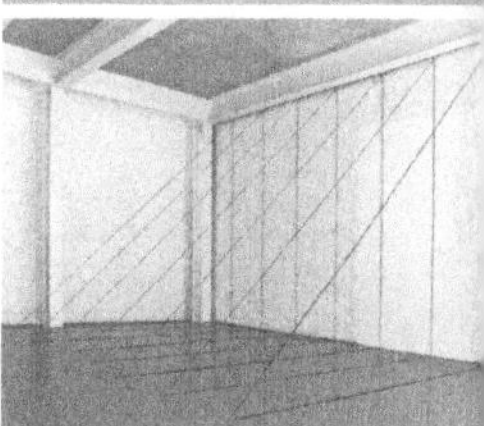

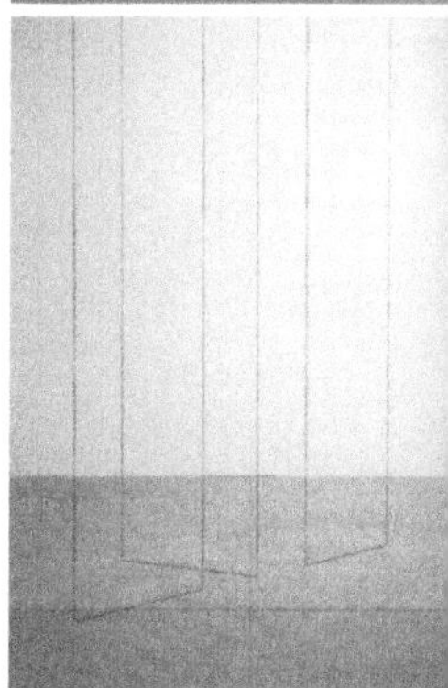

Installation of Sandback's sculptures in the Dia Art Foundatio[n]

space'.[50] Sandback's line constructions always complicate or complexify the spaces in which they occur. They sculpt the space differently. Rajchman's description of his sculptural practice makes clear that his pieces should not be seen in terms of objecthood but from a phenomenological perspective:

> Sandback's spatial actualities of facts set up discrete little virtual spaces that undo our ordinary sense of being inside the four walls of a room, seeing outside a window, moving within a frame, which we can momentarily inhabit. That is the kind of pedestrian nonillusionist space drawn or constructed by his lines of yarn. One sees with new eyes, one is strangely affected by inhabiting the virtual spaces drawn by these fraying lines of string that unmoor the usual parameters of the room.[51]

The lines of string change the space in which they occur; they do not only form a construction, but also sculpt the space by modifying its parameters.

The usual parameters are the four walls of a room, the corners, a window, a door, and more. Sandback's line constructions of string undo, however, the viewer's sense of the room as container, and they serve to free the viewer from the idea of a 'perspective on an object', or a room, that is. The viewer no longer occupies the space. As a result, the viewer enters a kind of virtual space and is immersed in a space without beginnings or endings, 'in an unlimited, unframed manner, while yet being there, even more in the spatial situation than one ordinarily is'.[52] Through the sculpting of space a new, virtual space is opened up. And this opened-up space is not the illusion of a three-dimensional space that is not actually there; it is the discovery of an extraordinary diagrammatic virtuality in a room. But this virtual space is at

Rajchman, 'Fred Sandback's ne of Thought', p. 11.

Rajchman, 'Fred Sandback's ne of Thought', p. 13.

Rajchman, 'Fred Sandback's ne of Thought', p. 14.

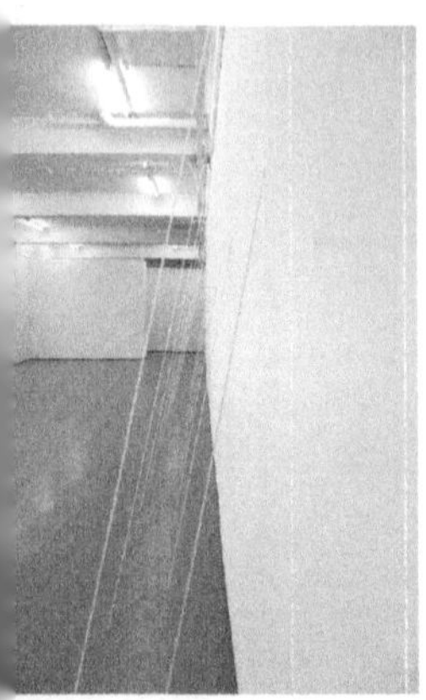

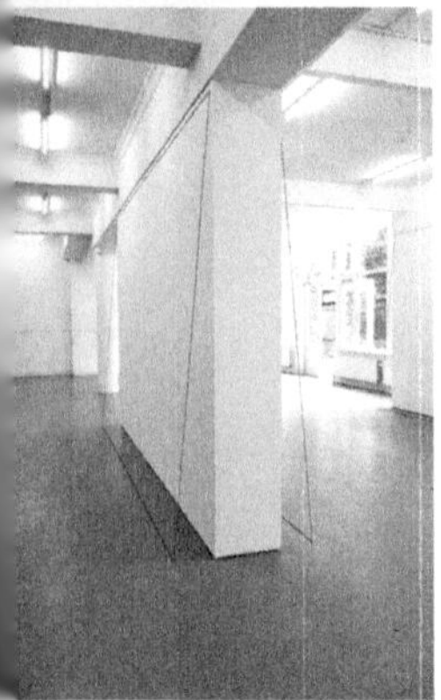

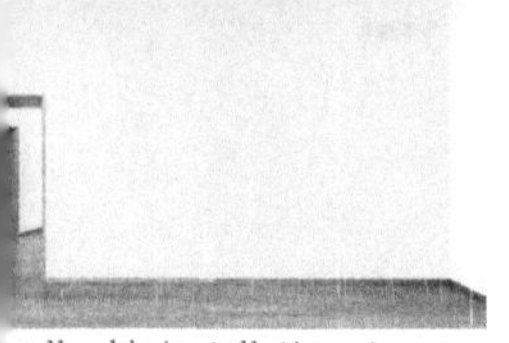

ndback's installation at unstmuseum, The Hague

the same time necessarily material. His ideas are material because one has to be in the room to experience the virtual space, one has to actually inhabit them. This is why photographs of Sandback's pieces fail in generating this experience. They are poor substitutes, because they only give an idea of the factuality of an idea.

Negative Space: Bruce Nauman and Rachel Whiteread

There is one specific mode of sculpting space that takes this logic rather literally in the sense that it can be seen as a circumscription of negative space: it makes visible and shapes the space that is 'empty' but enclosed by a three-dimensional object. This was first done by Bruce Nauman, who in 1965 made a work titled *A Cast of the Space Under My Chair*. The solid block is the negative of a chair: the empty space under the seat of the chair has materialized and form and shape have been bestowed upon it. Nauman's concrete cast was probably the inspiration for Rachel Whiteread's *Untitled (One Hundred Spaces)* from 1997. This work consists of a series of hundred resin casts of the spaces underneath chairs.

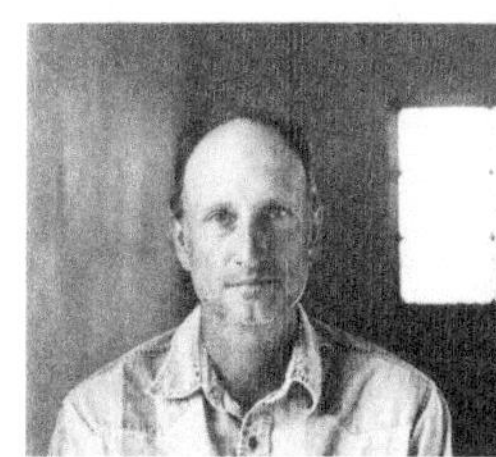

Bruce Nauman (1941)

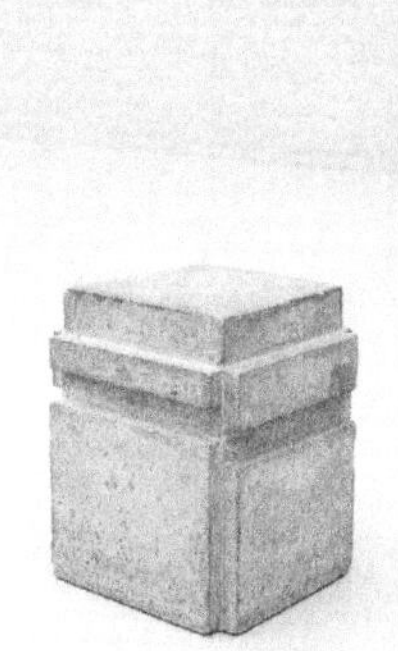

Bruce Nauman, *A Cast of the Space Under My Chair*, 1965

Yet already in 1993 Whiteread had made *House*, perhaps her best-known work. This was a concrete cast of the inside of an entire Victorian terraced house, exhibited at the location of the original house—193 Grove Road, in East London. The negative cast of the house was the only house left in the street because all the other houses had been knocked down earlier. The emptiness of the street was given form by the negative cast of the house. Whiteread has made the sculpting of negative space her trademark. The negative spaces of all kind of architectural spaces and elements are made visible by her, from complete staircases to library shelves and books.

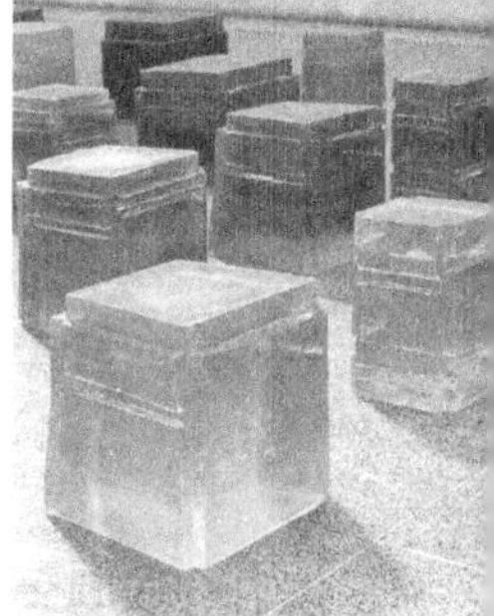

Rachel Whiteread, Casts of undersides of chairs, 1995

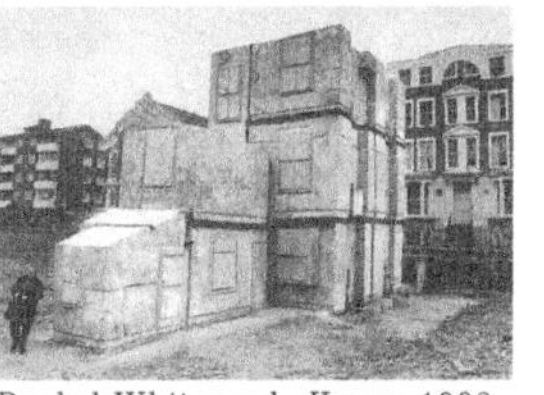

Rachel Whiteread, *House*, 1993, London.

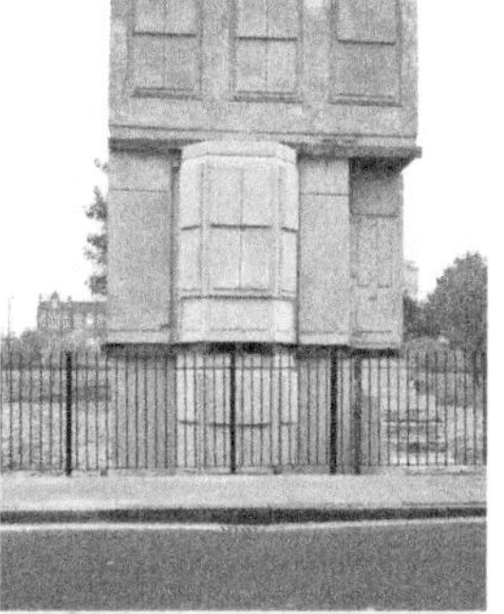

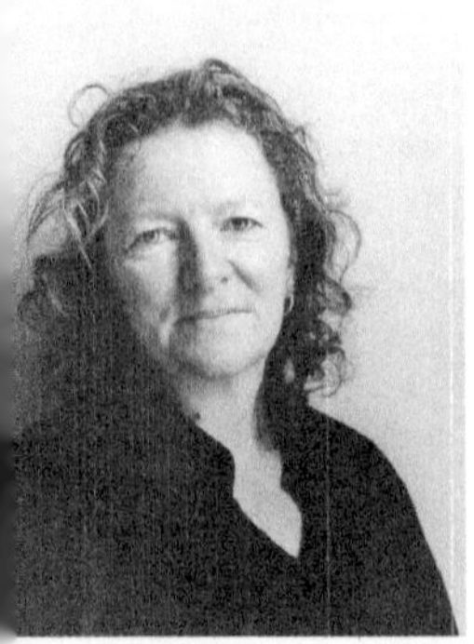

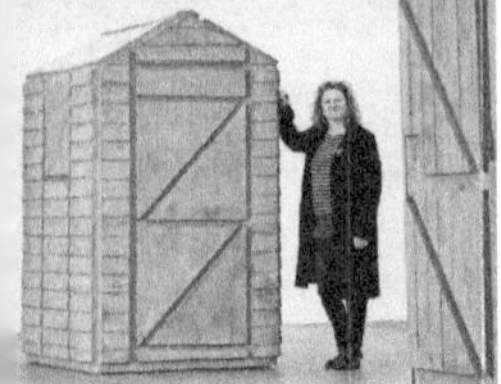

achel Whiteread (1963)

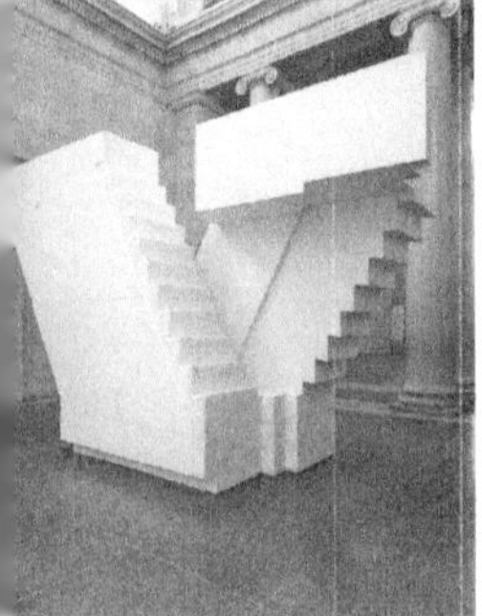

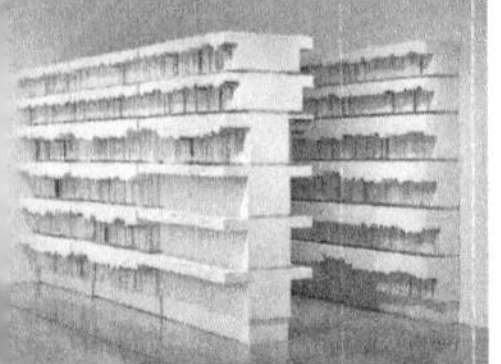

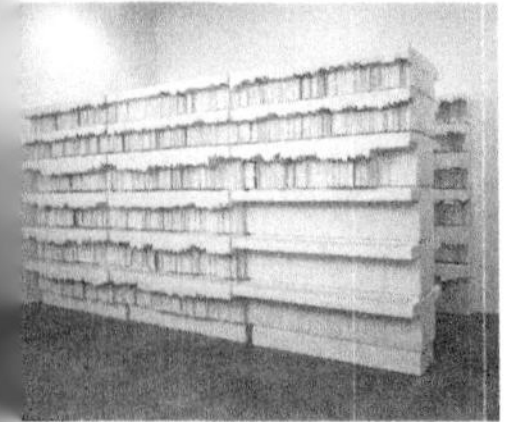

achel Whiteread, *Untitled tairs)*, 2003; *Untitled aperbacks)*, 1999

She was the first woman to win the prestigious Turner Prize in 1993. Whiteread's sculpting of negative space has also resulted in a very impressive Holocaust memorial. She was asked to make a memorial in Vienna for the 65,000 Austrian Jews who were killed in Austria during the Second World War, with the condition that this memorial could not be figurative. The commissioned monument was erected on the Judenplatz square in 2000. It is called *Nameless Library* and appears like an enormous tomb as well as an inside-out library. The bookshelves and corners of the room are not included, which makes it a negative space. But the logic of sculpting negative space is not followed in all details because the books are suggested by their volumes, by the space they occupy. The books do not fill the inner space of a room, but form the exterior of it, and are placed with their spines facing inwards. The spines cannot be read and as a result the books allude to the lost lives of the 65,000 Austrian Jews whose stories cannot be told. Their stories and lives are lost and absent. These books have also been seen as a reference to the Nazi book burnings.

Turning a library space inside out provides a monumental shape to the logic of sculpting space. Absent lives and empty space become voluminous. The negative space of the library shelves and the corners of the room suggest that memorials do not necessarily depend on countering and reversing absence by solid objecthood. The negativity of loss and death is in this work suggested by negative space, by making visible what is not there. The sculpting of negative space is not just a formal or conceptual issue, but an effective way of embodying and commemorating absent lives.

All artists discussed in this chapter do not consider sculpture as solid matter or a solid object, but as a dynamic of object and space. This dynamic of space and object can be seen as sculptural logic that differs from the other logics discussed in this book by its notion of space. Space is not the context of sculpture, but space is the dimension that is shaped by sculpture and in that sense is part of sculpture. The difference between these artists can be understood in terms of the gestures they perform in order to shape space: gathering space by Serra, cutting space by Andre, unifying space with sculpture by Kobro, drawing space by Sandback, and making negative space visible by Nauman and Whiteread.

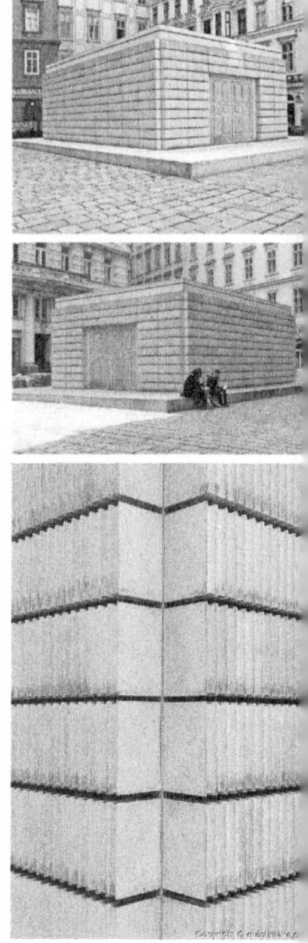

Rachel Whiteread, *Nameless Library*, 2000. Vienna, Judenplatz

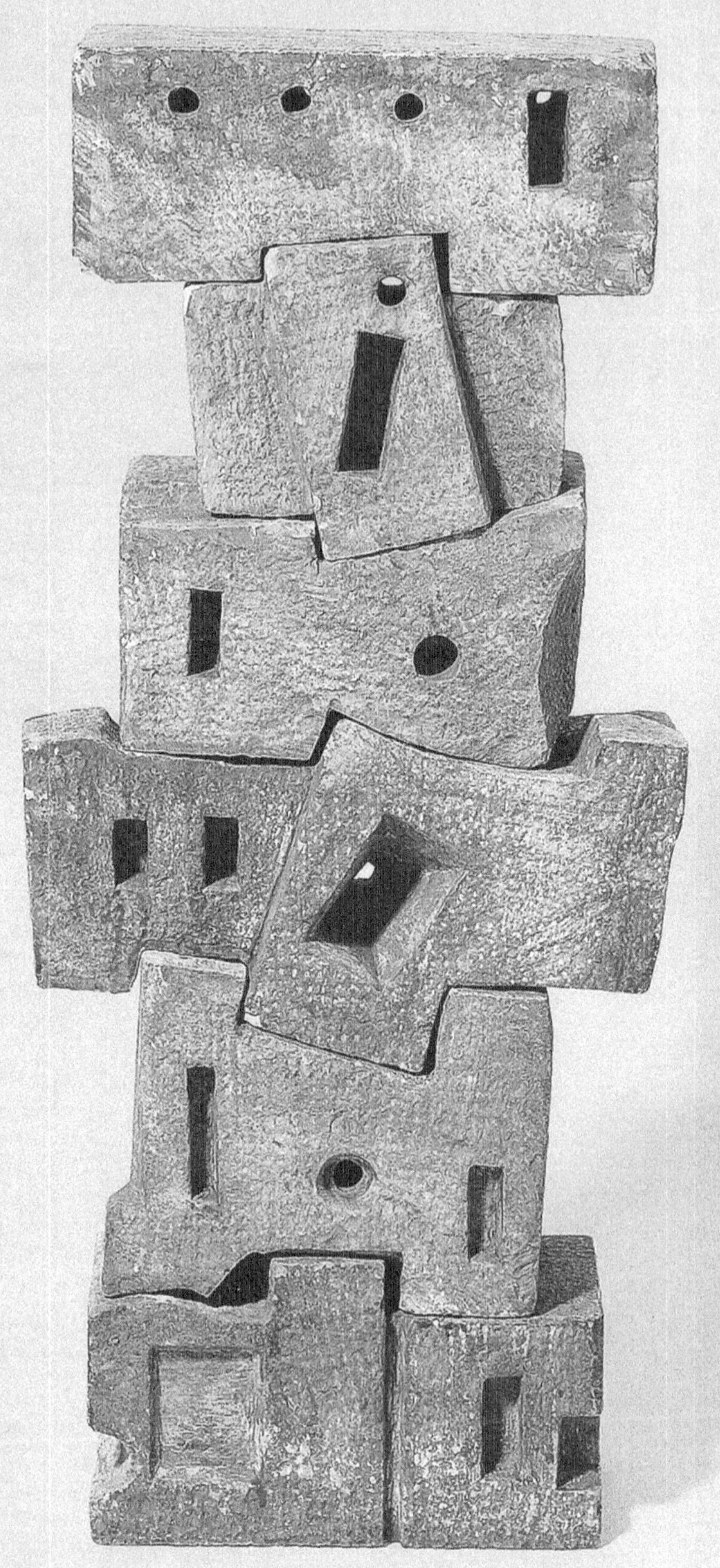

Building Blocks

From Body to Solid

Trying to assess Minimalist sculpture, Rosalind E. Krauss understands the work of Donald Judd as taking distance from the idea that sculpture should be understood in terms of the appearance and meaning of the (human) body. Judd's work implies, then, a radicalization of the thinking of two crucial figures in the early history of modern sculpture: Auguste Rodin and Constantin Brancusi.

> The art of both men represented a relocation of the point of origin of the body's meaning—from its inner core to its surface—a radical act of decentring that would include the space to which the body appeared and the time of its appearing.[1]

1 Krauss, 'The *Double Negative*', p. 279.

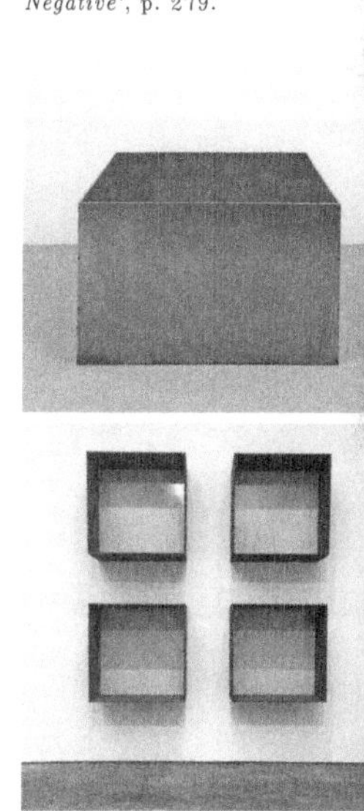

Donald Judd, *Untitled*, 1972; *Untitled*, 1979

In this chapter I will try to answer the following: when sculpture does not rely any more on the body, or rather the body's meaning, the question emerges: What are sculpture's 'building blocks'? In modern sculpture a search for the fundamentals of sculpture can be recognized in Minimalism,

Saloua Raouda Choucair, *Poem/ Bench Model*, 1963–1965

especially in the work of Carl Andre. In his case, the notion of building block is taken quite literally. He builds his sculptures with bricks, wooden blocks, or iron plates. The material he uses for sculpture is no longer the transcendental matter of marble, bronze, or ivory, but industrial building blocks like brick, iron, or wood. And these industrial materials are what they are. They do not rely on an inner meaning. The notion of building stone is not only taken literally in modern sculpture, however; a building stone is also something elementary or essential, whether material or not. It is a basic element of sculpture or the process of making or looking at sculpture. It is this figurative point of view on the building blocks of sculpture that will be addressed through the work of Belgian artist Didier Vermeiren.

From Pure Form and Materiality to Ornament: Carl Andre and Per Kirkeby

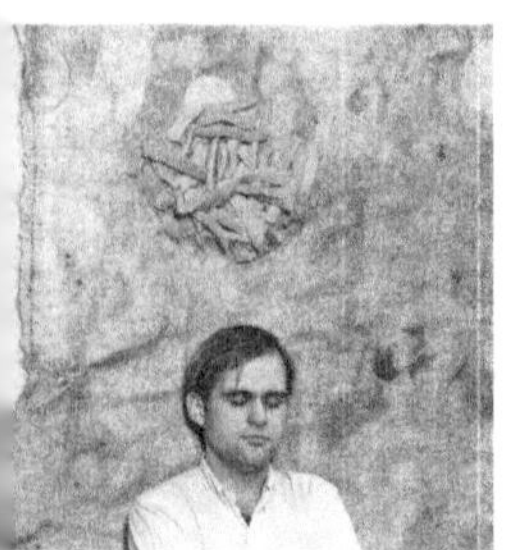

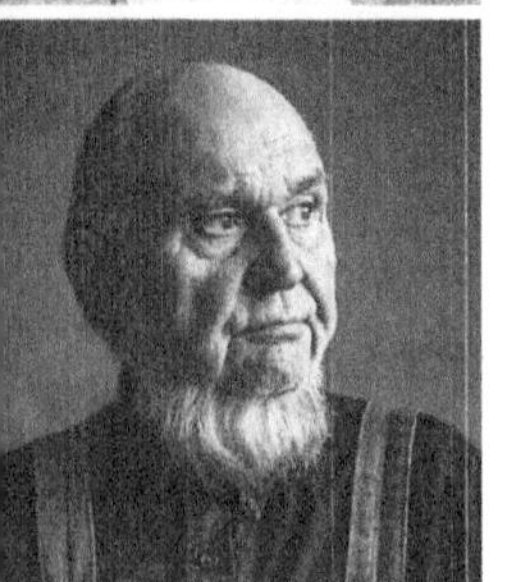

arl Andre (1935)

Carl Andre's sculptures consist of stacked wooden blocks, sandstone bricks, or iron plates. They counter classic sculpture by not suggesting any physical appearance or relying on inner meaning or essence. There is no narrative dimension either; what counts is the raw and silent material. His pilings or serial compositions also lack any artistic manual dexterity—he uses plainly industrial materials. The perception of the viewer should be constituted simply by the physical qualities of the building blocks; not by any indirect, associative elements that participate in vision. Andre's approach is quintessentially Minimalist in all respects, but because his sculptures can also be seen as objects that sculpt the space surrounding the blocks that build them, I will discuss them more elaborately in the chapter Sculpting Space.

arl Andre, *Uncarved Blocks*, 75

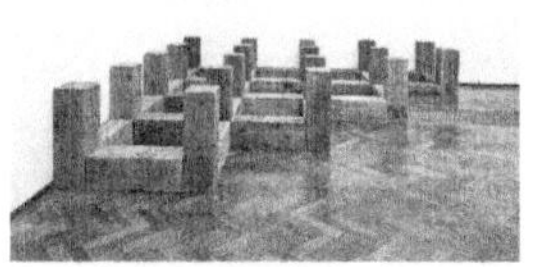

Carl Andre, *Bloody Angle*, 1985

Per Kirkeby made his first brick sculpture one year before Carl Andre began making them. Kirkeby's first pile of bricks date from 1965 and Andre's first one, *Equivalent I–VIII,* from 1966. Kirkeby's pursuit was, however, not in understanding and presenting pure form or materiality; he was interested in spatial arrangements, or in ornamentation, or rather spatial arrangement as ornamentation. The building blocks of brick are ideal for this interest.

Kirkeby conducted systematic research into a typology of spatial arrangements. He was fascinated by brick buildings in his homeland Denmark, for example the Grundtvigs Church in Copenhagen, built by the architect P.V. Jensen-Klint. But he also took his inspiration from Maya architecture. What fascinated him in simple brick arrangements was not the simple, pure form or materiality of the brick, but as part of that, the associative power of expression of brick arrangements and their history in different cultures. Wherever a brick sculpture was commissioned to him, he would always use local bricks with their own size, colour, and matter. The ornamental nature of these brick arrangements is described by Otto Kapfinger as follows:

> The patterns of the brick work finally form a kind of natural ornament, a linear, two-dimensional, spatial, graphic design composed of the repetition of simple parts. Through the laying of the individual parts, the network of joints develops into a simple rhythmic fabric which, due to its geometric independence, subtly contradicts the volume of the wall it produces. Through the graphic ornament of the joints the materiality of the volume is relaxed as it were, the substance of the body relieved.[2]

Although working in the period when Minimalism was dominant in contemporary arts, Kirkeby preferred the term

2 Kapfinger, 'The Art of Building in Brick', p. 23.

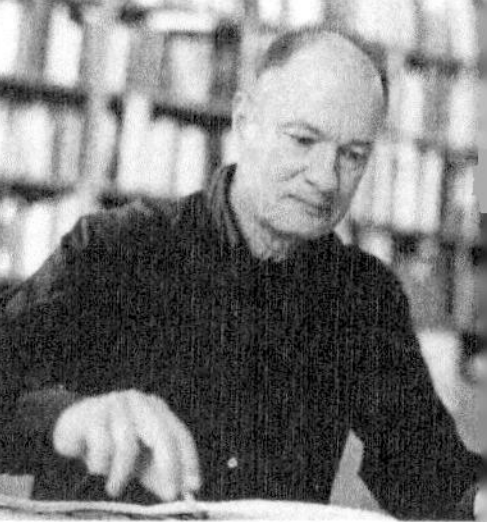
Per Kirkeby (1938)

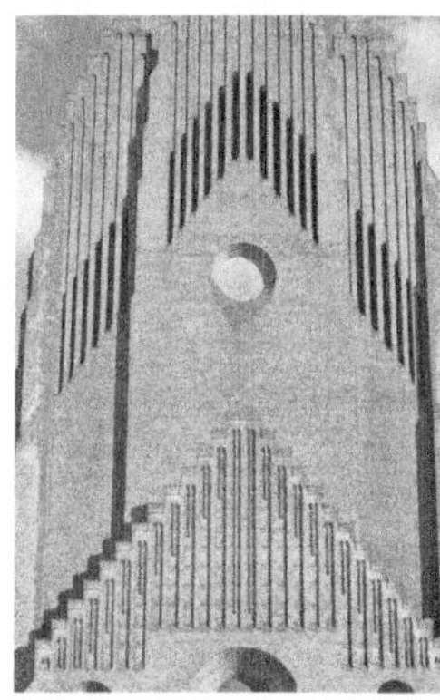
P.V. Jensen-Klint, Grundtvigs Church, Copenhagen

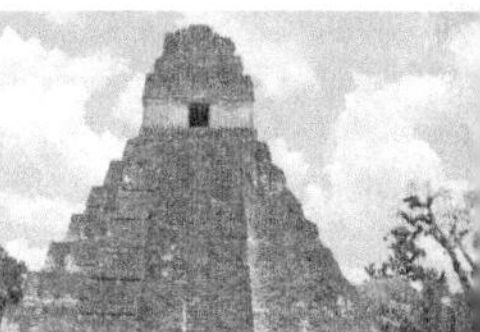
Temple 1, Tikal, Maya architecture

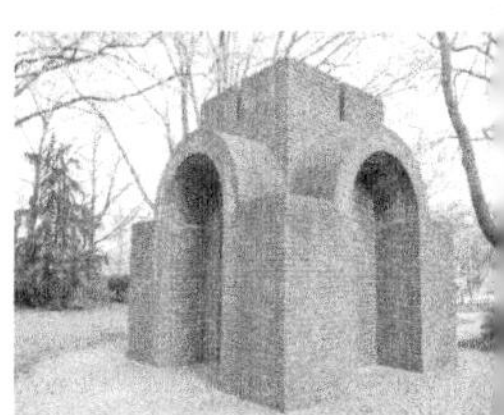
Per Kirkeby, *Untitled, Bielefeld* 1988

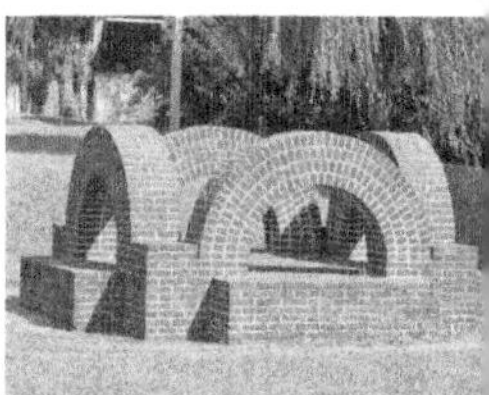
Per Kirkeby, *Untitled, Rotterdam*, 1987

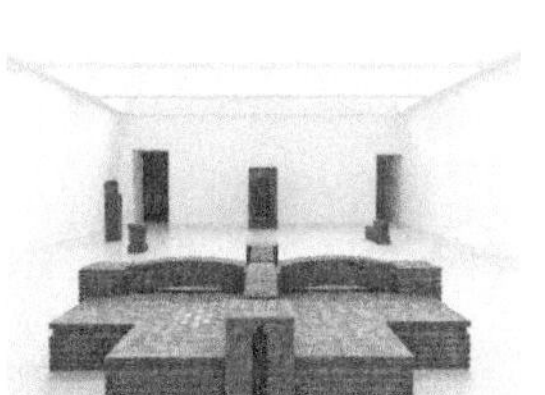
Per Kirkeby, *Brick Sculpture*, 2020

Hejlskov Larsen, 'Between Minimalism and Romanticism', 33.

ornamentation to seriality for these arrangements of bricks. Like the Minimalists, he looked for a non-hierarchical and non-subjective compositional principle. He was not a hard-core Minimalist, however, because pure form and materiality did not take precedence. Rather, he was fascinated by (historical and regional) associations of form and matter.

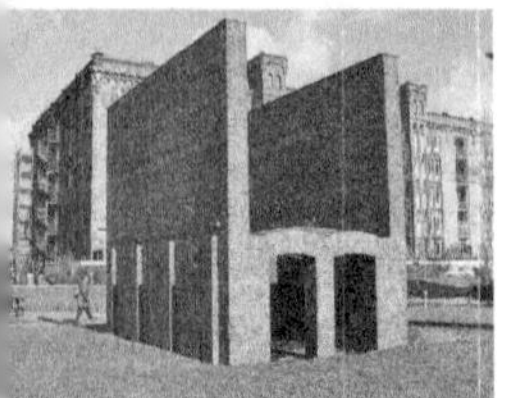

er Kirkeby, *Untitled*, 1990

The question his brick arrangements raise is, of course: Are they still sculptures, or is it more productive to see them as architecture? Or, as a compromise, and discussed in a separate chapter in this book: Does his work belong to the logic of architectural sculpture? Not always, but sometimes his brick arrangements seem to *represent* architectural constructions; they look then like little houses or spaces you can dwell in. In a sketchbook from 1969, he lists the architectural types which can be recognized in his art in general: tents, houses, and caves. The caves only appear in the form of contrasts between light and dark in the brickwork, whereas tents and houses can be recognized as being represented.[3]

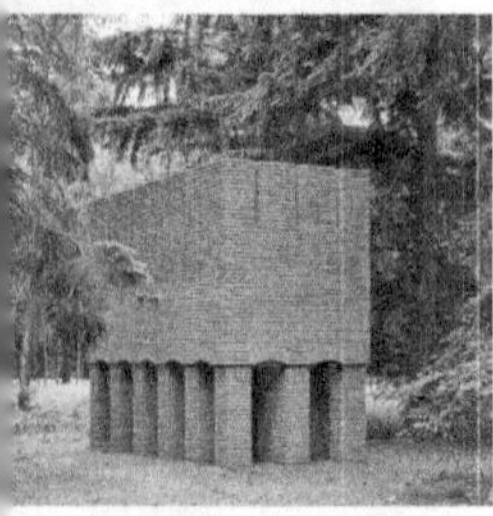

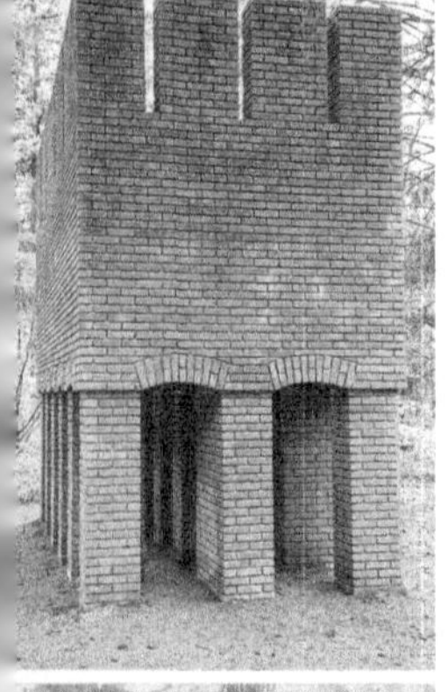

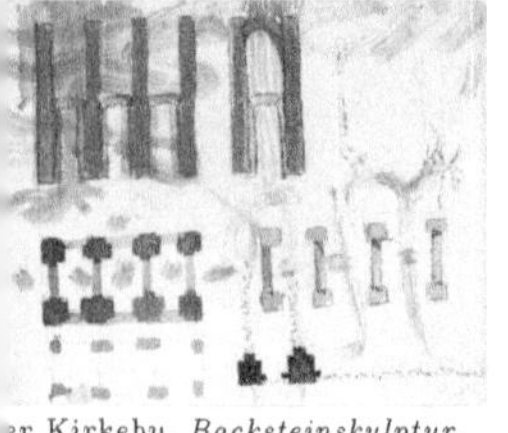

er Kirkeby, *Backsteinskulptur*, nhem-Otterlo, 1988

But when Kirkeby began making these brick arrangements, they were monolithic forms. It was only later that these forms became penetrable and that they could also be experienced from the inside. But even when one can experience the brick arrangement's inside, it does not mean that it is a volume. For example, when one looks at the brick sculptures he made in Amsterdam, Groningen, and Otterlo, the viewer is not guided through them by their volumes, but along a sequence of walls displaying one arrangement of bricks, or rather, one ornamental arrangement.

Kirkeby uses the term 'architecture' not only for his brick sculptures, but also for his paintings. This makes sense if we realize that he uses the term architecture as an equivalent for structure. This becomes clear, for example, in 1991 when he writes the following in his *Handbook*:

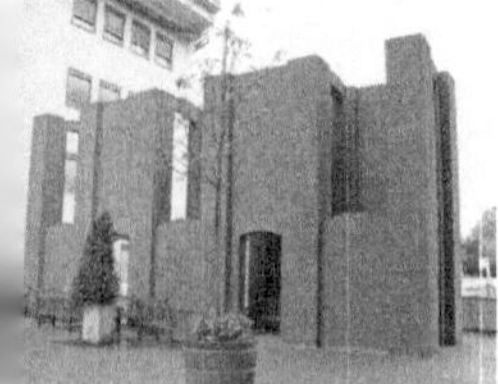

er Kirkeby, *Untitled*, 1990

> [...] the brick masses are the structure in my pictures, their inner scaffolding, their skeleton [...]. In the metaphysical layer of growth in the works there are some architectural principles, some structures which with almost literal clarity reveal themselves in the brick sculptures. But which are also present in the paintings [...].[4]

4 Per Kirkeby, *Haandbog*, quoted in Hejlskov Larsen, 'Between Minimalism and Romanticism', p. 30.

5 Hejlskov Larsen, 'Between Minimalism and Romanticism' p. 40.

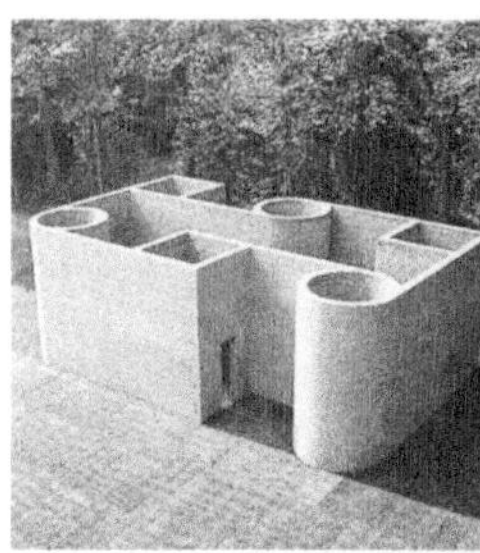

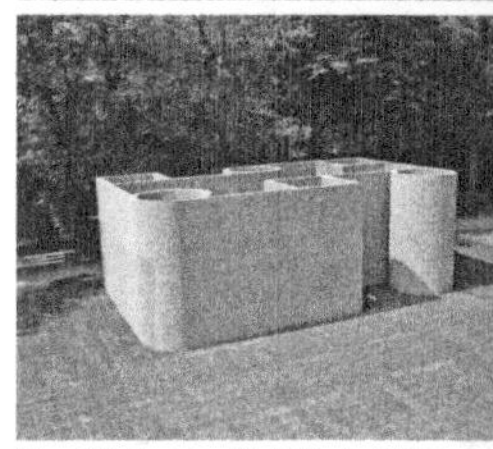

Per Kirkeby, *Untitled*, 1993

As Ane Hejlskov Larsen argues, for Kirkeby structures are architectural principles; so, there is an architectural element in each of his paintings.[5] His creation of sequences, modules, and ornamentation by means of bricks is a deployment of architectural principles, but that does not mean that his brick arrangements should be seen as architectural sculpture. Because of his very broad notion of architecture as structure, it is more productive to understand his brick arrangements as belonging to the logic of building blocks. These arrangements create a very specific texturality; the ordering of building blocks, of bricks in Kirkeby's case, is one big ornamental sculpture.

One final argument to consider his brick arrangements as architecture would be that one can often recognize architectural elements like doors or columns in his constructions. That said, one essential architectural element is always conspicuously missing: the roof. But an element like the door is detached from any function; it is used as a structural element, often by repeating it several times, so that a pattern or structure comes about. The door is not used because it makes it possible to enter the space (although most often that is also at stake), because it generates a specific pattern in the ornamental sculpture. What the openings, or doors, and the columns also do is stage light in very specific ways. The texturality of his brick sculptures is not only constituted by his arrangements of bricks, but also by how these arrangements stage shadows and the fall of light. All those elements that make one think of architectural elements (even though they are not), in particular, are responsible for turning light and shadow into a building block of sculpture. To further elaborate and substantiate Kirkeby's implicit treatment of light as building stone of sculpture, further on in this chapter I will discuss the work of Ann Veronica Janssens, who has devoted her whole career to demonstrating that light is one of the most fundamental building blocks of sculpture.

Modular Arrangements: Saloua Raouda Choucair

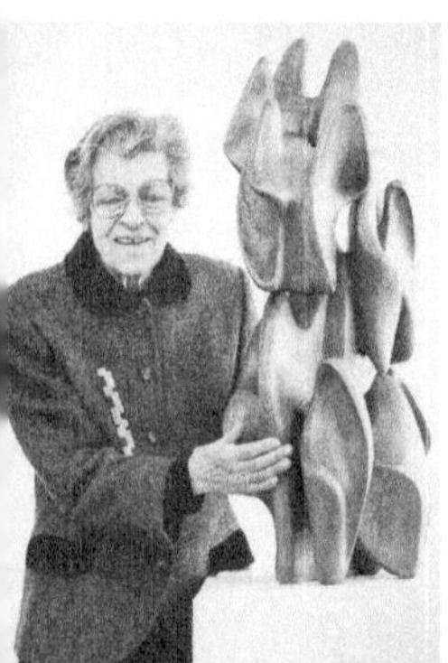

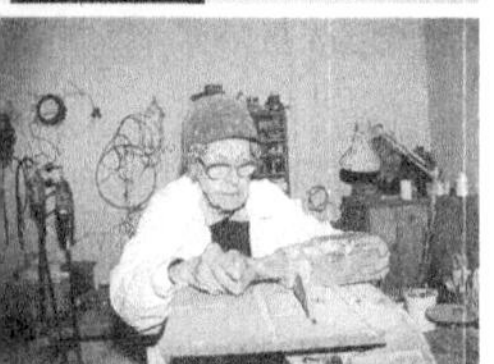

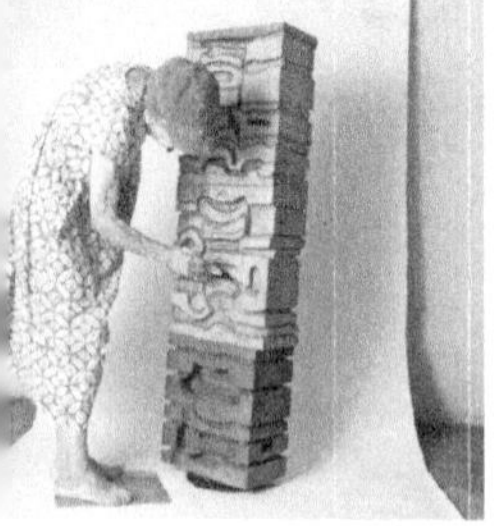

aloua Raouda Choucair
916–2017)

While Carl Andre and Per Kirkeby always used the same building blocks (bricks, iron plates, wooden blocks) in their work, the sculptural arrangements of the Lebanese artist Saloua Raouda Choucair consist of building blocks in the same material, but with a slight difference. She created interlocking shapes and built modular forms. With her Arabic background she was rooted in very different sculptural traditions to Carl Andre and Per Kirkeby. Choucair's work is considered as one of the best examples of the spirit of abstraction characterizing Arabic visual and geometric art, seemingly disconnected from the observation of nature. Believing in the arithmetical basis of Islamic art, she rejected figurative, bodily thinking and relinquished all symbolic references to the human body. While Andre's and Kirkeby's work can be seen as a polemic refusal of the Western tradition according to which the meaning and appearance of sculpture relies on the body's interiority, Chocair's sculptures do not differentiate themselves from this tradition, but materialize a new abstraction within Arabic geometric art.

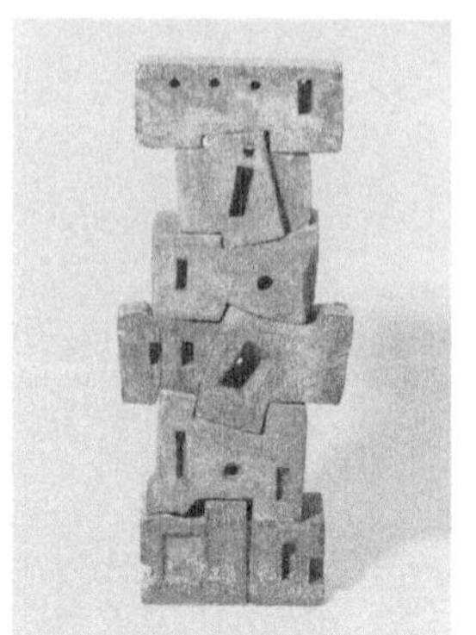

Saloua Raouda Choucair, *Poem/ Bench Model*, 1963–1965

In 1948 she left Lebanon and went to Paris, where she studied at the École nationale supérieure des Beaux-Arts and attended Fernand Léger's studio. Although having been exposed to Western traditions of art and sculpture, she mainly connected to the relatively new abstract movement in Paris. After returning to Beirut, in 1962 she began to concentrate solely on sculpture. Until then she had made design objects as well as art objects, for example paintings and drawings. The abstract sculptures she went on to make consisted of interlocking shapes and she built modular forms in different materials: wood, concrete, marble, stoneware. The shapes interlock in such a way that the modular shapes form a rhythmic pattern. Each form is shaped slightly differently, emphasizing similarity as well as difference. Forms never repeat themselves, and geometry manifests itself in this work in an organic manner. Many of these sculptures have the title *Poem*. They do not translate poetry into sculpture, but the arrangement of building stones or blocks create a rhythmic pattern comparable to Arabic poetry.

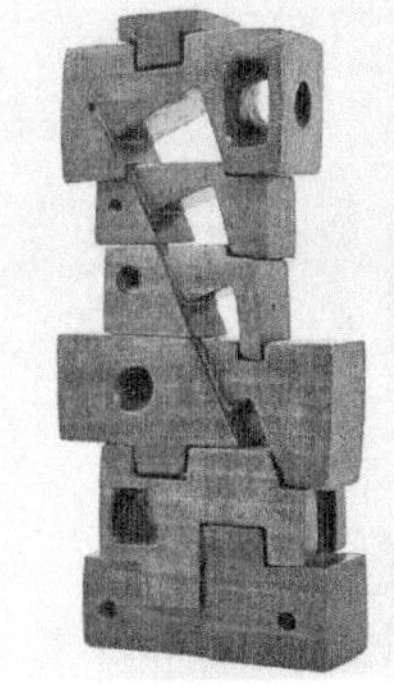

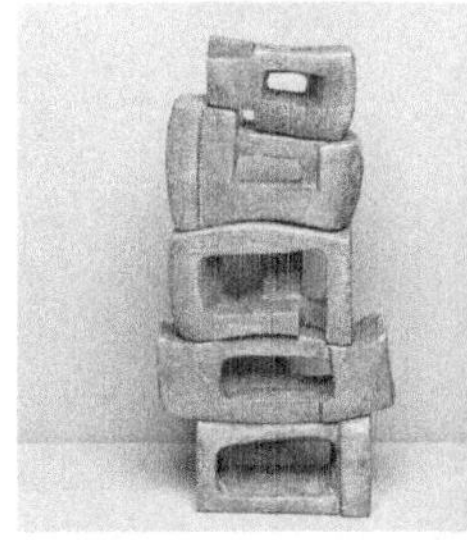

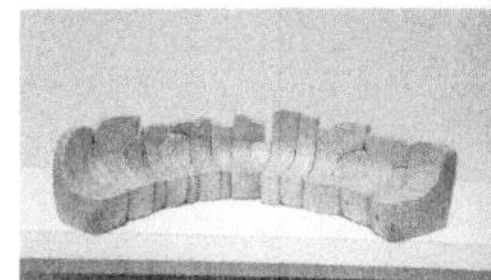

Saloua Raouda Choucair, *Poem*, 1963–1965; *Poem*, 1963–1965; *Bench Model*, 1963–65

Heads as Building Blocks: Marien Schouten

As my discussion of architectural sculpture will make clear, it is the positioning of the viewer's body that is a central element in the understanding of this hybrid medium. In that chapter the rooms of Dutch artist Marien Schouten will play an import role. In this chapter I would like to pay attention to other work he made that can be better understood in terms of the building blocks of sculpture. Schouten's so-called *Heads* decentre the body by replacing the inner or internal structure with bricks, poles... in other words, with building blocks. He deconstructs the internal structure, and by doing so suggests

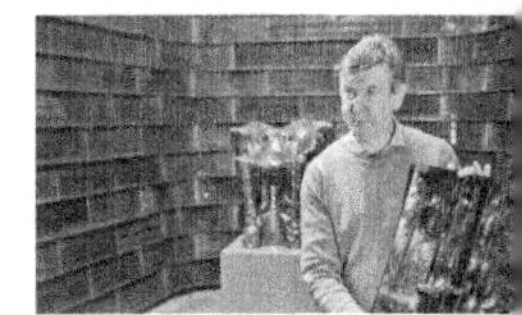

Marien Schouten (1956)

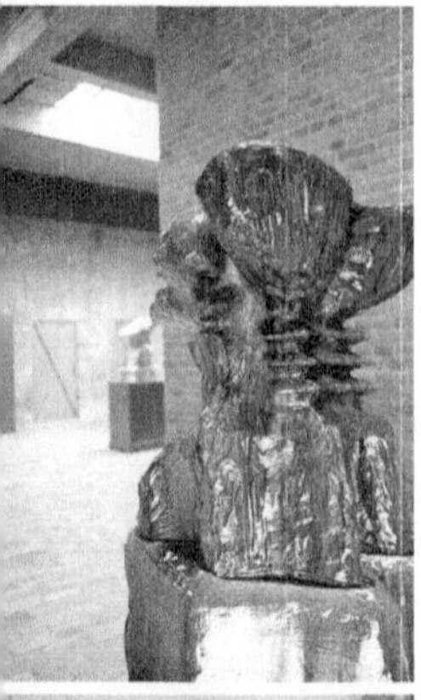

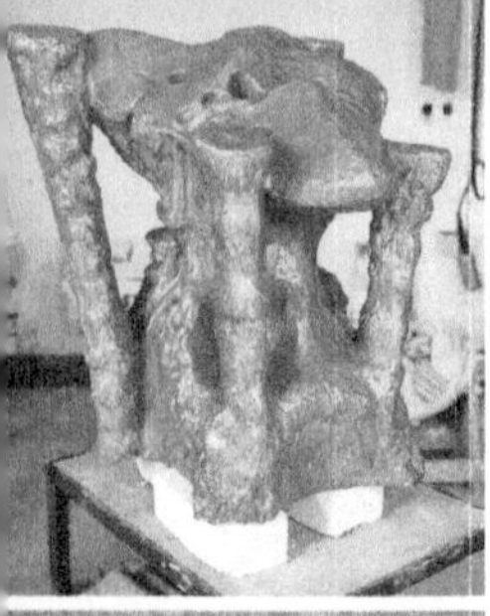

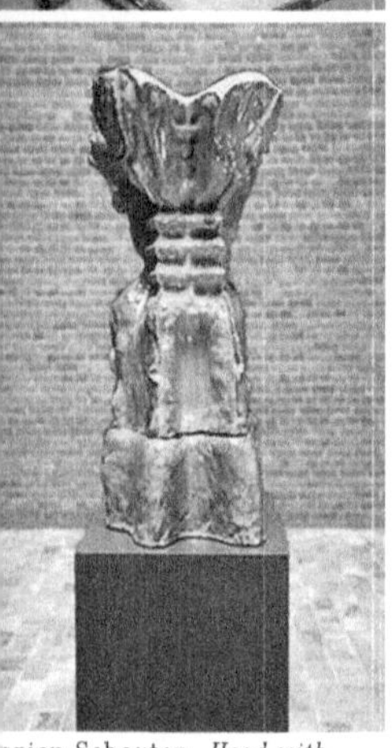

arien Schouten, *Head with edium-sized pedestal*, 2003; *ad with logs*, 2005; *Head with all pedestal*, 2003

another sculptural logic. He decentres the body not from internal essence to outward appearance, nor to the viewer's body, but by replacing the internal essence with structure in its most material sense. All metaphysical associations and connotations are cancelled by this sculptural practice.

His sculptures give thematic emphasis to the relationship between internal structure and outward appearance. This occurs in two ways. On the one hand, this relationship is ostentatiously ignored, as is often the case with Art Nouveau objects. Occasionally the surface of his *Heads* is indeed reminiscent of Art Nouveau. The movement, the commotion, and the changeability evoked by the organic surface of his sculptures suggest natural, external forces like water and wind.

On the other hand, at other times and in other areas of the same *Heads,* internal structure is made visible in the most concrete, material way: not as an expression of an inner feeling, or as a skeleton, but as the architectonic structure of the body. The idea that the inner structure should be regarded as having been built is emphasized especially at the back of some *Heads*. Here the surface sometimes looks like vertebrae. But looking more closely, there are also places where brick-like forms come to the surface and, in that sense, determine the outward appearance. In addition, some of the *Heads* have grid-like structures inscribed into the clay, as if the organic, Art Nouveau surface of them needs rationalistic ordering. These rationalistic elements provide a radical counterweight to those aspects of the *Heads* which can be understood on the basis of Art Nouveau principles. Yet it is impossible to decide which principle predominates. Seen in this way, Schouten's sculptures are the result of two antithetical principles. But both principles cancel the logic of sculpture according to which the appearance is caused by, and can be understood as the result of, an inner world or essence. The appearance of Schouten's *Heads* cannot be explained by an inner essence of the building block that they show. The poles lean the weight of the head while making it; they emphasise the heavy matter out of which the sculpture is built. And the arrangements of bricks replacing the ribs in 'real' bodies emphasize that these heads are not representations of heads but have been built as constructions. And to radicalize this notion of the head as building stone, Schouten also stacked in some of his works' heads as if they were bricks, resulting in a pile of heads.

Schouten's *Heads* embody another notion of sculpture that differs to his *Rooms*. His *Rooms*, which I will discuss in more depth later, are emphatic, outspoken architectural structures; they make the viewer's active positioning a crucial, central element of the work. In contrast, his *Heads* define the structural component first of all as works consisting of, made out of, building blocks. This notion radically undermines the idea of inner essence or structure. Hence the title of the last section of the current chapter: 'From Body to Solid'. His *Heads* no longer belong to bodies; they can no longer be understood as being part of bodies. They have been constructed out of building blocks.

To better understand Schouten's *Rooms* and his notion of architectural sculpture, I will now further consider some of his works more easily considered as sculpture, despite also having emphatic architectural elements: the pieces mentioned above and referred to as *Heads*. They are, in fact, not simply heads; each head has a neck and shoulders. They revert to the classical sculptural genre of the bust. Busts are pre-eminently classical as a genre; the shoulders function, after all, as a pedestal on which the head is placed. In that sense, the bust

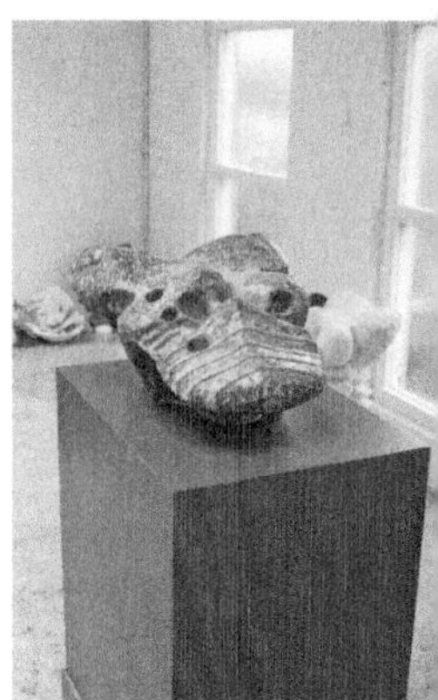

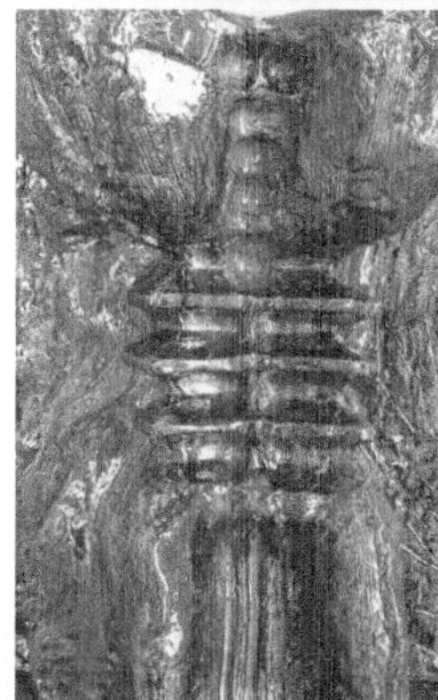

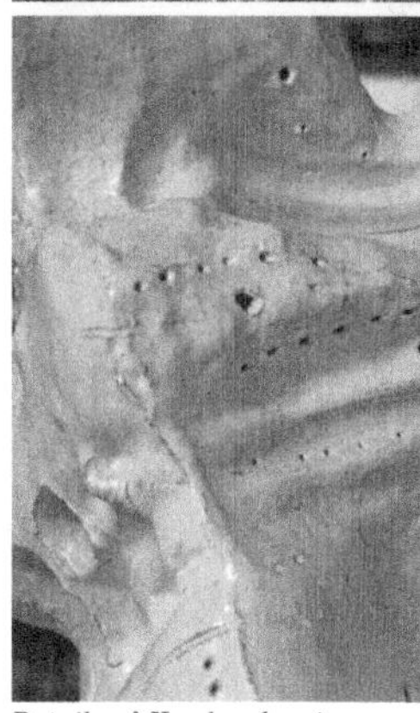

Details of Heads, showing bricks, holes, and grids

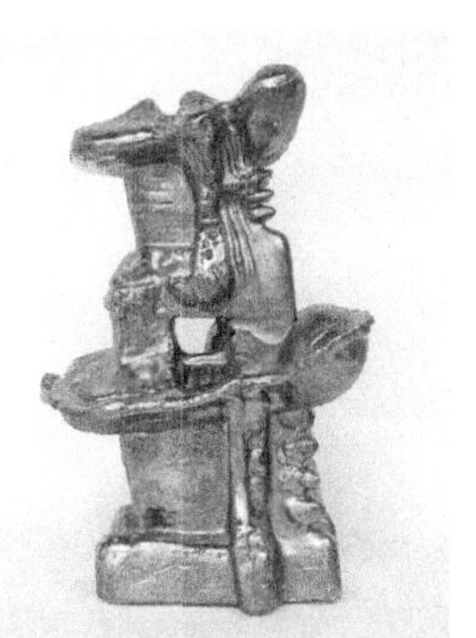

Marien Schouten, *Stacked Heads*, 2014

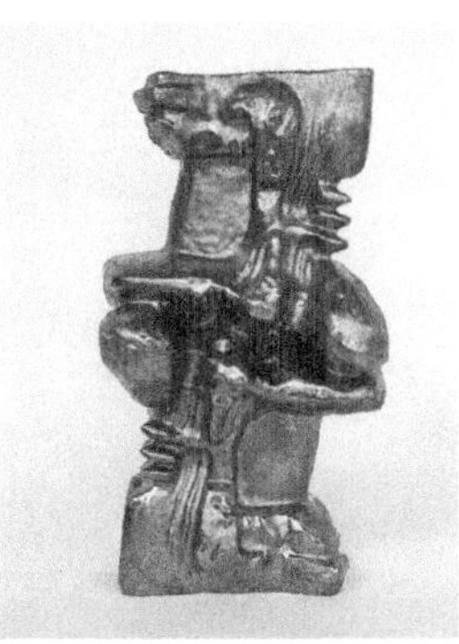

Marien Schouten, *Stacked Heads*, 2014

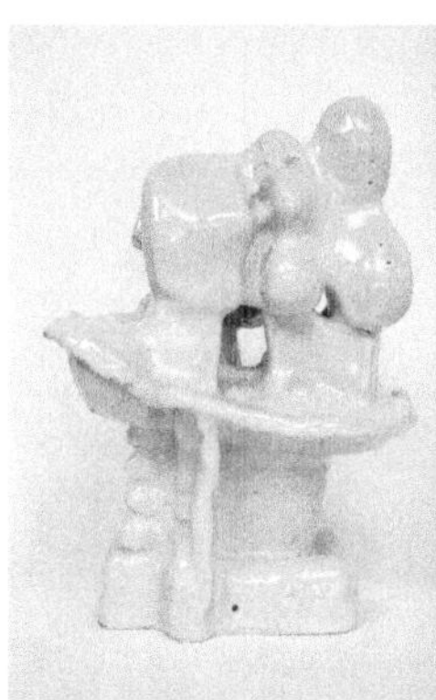

Marien Schouten, *Stacked Heads*, 2012

no longer requires a support. They can be put on a table or a cabinet without such anchoring. Nonetheless, Schouten has made separate pedestals for several of the *Heads*. The pedestal consisting of shoulders is doubled in these instances by a literal pedestal. This pedestal, however, does not mark a division that makes the sculpture relate metaphorically to the world. The problematics of the pedestal are rather intensified. The pedestal does not distinguish itself enough from the head placed on it. Like the head, it is ceramic, has the same texture, and is covered, as is the head, with a glossy glaze. What strikes the eye most of all is the similarity between pedestal and sculpture. That is why it does not function convincingly as a division that prompts us to see the figure metaphorically as a representation of a head.

Kop met console (*Head with Support*) (2003) intensifies the duality contained in all of the other *Heads*. The pedestal *is* and *is not* rejected. It is emphatically present but no longer functions as a division that makes the sculpture relate metaphorically to the world. Schouten's *Heads* can be compared, in that sense, to Francis Bacon's *Figures*. Bacon did not paint people or characters but rather figures in order to indicate clearly that his work was not about portrayal or representation. With his *Figures* he wanted to bring about something, to strike a nerve with the viewer. With the aid of the human figure, he did not wish to represent people or to make them present on the basis of analogy. In order to become free of the function of representation, however, he did not opt for what came to be seen in the twentieth century as the absolute antithesis of representation, namely abstraction. His *Figures* remain somewhere *between* representation and abstraction. Even though the starting point is a human figure, the human figure is not represented. In precisely the same manner, Schouten's *Heads* are not heads. The human (or animal) figure is present in a rudimentary way, not as a sign of a represented person or animal.[6]

This may suggest that Schouten's work has an affinity with the idealistic trajectory of modern sculpture. This is and is not the case. From a formalistic point of view, it is far removed from this. It lacks the purist tendency of this tradition entirely. But due to the fact that it is not aimed at representation, it does have something in common with this mode. Some of the ceramic *Heads* are covered with an extremely glossy glaze, and the materiality of these *Heads* becomes less visible, with an immaterial world of idealistic reflection coming into prominence. But the emphatically earthly colours of the *Heads* (deep green, moss green, sandy yellow), their organic forms, and the fact that some are made of plaster partially covered with wax, cause this work to belong, at the same time, to the materialist trajectory of modern sculpture. It is, in fact, within this materialist trajectory that Schouten's allusion to the traditional pedestal has an important function.

In materialist tradition, the pedestal has absorbed the sculpture by renouncing, as it were, precious and refined metals such as bronze or silver. Ordinary or industrial materials, such as steel or sheet iron, are used instead. Serra's work illustrates this development well. Schouten's relationship to materialist tradition is of a different nature, however. This is precisely where he plays on a dualist relationship between sculpture and painting. Like his paintings, particularly the most recent ones which are *built* with paint in the most physical sense, the three-dimensional spaces of his sculptural *Heads* are also emphatically the result of applying paint, wax, or glaze. His *Heads* cannot be seen, therefore, as a complete break with his paintings but rather constitute an extension of them. Ultimately, these are *painted* three-dimensional spaces.

6 Although Bacon's images ar[illegible] Schouten's Heads are made in different media, painting, and sculpture, their work has muc[illegible] in common—they both combin[illegible] architectural elements and organic elements. In the case [illegible] Schouten's sculpture, I prefer [illegible] call this organic quality 'Art Nouveau', because organic suggests that this quality comes from the inside out, whereas Art Nouveau forms are shaped from the outside. But what is important is that in both art practices the architectural an[illegible] organic qualities that shape form and space are combined and intertwined, instead of presented as opposites.

The treatment manifest with these *Heads* is one that evokes the flat surface and the illusionism linked with this.

Materialist tradition involves more, however. It is not merely about a different use of material—the spatial dimension also plays a role. That is distinctly human, earthly, specific. Sculptures become site-specific, respond to the specific environment, become part of it. Considered from this point of view, Schouten's pedestal is a paradoxical element. While the pedestal has always functioned as an element intended to free the sculpture from the spatial dimension in which it has been placed, Schouten's sooner anchors it in this. By way of the pedestal, his *Heads* do not relate metaphorically but metonymically to the spatial dimension in which they exist. After all, because of the decided contiguity of the 'earthly' head and the 'earthly' pedestal, the work then merges with the dimension of the viewer. As a three-dimensional object, it has become more an architectural element, since the viewer, or rather the user of the architectural space, relates by definition to that space in a metonymical way. The viewer of classical sculpture, on the other hand, looks at an analogous world and relates metaphorically to the sculptural space.

Deconstructing Sculpture: Didier Vermeiren

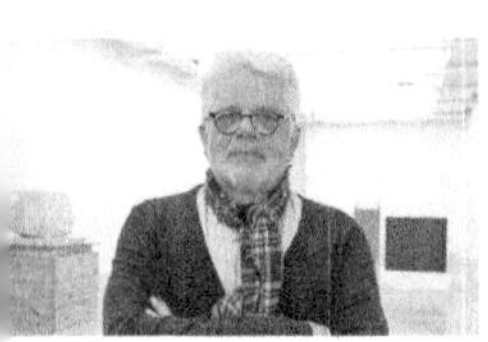
dier Vermeiren (1951)

Although most conventional sculptures look formally like a solid object, their appearance suggests otherwise. As I explained above, the appearance suggests an inner essence, structure, or experience that explains and causes the outer appearance. But when we consider sculptures as solids, it means that they are beings without an internal cavity, that they consist of a uniformly close and coherent texture. And of course, when we speak of inner essence, structure, or experience, this is metaphorically speaking; it concerns meaning as we derive it from the sculpture's appearance. There is no real cavity, no unfilled space within the mass of the sculpture.

So, when Belgian sculptor Didier Vermeiren uses titles like *Geometrical Solids* or *Solides plastiques* for his works, it is provocatively clear that he takes distance from Neoclassical sculpture and that he is less interested in how sculpture appears and what it means, and more in what sculpture is and consists of. One could say that his whole career has been motivated by a systematic deconstruction of the medium of sculpture; he explores the different building blocks of sculpture, rather than sculpture as an art in and of itself. According to Dominic van den Boogerd, Vermeiren's work addresses fundamental issues such as:

> What is sculpture? How do we recognize a piece of sculpture and what is that recognition based on? What makes it sculpture? How has that idea been formed over the centuries, and how is it changing today?'[7]

Until the late nineteen-nineties, Vermeiren explored elements of sculpture that are peripheral to it: he assimilated into sculpture aspects of the history of sculpture as well as its conditions of production, transportation, and exhibition. Sculpture is not yet considered as a solid object, but as a process or development.[8] The production, transportation, and exhibition of sculpture are not seen as *parergon*, as outside the essence of the medium of sculpture, but as building blocks that condition the specificity of that medium.

Vermeiren's so-called 'empty pedestals' are good examples of how he questions the conditions of exhibiting sculpture. But his pedestals are not empty or missing a sculpture on top of them; they are complete sculptures. They seem to

7 Van den Boogerd, 'Caryatid by Moonlight', p. 99.

8 Verhagen, 'Endogenous/Exogenous', p. 55.

address the following questions:

> Where does the sculpture end and the pedestal begin? Does the base produce the sculpture or the sculpture the base? At what point does that which is being exhibited become that which makes exhibiting possible? Does the base anchor the sculpture to the earth or raise it above the ground?'[9]

Whereas conventionally the pedestal is the separation of two different ontologies, the world in which the viewer is situated and the ideal world of art, Vermeiren's pedestals refuse a separation that gives access to an ideal world.

In his series of works titled Cariatides, base and sculpture have merged. The term 'caryatide' is derived from the Greek *Karyai,* a place on the Peloponnesus where young women danced in honour of the Goddess Artemis. In sculptural terms, it refers to the merging of a pillar with the image and body of a woman; they have become one. Vermeiren's *Cariatide à la pierre* (1997) shows a plaster base which exhibits its own mould in six parts. In the words of Van den Boogerd: 'Here the pedestal gives rise to the sculpture that gives rise to the pedestal.'[10] In another work with the same title, the base is turned inside out and upside down, so that the viewer can look into it. But those who look into it only see the exterior of the base. The so-called carts which he started to make in the nineteen-eighties reflect on sculptural practice in yet another way. He made all kinds of variations in different materials throughout the nineteen-nineties. These carts consist of four wheels on which an open structure is mounted. The structure of the first cart is open but later variations are closed off at one or more sites or have a drywall placed diagonally in the open structure. Although these carts cannot move and some of them are titled *Place,* they suggest

9 Van den Boogerd, 'Caryatid by Moonlight', p. 99.

10 Van den Boogerd, 'Caryatid by Moonlight', p. 100.

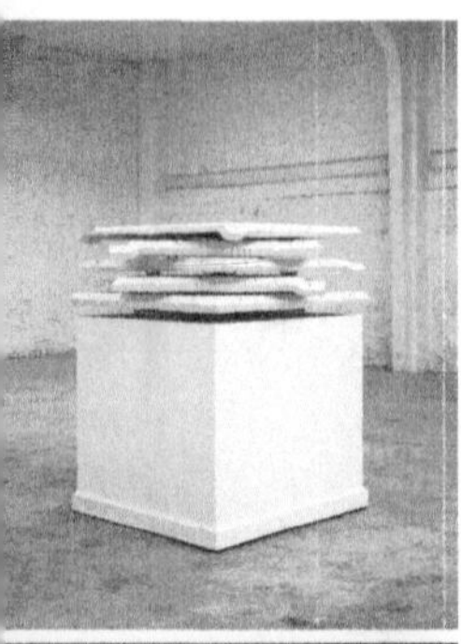

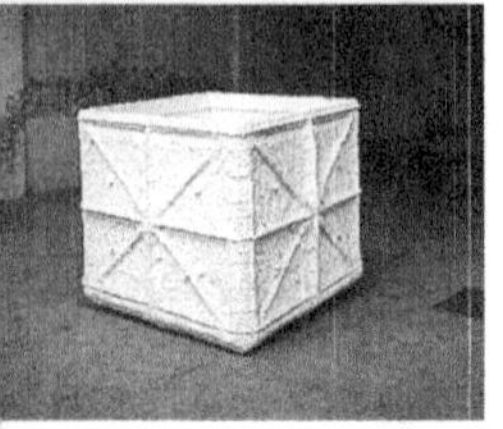

…idier Vermeiren, *Adam,* 1995; …ariatide à la pierre, 1995

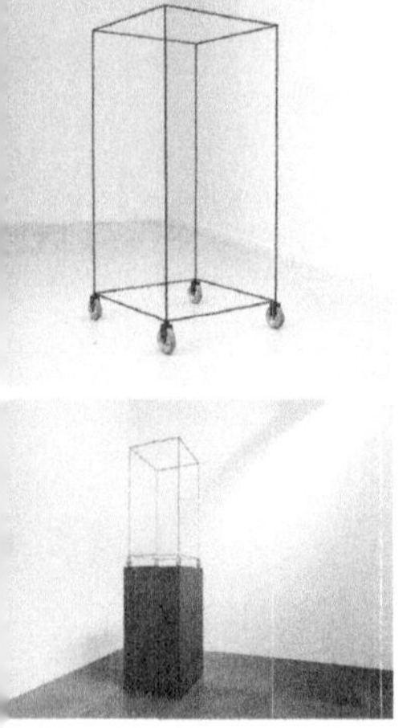

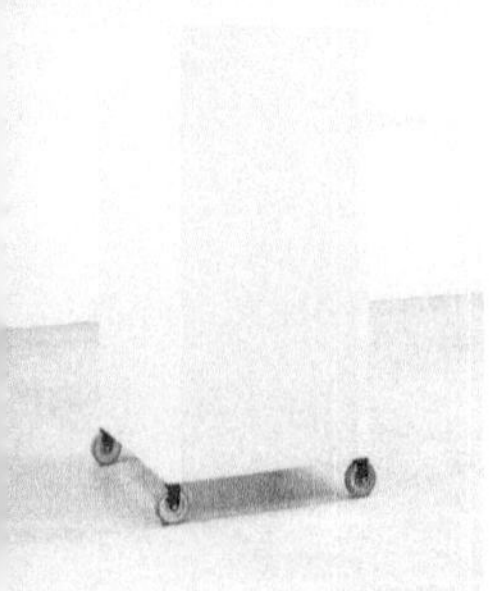

…idier Vermeiren, *Sans titre,* …99; *Place,* 2000; *Place,* 1994

that they are moveable. However, the carts can also be read more literally. For these little carts also belong to the tools of the sculptor. In most sculpture studios they can be found—they are used for moving materials or objects that are too heavy to carry.

These works reflect on the conventional logic of sculpture that grounds the sculptural object firmly on a plinth that functions as a hinge between the material world we live in and an ideal realm. Whereas the pedestal suggests the anchoring of a sculpture to a fixed place, these carts demonstrate another condition, namely that sculptures are being moved around a great deal. Instead, Vermeiren's carts are, in the words of Jean-Pierre Criqui, 'historically adrift and conceptually nomadic'.[11] In other words, they develop a new sculptural logic.

11 Criqui, 'A Brief Tour of 'Collections de Solides', p. 112.

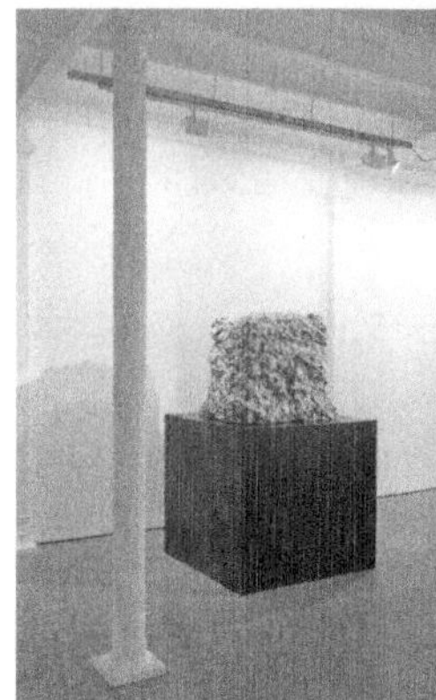

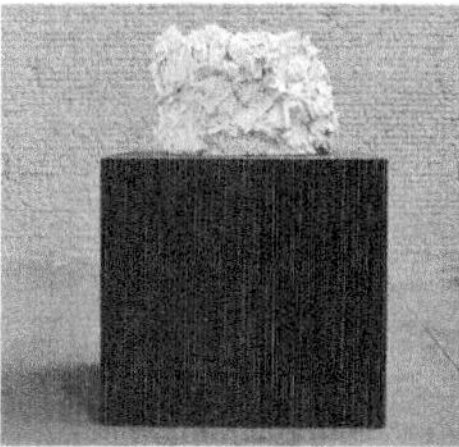

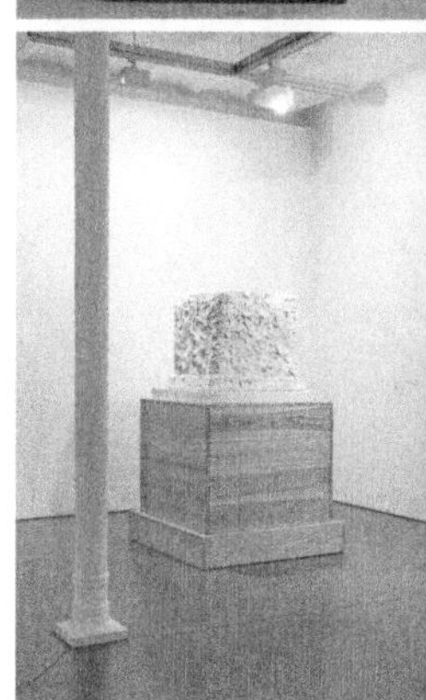

Didier Vermeiren, *Solide Géométrique #9*, 2006; *Solide Géométrique #14*, 2010; *Solide Géométrique #4*, 2005

His works titled *Solides géométriques* (2003–2004) do not create the illusion of having been shaped by an inner essence, nor by external forces: they are what they are; that is, solid clay objects, sometimes glazed. Some of these solids look as if they have been made of material leftovers. The stone, plaster, or clay cut or scraped away, in this case, is not thrown away; it is the matter that builds the sculpture. As a result, these objects do not create the illusion of having an inner essence that produces their outward appearance, nor do they suggest external forces like wind, water, or the hand of the artist. Because of the lack of these illusions, they really deserve the title 'solids'.

But Vermeiren's solids do not only consist of what sometimes looks like just matter or 'leftover objects'; the black plinths or pedestals on which they stand are part of the work. Each object is described as 'glazed, fired clay, and painted wood'. So, the plinth is no longer a hinge between the world we live in and an ideal world opened up by art and

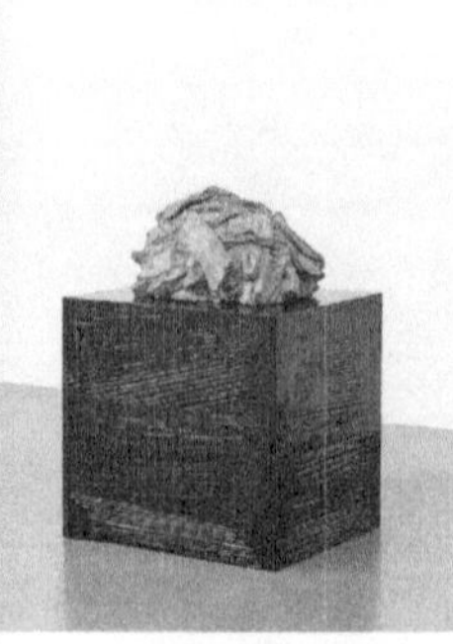

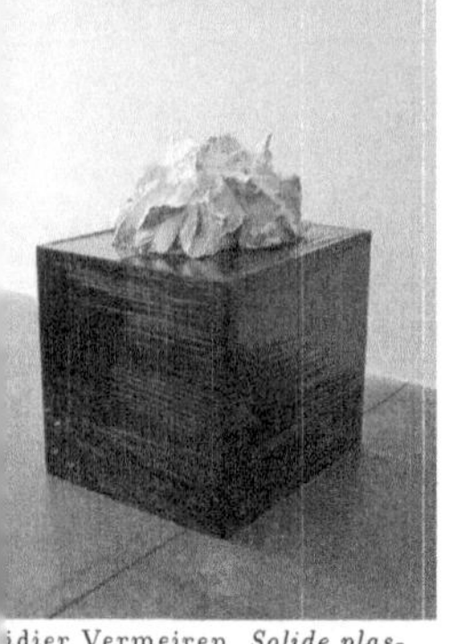

idier Vermeiren, *Solide plastique #14*, 2001; *Solide plastique 1*, 2001; *Solide plastique #23*, 001

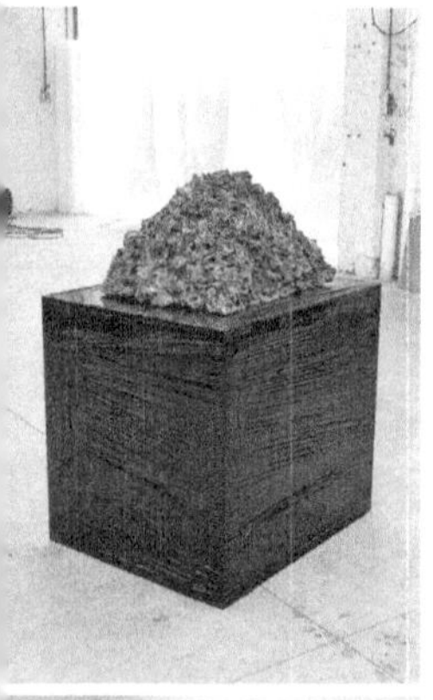

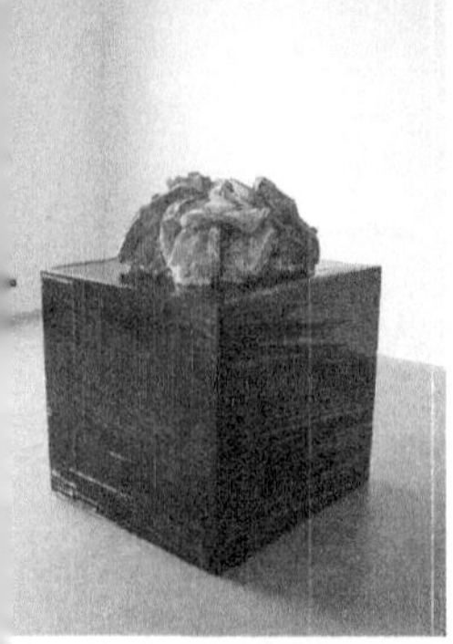

idier Vermeiren, *Solides plastiques*, 2001; *Solide plastique 16*, 2001

sculpture; the plinth is just another 'solid', although probably completely empty inside. Whatever the content of the plinth, it is not relevant, because Vermeiren's sculpture does not depend on illusions: it is real and solid, or at least it appears so.

The clay objects placed on the black wooden plinths are geometrical because they are more or less cubes. 'More or less' is important because they are not shaped on the ideal, underlying principle or form of the cube; instead they are heaps of leftover material. The black wooden boxes on which these imperfect cubes stand are more perfect as geometrical objects; they are real cubes. But in this case, the geometric shape does not create the illusion of an underlying ideal, a rational principle, because it is just a support, nothing more, despite being presented as part of the sculpture.

The suggestion that these works are heaps of leftover material is even more convincing in the case of an earlier series of works titled *Solides plastiques* (1998–2001). These works do not stand on black painted wooden plinths but on cubes that are covered by shiny black polyethylene. This packaging material is used in freight transportation, and alludes to the fact that sculptures are not at all anchored to the earth by a base or plinth but are being moved around all the time. The objects on top of the black cubes do not suggest they are geometrical; instead of approaching an ideal, underlying shape, they are shapeless or formless. The weight of the matter pushes the shapes down on the pedestal. The glossy surface of the black cubes on which they stand is in sharp contrast with the sculptural matter they support.

The glossy surface of the black plastic that covers the wooden supports is significant. In sculptural traditions, reflecting surfaces are exceptional because they make the materiality of sculpture invisible. In Vermeiren's case, the glossy surface reminds me of the polished, reflecting surfaces of many of Constantin Brancusi's sculptures, for instance *Mademoiselle Pogany II* (1925) and *L'Oiseau dans l'espace* (1923). Hal Foster reads this kind of reflecting surface of Brancusi's sculptures as an attempt to merge with the material surroundings that are visible in the reflections.[12] However, the non-material nature of reflections compels me to regard them not as a material aspect of the work but rather as an idealistic one. Although Brancusi refused the plinth as a hinge between the material, real world and the ideal world by turning the plinth into sculpture, the reflecting surface of many of his objects reaches back to an illusion of an ideal non-material world. Thus, Vermeiren's use of the glossy, reflecting surface does not have the same effect as Brancusi's sculptural practice. Vermeiren's ironic use of shiny, reflecting surfaces deconstructs conventional sculpture in yet another way, namely by grounding the work in matter instead of idealism. And it challenges the idea that plinths function as hinges between two different ontologies, the world we live in and an ideal world to which art gives access. In Vermeiren's case, the plinth is not something that anchors but that can be moved around.

His work *Forme #1* uses this packaging material even in an abundant way; not only the plinth is covered by it, but the object on top of it consists of one large wad of black polyethylene. The upper part of the sculpture is anything but durable and will need to be made anew for each exhibition. Not only the conventional idea that sculpture is durable is under discussion in the work, but also its gravity, because the wad of package material is almost weightless. And the two conventional ideas are of course related: sculptures are durable because they have gravity. Making sculptures that defy gravity is a mischievous act.

12 Foster, 'The Un/making of Sculpture', pp. 180–81.

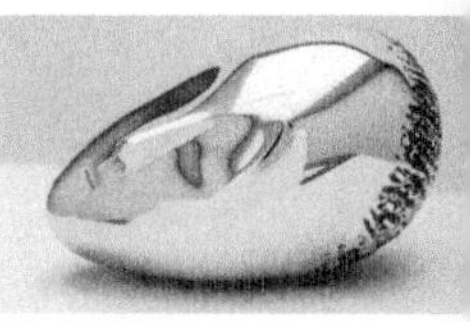

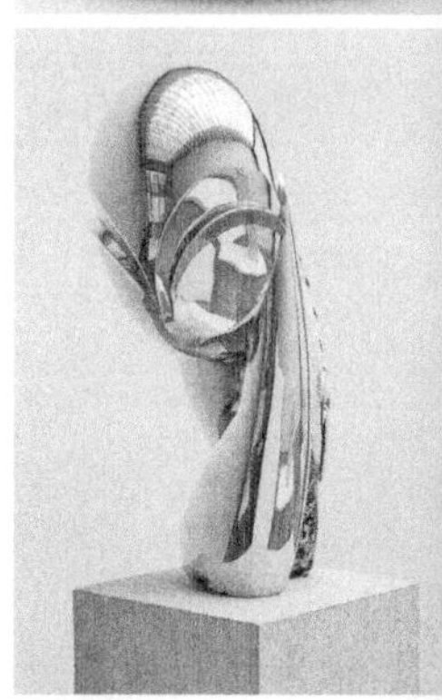

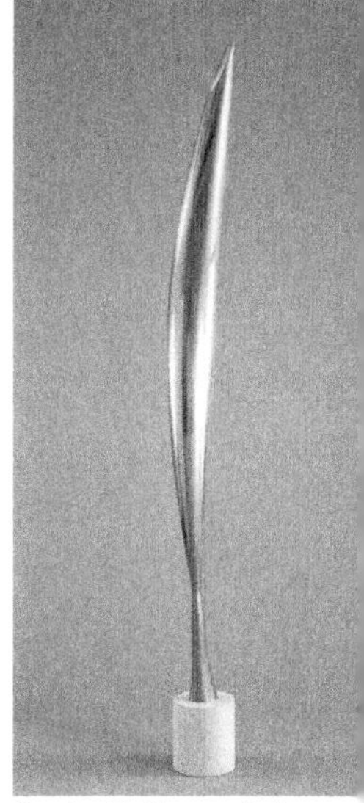

Constantin Brancusi, *La muse endormie*, 1923; *Mademoiselle Pogany II*, 1925; *L'Oiseau dans l'espace*, 1923

Vermeiren's work can be seen as self-reflexive, and as deconstructing the conventional logic of sculptural practice. The sculptural object is no longer limited to an object that is placed on a pedestal.

> Everything that is part of the modus operandi of sculpture is investigated in the work of Didier Vermeiren. Each component that is subject to further study is exposed to the risk of transformation. A pedestal can turn into a sculpture, a copy into an original, a sculpture into a mold, a mold into a copy, a copy into an original, an original into a negative, a negative into a positive.[13]

Vermeiren's investigation of the 'components' and 'building blocks' of sculpture focuses first of all on the process of making and exhibiting sculpture. But his work also takes the condition of viewing sculpture into consideration. For, in contrast to painting and photography, a sculpture cannot be seen in one single glance, from one single viewpoint. The viewers have to have multiple points of view. For this they need to walk around the sculpture, in order to understand the sculptural form, body, or solid they are looking at since sculpture unfolds in space and time. This means that the condition of looking at sculpture is highly specific and cannot be conflated with the modes of looking required for other media.

The question then is: How can the condition of viewing sculpture be investigated? Whereas Vermeiren investigates the condition of making and exhibiting sculpture within, by means of, the medium of sculpture, such a self-reflexive practice seems much more difficult when it concerns the condition of viewing. As Philippe Dubois has argued with regard to photography:

13 Van den Boogerd, 'Caryatid Moonlight', p. 102.

> I think we have never been in a better position to approach a given medium by imagining it in light of another, through another, in another, by another, or like another. Such an oblique, off-center vision can frequently offer a better opening onto what lies at the heart of the system. The thing is to practice this kind of oblique, sideways approach deliberately. We might begin with this simple idea: that the best lens on photography will be found outside photography.[14]

14 Dubois, 'Photography Mise en-Film, pp. 152–53.

15 Van den Boogerd, 'Caryati by Moonlight', p. 100.

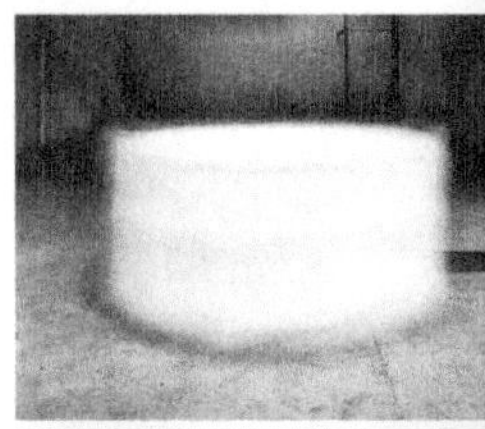

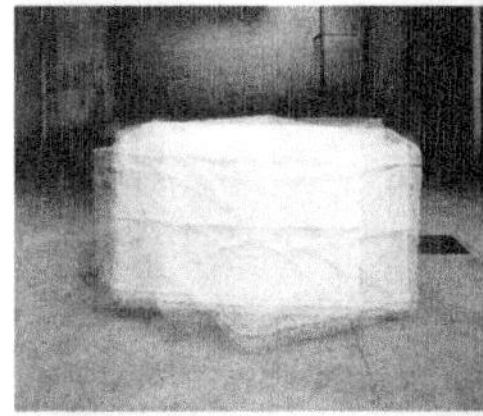

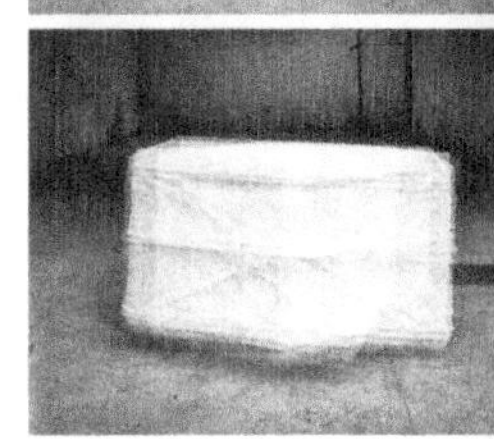

Didier Vermeiren, *Modèles #1* 1999

It is in the medium of photography that Vermeiren finds the best lens on sculpture. In his series *Profils, Cariatides à la pierre* (1998) and *Modèles* (1999) he looks at his sculpture *Profils, Cariatides à la pierre* through the viewfinder of a camera.

> He opens the shutter, walks over to the sculpture, manoeuvres the object on its underside's bulging point and gives it a swing with his arms, so that it rotates on its axis. Then he walks back to the camera and shuts the lens. All of this takes about three minutes. The camera has not been able to capture the artist's presence.[15]

In these photographs Vermeiren has turned positions around. It is the sculpture which turns before an observer who stands still, instead of the observer walking around a motionless sculpture. The photographs condense the time, the movement through space, it takes to look at a piece of sculpture in one single image. We see a diversity of profiles encapsulated into one form. The implication of this viewing condition is that there is no single perspective or angle that offers the best view on a sculpture; in contrast, Neoclassical sculpture, especially, suggests that this would be the case.

Non-Material Conditions of Sculpture: Ann Veronica Janssens

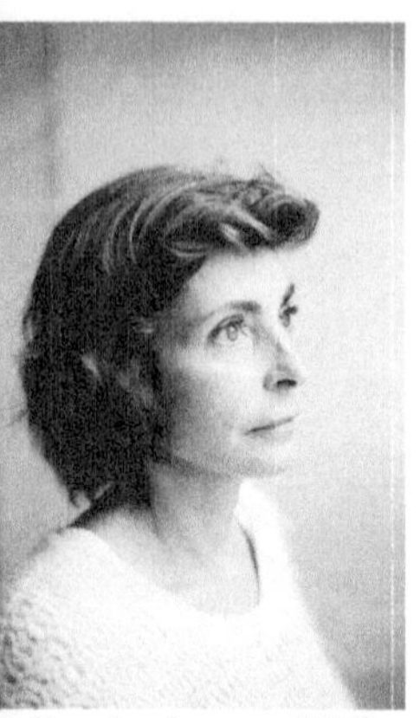
…n Veronica Janssens (1956)

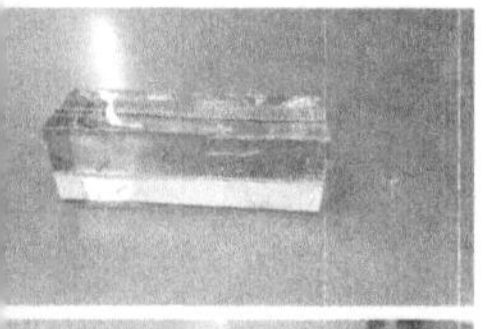

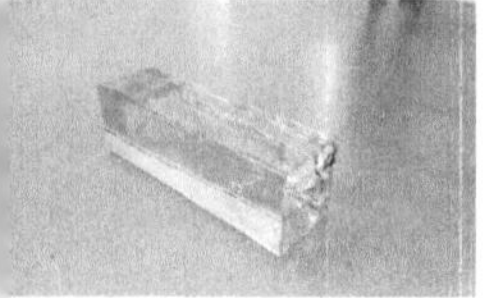
…n Veronica Janssens, …titled, 2019

When we consider viewing positions as a condition of sculpture, we have transgressed the simple notion that all there is to say about this medium is that sculpture consists of matter in the form of either a body or solid. A specific modality of looking is, as I argued on the basis of Vermeiren's work, one of the building blocks of sculpture that makes sculpture a specific medium that differs from other media. Belgian artist Ann Veronica Janssens has focused on other apparently non-material elements that constitute sculpture: light and colour. Whereas painterly traditions have revelled in the representation of light, Janssens demonstrates how non-material light and colour should be considered as material conditions of sculpture. This sounds paradoxical, but she does make visible light and colour something material. Similar to that which Philippe Dubois asserts in investigations of the specificity of media, that the best lens on photography will be found outside photography, Janssens demonstrates that non-material qualities of light can be best investigated through the material qualities of, for instance, glass.

At first sight, it seems a truism to say that sculpture depends on light, because it is due to light that we can see sculpture. But Janssens does not investigate light as contextual to sculpture but as building stone: light constitutes sculpture in the literal sense. In *Untitled* (2019) she presents a bar of optical glass. Optical glass is the most perfect kind of glass, having no imperfections in any kind of form. It is used, for example, for cockpit windows of airplanes. The materiality of this bar of glass is undeniable: it is very heavy, and as a result it rests on the gallery floor. The four sides of the bar are not completely flat; in consequence, we see light reflected in the glass in unexpected, baroque forms. The light is not reflected on the surface of the glass bar, but is materialized within the glass. Light is materialized due to being caught within matter; it is luminous matter.

Janssens's *Incandescent Glass Bar* from 2009 demonstrates that luminous matter also has colour. The bar made of incandescent Anla glass glows with luminescent green light. Although light and colour are seen as different qualities, these allegedly unmaterial elements cannot be distinguished from each other. The glowing bar radiates light through colour, or colour through light. Janssens exhibited this work at the Kijkduin Biennale on the beach near The Hague in 2011. The glass bar was especially visible during shimmering twilight, when the little light there was at that time of day was all caught within the glass; as a result, the glass became incandescent.

Janssens's work is often compared to that of the American artist James Turrell. Similar to Janssens, Turrell's work investigates different manifestations of light. In his own words:

> I have an interest in the visible light, the light perceptible only by the mind. A light which seems to be undimmed by the entering of the senses. I want to address the light that we see in dreams and make spaces that seem to come from those dreams and which are familiar to those who inhabit those places.[16]

An important difference between Janssens and Turrell is the media they work in or with.

Janssens embodies light as luminous matter whereas Turrell demonstrates the visual force of illuminated spatiality. This difference determines and differentiates the nature of their work. Janssens is a sculptor while Turrell makes installations. The same can be said of another American artist

16 Julia Brown, 'Interview wit James Turrell', p. 42.

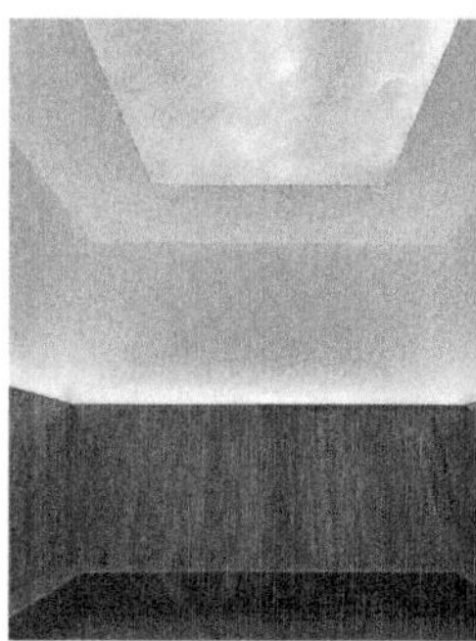

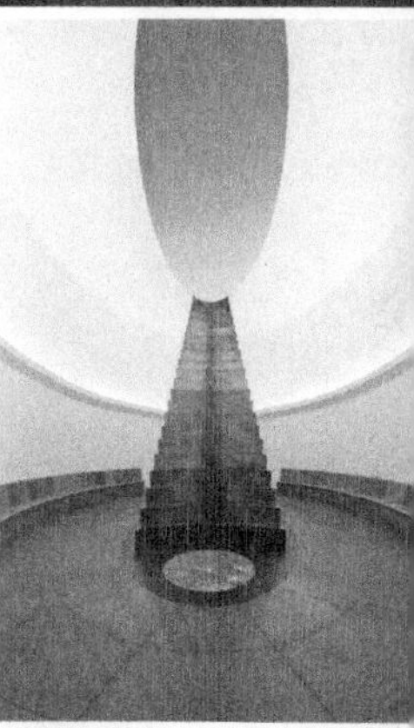

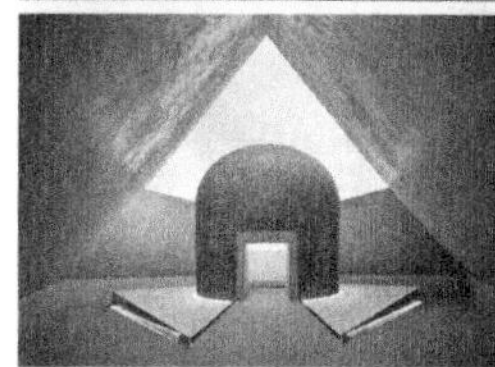

James Turrell, *Skyspace*, 2016, Wassenaar, Museum Voorlinden; Roden Crater, Arizona, *Within Without*, Canberra, National Gallery of Australia

working with light: Robert Irwin. He makes installations that deploy light in such a way that it changes and determines perception. In his works, light manifests itself spatially; not luminous matter, but luminous space.

Another striking instance of Janssens's work with light is IPE 535 (2009). This consists of a steel beam; the kinds of beams used in the construction of architecture. The beam is a 'found object'. Her intervention onto the beam is very simple. She has polished the upper side of the beam, which means the surface is very glossy and has an extreme sheen, opening up to the workings of light. The light is captured and reflected. In contrast with the glass bars with which I began my discussion of Janssens's work, light is not captured within the bar, but is fixated on its surface. The glossy, reflecting surface of the beam makes one forget its weight and materiality. Unmaterial light and heavy material steel have been unified. Opposing qualities can no longer be distinguished from each other. The conventionally heavy matter of sculpture has metamorphosed into light luminous matter.[17]

Another work by Janssens challenges the weight of sculpture in yet another way. The sculpture *Aerogel* (2000) is named after the material it is made of, which is the lightest material ever made by man. It weighs almost nothing and is 99.5 to 99.9 per cent air.

> Its lightness affects all aspects of its existence. Translucent, it looks a bit like clouds or mist [...]. Almost being weightless, it can carry up to 1500 times its own weight, and isolate down to minus 270 degrees Celsius. As an object or thing, its extreme porosity makes it utterly fragile; its tentative shape is arbitrary, and it can crumble at any moment. Materiality and objecthood are in fierce tension.[18]

' For a discussion of IPE 535, e Bal, *Endless Andness*, 181–82.

Bal, *Endless Andness*, 125.

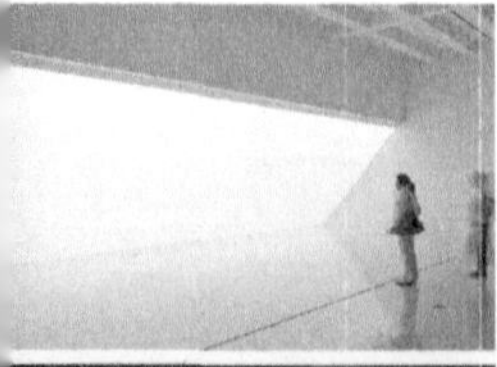
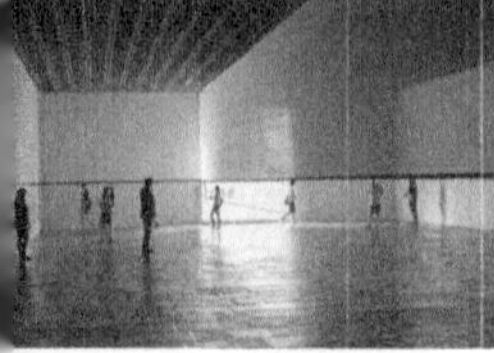

obert Irwin, exhibition views Minneapolis, Walker Art enter; New York, Whitney useum of American Art

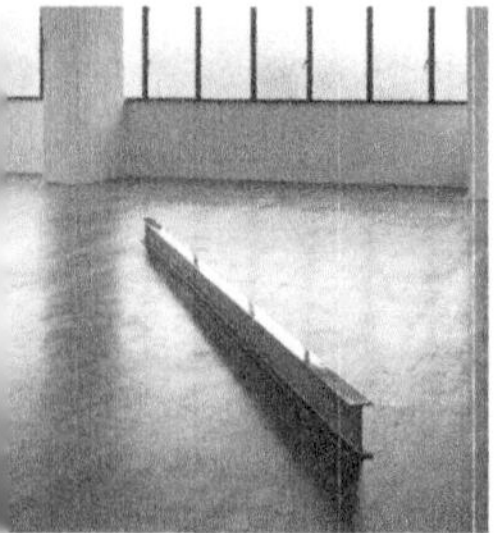

ın Veronica Janssens, *IPE 535*, 09

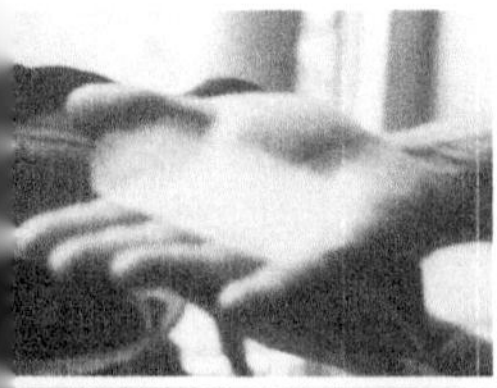
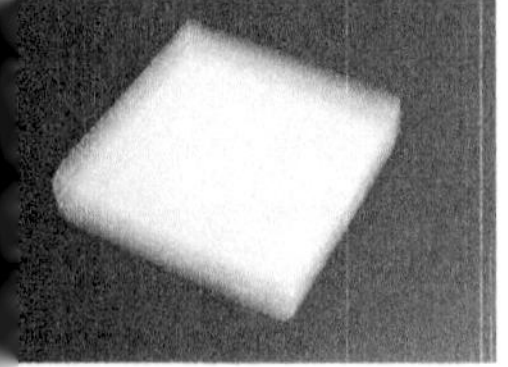

ın Veronica Janssens, *rogel*, 2000

According to conventional logic, weight and materiality define the objecthood of sculpture. *Aerogel* challenges both; its edges are undefined and, as a result, viewers find being sure of what they see difficult. The work lacks all features of solid matter and solid objects, 'such as form, color, fixed dimensions, and durability'.[19]

As Mieke Bal has argued, *Aerogel* is an 'almost thing that is on the side of thingness' (instead of objecthood); it is not a negation of weight and objecthood but 'a-radical almost-but-not-quite-yet'. It is a piece of matter with a non-form, but this does not imply that it is formless; it has a near-colour that is too unstable to be a proper one.[20] Janssens has said the following about her work in general: 'If my work has any meaning, it's about relinquishing control, the absence of authoritative materiality, and a tentative attempt to escape the tyranny of objects.'[21] It is rather amazing that she has pursued these goals in the medium of sculpture, which has always been defined by authoritative materiality and solid objecthood. But *Aerogel* is a good example of how successful she is in this pursuit.

Although far from being almost weightless like *Aerogel*, Janssens's *Blue Glass Roll* (2019) presents air as a building stone of sculpture in yet another way. When one looks closely, one sees tiny air bubbles in the glass roll. One could think these bubbles are imperfections resulting from the production process. However, the artist has materialized air, just as she has materialized light in many of her other works. The bubbles of air are caught in glass and have become matter. The sculpture is a solid of air/glass.

The 'near-colour that is too unstable to be a proper one' is also addressed by a work that cannot be considered as sculpture, materially, but by means of language demonstrates the impossibility of identifying colours in the sky. Janssens's

19 Bal, *Endless Andness*, p. 126.

20 Bal, *Endless Andness*, p. 127.

21 Rousseau, 'Ann Veronica Janssens'. 'Si mon travail a un sens, il est là, dans cette perte de contrôle, cette absence de matérialité autoritaire, cette tentative d'échapper à la tyrannie des objects.'

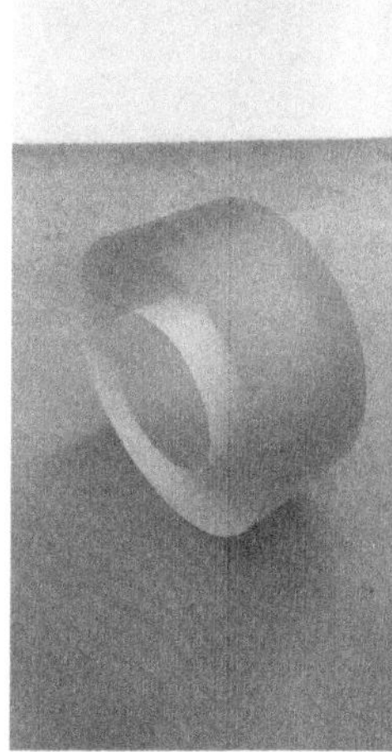

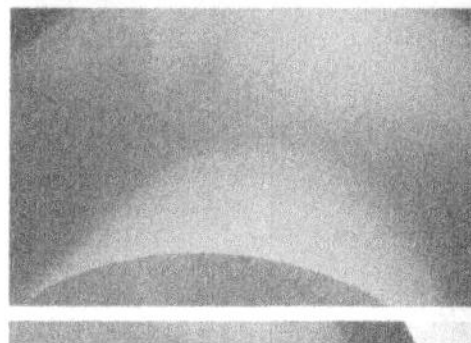

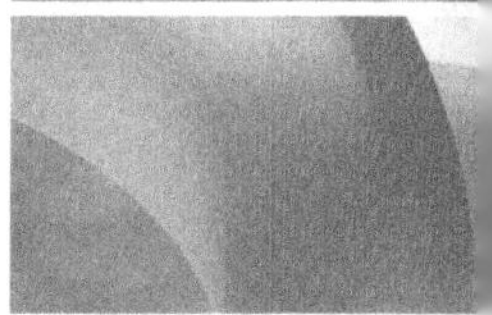

Ann Veronica Janssens, *Blue Glass Roll 405*, 2019, details

The Skeis... (2019) is a printed text on paper. The text is a scientific description of the sky, and attempts to capture all the changing colours and movements in the sky. But although one can see and 'grasp' the sky, it is impossible to identify all colours in their specificity. Janssens's text is a transcription of a scientific text from the beginning of the twentieth century describing the chaos of colours after a huge fire. Her text reads as follows:

> The skeis took on starnge
> cloors; terhe was an ereie
> srot of lgiht, fololewd in
> smoe palces by amlost
> copmltee dakernss...
> Sahdes vyaring from pnik
> and oarnge to ylleow and
> borwn wree uesd to
> decsribe the sky... The
> sun dsic wehn vsiible
> apepared blue or puprle.
> As it apeapred and
> dispapeared trhough brekas
> in the coluds it semeed to
> be in motoin.

The quality of near-colourness has been transposed into language. Although one can grasp the sky as a unified entity and say that its colour is blue or grey, one cannot identify the range or diversity of colours that the sky contains. Similarly, one can read and grasp this text as a whole, as long as one does not slow down to focus on individual words. Many words are unreadable and make no sense. But strangely enough this problem dissolves when reading the text as a whole. Although *The Skeis* is a text and not a luminous, colourful solid, one can draw the conclusion that it is not only weight and objecthood challenged by Janssens given that fixed, identifiable colours are also questioned. The impossibility of identifying colours does sometimes take on the condition of 'near-colourness', as in *Aerogel*; other works demonstrate this impossibility by means of a multiplicity of colours, or more precisely, kaleidoscopic colour effects. This phenomenon challenges the conventional idea that sculpture *has* colour, suggesting instead that sculpture adopts colour. In a series of works she has been making since the first decade of the twenty-first century, consisting of annealed glass with ribs covered by a PVC filter, colours are completely unstable. When the viewer walks by, the colours change from bright pink to purple to yellow. This kaleidoscopic effect is not just in the eye of the beholder, because colour is materialized into the glass.

But claiming that colour has been materialized into the glass does not mean that the viewer has no role in this effect. Bal has introduced the term 'deictic looking' for the mode of looking that is activated by many of Janssens's works. 'Deixis' is known as a term for linguistic markers such as I/you, here/there, yesterday/today/tomorrow that only acquire meaning within a specific situation or utterance. They require the subject's presence.[22] It is only from her/his being positioned in relation to someone else, in the present, or at a specific location, that these markers become meaningful. In other words, deictic looking is bodily; it is anchored in the viewing body.

At first glance, it seems rather self-evident that looking at sculpture is anchored in the viewing body. Although conventional, Neoclassical sculpture usually proposes a privileged point of view towards it, and it is assumed that one walks around a sculpture and see it from all sides. As I mentioned,

22 Bal, *Endless Andness*, p. 58

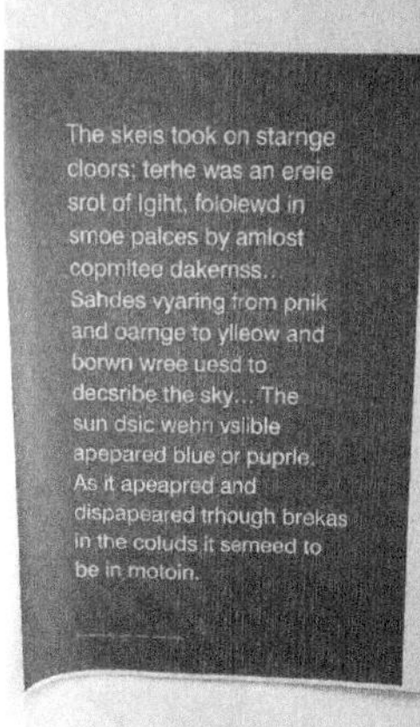

Ann Veronica Janssens, *The Skeis...*, 2019

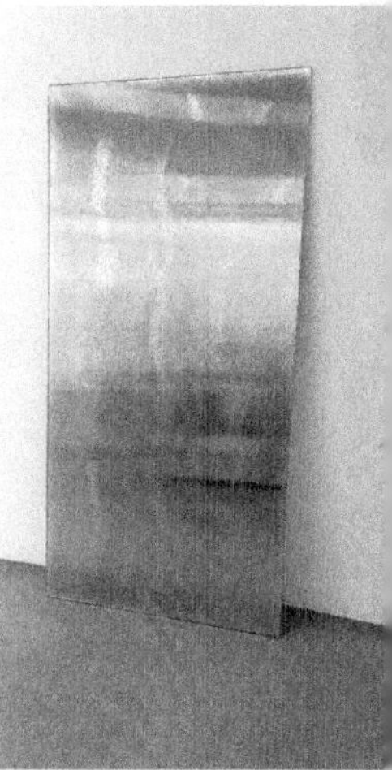

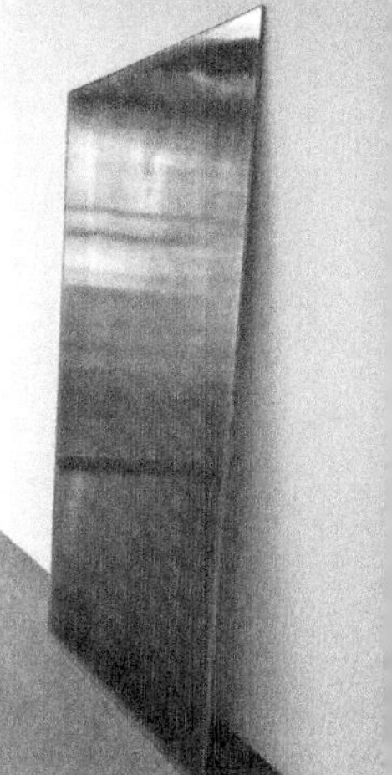

Ann Veronica Janssens, *Bright Pink*, 2020

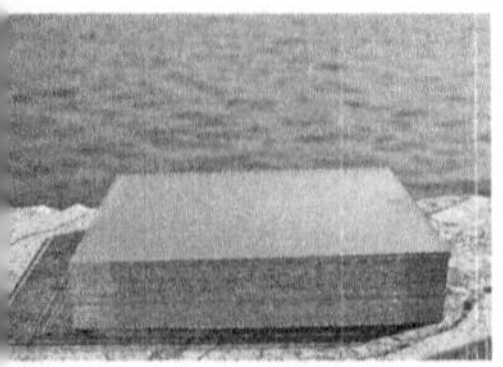
nn Veronica Janssens, *Casa rollo*, 1988

due to its three-dimensionality it is impossible to see and gain an overview of a sculpture in one single glance. But this acknowledgment of bodily looking in the case of viewing sculpture is very general. Regarding viewers, it assumes a stable body or a solid and moving body. They should adopt different perspectives in relation to the sculpture. Although in Janssens's work the viewer is also assumed to be in movement, the deictic looking in relation to her work also activates challenges to the solidity of the solid. When her works adopt different colours as the viewer moves before it, not only the viewer but also these works are far from stable. This makes the interrelationship between work and viewer more intense, and more difficult to grasp. It does not concern just a positioning of the viewer, but a dynamic relationship between two equal partners.

Janssens made a kaleidoscopic solid of glass, titled *Casa Frollo* (1988), for the Venice Biennale in 1988. She piled up eighteen panes of glass on a windowsill of one of the *palazzi*, Casa Frollo. This pile of glass was located at the edge of the quay in front of the water. The totally flat and crack-free shiny surface of the pile of glass panes contrasted with the old, cracked, uneven surface of the old stone of the sill. But there is more than a striking contrast between two different materials. The visual qualities of the glass are not stable but adapt themselves to those of the stone and of the water. Bal's description of unstable visual qualities is informative:

> The sides of these thin panes were not polished. As a result, the rough edges sculpted the blue into various tones, hues, and scintillations that echoed the infinite variation of the waves of water beyond it. However, whereas water moves and thus possesses a degree of variability unrivaled by any hard material, the grain of the

> edges was tiny, modest, and mute. At the same time, the rough edges were double-edged, so to speak. They were also responsive to the beauty of the old, rough stone on which the panes were stacked. [...] In terms of temporality, these unpolished edges of the glass panes mediate between the durability of the stone and the ephemerality of the waves. This in-betweenness turns them into a threshold of sorts.[23]

The deictic looking at stake here does not only involve the viewer's position towards *Casa Frollo*, but also the echoing and resonating water and stone. The anchoring of this look in the subject of looking also implies that the space surrounding the work becomes part of the work itself. As a result, the solid pile of glass never stops showing new visual qualities. The durability of the objecthood of sculpture is bracketed by Janssens; this solid of wavering light and colour forces us to rethink the conventional notions of solidity and durability.

All Janssens's works discussed so far engage light as material to make deictic looking possible and attractive. Light is never represented or created, nor is it depicted in its shades or nuances, as is common in painting and photography. Instead, light is dealt with as matter. Let me discuss one other work that deals with light as its main matter. *Grand disque* (1996) consists of a flat piece of metal, a perfect circle, with circular lines engraved on it. The only element that, so to speak, 'engraves' the plaque with design, volume, and depth is light. That light, however, challenges our sense of what the 'work' is, and also what light is. In this work, light takes on weight, dimension, form, and movement. The light emanates from the centre, in rays that grow wider as they move away from it.[24] The rays move, and there is no stable position offered from which one can view the rays at leisure. The

23 Bal, *Endless Andness*, p. 74

24 Bal, *Endless Andness*, p. 77

25 Bal, *Endless Andness*, 136.

tiniest movement, even of the eye itself, changes the rays of light. In this work, deictic looking involves an intimate dynamic between bodily looking and the materialization of light.

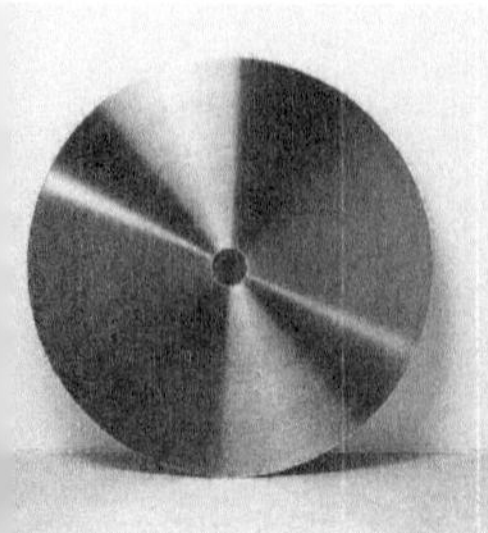

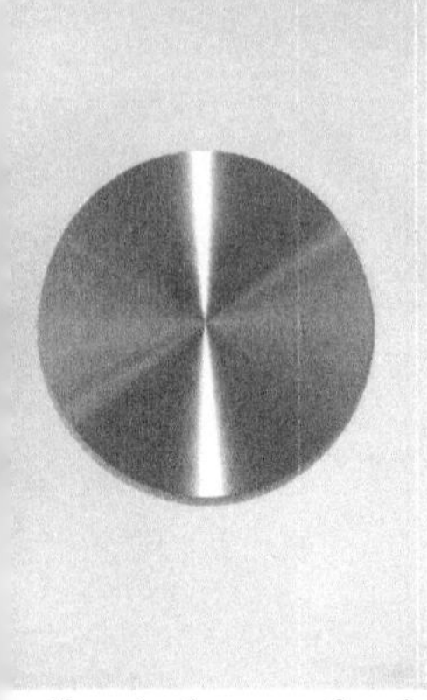

ın Veronica Janssens, *Grand* ˌsque, 1996; *Brass disque*, 2010

Let me end my discussion of Janssens's luminous solids with her most radical one in terms of solidity, her 'hollow sculptures', or rooms with mist.[25] A good example of these hollow sculptures is her *Horror Vacui*, which she made for the Belgian Pavilion at the Venice Biennale in 1999. Why is it important to assess these mist rooms as sculptures? What does considering this ungraspable 'object' as a condition of sculpture contribute to our understanding of sculpture? The mist rooms consist of a mixture of artificial mist and natural light, sometimes filtered through coloured filters. The viewer has to enter the room and as a result s/he has the feeling of being inside a cloud. The substance one enters is clearly not solid, because one can walk in it or through it. It feels slightly moist. The mist cannot be called matter, but Bal's phrase 'a-radical-almost-but-not-quite-yet' seems more than appropriate. It is almost matter but not quite yet.

Natural light enters the room and makes the mist luminous. One can distinguish other people walking around in the room, but only when one is close to them. These people have, however, no clear form or shape. They do not appear as bodies, but rather as silhouettes; and these silhouettes dissolve. The room is clearly a space, but it is filled with mist that is not evidently matter; or as I just formulated, it is almost matter but not quite yet. This suggests that we should not see this work as a luminous space, but as luminous matter, implying that the mist rooms belong to the medium of sculpture and not to that of installation. They are solids of light that challenge the notion of sculpture according to which solidity, weight, and objecthood are the only building blocks of the sculptural medium. As Janssens demonstrates again and again, light and colour are equally important as building blocks of sculpture. They are material.

The Art of Building: Lygia Clark

In the work of Brazilian artist Lygia Clark, the logic of building blocks has an entirely different dimension: a literal one. Her artistic practice belonged to so-called Brazilian Neoconcretism, which distinguishes itself from abstraction as non-figuration; non-figurative art is a creation of the mind, but becomes concrete when materialized. Her practice was not focused on the building blocks of sculpture, in any kind of material, solid or not; she made sculpture that had to be built by the viewer, or better, by the beholder, the person who 'holds' the object physically. This meant a shift from the art object as something intended to be merely looked at, to the art object as something that demanded to be touched and physically interacted with, effectively requiring the body of the beholder to construct or complete the work. This engendered a conceptual shift from the audience as passive viewers to the audience as active participants. According to Clark, art should be experienced not just with the eyes, but as a bodily encounter. By means of her art works, she staged an interaction between viewer and artwork akin to a meeting of two bodies. By doing so she activated the viewer's embodied, sensorial, and emotional response. Her artistic practice was a critique of art's institutional constraints; it embraced the potential value of art as a social practice. This social practice of art has a literal dimension when performed in sculpture: the beholder builds and completes the sculpture; the building blocks for these social artworks have been provided by the artist.

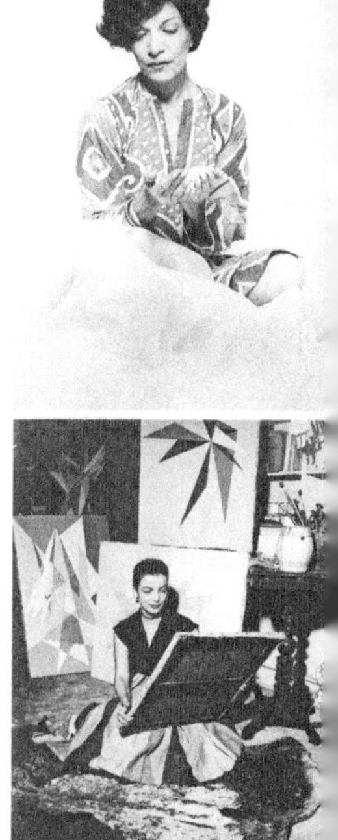

Lygia Clark (1920–1988)

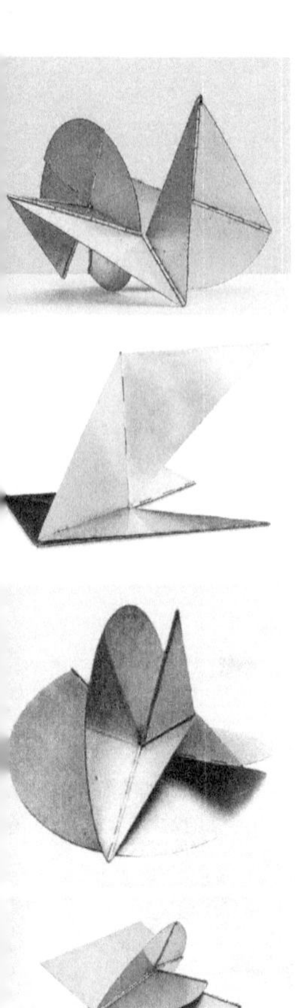

ygia Clark, *Bichos* or *Critters*, 960–1963

Although Clark worked with different media, especially painting at first, her sculptures realized her ambition most concretely. She aimed to achieve the idea that the beholder should build and complete the object. Between 1960 and 1963, she made the so-called *Bichos* or *Critters* (usually translated as *Beasts* or *Animals*). At the 1961 São Paulo Biennial, she won the first prize for sculpture. These sculptural objects are small enough to be held in two hands, and are made of flat circular and triangular aluminium sheets attached by hinges. She called these hinges 'spinal columns', emphasizing a bodily notion of sculpture. The works have no predetermined form; instead, the hinges allow them to assume a variety of three-dimensional configurations in response to handling by a viewer-participant. The artist envisaged a physical, mutually responsive interaction between art object and user; each *Critter* has the potential to react to manipulation in a multitude of unpredictable ways, forcing the user to adapt and respond in turn. Although this interaction is playful, it is not entirely without risk: one user described his experience of handling a *Critter* as akin to 'engaging in combat', and indeed, the artist did not think of these works as passively malleable toys, but as naughty, mischievous creatures capable of unexpected or unwanted reactions.

The *Critters* are groundbreaking in their rejection of the static qualities of sculpture. Unlike a traditional museum object, they are designed to be handled, with the meaning of the work ultimately residing not in the fixed form, but in the dynamic relationship between object and user. They build sculpture by being handled: the activation of the work completes it. Clark was disappointed whenever a *Critter* was transferred from a gallery to a private collection, because there it would usually be looked at but no longer handled or touched.

In this chapter I have dealt with a sculptural logic that no longer relies on the body, or rather the body's meaning. Instead, it develops a logic that is based on the notion of the building block. This notion should be taken literally as well as figuratively. A Minimalist sculptor like Carl Andre searches for the fundamentals of sculpture in a literal way and builds his sculptures with bricks, wooden blocks, or iron plates. The material he uses for sculpture is no longer the transcendental matter of marble, bronze, or ivory, but industrial building blocks like brick, iron, or wood. And these industrial materials are what they are. They do not rely on an inner meaning. Similarly, but not in a Minimalist way, Per Kirkeby builds his sculptures out of bricks. The modular arrangements of Saloua Raouda Choucair also arrange building blocks, but in contrast with Kirkeby her building blocks are not identical and industrially made; they are all slightly different and handmade.

But the pursuit for the fundamentals of sculptures can also be understood figuratively, as in the work of Didier Vermeiren and Ann Veronica Janssens. Vermeiren makes sculptures of the contextual and processual factors that result in sculpture; they are presented as sculptures in themselves. It is the process of making as well as looking at sculpture that he determines as being fundamental to sculpture. Janssens presents the non-material conditions of sculpture as sculpture; light, reflection, and air become matter out of which sculpture is made. Lygia Clark's objects do not undermine conventional ideas about sculpture's matter, but rather its solidity—sculptures are not necessarily static objects with a fixed shape and form.

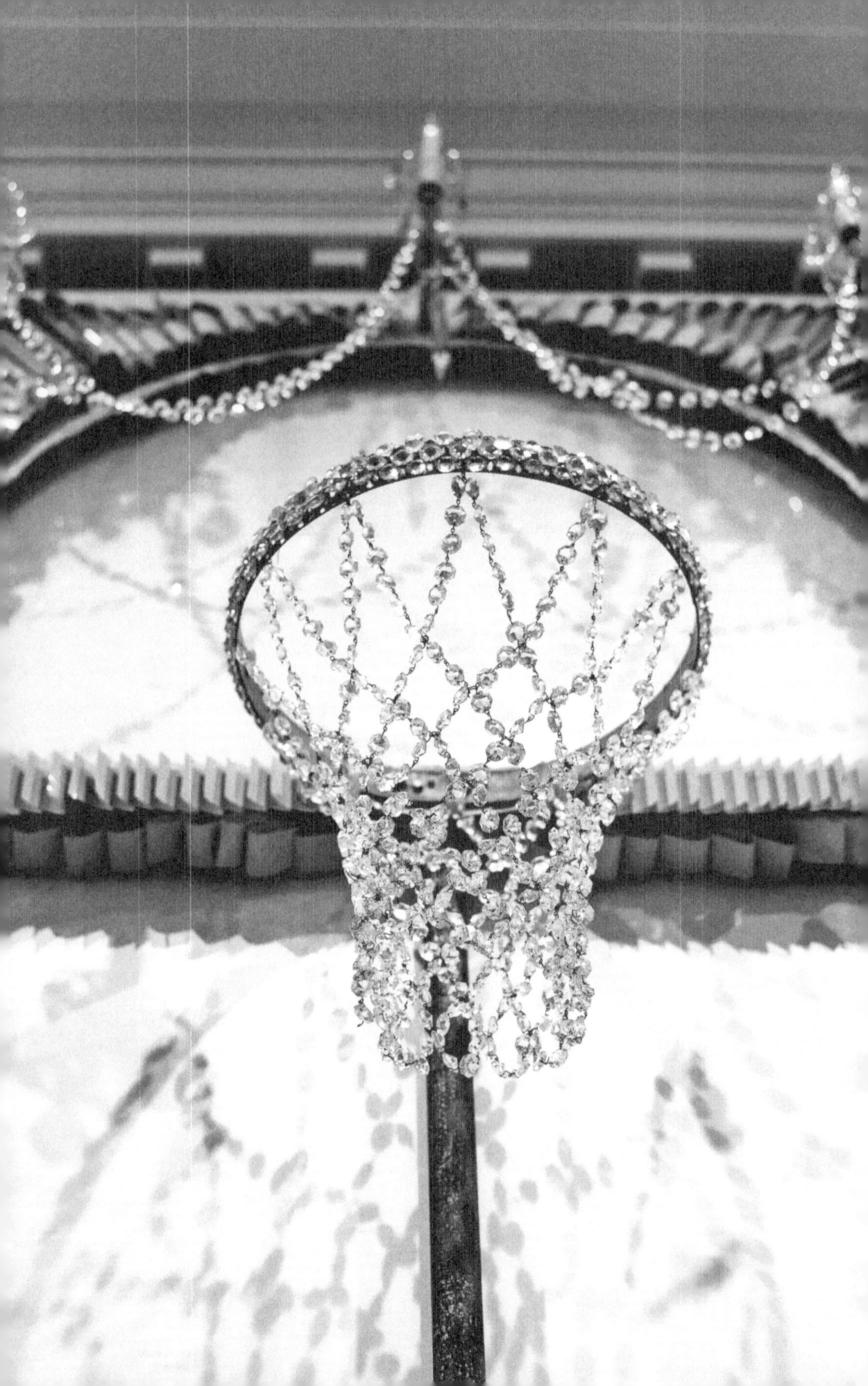

Assemblage

The Emergence of Assemblage Sculpture

The logic of assemblage came about at the beginning of the twentieth century in painting as well as in sculpture. At the beginning, the planar version was called collage. Compositions made in the nineteen-tens by Kazimir Malevich, Pablo Picasso, Georges Braque, Juan Gris, and Gino Severini (among many others) were collages comprising diverse materials and elements. The same method, however, was employed in the making of sculpture. Raoul Hausmann's *Mechanical Head*, realized in 1918, is a prime example of sculptural collage that consists of an arrangement of a wooden head with metal, leather, and cardboard. Yet previously, Auguste Rodin had made sculptures out of assembled antique remains from his own collection and also other plaster figures, or parts of them, he had made himself.

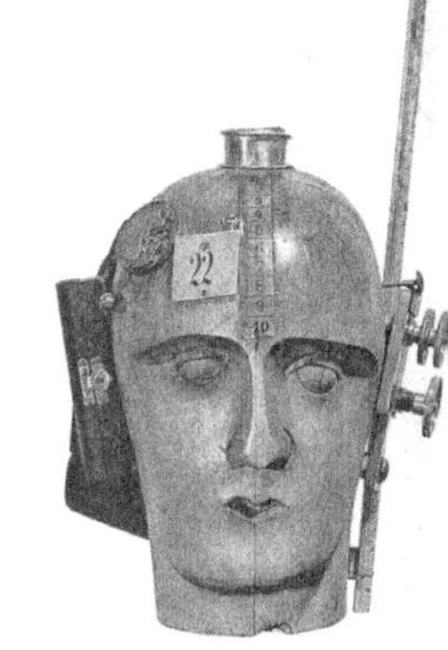

Raoul Hausmann, *Mechanical Head*, 1918

Between 1912 and 1914, Picasso made *Guitars* from cardboard and string. These are not illusionary representations of guitars but rather guitars made out of materials other than those one is accustomed to. Of course, they are less than

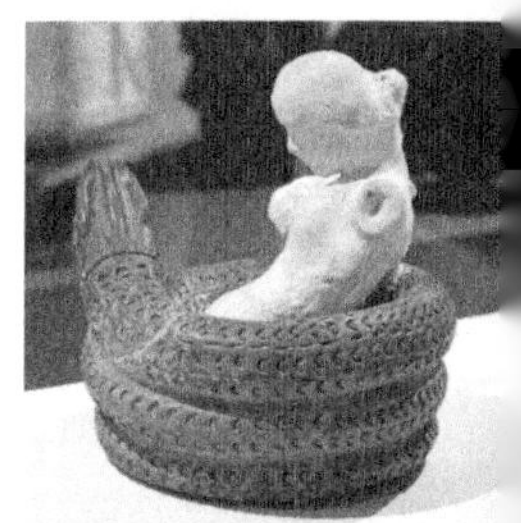

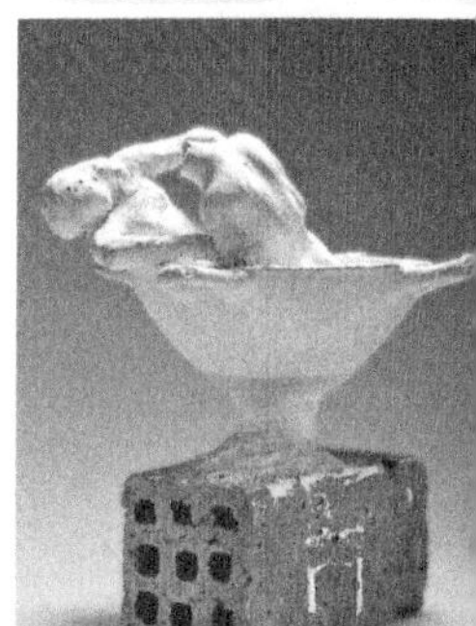

Auguste Rodin, *Assemblages*, 1890–1905

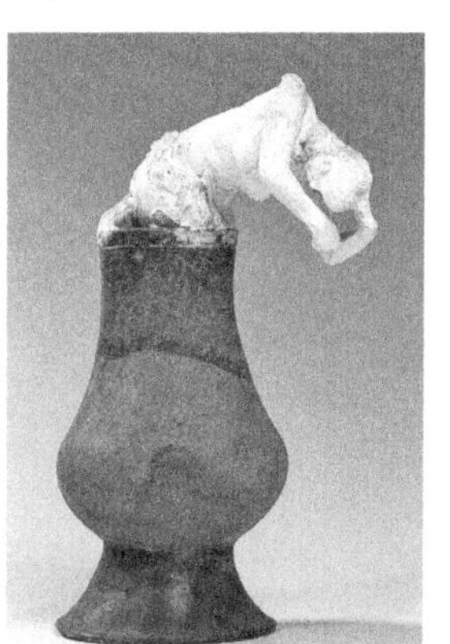

David Hammons, *Basketball Chandelier*, 1997

Seitz, *The Art of Assemblage*, 150, no. 5.

Elderfield, 'Preface', *Essays* *n Assemblage*, 1992, p. 7.

Seitz, *The Art of Assemblage*, 6.

Seitz, *The Art of Assemblage*, 10.

perfect and thus evoke only the idea of a guitar, instead of actually being one. But it is important to realize that these works are sculptural objects instead of representations.

Although the term assemblage had been used earlier, it became the common term, especially for sculptural collage after curator William C. Seitz had used it in 1961 in the title of an exhibition in the Museum of Modern Art in New York. The exhibition 'The Art of Assemblage' presented both three-dimensional and planar works, covering 'all forms of composite art and modes of composition'.[1] As John Elderfield makes clear, the term assemblage is more specific than the term construction because it stresses the accumulation of found elements in such a way that they remain separately recognizable.[2] Seitz describes assemblages in two points:

1. They are predominantly assembled elements rather than painted, drawn, modeled, or carved.
2. Entirely or in part, their constituent elements are preformed natural or manufactured materials, objects, or fragments not intended as art materials.[3]

In short, conventional artistic techniques (such as carving, painting, drawing) and materials (marble, wood, paint and more) are bracketed, and custom-made objects or materials are 'assembled'. According to some, this new artistic practice of assemblage was the most important artistic invention of the twentieth century. Seitz writes:

> Just as the introduction of oil painting in fifteenth-century Flanders and Italy paralleled a new desire to reproduce the appearance of the visible world, collage and related modes of construction manifest a predisposition that is characteristically modern.[4]

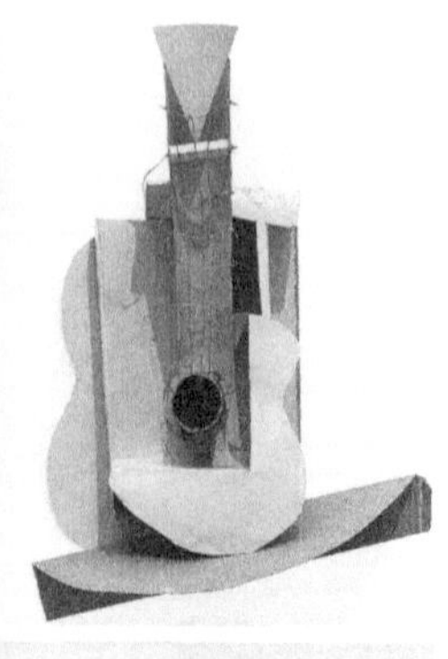

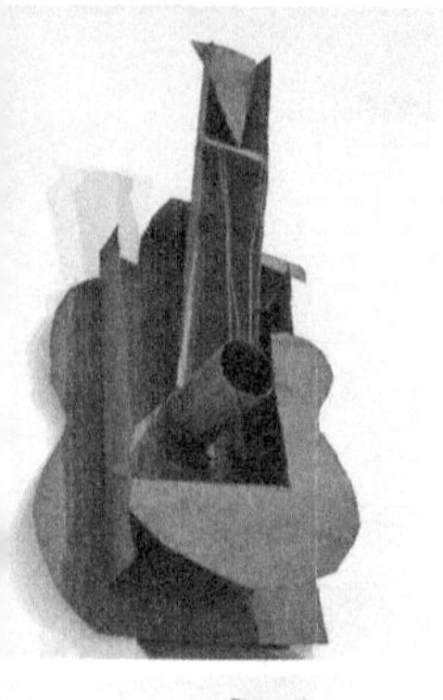

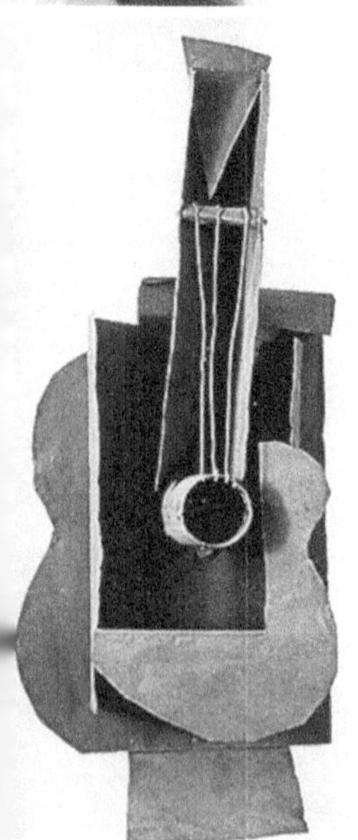

ablo Picasso, *Guitars*, 12–1914

The background of assemblage originates from literature, particularly in the poetry of Apollinaire, and in painting from Cubism, which tried to reconcile the conflict between representation or illusion and structure. Already in his poems of 1908, Apollinaire had explored the 'freedom in assembling a poem out of disparate parts'.[5] In his 'calligrammes', routine phrases and clichés are combined with snatches of conversation without the transition of thematic connection. He sometimes realized this juxtaposition of verbal fragments visually, placing them not linearly in sentences or poetic lines, but visually dispersed over the page.

As Seitz explains, the shock this kind of assemblage caused was not that diverse literary or poetic phrases were juxtaposed, but that these verbal fragments were actual in describing or referring to the real world. This important element of the art of juxtaposition is foregrounded in Georges Duhamel's review of Apollinaire's book of poems *Alcools* (1913). I will quote him at length because his description of poems is emblematic for assemblage from the first half of the twentieth century:

> Nothing could remind one more of an old junk shop than these collected poems [...] I call it an old junk shop because a mass of heterogeneous objects has found a place there, though some of them are of value, none of them has been made by the dealer himself. That is just the characteristic of this sort of industry: it resells but does not produce. Sometimes there are strange objects for sale; on its grimy shelves one may discover a rare stone hanging from a nail. All this comes from afar, but the stone is pleasant to look at. The rest is a collection of faked paintings, patched exotic garments, bicycle accessories and articles of intimate hygiene. A truculent and

5 Shattuck, *The Banquet Years*, p. 245.

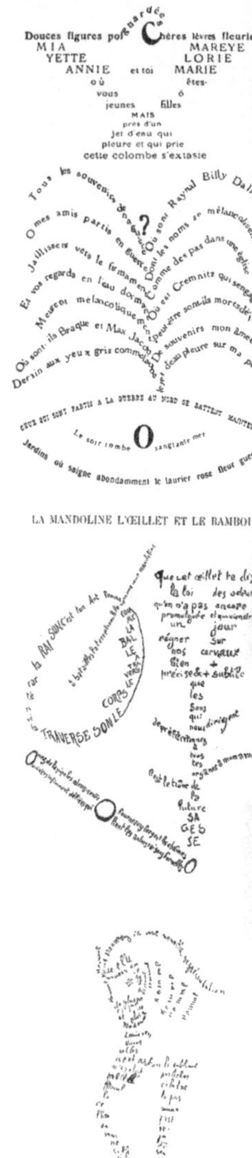

Three poems from Apollinaire's *Calligrammes*, 1918

bewildering variety takes the place of art in this assemblage.[6]

The collection of poems is compared with a junk shop in which heterogeneous objects are sold, and which have not been made or produced by the shop owner, but collected or assembled. The discourse is not artistic but economic; it uses the terms of modern capitalism that surfaced at the end of the nineteenth century. Some objects are very attractive and come from afar. Their attraction seems to be exotic and is probably the result of colonialism, which was at its peak at that time. The materials of the objects in the junk shop are again not artistic, although some fake paintings can also be found there. Many are of little value, a combination of dated, old objects, objects that connote modern life but ended up in the junk shop owing to the fast circulation of goods in the modern economy.

There is one other important characteristic of the logic of assemblage that is only implicitly suggested by Duhamel's discussion of Apollinaire's poems, namely that it occupies real space. The sculptural object does not represent by means of illusion but is real and actual. This is also the case in assemblage painting and becomes clear in the words of one of the most renowned post-war assemblage artists. Asked in Paris why he adds objects to his paintings, Robert Rauschenberg answered: 'Paint itself is an object, and canvas also. In my opinion, the void which must be filled does not exist.'[7] The void is filled by the strategy of no longer dealing with paint and canvas as something artistic, something which belongs to a realm other than objects in the real world.

One question that imposes itself on the maker as well as the viewer of assembled artworks is: Does it form a unity or is it just an assemblage of diverse and usually fragmented

Georges Duhamel, quoted in Seitz, *The Art of Assemblage*, 15.

Seitz, *The Art of Assemblage*, 25.

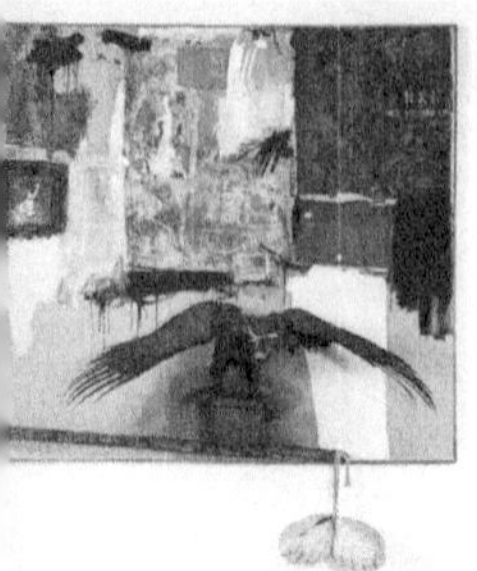

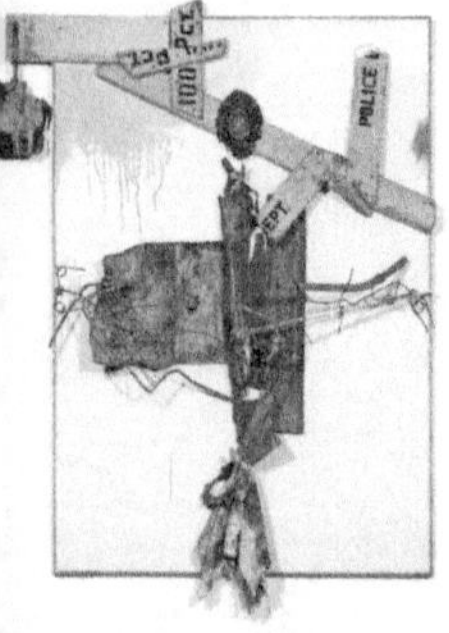

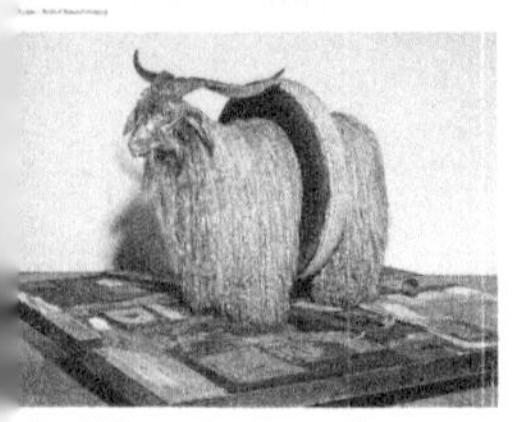

Robert Rauschenberg, *Canyon*, 1959; *Co-Existence*, 1961; *Monogram*, 1959

objects and materials? The type of unity that results from juxtaposition, however,

> [...] can never be entirely preordained, for an assembled work grows by testing, rejection, and acceptance. The artist must cede a measure of his control, and hence his ego, to the materials and what transpires between them, placing himself partially in the role of discoverer or spectator as well as that of originator.[8]

These processes of testing, rejection, and acceptance provide us with criteria for evaluating and understanding different assemblage practices. Therefore, relevant questions are: What is the nature and meaning of the used objects and materials? Where were they found or collected? It is only on the basis of the answers to these questions that the unity of the diversity of elements can be assessed. The assemblage practices of Louise Bourgeois, David Hammons, and Heringa/ Van Kalsbeek, which I will discuss later in this chapter, are explored on the basis of these questions.

Also, the dreamlike juxtapositions of Surrealism combine a diversity of objects and motifs. But according to Seitz, these juxtapositions are produced by automatic expression: they are the result of the artist's unconscious, and as a consequence there is a pre-established unity, albeit implicitly given that it is unconscious. 'Real assemblage' differs from Surrealist juxtaposition by the way it originates in unrelated fragments and does not draw from the unconscious but from the world around us.[9] According to Max Ernst, Surrealist collage is an exploration of 'the fortuitous encounter upon a non-suitable plane of two mutually distant realities'.[10] This results in what is famously known in Surrealism as 'a convulsive image', explained by the poet Le Comte de Lautréamont as the unexpected beauty of 'the chance encounter of a sewing machine

8 Seitz, *The Art of Assemblage* p. 39.

9 Seitz, *The Art of Assemblage* p. 39.

10 Ernst, *Beyond Painting*, p. 21.

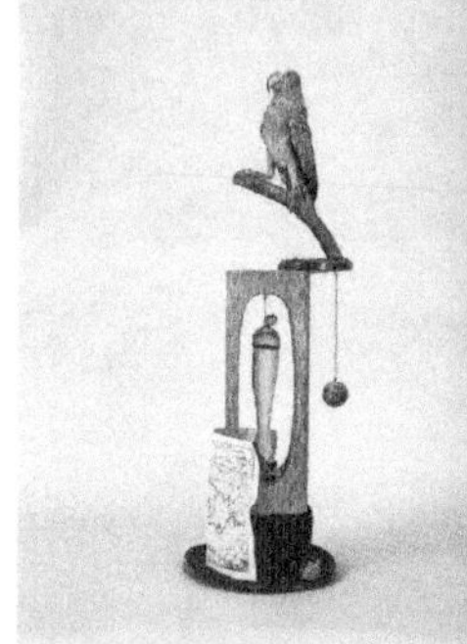

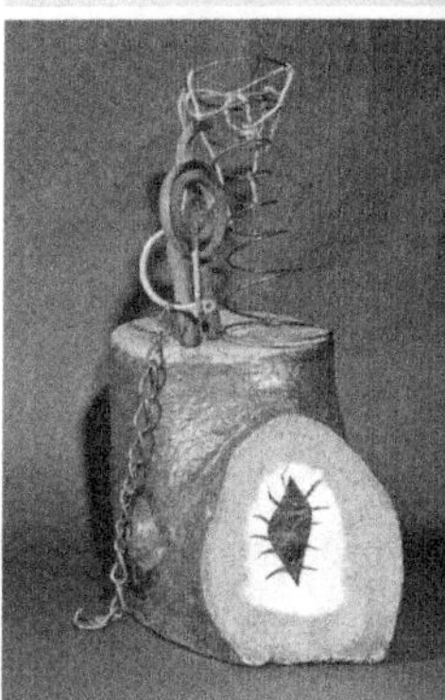

Joan Miró, *Objet poétique*, 193
Objet du couchant, 1932

Le Comte de Lautréamont
sidore Ducasse), quoted by
itz, *The Art of Assemblage*,
40.

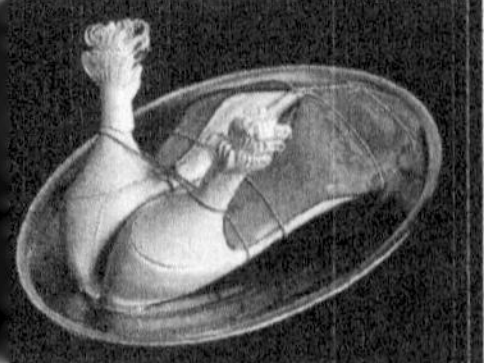

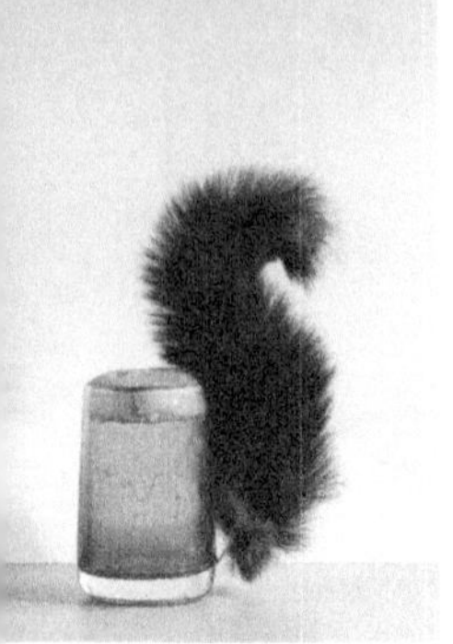

éret Oppenheim,
gouvernante—My Nurse—
in Kindermädchen,
36/1976; *L'écureuil*, 1969

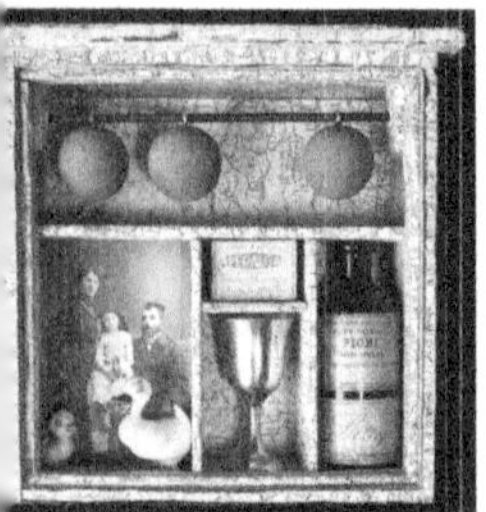

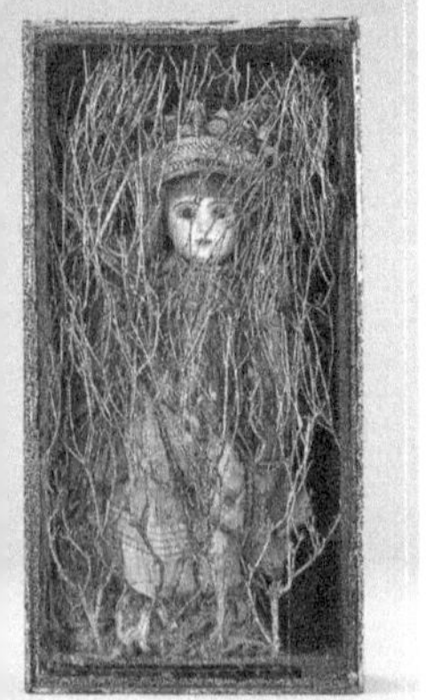

xes by Joseph Cornell

and an umbrella on a dissecting table'.[11] The kind of unity that comes about performatively in the encounter is aesthetic or bodily: it results in an unexpected beauty or eroticism. The best-known Surrealist artists who made assemblage sculptures are Joan Miró, Méret Oppenheim, Salvador Dalí, and Joseph Cornell.

One important issue still to be addressed is the role of the readymade artefact in the logic of assemblage. According to Seitz's definition of assemblage, such works can be understood as manufactured objects not intended as art material. But in the best-known cases, the *Fountain* (1913) and the *Bottle Dryer* (1913) by Marcel Duchamp, art objects are not assembled but consist of one object: a urinal and a bottle dryer. Some of his other readymades fit the definition much more easily, like *Bicycle Wheel* (1917) and *Why Not Sneeze, Rose Sélavy?* (1921). The former consists of an assemblage of a bicycle wheel on a stool, the latter sugar cubes in a bird cage. But because so many assemblages include readymade objects, I don't think we should take this definition too strictly and also consider unassembled, readymade objects as complying with the logic of assemblage.

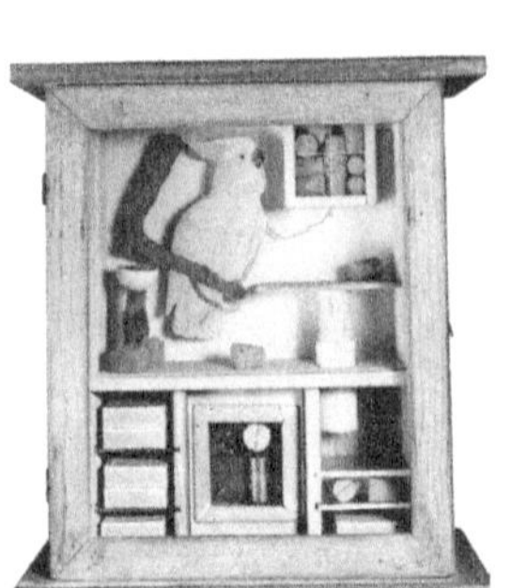

Box by Joseph Cornell

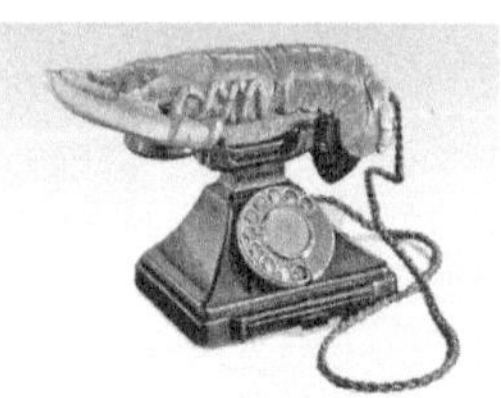

Salvador Dalí, *Lobster Telephone* (collaboration with Edward James), 1938

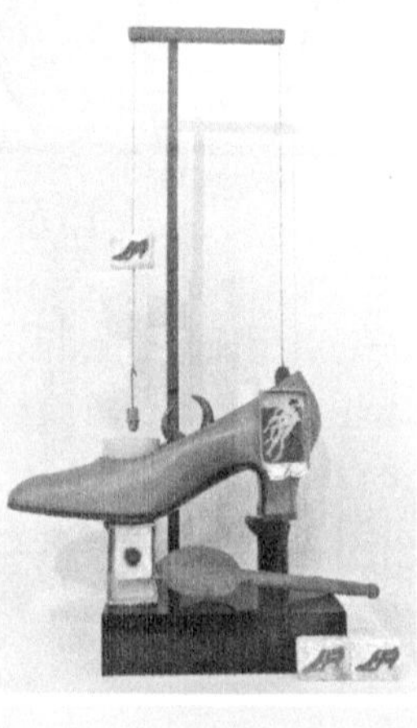

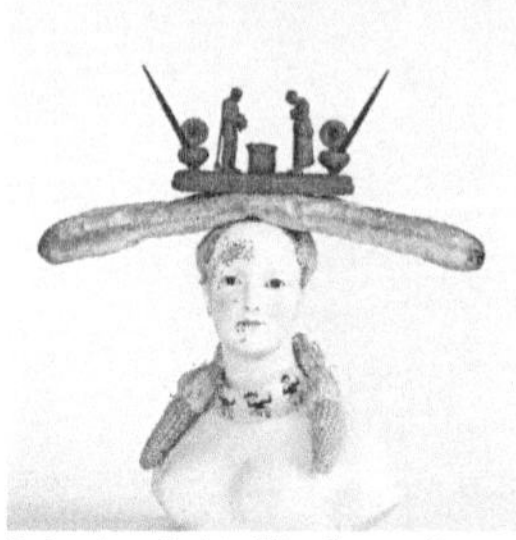

Salvador Dalí, *The Surrealist Shoe*, 1931; *Retrospective Bust of a Woman*, 1933

It is important to notice that Duchamp's ready-mades always consist of objects that could have been bought in a hardware store. All these objects are manufactured and hand-made and, therefore, man-made. His readymade artefacts differ from natural 'found objects' like shells, weathered wood, butterflies, or stuffed birds, as found in the assembled boxes by Joseph Cornell. This is why there is a hint of Cornell's assemblages being modelled on the *Wunderkammer* or cabinets of curiosity, whereas Duchamp's readymade assemblages should first of all be understood as an institutional critique of the art object.

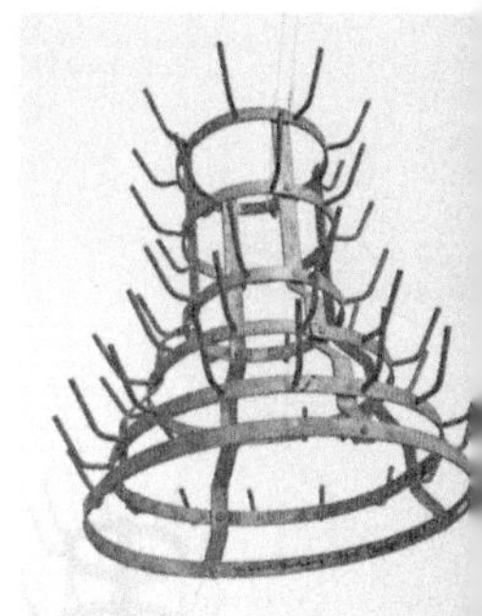

Assemblages of Existence: The Cells of Louise Bourgeois

French-American artist Louise Bourgeois had been making sculptures in plaster, wood, marble, and bronze when she turned sculpture inside out by introducing an entirely new category of sculpture: her so-called *Cells*. These *Cells* have been called 'environmental sculpture' by Rainer Crone, and indeed, the *Cells* deny or complicate objecthood and instead form a closed environment, consisting of a wooden or iron construction; in the interior of these constructions a variety of objects is assembled. Some of these objects were made by Bourgeois herself, like a marble sculpture of three hands in *Cell (You Better Grow Up)* (1993), an ear cut out of a block of marble in *Cell IV* (1991), or a bronze female figure in *Cell (Arch of Hysteria)* (1992–1993). But most often the objects are artefacts that could have been collected at a flea market or hardware store, like old mirrors, an old bed, or old clothes. The logic of assemblage realized in Bourgeois's *Cells* differs from conventional assemblage sculpture through the unity that the collected and assembled objects, fragments, and

Marcel Duchamp, *Bottle Dryer* 1913; *Fountain*, 1913; *Bicycle Wheel*, 1917

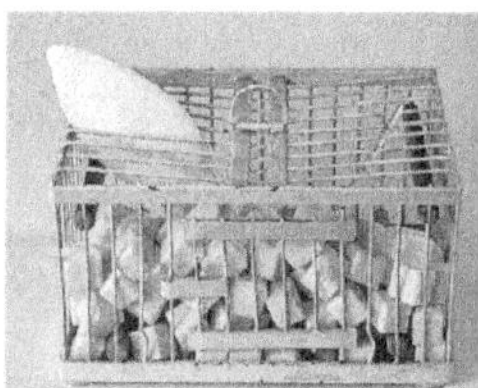

Marcel Duchamp, *Why Not Sneeze, Rose Sélavy?*, 1921

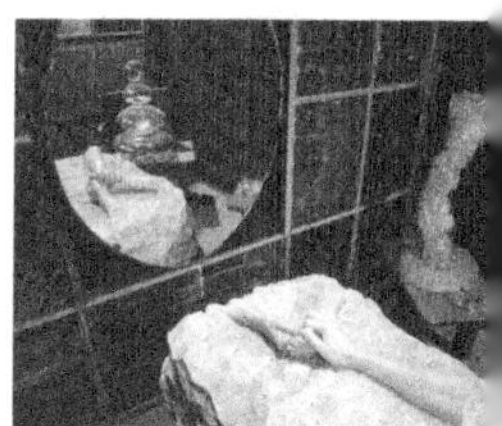

Louise Bourgeois, *Cell (You Better Grow Up)*, 1993

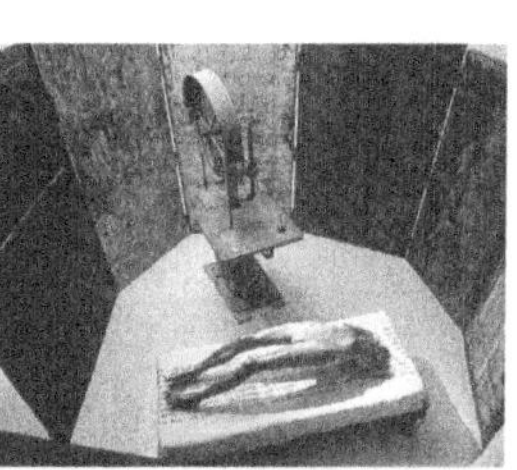

Louise Bourgeois, *Cell (Arch of Hysteria)*, 1992–1993

A.B. Novikoff and E. ltmann, *Cells and Organelles* 970), quoted in Crone and af Schaesberg, *Louise urgeois*, p. 88.

Louise Bourgeois, quoted in one and Graf Schaesberg, *uise Bourgeois*, p. 105.

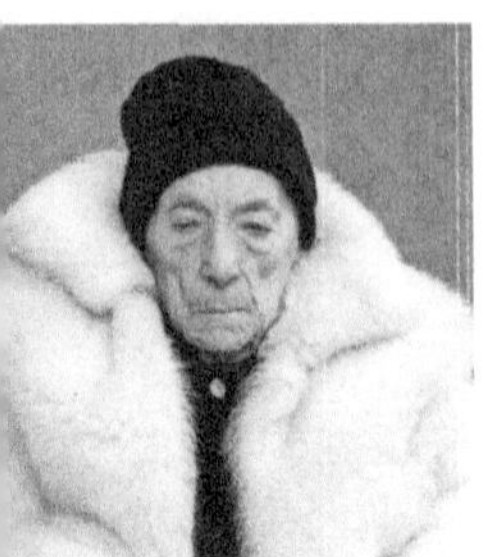

uise Bourgeois (1911–2010)

materials establish. To better understand that unity, one should assess the generic title of these assemblage sculptures: *Cells*.

The noun 'cell' has several meanings and connotations and they all seem relevant for an understanding of Bourgeois's *Cells*. First of all, a cell suggests an architectonic structure or space of which it is part, like a prison, a cloister, or a honeycomb. These spaces may connote a friendly as well as hostile living space with psychological repercussions, such as voyeurism and imprisonment, but the cell is also a biological and physical element, a prototype of life: the smallest physical or biological structure that condenses all ramifications and features of life into one single cell. According to the scientific discipline of cell theory, 'an intact cell is the simplest structure that displays all the characteristics of life'.[12] This suggests that Bourgeois's assemblage sculptures display all the features of her own, personal existence, because her own life and that of her family is the 'smallest structure' which can be seen as 'a prototype of life'. The unity of her assembled constructions brings together elements, objects, and histories which have determined her existence in life. The family she was born into is central to her perspective on her own existence. Bourgeois defines the pursuit she tried to realize in the *Cells* as an effort 'to understand what we are about, to scrutinize ourselves':

> [...] because of the symbolic quality of the thing.
> I worked with found objects, and I found a magic overtone in them. What counts, our whole purpose, is to try to understand, what we are about, to scrutinize ourselves. Art is an aid to this.[13]

In these sentences, Bourgeois does not only articulate what she wanted to convey with her *Cells*, but she also explains why she used the sculptural logic of assemblage. Although her *Cells* do not exclusively consist of found objects, she explains why an assemblage of found objects is effective in her effort to understand herself. It is the symbolic overtone of things that brings about this understanding performatively. The fact that she describes her *Cells* as consisting of 'found objects' can also mean that she might use works she had made in the past and 'found' in her studio.

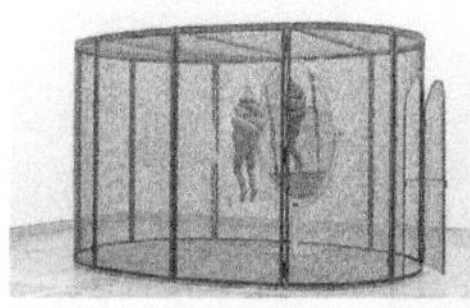

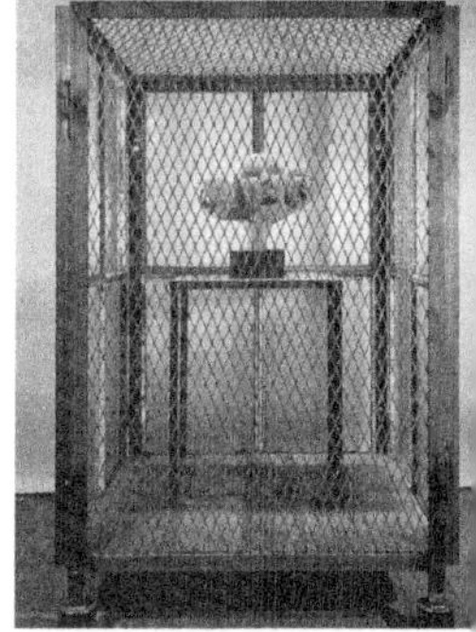

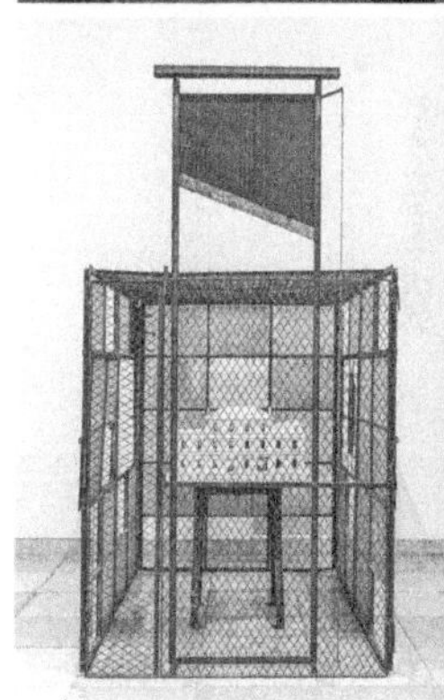

Louise Bourgeois, *Cell XXVI*, 2003; *Cell XIV (Portrait)*, 2000 *Cell (Choisy)*, 1990–1993

Dadaist and Surrealist assemblages were less emphatically personal: they used and made manifest various elements that constituted modernity and fuelled erotic and political desires. At first, the boxes of Joseph Cornell (often categorized as Surrealist) look like miniature versions of Bourgeois's *Cells*, but his boxes do not confine or imprison like her cells do. We do not voyeuristically look into an inner world, but gaze with wonder into a *Wunderkammer*, a cabinet of curiosities, which displays for the public eye a wide variety of objects that can be encountered in modern life. Bourgeois's assemblages are sculptures we do not look at but look into. In that respect, they do not belong generically to the medium of installation, although a diversity of elements is 'installed' in iron cages or confining structures constituted of old wooden doors and window frames. As explained before, the viewer relates in a different way to sculpture than to installation. Whereas the viewer stands before and walks around sculpture, s/he walks through an installation that surrounds her. We are not supposed to walk into Bourgeois's *Cells*; we can peep into or investigate them. That difference defines them as sculpture instead of installation.

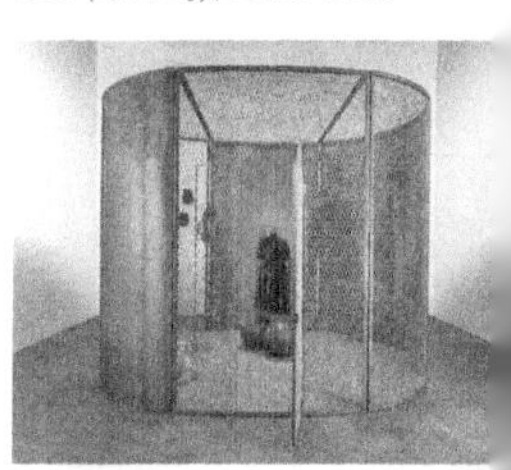

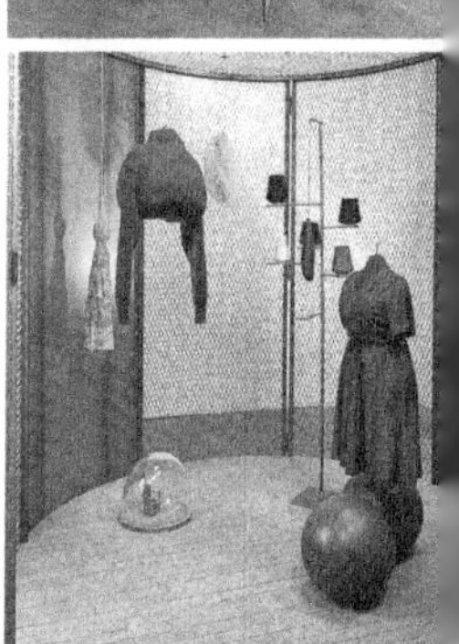

Louise Bourgeois, *Cell (Black Days)*, 2006, and its interior

As already said, Bourgeois's *Cells* invoke a personal world. But what 'personal' exactly means is not yet clear. What is it that generates this enclosed space? I will quote Bourgeois at length, because she is very articulate on the specific meaning of the *Cells*, on what they share with her other sculptures, and also, conversely, how they differ from them.

> The subject of pain is the business I am in. To give meaning and shape to frustration and suffering. What happens to my body has to be given a formal shape. So you might say, pain is a ransom of formalism. The existence of pains cannot be denied. I propose no remedies or excuses. I simply want to look at them and talk about them. I know I can't do anything to eliminate or suppress them. I can't make them disappear; they're here to stay.[14]

In the quote that follows she throws light on how the *Cells* deal with the more general 'business' of pain in a very specific way:

> The Cells represent different types of pain: the physical, the emotional and psychological, and the mental and intellectual. When does the emotional become physical? When does the physical become emotional: It's a circle going around and around. Pain can begin at any point and turn in either direction. Each Cell deals with fear. Fear is pain. Often it is not perceived as pain, because it is always disguising itself. Each Cell deals with the pleasure of the voyeur, the thrill of looking and being looked at. The Cells either attract or repulse each other. There is the urge to integrate, merge, or disintegrate.[15]

The pain her work addresses is personal and happens to her body. The *Cells*, however, represent different pains, the physical, the emotional, the psychological, the mental and the intellectual in intimate interaction with each other. Her remarks make clear what the 'business' or 'stuff' of the *Cells*

Louise Bourgeois, quoted in …rone and Graf Schaesberg, …ouise Bourgeois*, p. 81.

Louise Bourgeois, quoted in …rone and Graf Schaesberg, …ouise Bourgeois*, p. 81.

is, in other words, what they represent. Another remark made by Bourgeois reveals what enables these representations of different pains:

> I need my memories. They are my documents. I keep watch over them. They are my privacy and I am intensely jealous of them. Cézanne said: 'I am jealous of my little sensations'. To reminisce and woolgather is negative. You have to differentiate between memories. Are you going to them or are they coming to you here? If you are going to them you are wasting time, you are wasting time. Nostalgia is not productive. If they come to you, they are the seeds for sculpture.[16]

Memories that stalk her cause the diversity of pains and make her aware of them. These memories are utterly productive: they produce her private as well as her artistic world. This explains Bourgeois's jealousy, because although these memories are hers, she owns them, one could say; they cannot be conflated with her.

Her working method of assemblage is effective in this respect because it is relational. Through assembling different objects in an enclosed space, she connects different memories, relating herself to different surroundings and different persons. Memories of the small family she came from, of her father and mother, are the ongoing preoccupation in most of the *Cells*. *Cell I* (1991), for example, is a spiral-shaped space that consists of old doors, linked together by hinges. One of these doors has glass panels through which the viewer can peep in. The doors themselves are highly symbolic: 'These doors have endured outbursts of rage, have stood open as mediators, been pushed shut to create division, been locked to keep secrets, have kept out prying eyes.'[17] But now the handles and locks have been removed; in the assemblage the

16 Louise Bourgeois, quoted in Meyer-Thoss, *Louise Bourgeois*, p. 155.

17 Crone and Graf Schaesberg, *Louise Bourgeois*, p. 92.

[1]8 Crone and Graf Schaesberg, [L]ouise Bourgeois, p. 94.

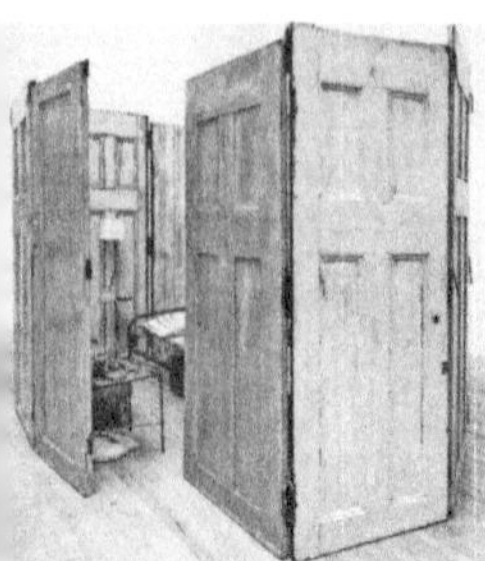
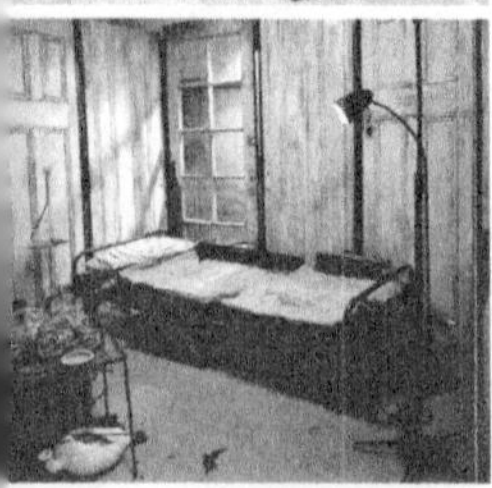
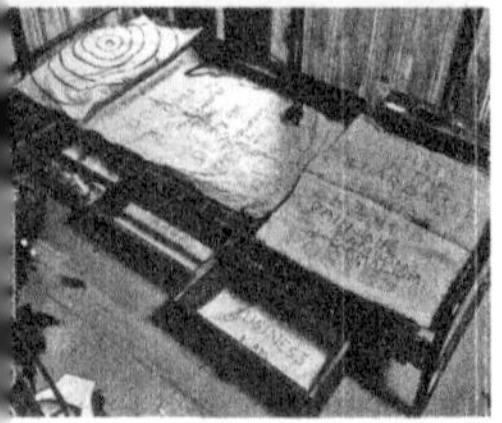
[L]ouise Bourgeois, *Cell I*, 1991

doors remain unlocked. This changes their status as mediators: the spiral structure is open to the public, although only through one opening between two doors and through the glass panels of one door.

When we look through the gap between two doors we gain a partial view of the inside and discover an iron bedstead, a standing lamp, a clothes stand, and a table with a lot of objects on top of it. Through the glass door one can get a better overview of the interior space of the *Cell*. One window frame turns out to be without glass, so the viewer can even stick her head inside and look around. The impression one already had becomes a reality. In the narrow space objects crowd together. In this cluttered environment what immediately catches the eye are folded sacks from the French mail service POSTES FRANCE lying on the springs of the iron bed and in drawers hidden under this bed. Like the old doors, these sacks are highly symbolic: 'Now torn and partly patched, these sacks once crossed the Atlantic filled with letters of hope, anxiety, trust, dreams, congratulations, and bereavement.'[18] Onto these sacks Bourgeois has embroidered short sentences in red thread. There is a mix of print capitals and handwriting, as if written, or in fact embroidered, by a child who has just learned to write. The short, embroidered texts on the sacks on the bed run as follows: 'I need my memories, they are my documents', 'Art is the Guarantee of Sanity', 'Pain is the Ransom of Formalism'; the texts on sacks in the drawers are: 'Rage' and 'is the Business I am'. All these texts seem to assess the inner life of Louise Bourgeois, the artist with a painful youth in France who subsequently migrated to New York. This installation seems to work through the memories of this past. These memories are clearly not just pleasant, but also traumatic, as the words 'pain', 'rage', and 'sanity' suggest. At the head of the bed lies a cushion on

which a spiral of circles is painted. Also, the old doors are placed in spiral form. Bourgeois has made many sculptures in which the form of a spiral can be recognized, such as *Spiral Woman* (1984) and *Spiral/Summer* (1960). In *Cell XXVI* (2003), a spiral woman hangs from the ceiling, this time made from textile. In 2019, the publisher Damiani published the book *Louise Bourgeois: Spiral,* which collects a great number of her works with spirals, among them many drawings. This recurrent motif in Bourgeois's work can be recognized in the macro-structure of *Cell I* (1991), as well as in its details.
The form of the spiral is for Bourgeois chaos and order at the same time, or rather, it is the attempt to order chaos:

> To me the spiral is a form of arranging chaos. The spiral is completely continuous, predictable or infinite. It is a form of disorientation: you don't know whether its direction comes from the right or the left, [...]. The references that man needs to live in an orderly way disappear.[19]

The arranging of chaos is also clearly at stake on the seat of the chair and on the low wooden table next to the iron bed. Both are being used as storage space for screws and fittings, frayed rope, glass bottles, bulbous retorts and long-necked phials, pliers, a whisk, and a machete. The instruments of chemical analysis and synthesis seem to be life-destroying and life-bringing at the same time. The chaos is not complete, because there is a suggestion of coherence between the cluttered objects. Under the chair is a white chamber pot and next to the wooden table a dusty kettle; on the bedside table lies a book with the word 'tuberculosis'. Many more objects are part of this ordered chaos, but the overall impression it makes is one of frailty, illness, and suffering.

Cell I is emblematic of Bourgeois's notion of assemblage. The chaotic ordering of assembled objects prevents the

19 Louise Bourgeois, in Gorovoy and Asbaghi, *Louise Bourgeois*, p. 170.

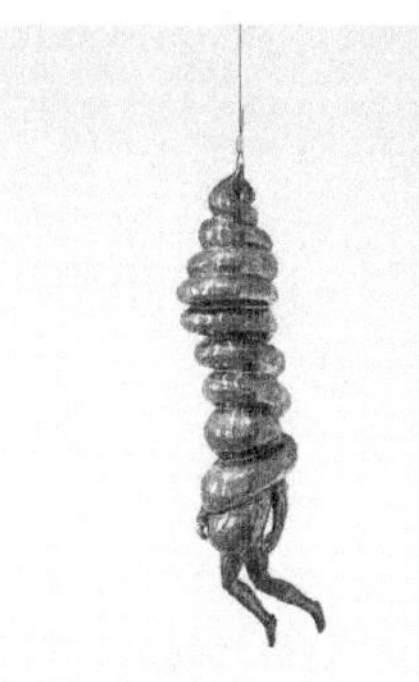

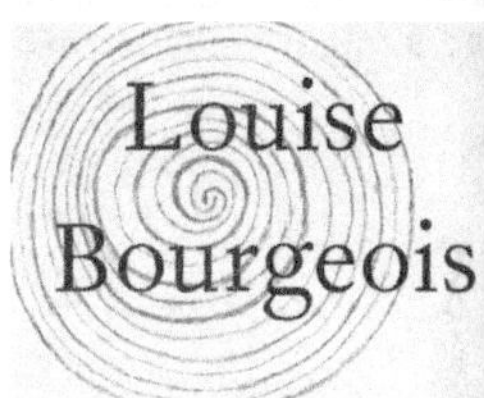

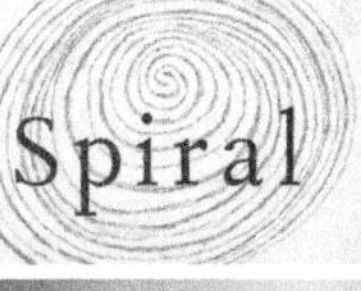

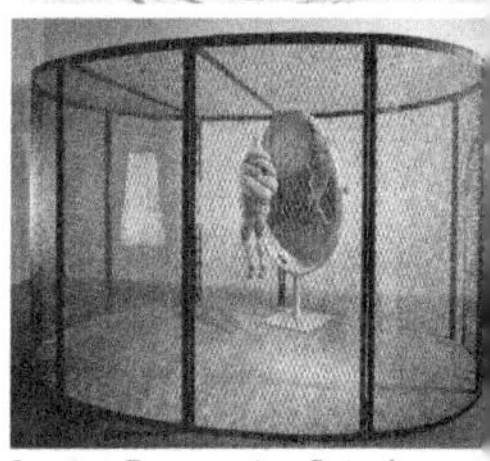

Louise Bourgeois, *Spiral Woman*, 1984; *Spiral*, publication 2019; *Cell XXVI*, 2003

viewer's gaze from paying too much attention to each individual object. No clear or fixed image comes about before our eyes. In the words of Crone and Schaesberg:

> [...] it invalidates the attempt—taking place in our heads—to create some kind of logical structure. As it is not possible to distinguish any fully worked-out composition, the chaos that we are to experience must not be structured—the form must be such that it admits of chaos, a form that must be compatible with disorder.[20]

Although not all of Bourgeois's *Cells* are as cluttered with such diverse objects as *Cell I*, one can say that this environmental sculpture aptly demonstrates her contribution to the logic of assemblage. The kind of unity that her assemblages performatively bring about is 'chaotic and dispersed'. But that is exactly the point: the unity is that of Bourgeois's privacy, her personal, inner world. That world is chaotic because it is a mixture of hope, anxiety, trust, dreams, anger, pain, and bereavement. The assembled objects imprison her and display all the characteristics of her life—the cell itself provides the unity. It is important to note that the unity is not based on narrative, on a representation of a coherent sequence of events.[21] The assembled objects have symbolic meanings and it is the interaction between these symbolic meanings that brings about, performatively, the personal inner world of Louise Bourgeois. The more uncluttered *Cells* she made after *Cell I* include *Cell (You Better Grow Up)* (1993), which does not consist of a spiral of old wooden doors, but rather a cube and a steel cage with a steel raster, and contains relatively few objects. Two following *Cells*, *Red Room (Parents)* (1994) and *Red Room (Child)* (1994) consist again of spirals of old wooden doors and are much more cluttered with objects than the *Cells* consisting of steel cages. But the relative

Gorovoy and Asbaghi, *[Lo]uise Bourgeois*, p. 97.

For a clear notion of story[te]lling and narrative, see Bal, *[Na]rratology*. In her *Narratology [in] Practice* she analyses [Bo]urgeois's *Cell Spider*, [pp]. 47–51.

difference between disordered and more ordered *Cells* has no implication for how these assemblage sculptures work on the basis of an interaction between connotations and symbolic meanings of the assembled objects.

The viewer gains easy access to *Cell (You Better Grow Up)* through the iron raster that covers the steel cube. In contrast to *Cell I*, this sculpture radiates not feelings of chaos and rage, but well-being and care. Centre stage is a perfectly crafted marble sculpture of three arms.

> Two tiny hands lie folded, relaxed and composed, almost meditating, in their own lap. They activate no reference beyond themselves; they do not aspire to mean. Solemnly they receive the blessing of the large hand that tenderly touches the others and protects them.[22]

22 Crone and Graf Schaesberg *Louise Bourgeois*, p. 100.

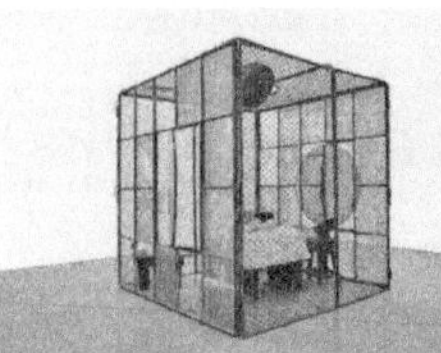

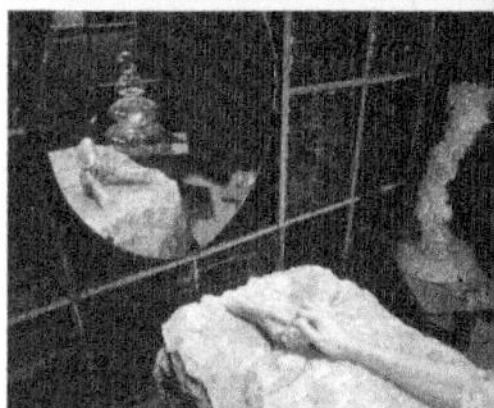

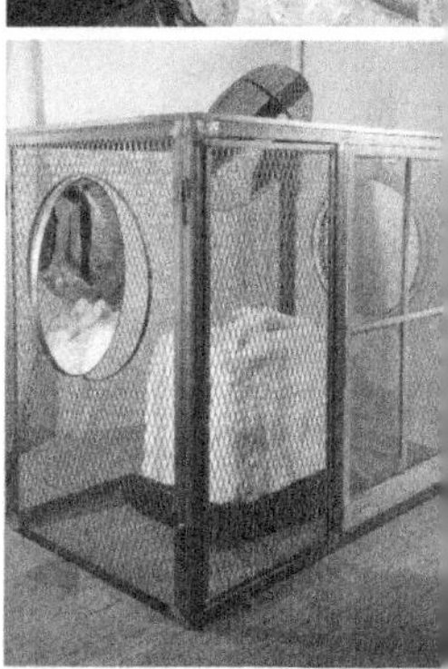

Louise Bourgeois, *Cell (You Better Grow Up)*, 1993

These tender and fragile gestures of three hands rest upon a ton-weight of unpolished pink marble that on its turn rests on heavy steel carriers. The impression of the lightness of the hands and the heaviness of the double consoles on which they are placed are in sharp contrast. The base is solid and will last forever. A glass vessel comprising three bulbous, stacked shapes contains a glass and a transparent female figure with her arms missing; just a torso. Three perfume bottles are placed on a plateau. Three adjustable mirrors are placed within the cage, one fixed to its ceiling. These mirrors do not confirm the image the viewer has of this *Cell*, but introduce many new perspectives that fracture the image one has. Bourgeois herself has provided a reading of this *Cell* that suitably demonstrates how this assemblage sculpture evokes symbolically and connotatively her inner world occupied with memories of her youth:

> The tiny figure inside the stacked glass shapes is cut off

3 Louise Bourgeois, quoted in
rone and Schaesberg, *Louise
ourgeois*, p. 101.

4 For an extensive reading of
pider (Cell) see Bal, *Louise
ourgeois' Spider.*

5 David Hammons, quoted in
booklet from the Pinault
ollection, Paris.

> from the world. That's me. The little hands are mine. They are self-portraits. I identify with the dependent one. The world that is described and realized is the frightening world of a child who doesn't like being dependent and who suffers from it. So the moral of this Cell is, you better grow up.[23]

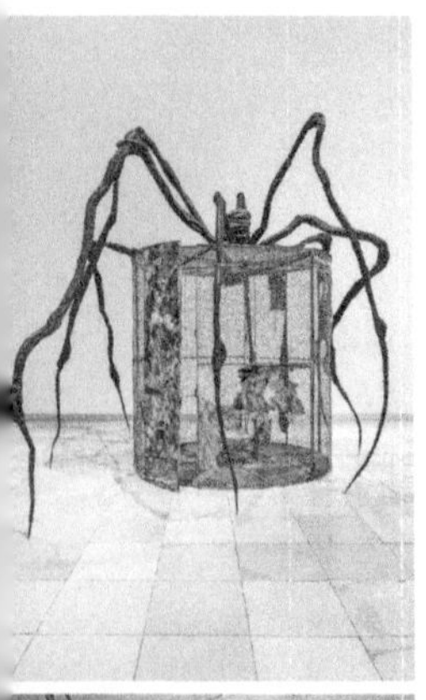

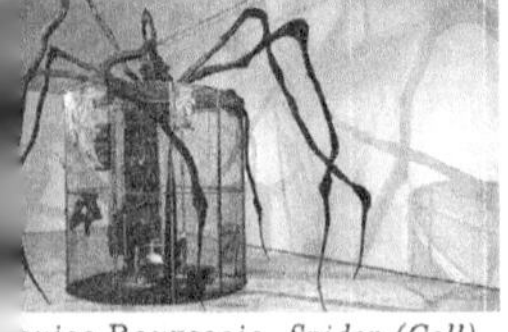

ouise Bourgeois, *Spider (Cell)*,
97

The transparent female figure without arms embodies this problematic dependency symbolically. Although the first impression one gets, especially on the basis of the three arms, is one of well-being and care, the other assembled objects introduce conflicting connotations and meanings. The care with which the girl was treated was exceedingly 'heavy' and 'loaded', which explains the extremely solid base of a giant block of marble on two iron carriers. The *Cell* titled *Spider* (1997) evokes the heaviness of care, this time maternal care in yet another way. On top of a steel cage an enormous spider seems to protect the cell on which it rests. The spider is a recurrent motif in Bourgeois's work. She has made many spider sculptures, similar to the one here which is part of this *Cell*. Her ambivalence towards her mother is embodied by the ambivalent insect of the spider. The spider/mother's protection is at the same time imprisonment.[24]

Harlem Rubble: David Hammons

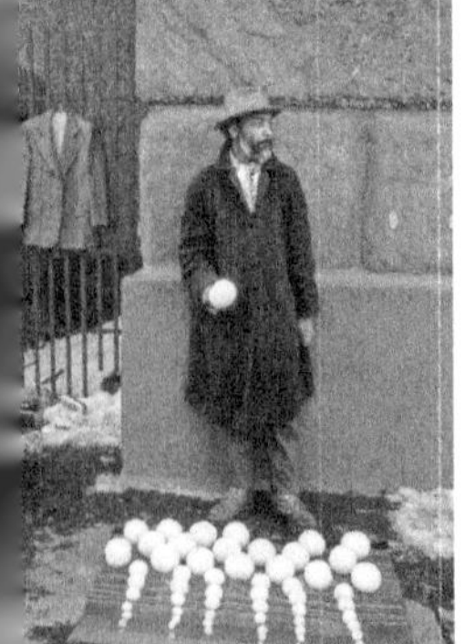

avid Hammons (1943), during
e of his performances in
HO in 1983 selling ice balls
different sizes

American artist David Hammons frames his own work in the most astute way via the following remark:

> It's not new. What I'm doing, these are old tools that the white boys have been using, but I'm using it to bring my culture through theirs, like we bring our culture through the European ancestors.[25]

Although very astute, he forgets that white girls have also been using the tool or technique of assemblage, for instance Méret Oppenheim and Louise Bourgeois, among several others. In Hammons's works of assemblage one can recognize the Duchampian legacy of readymade objects and materials, and witty puns, in addition to the Situationist engagement with street life. But here what is new is that all the materials and objects he assembles are from a black neighbourhood, Harlem; all these objects are old and used and are testimonies of black life in the US. For instance, after having moved to New York (Harlem) in the nineteen-eighties, he made a series of works related to basketball. This sport is synonymous with black culture, first of all because it is pervasive in urban street culture, particularly in black neighbourhoods like Harlem and the Bronx. Second, because of the systematic issue that predominantly African-American players perform in predominantly white-owned professional teams. For one of his best-known works he made for public space he transformed some towering telegraph poles in Brooklyn into basketball hoops, giving these assembled hoops the title *Higher Goals* (1986). This title poetically refers to 'African-American aspirations toward careers in professional sports, one of the few avenues to meteoric success for young Black men'.[26] The work *Basketball-Chandelier* from 2000 evokes this glorious future of young black men in yet another way: through the festive lights of baroque chandeliers connoting wealth.

26 Quotation from a booklet published by the Pinault Collection, Paris.

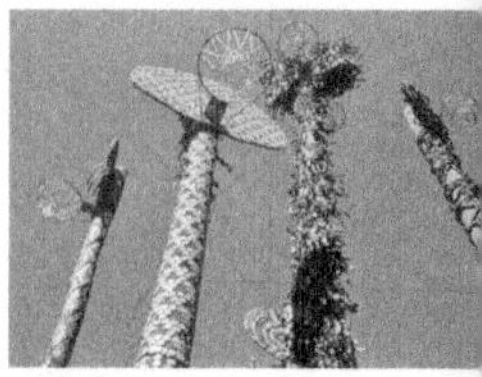

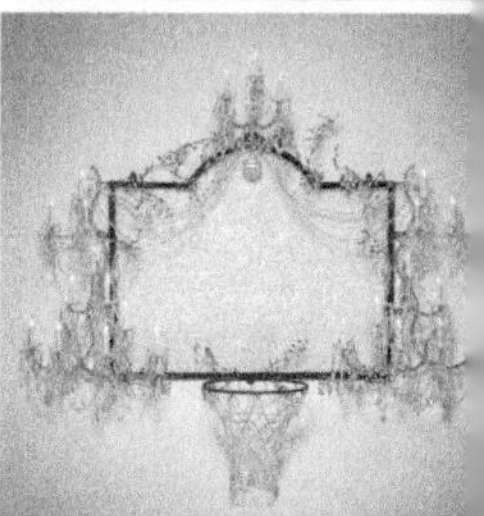

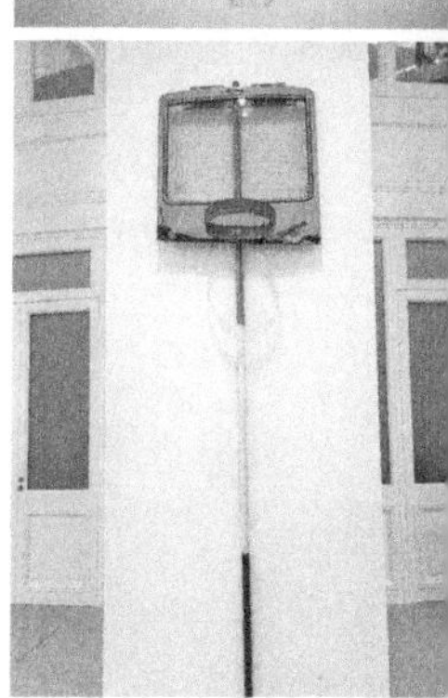

David Hammons, *Higher Goals* 1986; *Basketball-Chandelier*, 2000; *Untitled*, 1989

The telegraph poles of the work *Higher Goals*, topped with basketball hoops, were covered with thousands of bottle caps, especially from beer bottles.

> Some of these regal obelisks carried diamond, zigzag, and chevron designs on their mosaic-like surfaces, their

tight configurations reminiscent of snakeskin, Islamic decoration, African textiles or even the patterns on Hammons' earlier hair quilts.[27]

Jones, 'The Structure of ...th and the Potency of Magic', 28.

Jones, 'The Structure of ...th and the Potency of Magic', 31.

Jones, 'The Structure of ...th and the Potency of Magic', 33.

Besides the bottle caps he collects on the streets of Harlem, Hammons also uses bottles, bricks, cereal boxes, trees, chicken bones, gold chains, and reproductions of Louis Vuitton bags (real ones cannot be found in Harlem) for his assemblages. For a period of time, he preferred to work with empty wine bottles, especially Night Train and Thunderbird varieties, the least expensive forms of alcohol available in Harlem and, therefore, the most pervasive brands found on the streets. He fashioned the sea-green glass bottles into arches and circles; sometimes these curves were interrupted by one or two bottles still contained in their brown paper bags.[28]

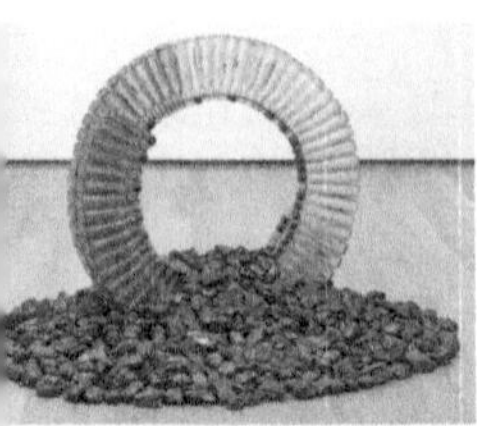

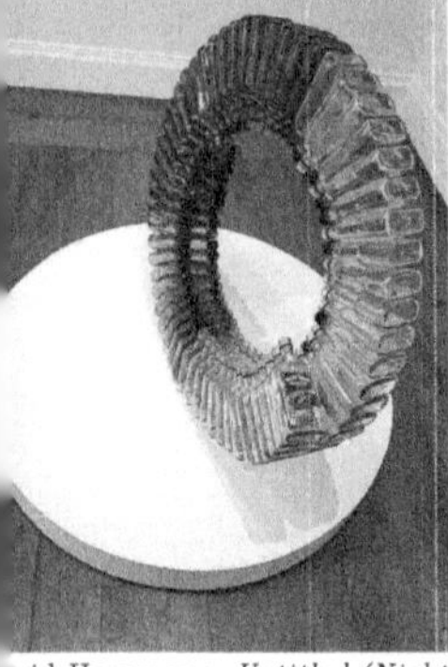

...vid Hammons, *Untitled (Night ...ain)*, 1989

The Night Train and Thunderbird bottles are not just fascinating in their form and colour; they also tell stories and allude to black history in the US:

> The train figures prominently in African American culture and lore: there's the underground railroad (the network by which slaves escaped to freedom); Freedom train (metaphorically 'ridden' by "freedom riders" during the 1960s); train porters (this was a respectable job for African American men in the twentieth century). The blues is full of train metaphors, which are also used in jazz and rhythm and blues. The 'A train' (the song by Duke Ellington about the subway line that goes to Harlem); 'Night Train' (in addition to being a cheap high, popular with those down on their luck, is an early piece by James Brown); John Coltrane (the legendary jazz saxophonist is often referred to as Trane). Finally, there is the idea of African Americans "living on the other side of the tracks" in a segregated society.[29]

Through these allusions to African American culture in the US, his assemblages with Night Train and Thunderbird bottles function as visual puns.

30 Jones, 'The Structure of Myth and the Potency of Magic', p. 34.

Hammons employs the logic of assemblage by recycling materials, objects, ideas, images, and stereotypes. By reusing them he disarms and deconstructs stereotypical images; he recontextualizes them, an act by which their meanings change or take on different connotations. His visual puns do not work in the same way for his audience. As Kellie Jones explains: 'There are gestures for both the initiates and non-initiates of African American culture; there is visual stimulation for different levels of cognition, something for everyone.'[30] Steve Cannon has described beautifully how Hammons's visual-pun-assemblages work—in the rhythm of African American hip-hop. I will quote him at length because his description is a great, impressive demonstration of the artist's use of assemblage:

> Say, U are into modes—in your solitude—The A Train—Coltrane—The F train—The D—straight to Queens—travelling undersound of Jass—Like, Jass Me, Jass me baby, all night long! Into Nightrain—Into provokin' emotions all day long—Like take that Isle of Manhattan—that twelve miles isle, & make it Over in yr own image, like Wynton Marsalis like Miles, Clifford Brown, Cat Anderson, Diz & Fats Navarro! Like those B-boys on Home-boy turf—the quickest way to get from Harlem—say U'r into art the High & the Low—into trashing whole cultures! Into Putting on the Ritz—into sledge hammers & Axes—say Lucky Strikes into scenes— Fashions, styles, attitudes—into modes of Higher Goals—Jailhouse Blues—the Mayor as a Dunce—the President, a Fool, the original Fall guy—

Cannon, 'David Hammons' ew York', pp. 41–42.

Cannon, 'David Hammons' ew York', p. 55.

David Hammons, quoted in nkelpearl, 'On the Ideology of rt', p. 79.

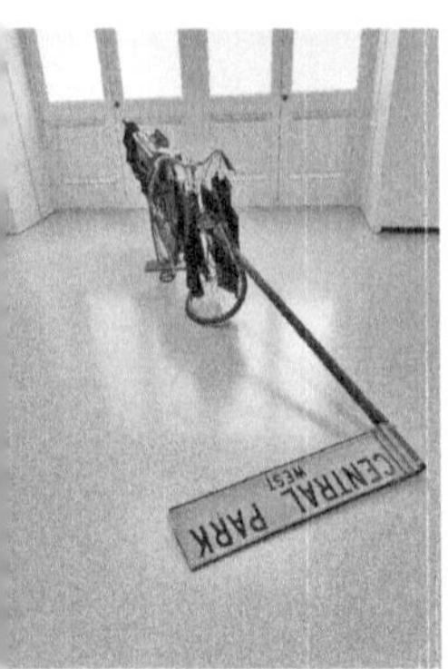

avid Hammons, *Central Park est*, 1990

> Putting on the Culture walking round Harlem![31]

Moreover, I cannot resist quoting Cannon's evocative description of Hammons's assemblages in public space, this time more in the style of John Dos Passos's novel *U.S.A*:

> Public art works Latrines and an assortment of places in space to relieve one's self nobody's nobody check the body language made over into features those most sacred of ancient traditions into monkey shines into shoeshines Got a dime? She's so fine![32]

Although not all of Hammons's works are made for public space, it is understandable that he prefers to see his work there, because it is the same public space where his assemblages originate:

> I think I spend eighty-five percent of my time on the streets as opposed to in the studio. So, when I go to the studio, I expect to regurgitate these experiences of the street. All of the things I see socially—the social conditions of racism—come out like a sweat.[33]

One could also understand Hammons's assemblages as environmental art: he works with the social meaning of specific sites, especially his neighbourhood Harlem. The site of Harlem is segregated, poor, unfinished, and in many respects dirty. He transforms the site by adding assemblage sculptures to its social space. The distinction between social meaning and aesthetic meaning becomes fluid, since the aesthetic of these works transform the social meaning of the site.

Cluttering Time and Space: Heringa/Van Kalsbeek

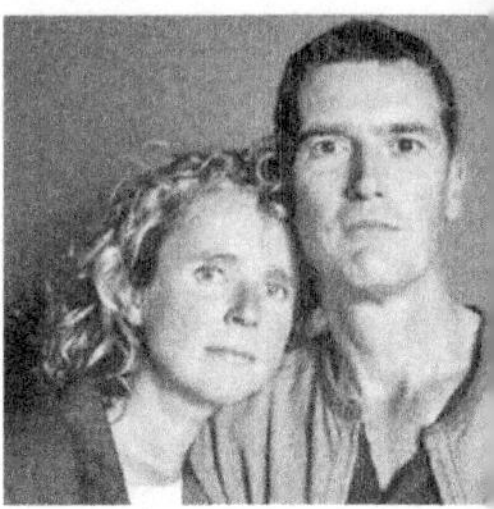
Heringa/Van Kalsbeek (1966 and 1962)

The assemblage works of Dutch artists Liet Heringa and Maarten van Kalsbeek offer a new dimension to assemblage sculpture. Their works consist of assembled material, objects, or fragments of them, and also techniques. Usually works that combine different techniques are not called assemblages but 'mixed techniques', but because Heringa/Van Kalsbeek assemble everything possible, not only materials and objects, 'assemblage' as an overall sculptural logic is more to the point. And as I will argue later, they also assemble 'forms'—their work is assemblage in the extreme, or rather, hyper-assemblage.

Another important feature of their assemblages is that they are cluttered. In the tradition of assemblage sculpture, the assembled materials and objects form a new unity; in that respect, they create order out of chaos. In the case of Heringa/Van Kalsbeek, this newly created unity is never fully convincing: they remain cluttered and disordered, and it is precisely their clutteredness that makes them powerful and fascinating. They violate the most basic principles of aesthetic perfection. What does that mean?

Conventional assemblages as we know them now from Dada and Surrealism mostly select objects that can be found in the dump store or the hardware store. David Hammons assembles objects that he finds on the streets of the black neighbourhood Harlem. The assemblage work of Heringa/Van Kalsbeek consists of materials and objects that are old as well as new, traditional as well as modern or ultra-modern, man-made as well as natural. The techniques they employ and 'assemble' in their works sometimes belong to the traditional sculptor, like casting, carving, or modelling clay or porcelain, or can be hyper-modern, like the modelling of glass fibre or polyurethane. The materials they use are

34 Marjan Boot, booklet on the occasion of the exhibition *Cruel Bonsai* in the Stedelijk Museum Amsterdam, 2007–2008, n.p.

time-honoured ones, such as stoneware and porcelain, and very modern ones, like the aforementioned glass fibre and polyurethane. 'The qualities of the materials are exploited to the utmost: the fragile white porcelain is gossamer thin; the elastic polyurethane is subjected to the maximum distortion.'[34] And they do not limit the objects for their assemblages to those that are handmade, like Duchamp did, but also use natural ingredients like bird wings, plant stems, or flowers. Their assemblages are hybrid in all respects.

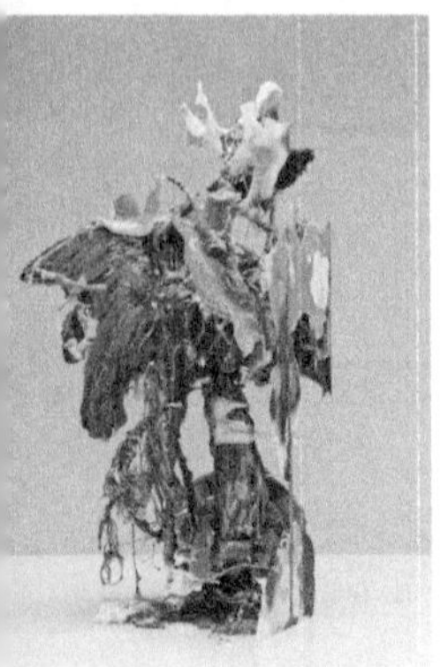

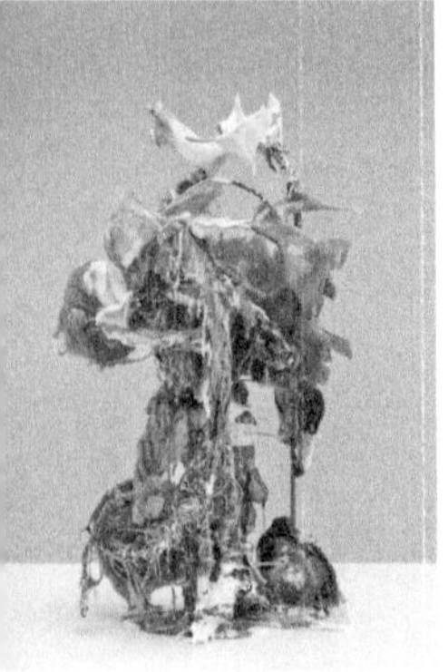

Heringa/Van Kalsbeek, *Untitled*, 2007

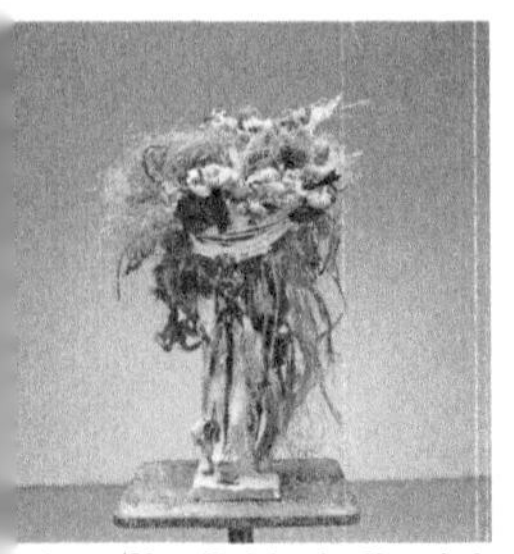

Heringa/Van Kalsbeek, *Untitled*, 2002

Heringa/Van Kalsbeek have also made works in only stoneware or porcelain. At first, these works cannot be considered as assemblage because there is no diversity of objects, materials, or even techniques combined in them. But still, they look like assemblages, even though they consist of one single technique and material. The only conventional element that evokes the idea of assemblage is that in many of the stoneware works a Chinese porcelain statuette forms the base on top, and around which stoneware or porcelain forms are assembled. Sometimes these forms represent something, and when they do they are often produced by a mould. Found objects from the natural world, such as pieces of coral and fresh buds, have been pressed into a mould and then cast in porcelain or synthetic resin. Yet the objects do not always stem from the natural world. The artists have also pressed the drippings under the lid of a tin of paint in a mould, the moulded forms subsequently assembled in a work with the iron frames of found leftovers of broken and discarded umbrellas and other stuff. But more often than not, the rather exuberant forms do not represent anything. We can conclude that their assemblages do not only assemble objects, materials or techniques, but also forms: sometimes these forms represent something, at other times they do not. So, even the works realized in one technique can still be called assemblage. Usually, the fragmented elements of an assemblage work are only the constituents of the final form of the work. In the case of Heringa/Van Kalsbeek, different forms, figurative or not, are assembled, and together they create a new hybrid form and object.

A Chinese porcelain statuette is a figure that repeatedly runs through their work. Years ago, they were able to buy a large number of these statuettes and ever since have used them as a central element in many of their sculptures. The porcelain figure is not an authentic artwork but an article mass produced by the Chinese ceramics industry. This simple, worthless, recurrent element in their works is in many respects emblematic of their notion of assemblage. Their assemblages are hybrid and globalized, or globalized and, as a result, hybrid. They do not simply bring together just man-made things (versus natural objects), nor things that signify modern life, Western life, that is (as Dadaist and Surrealist artists did, albeit sometimes with a bit of African 'primitivism'); they assemble whatever and from wherever.

This artist duo travel a lot, all over the world—they have had working visits to France, Italy, South Korea, Japan, New Guinea, and more. Their exhibition in the Stedelijk Museum in Amsterdam bore the appropriate title 'Cruel Bonsai', because part of that show was the result of a working visit to South Korea, and also because their works often look at once like miniature landscapes or trees and also artificial and handmade. Their 'bonsai' are cruel, because they look less like idealized, perfect landscapes and more like 'hysterical' landscapes: they violate all criteria for aesthetic and natural perfection. They make cluttered compositions, sometimes looking like 'dismantled machines, turned inside out'.[35] Their assemblages are triggered to an excessive degree by unlimited travelling, including virtual travelling on the internet.

35 Boot, 'Preface', n.p.

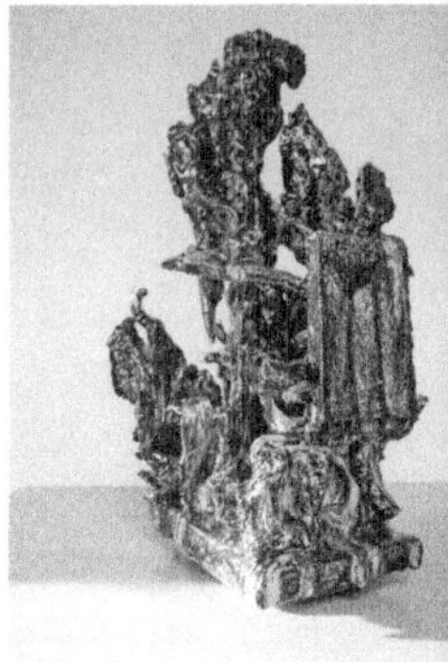

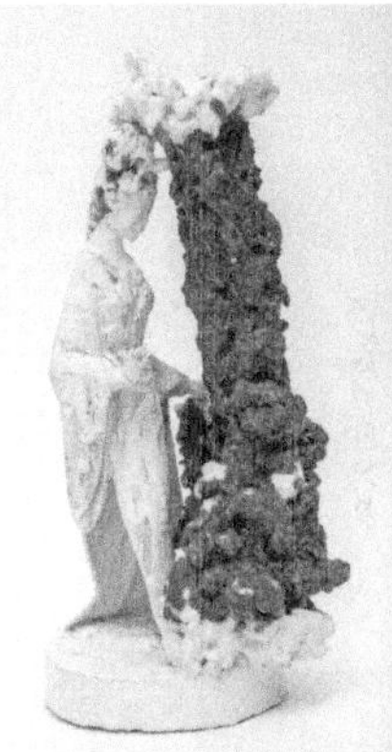

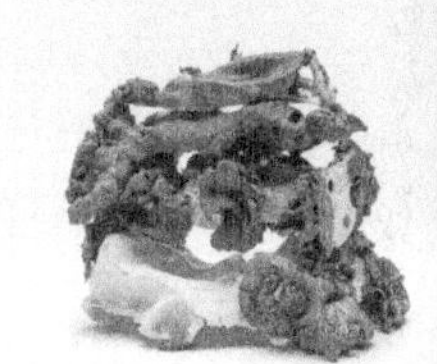

Heringa/Van Kalsbeek, *Untitl*[cut off] 1999; *Untitled*, 1999

Boot, 'Preface', n.p.

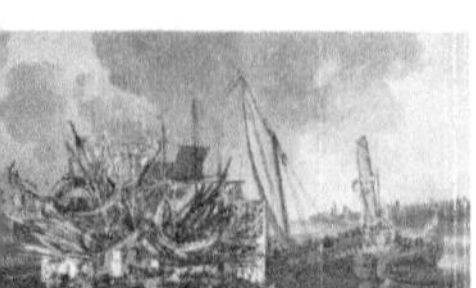

ringa/Van Kalsbeek, *rrowing Scenery* (2018), with eascape by Jan van de ppelle as the background

Globetrotting has become perfectly normal and the unfamiliar is now within anyone's reach:

> At the same time, the sensation of the unfamiliar has diminished in intensity. In mass tourism everything other, unfamiliar has been flattened. Traveling has been reduced to 'all-inclusive', all risks insured 'adventure' travels; to prefab experiences.[36]

Not only mass tourism contributes to the flattening of the unfamiliar and the exotic; the whole world is attainable via the internet. Heringa/Van Kalsbeek are children of their time, a time which is completely globalized and digitized.

Objects from the past found in second-hand stores, flea markets, or just in the street (like old umbrellas) are combined with Chinese porcelain statuettes, dead parakeets, and materials that are far from conventionally artistic and are hyper-modern, such as glass fibre and polyurethane. The assemblage of different materials and objects condenses time and space. The globalized world is all within reach and everything exists within one extended present. Past and future have ceased to play any role. It is this element that makes the assemblages of Heringa/Van Kalsbeek disturbing and critical in a very specific way.

When Duchamp presented an old umbrella on a stool in his *The Sculptor's Wife* it was a statement about art and artefacts; art is nothing other than an artefact, man-made. When Heringa/Van Kalsbeek include old umbrellas in the work *Borrowing Scenery* (2018) they are combined with objects and materials from very different contexts and temporal dimensions. Time and space are assembled and condensed in one single object embodying an extended present.

When the work *Borrowing Scenery* was shown in the old art gallery De Boer in Amsterdam, it was placed in front of a Dutch seventeenth-century seascape painting by Jan van de Cappelle. The work itself included a glass mirroring background as if it formed the stage of a theatre—the seascape was more than a nice background for this 'theatre'. Sculpture and seascape resonated so intensely that the old painting and the hyper-modern sculpture became one in colour and form. By means of their spatial proximity, their temporal distance was cancelled; they existed in one temporal present. The staging of this work in front of the painting was an assemblage in itself; a curatorial one.

The assemblage sculptures of Heringa/Van Kalsbeek are at their most powerful when they are disturbing, because they look like a cluttering of objects, materials, techniques, and forms. Cluttering implies disorder, and it is indeed the lack of order that makes their work critical about our present time of globalization and digitization. The extended present and place we live in has levelled difference in time and locality. The fact that it is, strangely enough, pleasing and pleasant to look at their cluttered assemblages demonstrates how unaware we are of the impact of globalization and digitization. The disorder of clutteredness has become a fact of our lives.

The artistic practices making use of the logic of assemblage discussed in this chapter commonly assemble elements, objects, and fragments, instead of being based on drawing, painting, modelling or carving. And entirely or in part, their constituent elements are preformed natural or manufactured materials, objects, or fragments not intended as art materials. These characteristics define them as assemblage. Yet as we have seen, they also differ in important respects: Bourgeois, Hammons, and Heringa/Van Kalsbeek deploy this logic in different ways, especially by evoking different unities between the assembled objects or elements. And although we can only speculate about where they assembled these objects and elements, their practices of assemblage also suggest that they derive from very different sources. Further, that difference has implications for how the viewer processes these assembled sculptures. Most conventional assemblages as we know them now from Dada and Surrealism select objects that can be found in the dump store or the hardware store. Although they can be found in the dump store, they connote modern life, because of the fast circulation of goods in the modern capitalist economy. The kind of unity that comes about performatively in these Surrealist and Dadaist encounters is aesthetic or bodily: an unexpected beauty or eroticism is the result.

I examined the *Cells* of Louise Bourgeois as assemblage sculpture because they are environmental sculptures consisting of different assembled objects. Some of the assembled objects were found or made in her own studio, while others were probably found in a dump store. This mixture of found objects gives rise to a world that is utterly personal. Instead of evoking modern life, economically or erotically, it opens the privacy of Bourgeois's youth and the small world of the family she grew up in. There are many documentaries and books about Bourgeois in which the details of her family history are revealed. I have not provided this biographical information because her assembled sculptures called *Cells* are powerful enough to open up her private world of their own accord.

The assemblages of David Hammons assemble objects that he found on the streets of Harlem. This location signifies an iconic place of black African history in the United States, and the objects he assembles in his sculptures reveal those very specific histories. It is these histories that form their unity.

The assemblage work of Heringa/Van Kalsbeek consists of materials and objects that are old as well as new, traditional as well as modern or ultra-modern, man-made as well as natural. Their work is in a certain sense hyper-assemblage, because it does not only assemble objects, fragments and different materials, but also different forms and techniques; and they come from all over the world and from different cultural backgrounds. It is this hyper-hybridity of their work that makes their assemblages emblematic for the globalized time and space we live in. The specificity of each of these bodies of work demonstrates how variations within the larger logic of assemblage clarify what the logic itself comprehends.

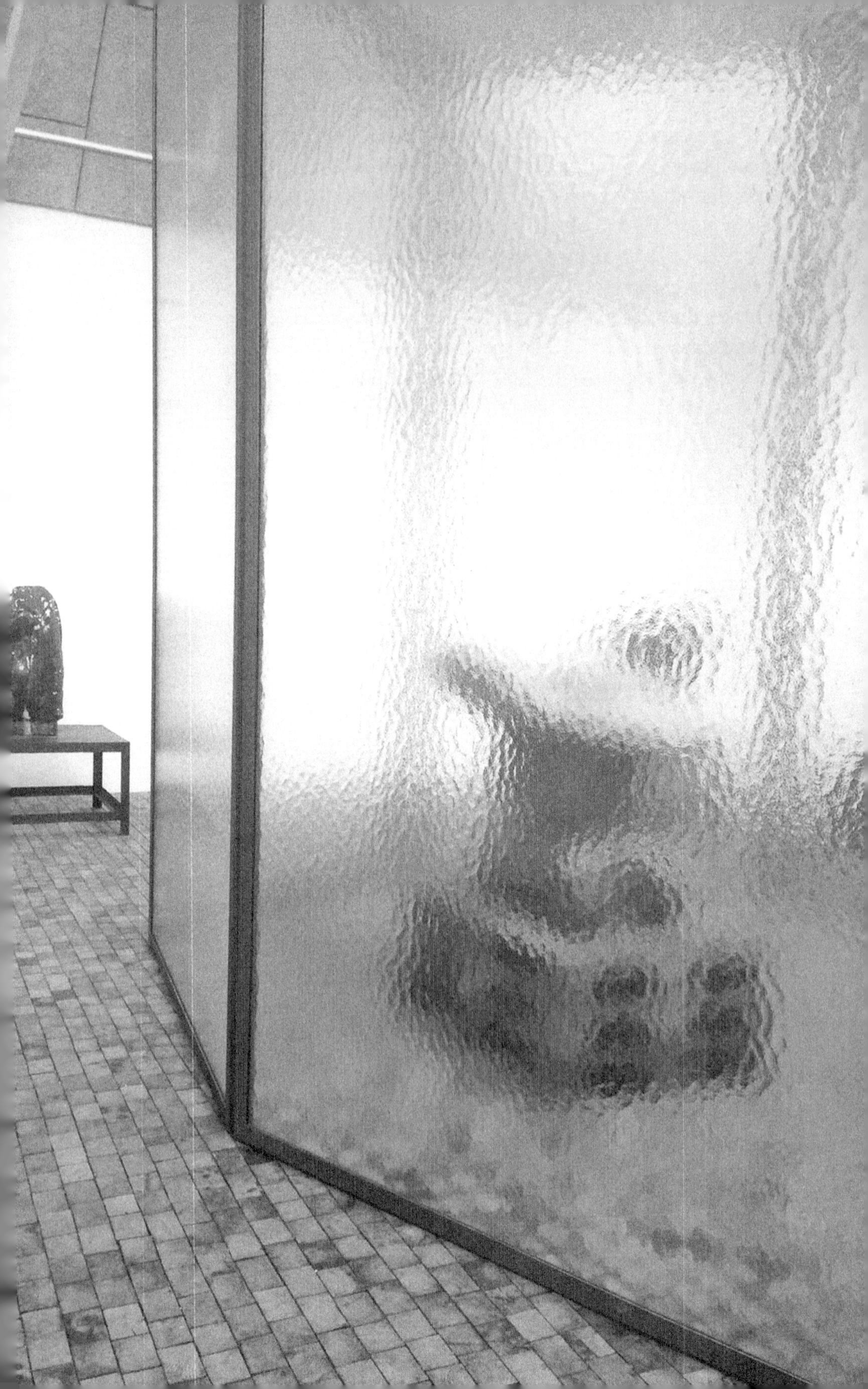

Architectural Sculpture

Viewing Positions and Viewing Modalities

When, in the nineteen-eighties, Dan Graham began to make his series of freestanding sculptural objects called *Pavilions* he blurred the line between sculpture and architecture. His *Pavilions* are glass and steel sculptures which viewers can walk into, as if in a small room. One associates the materials out of which the pavilions are made more with architecture than with sculpture, and the fact that these sculptures have an inner space which one can enter suggests that they *are* a kind of architecture. The glass panels are transparent, mirroring, or half-mirroring; that is, both reflective and transparent. Upon entering the space of the *Pavilions* viewers tend to get disoriented: the enclosed space differs slightly, but not radically, from their usual knowledge and experience of space. To categorize this kind of artistic practice as architectural sculpture seems self-evident because of the blurring of those two media. Although the embodied position of the viewer is always of great importance to sculpture, as I argued in the introduction to this book, in the case of architectural

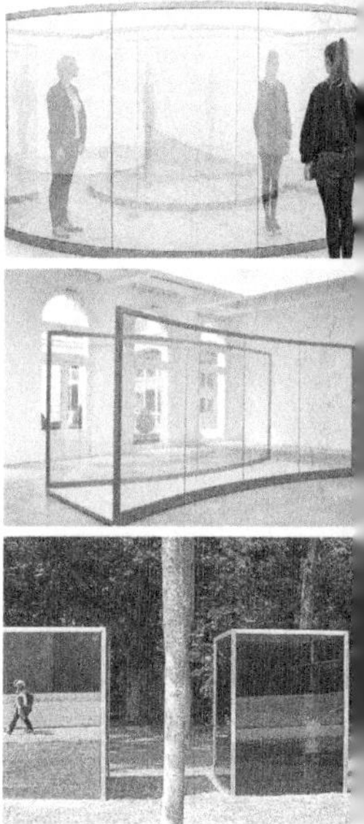

Dan Graham, *Tunnel of Love*, 2014; *Passage Intime*, 2015; *Tw Adjacent Pavilions*, 1978–2001

Marien Schouten, Museum Jorn, Silkeborg, Denmark, 2018

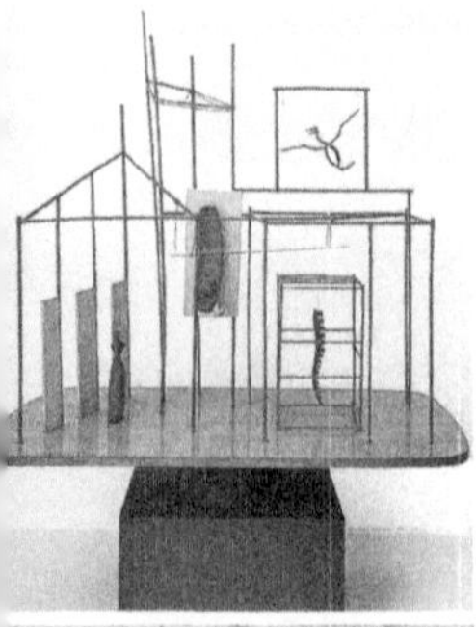

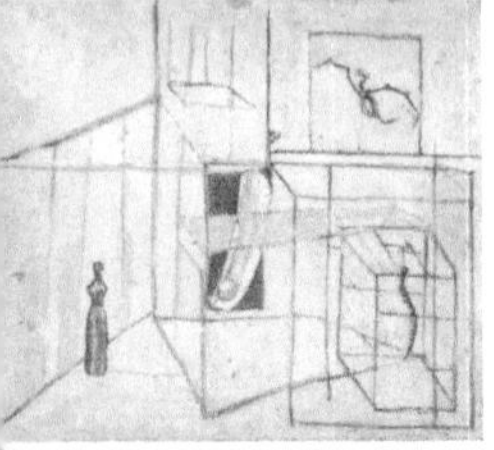

lberto Giacometti, *The Palace* *4 a.m.*, 1932; *Drawing of The* *alace at 4 a.m.*

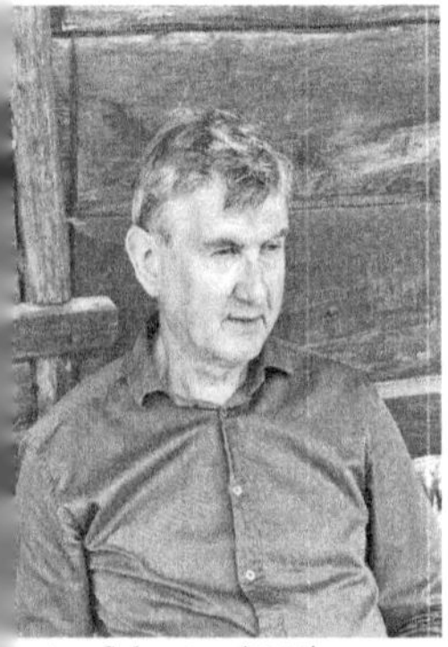

arien Schouten (1956)

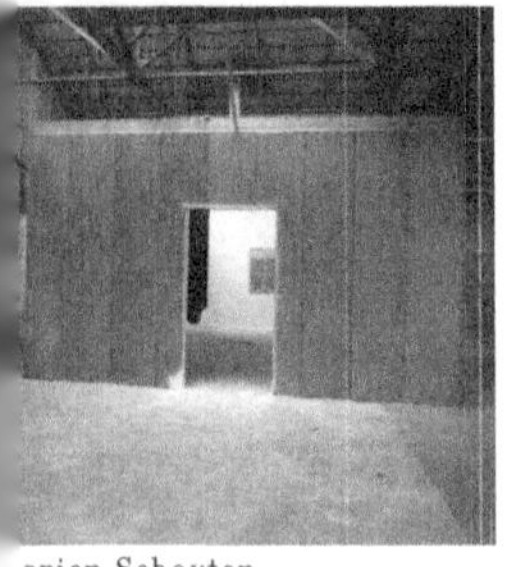

arien Schouten, *econstruction Studio*, 1987

sculpture the viewer's role plays an even more emphatic and explicit role.

Alberto Giacometti's well-known *The Palace at 4 a.m.* from 1932, now in the MoMA collection, also rises from the medium it belongs to; it is a sculpture, presented on a plinth, but what it represents is a room in which artworks are shown. It is like an architectural model of an exhibition space. In contrast with Dan Graham's *Pavilions*, the viewer relates in a rather conventional way to it, as with conventional sculpture. Although one can walk around it, the gestalt of the work is enough to understand it. Giacometti's work can be more easily understood as sculpture, albeit as an architectural space.

In this chapter I will assess the logic of architectural sculpture. What defines this logic and what are its fundamental elements? How does it differ from other sculptural logics intimately related to it? The format of the chapter differs slightly from the others in that instead of discussing several artists who all foreground different elements of the logic, I will mainly focus on one specific maker, the Dutch artist Marien Schouten. Although I will frame his work with other artists whose practice can also be understood as architectural sculpture, the main focus will be on Schouten's work, because in it the main features of the logic of architectural sculpture manifest themselves in all their complexity.

At the end of the nineteen-eighties, Marien Schouten made a work titled *Reconstruction Studio* (1987), an exact copy of the space of his own studio. In this 'room' Schouten displayed a framed drawing, a wall painting, and a drawing of a black surface covered by a grid of wooden slats. The reason why he displayed his own works in a reconstruction of his own studio was because his pieces 'need' a specific space and environment. The best way to see these works is in the space where they were made, for the work is conditioned by this space and depends on it.[1] One wonders if the notion of 'architectural sculpture' can also be applied to this 'room'. In the case of Dan Graham's *Pavilions*, the medial differences between sculpture and architecture are emphatically blurred. In the case of Schouten's *Rooms*, it is less clear which medium these objects/structures belong to and the kind of distinctions between media that are blurred.

1 Fuchs, 'Giotto's Circle'.

The work *A Reader's Bedroom* that he made in 2019 raises the same issues and questions: Is this work a room, or is it a representation of a room? Or is it not a real room, but an abstraction of a room? When we consider it to be a room, its medium is architecture. But when we consider it to be a representation or abstraction of a room, it can also be sculpture.

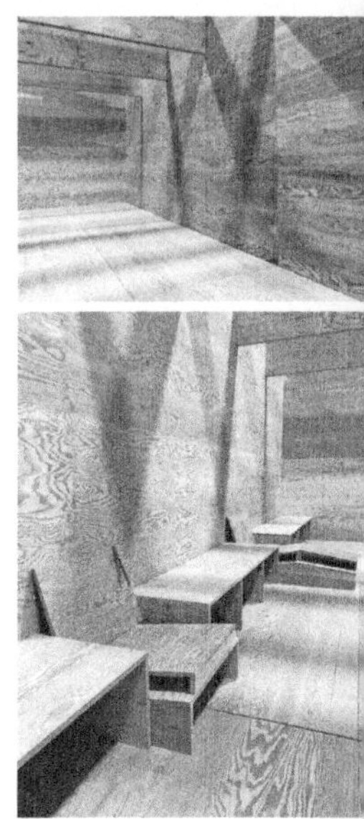

Marien Schouten, *A Reader's Bedroom*, 2019

Like *Reconstruction Studio, A Reader's Bedroom* is not a room in an existing building; it is a kind of wooden box with an entrance that looks like a door opening. It has a wooden floor consisting of wooden panels and it has a ceiling, made up of wooden beams, which compress the space and give it a strong horizontality. The room has no windows. Whereas the conventional room consists of the space demarcated by the walls, the floor and the ceiling, the space within, this room also has an outside. One can walk around the box-like room and see the outside structure of it. But the room is not empty: against the walls three wooden structures are extended from both the walls and floor. The room contains a chair, a small couch, and a bed. Next to the chair and the bed are constructions that look like bookshelves. These pieces of furniture are not moveable, but are built in, or part of the architecture of the room. The kind of architecture that is evoked here is very much like the houses of Frank Lloyd Wright, especially his so-called prairie houses, in which a great part of the furniture was built in and is actually part of the architecture. The fact that Wright built in some of the

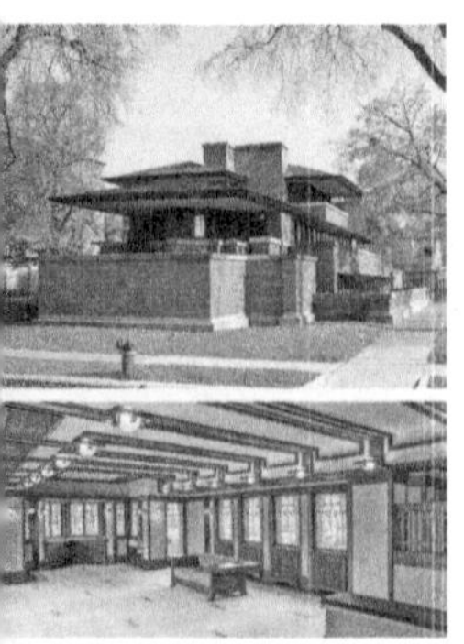

rank Lloyd Wright, Robie
ouse, Chicago, 1909

furniture is not arbitrary. It means that furniture is not seen as separate from his architectural concerns: it is part of the architecture, because the volumes of which Wright's kind of architecture consists translate themselves on a smaller scale in his furniture. This principle is even more recognizable when furniture is built in, and thus part of, the architectural construction. His moveable tables and chairs are, however, not fundamentally different because they also form volumes in the space (an empty, or negative volume) of the room. Hence, Schouten's chair, couch, and bed are not arbitrary additions to the room in order to suggest an interior for it; instead, they translate the architectural principles on a smaller scale. Wright's architecture is not only evoked by the built-in furniture, but also by the wooden beams that are used to create a ceiling. The strong horizontality suggested by these beams is a recurring feature of his prairie houses, for instance his well-known *Robie House* (1909) in Chicago. The horizontality emphasized by the wooden beams is almost 'felt' because of how it relates to the human scale: the ceilings in Wright's prairie houses, and also in Schouten's *A Reader's Bedroom*, 'feel' relatively low because they compress the space.

Because of its undecidability it seems appropriate to see *A Reader's Bedroom* as architectural sculpture, but the reasons to do so differ from why one understands Dan Graham's *Pavilions* in those hybrid terms. What Schouten's *Rooms* and Dan Graham's *Pavilions* have in common, however, is that they have an inside and an outside. From the perspective of sculpture, they take distance from traditional sculptural objects as closed solid shapes or objects. Their works are not self-supporting constructs but open structures of which each element helps to support the whole construction. This is why architectural sculpture seems to be the appropriate term for them.

The entanglement of the media of sculpture and architecture is relatively recent. Traditionally, sculpture and painting were considered to be similar, and in art theory the view was that they were both grounded in the mastery of drawing. The difference between painting and sculpture was grounded in different modes of execution—the execution of sculpture required different skills and was made of different material. Whereas sculpture was a solid thing, painting consisted of a painted surface and offered an image.

But as Alex Potts has argued, in the second half of the eighteenth century a modern notion of sculpture emerged.[2] Johann Gottfried Herder's *Sculpture: Some Observations on Shape and Form from Pygmalion's Creative Dream* (1778) is especially important because he distinguishes painting and sculpture not on the basis of different modes of execution and different materials, but on the basis of different modes of viewing activated by painting and sculpture, respectively. As already explained in the Introduction, his theory of sculpture is in fact one of the first phenomenological art theories, greatly inspired by Diderot's *Letter on the Blind* (1749) and George Berkeley's *Essay towards a New Theory of Vision* (1709).

According to Herder, as explained previously, sculpture is grounded in touch, whereas painting is grounded in sight. As a result, 'the distinctive effects and particular domains of these arts are to be explained with reference to the different perceptions of things we have through these two basic senses'.[3] The distinction between sight and touch is not absolute, however. It cannot be, because as we look and feel we rarely experience seeing and touching separately. Seeing things, Herder points out several times, 'carries an implicit sense of their shape and disposition deriving from our tactile contact with the world'.[4] This implies that the apprehension

2 Potts, *The Sculptural Imagination*, p. 29.

3 Potts, *The Sculptural Imagination*, p. 29.

4 Potts, *The Sculptural Imagination*, p. 29.

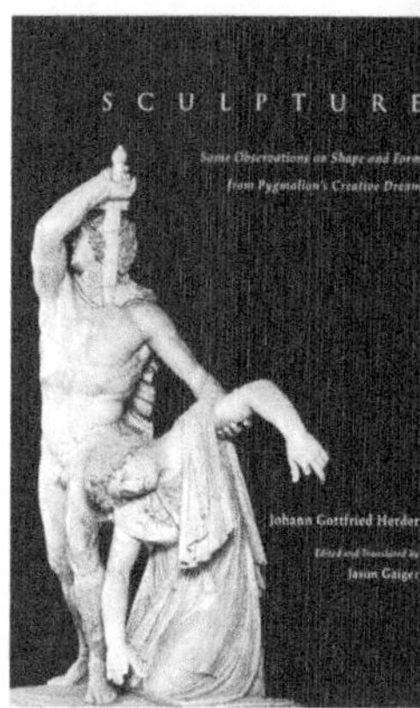

Johann Gottfried Herder, *Sculpture: Some Observations on Shape and Form from Pygmalion's Creative Dream*, 1778/2002

5 Potts, *The Sculptural Imagination*, p. 29.

of sculpture is not a literally tactile experience, but a mode of looking that assimilates itself to the 'dynamic of a tactile exploration'.[5]

Although Herder's distinction between a mode of looking grounded in touch and another grounded in sight does not seem to be particularly relevant for the kind of architectural sculpture I have discussed so far, the most important thing is that viewers and their mode of viewing are introduced into discussions about different media and arts. In the second half of the twentieth century, it was the role and function of the viewer that became the crucial factor for the understanding of specific art practices such as Minimalism, which I will discuss more elaborately in the chapter Specific Objects. And as I contend, the 'place' and 'role' of the viewer cannot be neglected either for a better understanding of architectural sculpture.

However, in my description of *Reconstruction Studio* with which I began this chapter, the active positioning of the viewer does not play any role. I said that Schouten's decision to reconstruct his studio was motivated by the fact that the works he was showing in that space were conditioned by the studio where they had been made. This could be understood as a formal issue, but implicitly this motivation also stages the viewer. For it is the artist-as-viewer of his work during its creation in the studio that stages the most ideal viewing position. Another studio, another space, would have enabled other viewing positions and would have resulted in a different work. So, even in the case of this room the place and role of the viewer cannot be neglected for understanding how it can be seen as architectural sculpture.

Between Idealism and Materialism

Before further exploring this notion of architectural sculpture, I must mention a major transformation in the history of sculpture as a medium. This transformation is important because it opens up the possibility of architectural sculpture. As Richard Serra and others have said, the history of sculpture has an absolute breaking point in the twentieth century: the point at which the pedestal, the support, was cast aside as the means of anchoring a sculpture in the world. Until then, the pedestal had enjoyed a dual status. On the one hand, it created a transition between sculpture and the world, and on the other, it comprised a rupture, a division between the two. It is this very twofold, ambiguous status of the pedestal which prompts the viewer to interpret the sculpture placed on it as a metaphor of the world, from which the work has been separated by the pedestal. The metaphor contains, after all, a resemblance between two things that basically differ. When sculptors rejected the pedestal as something on which to put sculptures, a totally new conception of sculpture became possible. From then on, sculptures were no longer monuments that embodied an idea or a memory in a metaphorical way, on the basis of analogy. From the moment at which the pedestal was cast aside, the sculpture began to become part of the same space as that of the viewer.[6]

6 Eisenman, 'Interview by Eisenman', p. 141.

This breaking point in history launched two new trajectories for sculpture. On the one hand, sculpture *descended* into the material world in which the viewer lived. The viewer's experience in time and space thus became the object of modern sculpture. On the other hand, though, by being removed from the pedestal it has become possible for sculpture to *ascend* into the idealistic world of absolute forms. Whereas the sculpture absorbs the pedestal in this second trajectory, in the first the pedestal absorbs the sculpture.

For Serra, Constantin Brancusi represents these two trajectories in an exemplary way. With some of his works, such as *Bird in Space* (1923), he was seeking to evoke a Platonic realm of thought. He dealt with the problematics of the materiality of these sculptures by making them out of highly polished bronze. Because of this, they became increasingly immaterial as they seemed to consist of sheer reflection.[7] Given that Brancusi allowed the pedestal of these works to become part of the sculpture itself, the work becomes 'detached' from its place in the world. As such, it is possible for the sculpture to become an allusion to an idealistic world of absolute thought and form. But at the same time Brancusi produced works that consist of nothing more than a pedestal. The sculpture has been absorbed, as it were, by its pedestal and has thereby become a lasting part of the material world. The sculpture *Caryatid* (1914) is a prime example of this. While modernism initially seemed to embrace the idealistic trajectory for the most part (Henry Moore, Barbara Hepworth), the materialist trajectory (Eva Hesse, Richard Serra) later became increasingly important.

Hal Foster interprets the lished, reflecting surface of ıny of Brancusi's sculptures an attempt, in fact, to merge th the material surroundings ıt are visible in the reflection. ıe non-material nature of flections is reason for me, wever, to regard them not as material aspect of the work t rather an idealistic one. See ster, 'The Un/making of ulpture', p. 180.

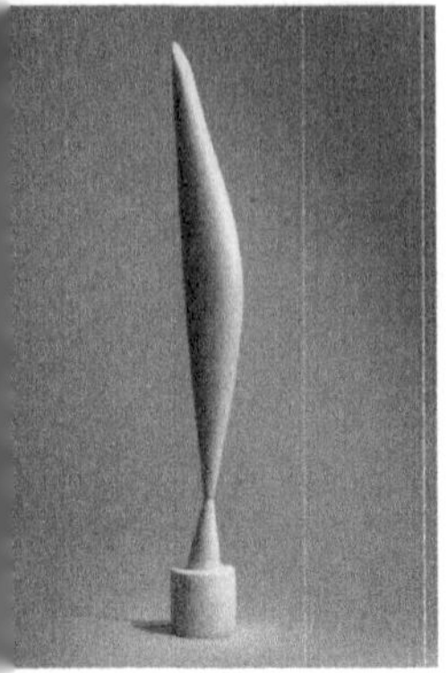

nstantin Brancusi, *Bird in ace*, 1923

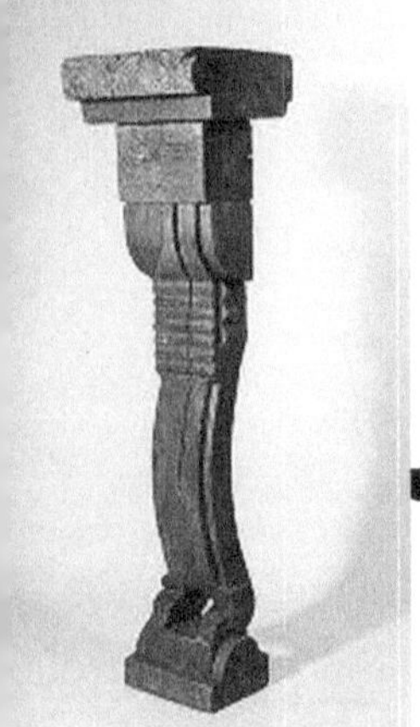

nstantin Brancusi, *Caryatid*, 14

Parallax, Fences, and Grids

Architecture does not have the two possible trajectories that sculpture has. Not being an autonomous medium but a functional one, architecture belongs unambiguously to the materialist domain. It is always part of the material world of the viewer, or rather, of the user who lives in or with architectural constructions. But one can ask if this is still the case when architecture and sculpture are entangled, for instance in architectural sculpture. Does architecture then become autonomous? Or is the role and active positioning of the viewer imposed on sculpture as a crucial, undeniable element of architectural sculpture?

Richard Serra has thoroughly explored the entanglement of sculpture and architecture:

> When sculpture [...] leaves the gallery or museum to occupy the same space and place as architecture, when it redefines the space and place in terms of sculptural necessities, architects become annoyed. Not only is their concept of space being changed, but for the most part it is being criticized. The criticism can come into effect only when architectural scale, methods, materials and procedures are being used. Comparisons are provoked. Every language has a structure about which nothing critical in that language can be said. To criticize a language, there must be a second language available dealing with the structure of the first but possessing a new structure.[8]

8 Serra and Eisenman, 'Interview', p. 15.

Here, Serra implies that architecture can be understood only by way of sculpture. And the reverse: that sculpture can be understood only by way of architecture. Architecture and sculpture are related to each other because they involve similar structures. Equally, there are real differences between the two media, whereby the one medium can offer an external perspective on the other as a metalanguage. As such, sculpture functions as a metalanguage of architecture, and, conversely, architecture can be put to use as a metalanguage of sculpture. It is that very relationship of correspondence between the two media which makes it possible for sculpture to provide insight into architecture, and vice versa. Thanks to the fact that they have something in common, they are able to 'communicate' with each other.

Bois, 'A Picturesque Stroll ·ound *Clara-Clara*', p. 65.

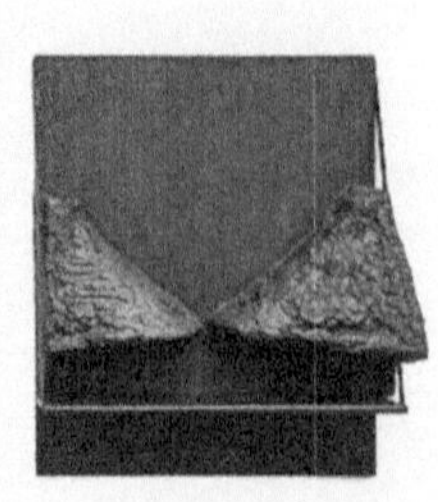

arien Schouten, *Bronze* ıinting, 1995

As Yve-Alain Bois makes clear, the common denominator of sculpture and architecture consists of what is usually referred to by the concept *parallax*. The word parallax, derived from the Greek *parallaxis*, or 'change', is defined as 'the apparent displacement of an observed object due to a change in the position of the observer'.[9] The parallax concept thus alludes specifically to the phenomenological similarities between sculpture and architecture. Here the viewer/user is positioned in the same active manner. This approach to sculpture on the basis of the parallax concept explains why Schouten's *Bronze Paintings* and *Plaster Paintings* from 1995 and 1996, respectively, should be seen as paintings and not as sculptures.

Although these works are three-dimensional rather than flat surfaces, they are fixed to the wall. No matter how three-dimensional they are, the viewer's position with respect to them is basically stable and not active. The three-dimensionality of both architecture and sculpture leads, however, to the position of the viewer no longer being a stable, abstract point but rather a space in which the body actively moves.

The parallax concept also suggests that architectural sculpture is based on, or enabled by, what the two media (can) have in common, namely a viewer who is actively positioned. There is no longer a fixed, ideal position from which architectural sculptures can be seen. The viewer has to move around in order to relate to them. A well-known architectural sculpture that most radically positions the viewer is Bruce Nauman's *Double Steel Cage Piece* from 1974, already discussed in the chapter *Sculpting Space*. This sculpture is made up of what its title suggests: two cages, one placed over the other. The outer gate has a door through which the viewer can enter. The space that opens up to the viewer and which s/he can walk through is the very narrow space in between the two cages. The viewer is confronted with the tension between space and her/his body. When you enter this sculpture, or rather the narrow passage, the experience differs greatly from seeing the double cage from a distance. The first experience is bodily, the second just visual.

The fences that Schouten installed in exhibition spaces during the nineteen-nineties (Galerie Konrad Fischer, 1991, Kunsthalle Bern, 1992, and the Stedelijk Museum, 1996), and again in 2019 in his exhibition with Martin van Zomeren gallery, are works that are outspokenly architectural. They position viewers in a very self-reflexive way: they are hindered if they wish to freely wander through the exhibition space and cannot ideally position themselves in front of the artworks hanging on the walls. This negation of free/ideal looking makes us aware of the fact that looking takes place from a certain position. This positioning is hindered by the fences, which we associate first of all with prisons. Our look is hampered and imprisoned by these fences, because we cannot approach the artworks hanging or standing behind them and position ourselves in front of them or walk around them. Schouten has not only used iron fences to define exhibition spaces, but also glass walls, for instance in *Witte de With* in 1993. These glass walls are usually half transparent because they are made of so-called 'oceanic glass'. The work *Cathedral*, which he made in 2018 as part of the exhibition 'Clay!' in the Museum Jorn in Silkeborg, Denmark, consists of such walls. By means of six five-metre high panels of oceanic glass, he made an architectural inner space. Inside as well as outside this space some of his ceramic sculptures were shown. Wherever the viewer was (inside or outside), Schouten's sculptures were partly visible through the half-transparent glass with ghost-like presences. Although Schouten uses glass walls as well as fences to define space

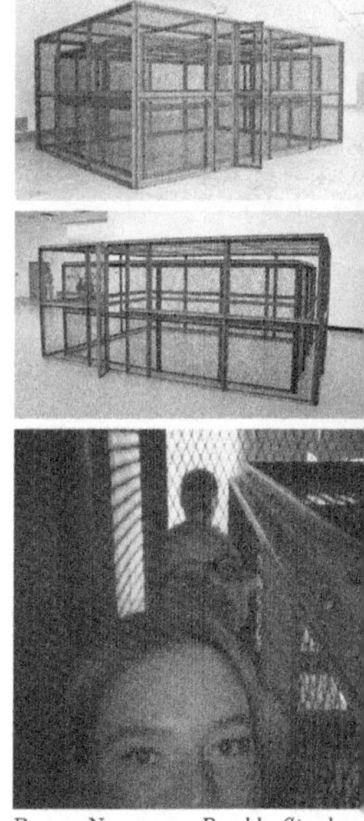

Bruce Nauman, *Double Steel Cage Piece*, 1974

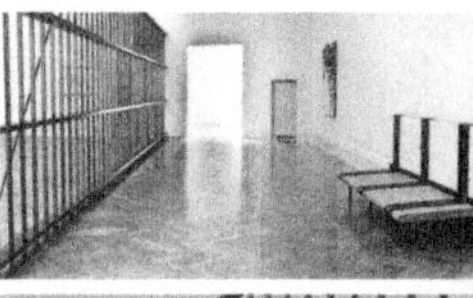

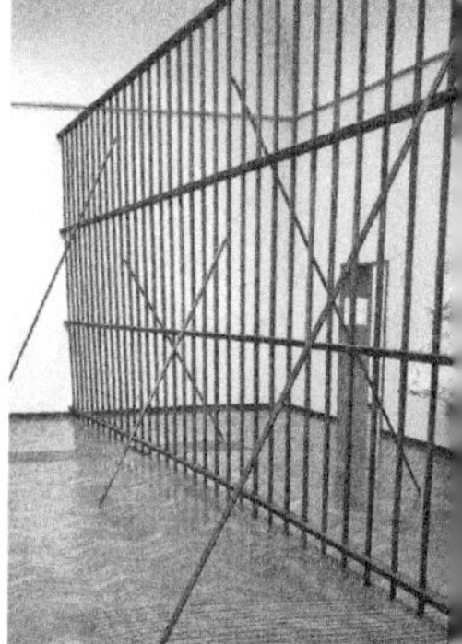

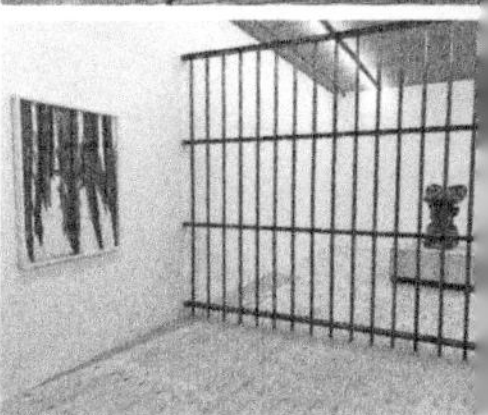

Marien Schouten, installation views *Steel Fence*, Kunsthalle Bern, 1992; Stedelijk Museum, Amsterdam, 1996; Martin van Zomeren, Amsterdam, 2019

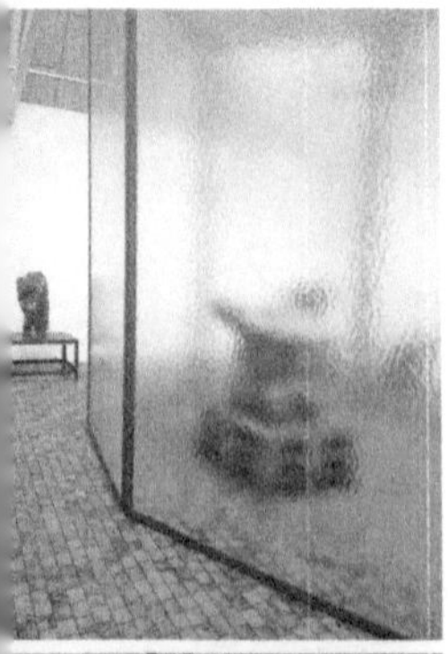

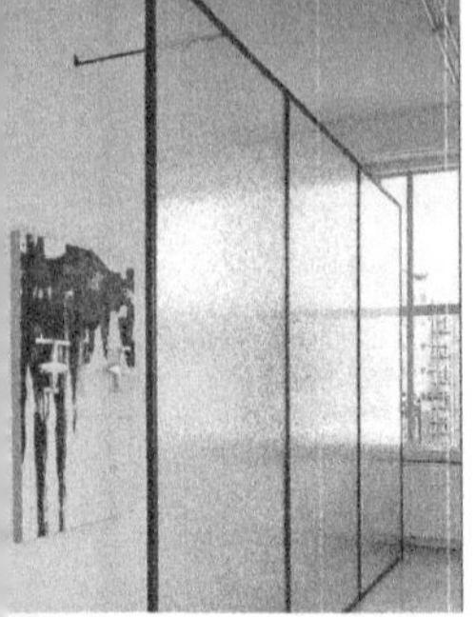

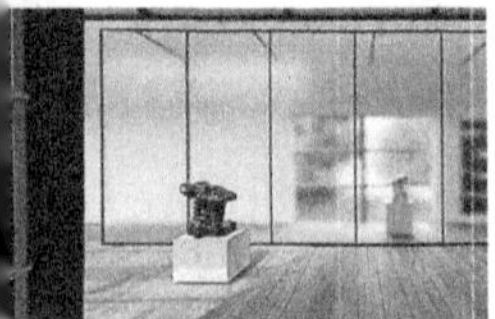

arien Schouten, exhibition
ews Museum Jorn, Silkeborg,
enmark, 2018; Witte de With,
otterdam, 1993; De Paviljoens,
mere, 2010

architecturally, the way the walls and fences do this differs. Whereas the grid-like structure of the fences imposes a perspectival organization on the space behind the fence, the glass walls impose the tension between visibility and invisibility on the space behind them.

The fences look formally like grids, enabling or enforcing a perspectival ordering of the space behind them. We know this kind of perspectival grid very well from renaissance tractates about linear perspective. They order the illusionary space of the image and create an almost perfect illusion of three dimensionality because they are based on perspectival principles. And representations of architectural spaces, especially, demonstrate the power of perspective most emphatically.

But Schouten's use of grids in his works is complex. Sometimes the grid orders 'real', that is three-dimensional, space, as with the fences, the illusionary real space, or it orders the image itself in its flatness. In the case of (illusionary) three-dimensional space the ordering takes place from where the viewer is positioned. When the image is reduced to a flat surface by a grid structure, the viewer plays no role, is not taken into consideration. Of course, introducing the flat surface of the picture plane and its illusionary possibilities of depth into the discussion concerns a new topic, namely the relationship between architecture and (perspectival) painting. Schouten's *Rooms* impel us, however, to reflect on the relationship between sculpture and architecture, but a short digression into another medium will highlight the possibilities of using grid structures.

Let me give one example of his complex use of grid structures on or in the picture plane. Schouten's drawing *Untitled* (1987) evokes the spaces of landscape as well as those of architecture. The viewer is confronted with a contrast between the geometrical forms, the black and grey horizontal beams, the grid-like structure in the centre of the image, and the organic, greenish/brownish forms on both sides of the image. The organic forms look like the mountains that flank so many traditional history paintings as coulisses, or that create the setting of a landscape painting. The grid, in contrast, evokes first of all twentieth-century works of art that have deployed it, for instance in the works of Agnes Martin.

The grid counters illusionistic space, stating the autonomy of the realm of art. In the words of Rosalind E. Krauss: 'Flattened, geometrized, ordered, it is antinatural, antimimetic, antireal. It is what art looks like when it turns its back on nature.'[10] This notion of the grid seems utterly materialistic, because it makes us talk about the material and formal qualities of the image's surface. However, this is not how artists deploying the grid talked about it when they introduced the grid into their painting:

> [...] Mondrian and Malevich are not discussing canvas or pigment or graphite or any other form of matter. They are talking about Being or Mind or Spirit. From their point of view, the grid is a staircase to the Universal, and they are not interested in what happens below in the Concrete.[11]

It may be evident that Schouten is not evoking this idealistic, metaphysical understanding of the grid when deploying it. When Schouten draws grids on his drawings or paintings, or when he attaches wooden grids or shelves in front of his works, he imposes the architectural medium on drawing or painting. The specificity of each medium is not lost but highlighted in interaction with another medium.

But the grid also alludes to Renaissance paintings, which projected the grid-like structure *within* the painting in order

10 Krauss, 'Grids', p. 10.

11 Krauss, 'Grids', p. 10.

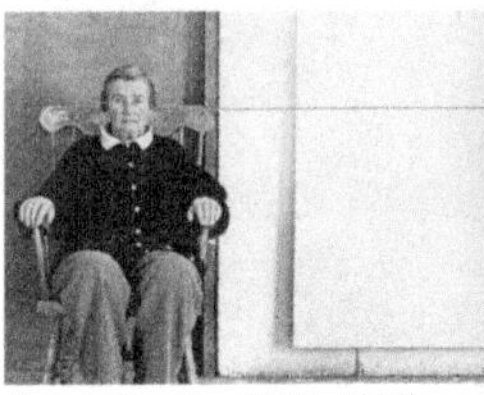
Agnes Martin (1912–2004)

Agnes Martin, *Untitled #1*, 19

12 See Damisch, *The Origin of Perspective*.

to create linear perspective. Whereas in twentieth-century art the grid maps the surface of the painting itself, in Renaissance painting the projected grid of perspective maps reality onto its representation. Perspective as such is also evoked in Schouten's work by the receding of organic forms on both sides. Renaissance perspective was, of course, explored or proudly practised not only within the genre of landscape painting, but especially within architectural painting. The tile floor, which creates the structure of a chessboard, also forms a grid, although now represented three-dimensionally. This quintessential motif most convincingly embodies the features of illusionist space as produced by linear perspective.[12]

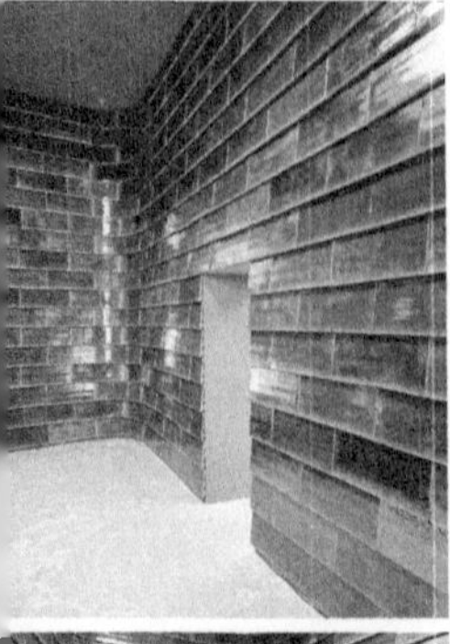

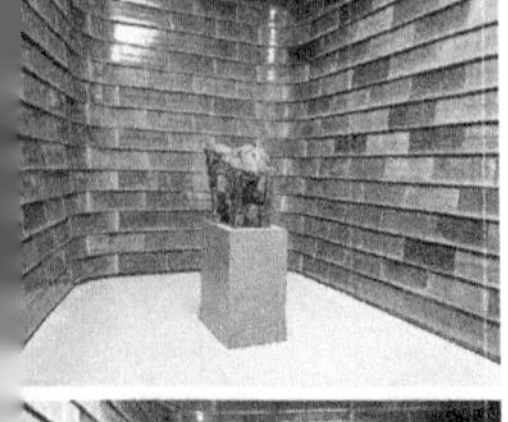

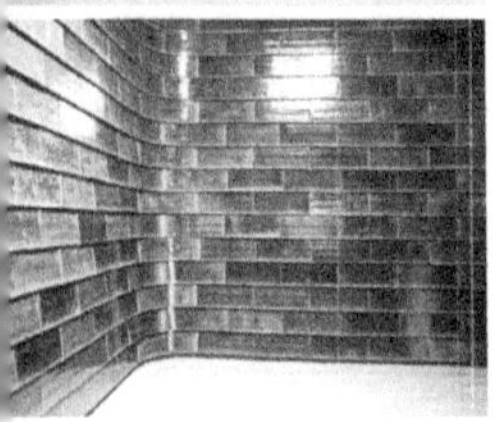

Marien Schouten, *Green Room/ Wake*, 2001–2002

When grid structures are used in real or illusionary three-dimensional space, they delimit, define, and direct the viewer's look into (illusionary) space. This results in an organization of space taking place before the eyes of the viewer. In Schouten's work, this use of the grid is deployed by means of fences: they direct and delimit the viewer's gaze in the most radical way. He does not deploy grid structures within his paintings or drawings for the creation of the illusionary depth of linear perspective. In his drawings and paintings, the grids map and delimit the surface of the works.

Ornamental Grids

As architectural elements the fences seem to install a different kind of viewer to Schouten's *Rooms*. Although they also present themselves as architectural structures, the viewer is not delimited in how she looks and what she can see. She can wander freely through the room, and in the case of *Studio* and *A Reader's Bedroom* also around it. The grid structure that can be recognized in the fences returns in *A Reader's*

Bedroom, but also in the *Green Room/Snake* that he made in 2001–2002 in De Pont Museum in Tilburg. The *Bedroom,* its floor and walls, consist of wooden panels that together form a grid structure. This grid structure is foregrounded because it contrasts with the baroque, curly pattern of the nerfs in each wooden panel. Schouten seems to have precisely selected those wooden panels for his *Bedroom* with the most intense baroque patterns. The *Bedroom's* ceiling is made out of a grid structure of wooden beams. The *Green Room,* meanwhile, is made up entirely of ceramic tiles—tiles are not only functional, but also ornamental. Behind Per Kirkeby's use of bricks, discussed in the chapter Building Blocks, is ornamentation. The grid pattern formed by tiles, likewise, has an ornamental function. The dark-green glaze on the tiles has an organic, baroque pattern that, like the baroque pattern of the wooden panels of *A Reader's Bedroom,* contrasts intensely with the formal pattern of the grid the wooden panels form together. These architectural rooms are clearly not made from a solely functional point of view; ornamentation adds another element that is difficult to negotiate with their status as architectural sculptures. For architecture and applied arts can have ornamental elements but sculpture certainly cannot.

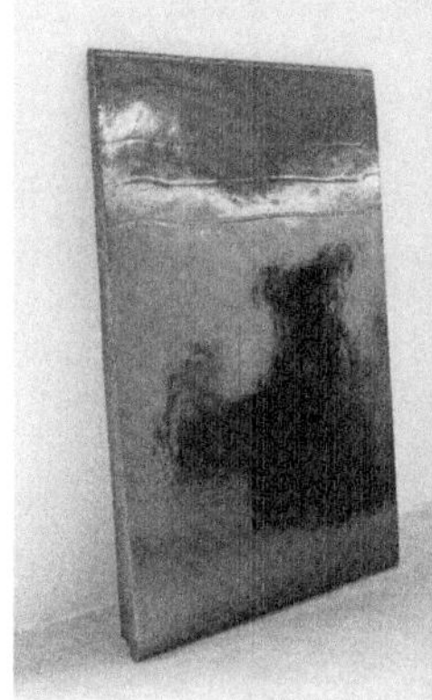

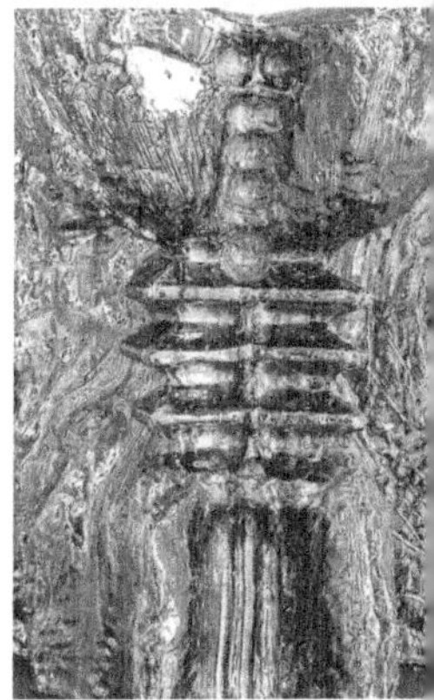

Marien Schouten, *Ceramic tile* 2003, 180 × 120 cm; *Head with wings*, 2008

Although in the Building Blocks chapter I differentiated between Schouten's *Heads* and *Rooms* as embodying different notions of architectural sculpture, what *Green Room* has in common with these Heads is that they foreground the building stones that give them body. The green, ceramic tiles lie overlapping with each other, like roof tiles, covering the four walls completely. Not coincidentally, this sculptural space or room has a second name: *Snake.* Reptiles not only have a skeleton as the body's internal architecture; their scaled skin is a kind of external architecture of the reptilian

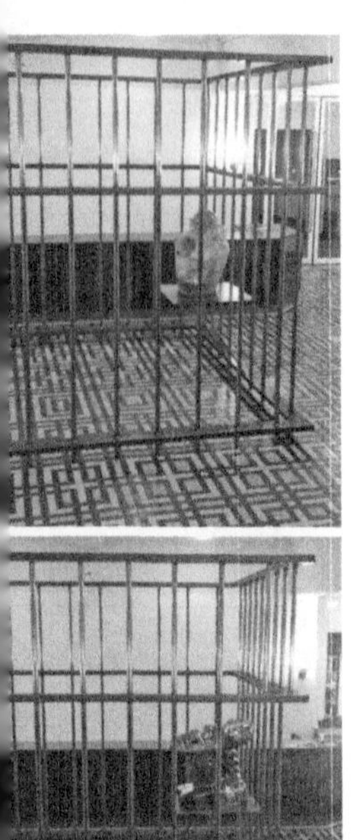

arien Schouten, *Chambres des* *ınaux*, 2013

body. The skin is no longer the surface on which the inner volume is expressed. Architecture and surface coincide here: the skin *is* architecture. Of course, one could argue that his two other *Rooms* have similar kinds of building stones—not ceramic tiles, but wooden panels and beams. In the case of the *Green Room*, the ceramic tiles *are* the architectural structure, whereas in *Reconstruction Studio* and *A Reader's Bedroom* the panels and beams are absorbed into the architecture and are less recognizable than the building stones that made them.

The *Green Room* differs in yet another way from the two other *Rooms*. The *Green Room* has no outside; it is a room in an existing former factory building, now De Pont Museum. The viewer can only enter the space of the room, but cannot walk around it. *Reconstruction Studio* and *A Reader's Bedroom* not only have a space which one can enter, but they also have an outside around which the viewer can walk. As a result, the viewer will have different reflections on, and experiences of, the space that is sculpted by architecture. Schouten also used the kind of architectural space that combines inside with outside in his proposal for the reconstruction of the factory building where the De Pont Museum was going to be established. The main space of the factory was too big and too undefined; it was impossible for artworks to have a productive relationship with the surrounding space. So, Schouten designed three islands of interconnected 'rooms' which could offer intimacy and contextual space for the displayed artworks.

Although Schouten's use of fences and *Rooms* install very specific viewer positions, these positions also differ radically. In the 'space' he made in 2013 for the exhibition 'Chambres des Canaux' in the new building of the Amsterdam City Archives, he combined the different viewing positions. This time he made a room out of fences, a prison-like box. Inside, at each end of the box, a ceramic sculpture was shown. The viewer was clearly delimited in what s/he could see, because s/he could only walk around the fenced-off space. But by walking around it, the viewer could see the sculptures from all sides—this time the viewer's look was not hampered by foreclosing certain perspectives on the sculptures, just as his fences in other installations do, but by determining the distance towards them.

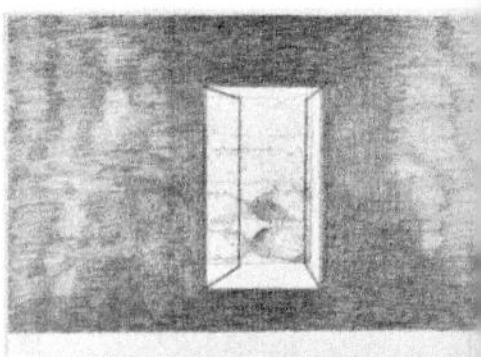
Marien Schouten, *Untitled*, 19

Another example of an architectural instalment of the viewing position can be recognized in a drawing he made in 1998. This drawing concerns a proposal to connect two rooms in the Van der Steur building of Museum Boijmans Van Beuningen, in Rotterdam, by means of a window. In the drawing the window is half open; the viewer can look through the half-open window and see one of Schouten's paintings in the other room. And of course, the viewer can also enter the second room in the usual way, and then look at the painting, choosing her own position in relation to it. Schouten's proposal was never realized.

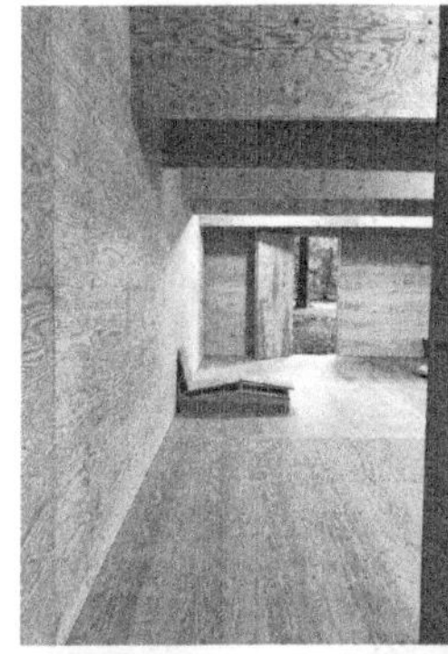
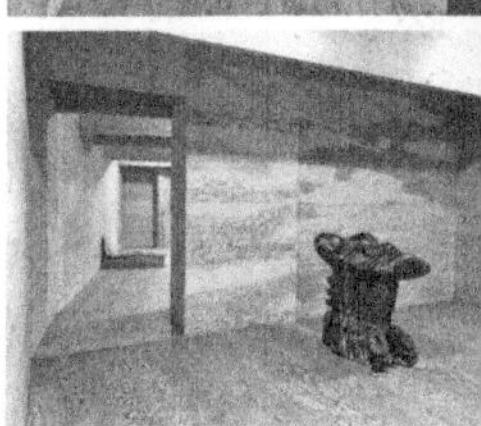
Marien Schouten, *Nocturnal Reading*, 2021

The most recent 'room' Schouten has made is the one with which I opened the discussion of his *Rooms*, and which he made for the yearly sculpture exhibition in Tilburg's De Oude Warande, titled *Nocturnal Reading* (2021). This room not only combines different viewing positions, but also different modalities of viewing. In fact, it consists of two rooms, one after the other, the second positioned slightly obliquely in relation to the first. When one enters the first room, one notices the passage towards the second. At first, one only sees a reflection of light on the side wall of the second room; however, one does not see the source of this light. The reflected light seduces the viewer to enter the second room, and after one has entered the second room, it turns out that the wall at the end consists of 'oceanic glass', the same kind of glass Schouten had used in the Asger Jorn Museum in Denmark. The fact that the two rooms are positioned one after another can be compared to how the fences determine viewing positions. The wall in between the two rooms blocks the viewer's sight: one only gets a glimpse of the second room through the passage to the next room. The in-between wall forecloses an open perspective on the second space. The glass wall at the end of the second space does not hamper specific perspectives on the space outside the room, but imposes the tension between visibility and invisibility upon it. One can see space outside the room, but one is not able to distinguish details of that space. The half-transparency of the outer world is a nice image of how one recalls the outer world while dwelling inside an architectural construction.

How Does Architectural Sculpture Sculpt Space?

One could argue that architectural sculpture equally belongs to the logic of sculpting space. For architecture is more than an assemblage of walls, ceilings, and floors; it also shapes the space inside and outside of the architectural construction. Yet, does it make sense to differentiate these two logics? In order to answer this question I will return to Donald Judd, already discussed in the Sculpting Space chapter, and his views on how his works sculpt space.

Donald Judd's absorption of space into the notion of the object was, according to him, 'new in art'; in other words, this was his contribution to art (he was probably not aware of Kobro's very similar artistic practice in the first half of the twentieth century). He distinguished his objects from conventional sculpture, which he described as totems or monoliths: with conventional statuary 'the space around the sculpture is only somewhere from to look towards the continuous solids'. In Judd's works, however, space is actively engaged and activated:

> I found that if I placed a work on a wall in relation to a corner or to both corners, or similarly on the floor, or outdoors near a change in the surface of the ground, that by adjusting the distance in the space in between became much more clear than before, definite like the work. [...] If the space in one or two directions can become clear, it's logical to desire the space in all directions to become clear. This usually requires more than a unit or it requires a space built around a unit or it requires a space built around a unit or it requires a great deal of space. This is so of some large indoor works and of most large outdoor ones.[13]

13 Judd, '21 February 1993', p. 812.

Schouten's *Rooms*, especially the two with an inside as well as an outside, can also be considered as 'sculpting space'. From the outside, the viewer bears witness to how space is demarcated by the box-like room, when inside space is enclosed by the walls, ceiling, and floor. *A Reader's Bedroom* sculpts the space not only by means of walls and ceilings, but with the aid of the chair, couch, and bed, which are part of the architecture, and not moveable parts in the room's interior. Incidentally, this suggests that Frank Lloyd Wright's architecture can also be seen as an architectural form of sculpting space. But an important difference between Kobro's sculptures and Schouten's architectural sculptures is that Kobro's objects can still be looked at as gestalts. Although they are three-dimensional, viewers will have an impression of the whole structure by standing in front of it, on the basis of their visual memory of similar objects. As with classical sculpture, walking around it is not absolutely necessary, because through visual deduction one can have an idea of how the sculptural object looks from other sides. This visual processing as gestalt is completely impossible with Schouten's *Rooms*: the viewer has to look actively and walk through and around the rooms in order to see how this architectural sculpture sculpts space.

This suggests that the emphatic active role of the viewer in architectural sculpture distinguishes the logic of architectural sculpture from the logic of sculpting space. Although the viewer always places an important role in the medium of sculpture through her embodied positioning, in the case of architectural sculpture the viewer is not only embodied but also actively moving around.

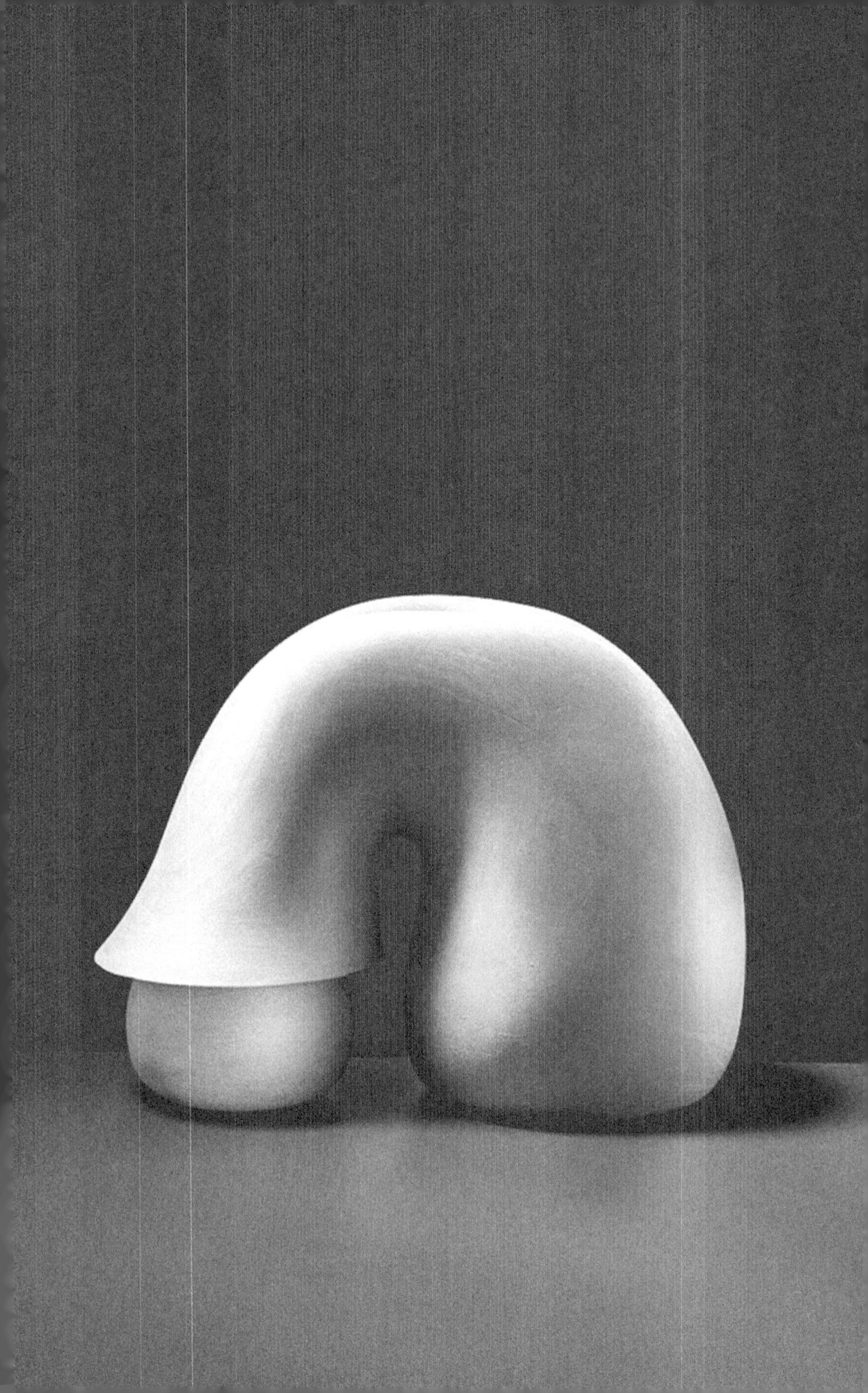

Specific Objects

Donald Judd and Minimalism

In 1964, Donald Judd claimed that the possibilities of sculpture and painting had been exhausted. Art should go into a new, different direction and he named the three-dimensional, geometrical work that materialized that new direction 'specific object'. The kind of cadmium red boxes and wall pieces he made around 1963 are good examples of specific objects, and because of the three-dimensionality of these works they are now usually treated as sculptures. But for Judd, these works in particular took painting in a new direction: 'the new work obviously resembles sculpture more than it does painting, but it is nearer to painting'.[1] They are nearer to painting because they fail to adhere 'to the demands of painting as they had been identified with the pictorial qualities of the expressive surface'. More specifically, it is because of this antagonistic relation to the expressiveness of painting that they took painting on a new course. The specific objects are not expressive; that is, they do not express the inner subjectivity of the artist, but they are literal: they

1 Judd, 'Specific Objects', p. 141.

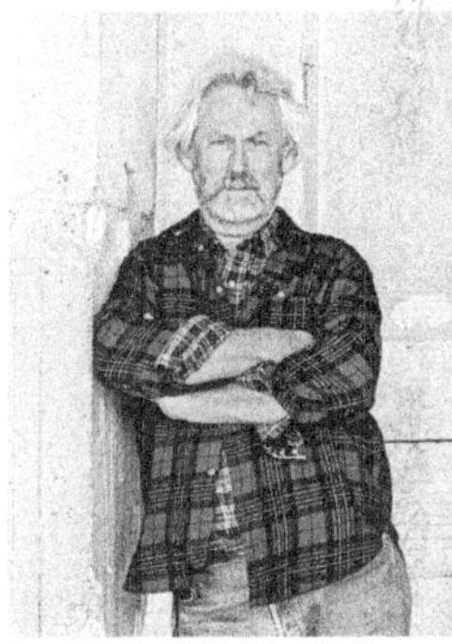
Donald Judd (1928–1994)

Donald Judd, *Untitled*, 1984–1986

Aldo Bakker, *Jug and Cup*, 2011, photo: Erik & Petra Hesmerg

2 Fer, 'Judd's Specific Objects', p. 131–32.

3 Judd, 'Specific Objects', 136.

4 Fer, 'Judd's Specific Objects', 133.

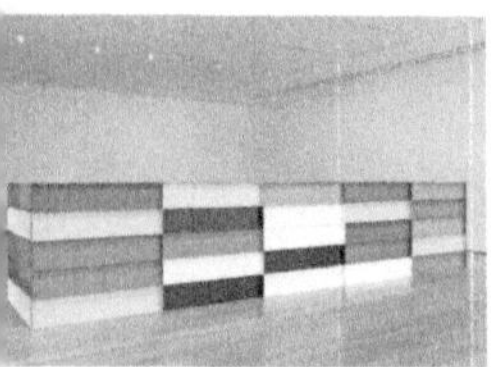

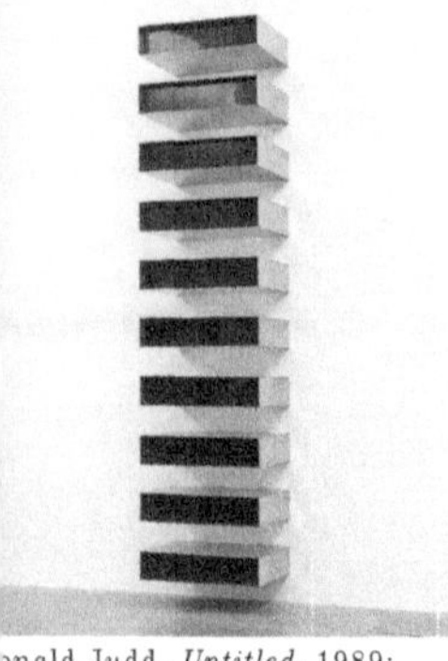

Donald Judd, *Untitled*, 1989; *Untitled*, 1973

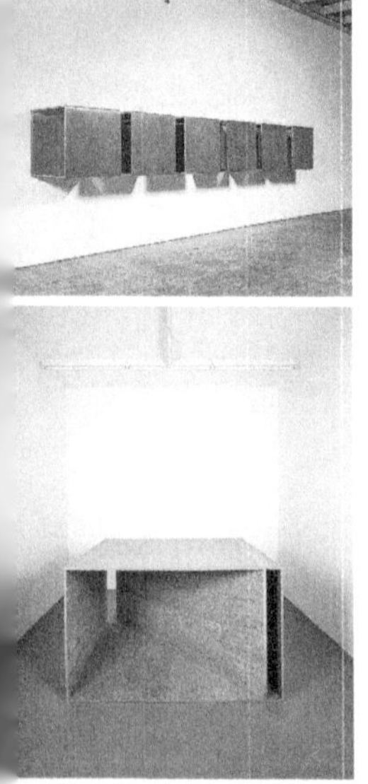

Donald Judd, *Untitled*, 1968; *Untitled*, 1977

are what they are, and the viewer should focus on 'what's there'.

> At stake here is not an opposition between a high modernist insistence on the value of the art object and a Minimalist rejection of art, but a shift of emphasis onto another way of attending to the object, of looking with a different set of interests in mind. This is a matter of redefining rather than rejecting the art object and claiming for it an interest other than the purely 'optical', with all the aesthetic values upon which that term depends.[2]

Judd believed the differentiation between sculpture and painting is not relevant; his term is 'the art object', whatever medium it belongs to. But because of the three-dimensionality of his objects his work inevitably tends to be understood as sculpture. So, what is the logic with which his sculptural objects comply, or rather, in his own words, what is the logic of a specific object?

In his text 'Specific Object', Judd opposes the 'part-to-part' organization of European modernism in favour of the 'singleness' of the specific object.

> The main thing wrong with painting is that it is a rectangular plane placed against a wall. A rectangle is a shape in itself; it is obviously the whole shape; it determines and limits the arrangement of whatever is on or inside it.[3]

This results in a 'part-to-part' organization, because in art prior to 1946 the edges of the rectangular frame constituted a boundary and a composition 'related to those edges. In order to unify the composition, what mattered most were the relationships between parts rather than the single whole'.[4] The backdrop against which Judd articulates his notion of the specific object is European modernism and abstraction.

Even the abstraction of Malevich and Mondrian continued to be dependent on relationships between parts. After 1946, with Abstract Expressionism, the rectangle of the canvas became more emphatic: 'The parts are few and so subordinate to the unity as not to be parts in the ordinary sense.'[5] The American Abstract Expressionist artists he explicitly mentions are Jackson Pollock, Mark Rothko, Clifford Still, and Barnett Newman. The unity of their works becomes nearly 'one thing' rather than an arrangement of parts. Because of this, his new type of abstraction is superior to the old European model, although for Judd even this new kind of abstract painting had already exhausted its limits. For him, the ideal of 'singleness' has a better future outside of painting, especially in his own 'specific objects'. Another important quality of his specific objects is their three-dimensionality, which consists of 'real space'. This solves the problem of illusionism and the space in and around marks and colours called literal space. Although the medium of sculpture also exists in real space, Judd rejects the term sculpture in favour of specific objects, because the work of the most important sculptors from that time, like David Smith and Anthony Caro, also used part-to-part composition: 'most sculpture is made part by part, by addition, composed'.[6] These compositions never form a single unity, because parts fall into a hierarchical organization. The relation between a specific object and 'real space' is of great importance to Judd, with the latter being modified by the former. Real space is not the context of the specific object; real space is shaped by the form of a specific object. This means that space is the medium of the specific object: the specific object's silhouette outlines space as volume. One must also conclude that the logic of the specific object has this notion of space in common with the logic of sculpting space.

5 Judd, 'Specific Objects', p. 136.

6 Judd, 'Specific Objects', p. 137.

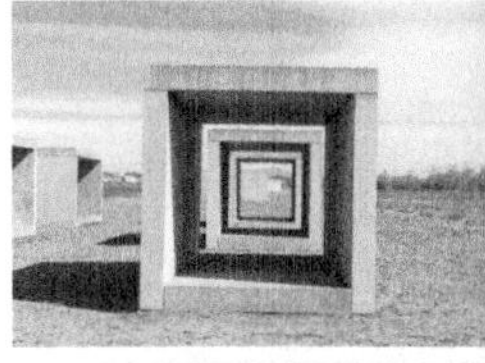

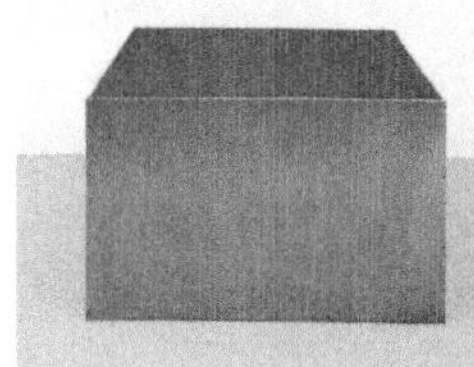

Donald Judd, detail of fifteen untitled works in concrete, 1980–1984, on the grounds of The Chinati Foundation in Marfa, Texas; *Untitled*, 1972

Fer, 'Judd's Specific Objects', 134.

Judd, 'Specific Objects', 141.

Chandler, 'Tony Smith and l LeWitt', p. 20.

Judd's writing both in his text 'Specific Objects' and in his other texts is utterly 'dry' and descriptive in the formal sense. As Briony Fer has suggested, Judd's writing is in itself a form of Minimalist criticism. 'Judd's commentaries stick to precise formal descriptions, to "what's there" and the plain, no-frills style corresponds to the "clarity" of the object.'[7] The clarity of the object (and of his writing), should, however, not be explained or understood in terms of a systematic or rational kind of formalism, because there is no underlying system that generates the work. His description of Frank Stella's shaped paintings is also appropriate as a description of his own specific objects: 'The order is not rationalistic and underlying but is simply order, like that of continuity, one thing after another.'[8] Whereas Minimalism is seen as utterly rationalistic, Judd rejects this idea explicitly because there is no underlying rationality that generates the work as its origin.

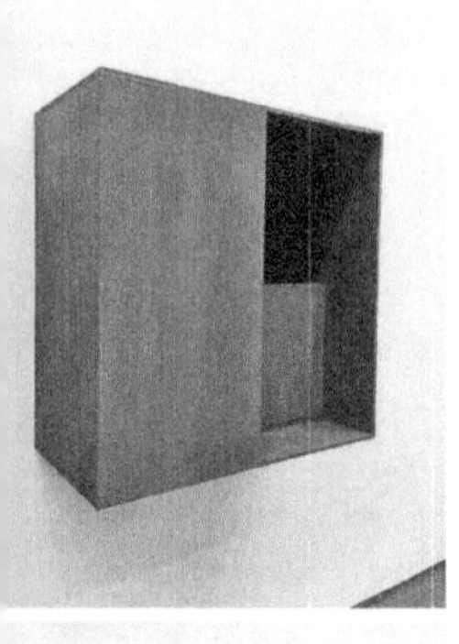

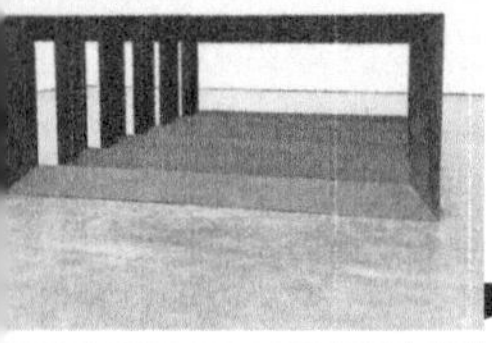

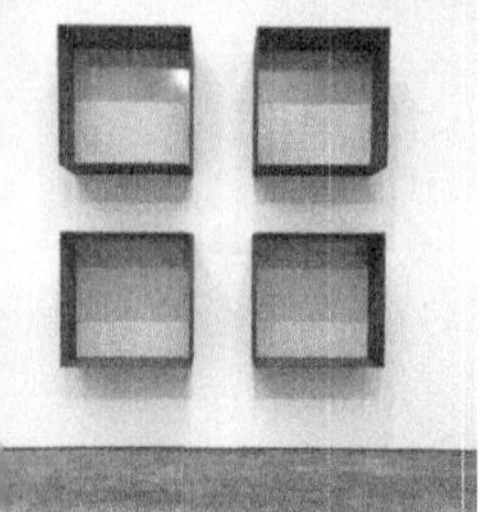

nald Judd, *Untitled*, 1987; *titled*, 1979; *Untitled*, 1979

Repetitions and Variations

Although Judd's work looks highly systematic, that does not mean it is the result of a systematic procedure. For, as I just argued, there are no underlying systems that produce his works as the origin from which they sprout. In order to better understand the systematic nature of Judd's work it is important to make a distinction between 'system' and 'method'. A method is a means of obtaining an end and never an end in itself; a system is both a means and an end. This implies, for example, that Schoenberg's twelve-tone technique is a method, not a system.[9] But how should we assess his method?

Judd said the following about the quality, in fact, the method, of repetition in both his own work and in the paintings of Frank Stella (his striped paintings): 'The order is not rationalistic and underlying, but is simply order, like that of continuity, one thing after another.'[10] Composition by means of 'one thing after another' replaces relational composition, which he identified with European art. In a joint interview with Frank Stella, they explain what relational composition involves: 'The basis of their whole idea is balance. You do something in one corner and you balance it with something in the other corner.'[11] As Rosalind E. Krauss concludes, 'one thing after another' was a way to escape from setting up relations.[12] Repetitive structures resist meaning, yet they also determine the viewing experience. The repetitiveness of 'one thing after another' is a compositional strategy or method, but it does not determine the composition of the work; instead, it determines its experience. The kind of meaning that is being resisted is not only that of the illusionistic, represented body, as in classical sculpture, but also that of the personality of the sculptor, his/her expressiveness. There are also no allusions to an 'inner life of form', 'the way eroded or chiselled rock in a sculptural context might allude to inner biological forces'.[13]

10 Judd'Specific Objects', p. 141.

11 Judd, '21 February 1993', p. 811.

12 Krauss, 'LeWitt in Progress', p. 244.

13 Krauss, 'The *Double Negative*', p. 250.

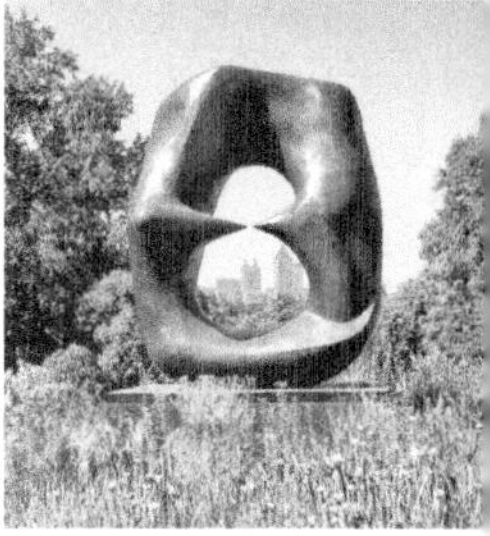

Henry Moore, *Oval with Points* 1968–1969

Henry Moore's work usually exemplifies this notion of sculpture as being the result of an inner life of form. When we understand the experience of the viewer, how his/her body is positioned in relation to the object, this meaning does not arise from an inner, private space, but from a space that is public. Krauss concludes:

> Minimalist sculptors began with a procedure for declaring the externality of meaning. As we saw, these artists reacted against a sculptural illusionism which converts one material into the signifier for another: stone, for example, into flesh—an illusionism that withdraws the

14 Krauss, 'The *Double Negative*', p. 266.

> sculptural object from literal space and places it in a metaphorical one. These artists refused to use edges and planes to shape an object so that its external image would suggest an underlying principle of cohesion or order or tension. As with metaphor, the implication of this order is that it lies beyond the simple externals of the object—its shape or substance—endowing that object with a kind of intentional or private center.[14]

Minimalist artists privileged composition by means of 'one thing after another'. To reach the result of this kind of composition, they favoured a specific method. They complied with the method of repetition, which comes in two forms: repetition of the same or repetition with difference. Minimalist artists usually call the latter 'variations'. Sol LeWitt often gave his work the title 'variations', yet Judd's work can just as well be understood as variations on a limited number of principles.

Systematic Intuition

However, as Krauss has argued, Minimalist artists are far less systematic than their works suggest. The systematicity of their work is not the result of an underlying, rational system that produces the work; in fact, it is just an effect or a look of systematicity. She opposes, for example, Donald Kuspit's perspective on the variations of Sol LeWitt. He claimed the following about LeWitt's work:

> In LeWitt there is no optical induction; there is deduction by rules, which have an axiomatic validity [...] Rationalistic, deterministic abstract art links up with a larger Western tradition, apparent in both classical antiquity and the Renaissance, the pursuit of intelligibility

> by mathematical means. This tradition is profoundly humanistic in import, for it involves the deification of the human mind by reason of its mathematical prowess.[15]

Krauss criticizes Kuspit's account of Sol LeWitt's work as being 'dedicated to a triumphant Cartesianism' as follows:

> His math is far too simple; his solutions are far too inelegant; the formal conditions of his work are far too scattered and obsessional to produce anything like the diagram of human reason these writers seem to call for.[16]

She describes his work not as rationalistic, but as the result of obsessiveness and a 'kind of mad obstinacy'.[17]

> The babble of a LeWitt serial expansion has nothing of the economy of the mathematician's language. It has the loquaciousness of the speech of children or of the very old, in that its refusal to summarize, to use the single example that would imply the whole, is like those feverish accounts of events composed of a string of almost identical details, connected by 'and'.[18]

Krauss's expressions 'mad obstinacy' and 'the babble of a LeWitt serial expansion' seem perhaps to be a negative evaluation of his artistic practice; however, it is in fact directed against the art critics who turn him into a rationalist. The text in which she argues this contains eleven quotations from Samuel Beckett's *Molloy* (1965), illustrating the obsessiveness and mad obstinacy of 'one thing after another'. Let me cite one of her quotations from *Molloy*.

> Good. Now I can begin to suck. Watch me closely.
> I take a stone from the right pocket of my greatcoat, suck it, stop sucking it, put it in the left pocket of my greatcoat, the empty one (of stones). I take a second stone

15 Kuspit, 'Sol LeWitt', p. 48.

16 Krauss, 'LeWitt in Progress', p. 243.

17 Krauss, 'LeWitt in Progress', p. 244.

18 Krauss, 'LeWitt in Progress', p. 244.

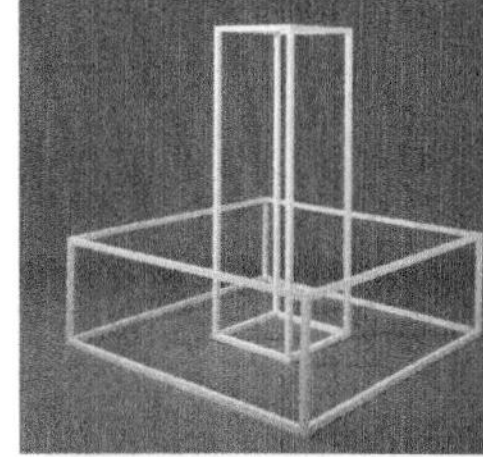

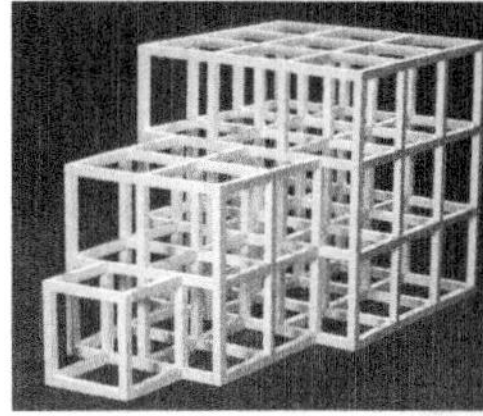

Sol LeWitt, *Maquette for One, Two, Three*, 1979; *Serial Projec[t] 1A*, 1967

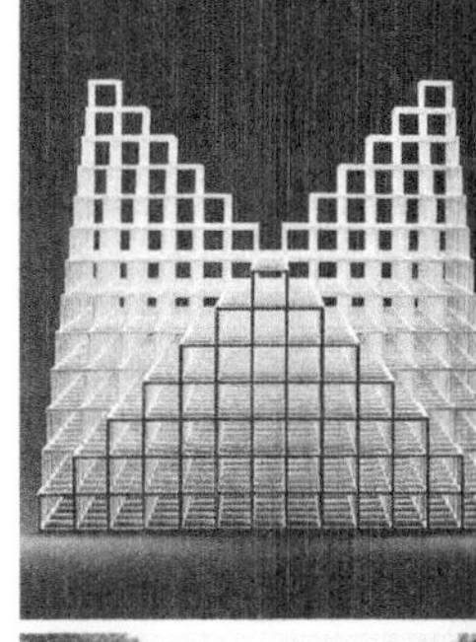

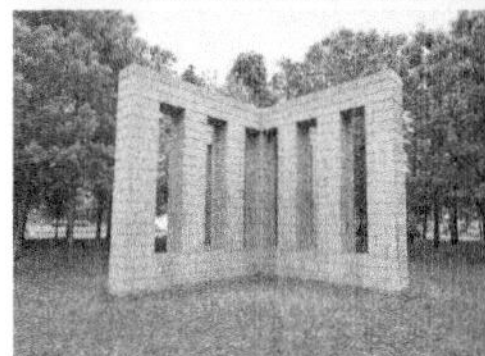

Sol LeWitt, *13/3*, 1981; *X with Columns*, 2015

Samuel Beckett, *Molloy* 965), quoted in Krauss, eWitt in Progress', p. 247.

LeWitt, 'Sentences on onceptual Art', pp. 88–90.

> from the right pocket of my greatcoat, suck it, put it in the left pocket of my greatcoat. And so on until the right pocket of my greatcoat is empty (apart from its usual and casual contents) and the six stones I have just sucked, one after the other, are all in the left pocket of my greatcoat.[19]

Although Molloy's sucking and displacement of stones from one pocket to the other is utterly systematic, this systematicity is clearly the result of an obsession, a mad obstinacy.

While LeWitt identifies less as a Minimalist artist and more as a conceptual one, his work also tends to be seen as Minimalist. Some of his 'Sentences on Conceptual Art' explain the methods of Minimalism very well:

1. Conceptual artists are mystics rather than rationalists. They leap to conclusions that logic cannot reach.
3. Irrational judgments lead to new experience.
5. Irrational thoughts should be followed absolutely and logically.
21. Perception of ideas leads to new ideas.
28. Once the idea of the piece is established in the artist's mind and the final form is decided, the process is carried out blindly. There are many side effects that the artist cannot imagine. They may be used for new works.[20]

Like Judd, LeWitt has claimed that his work does not originate from rationality, but from intuition. The quoted 'Sentences on Conceptual Art' illustrate that conviction, or those aesthetics, well. Irrationality is not seen as the negation of Minimalist and Conceptual Art, but as an important inspiration for it.

Can Furniture Be Specific?

Judd is not only known for his sculptures but also his furniture. In the nineteen-sixties, he made furniture for houses in which he was living at the time, but in the nineteen-seventies, after having moved to Marfa in Texas, he began to design furniture on a more regular basis and not only for his own use. In a text from 1993 he explains clearly why the making of a chair is not the same as the making of an artwork:

> The configuration and the scale of art cannot be the transposed into furniture and architecture. The intent of art is different from that of the latter, which must be functional. If a chair or a building is not functional, if it appears to be only art, it is ridiculous. The art of a chair is not its resemblance to art, but is partly its reasonableness, usefulness and scale as a chair. These are proportions, which is visible reasonableness. The art in art is partly the assertion of someone's interest regardless of other considerations.[21]

21 Judd, 'It's Hard to Find a Good Lamp', p. 7.

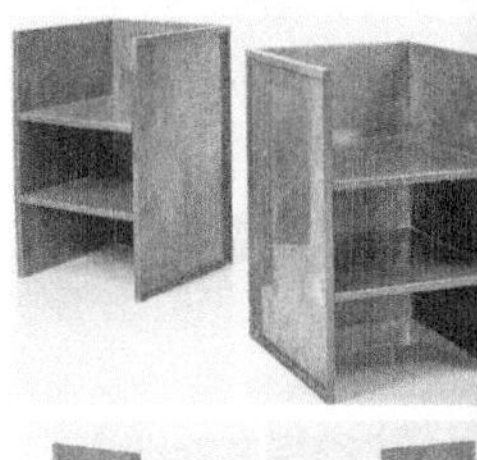

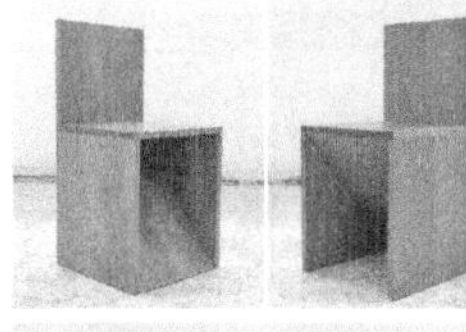

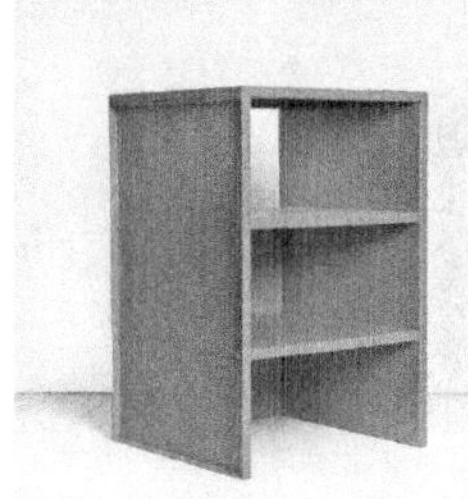

Furniture by Donald Judd, in metal and wood

Although there is the art of furniture and the art of art, art differs from furniture because it is autonomous and not functional, 'the assertion of someone's interest'. Judd speaks like a modernist for whom the distinction between media is sacred. But at the end of his essay, the distinction between art and furniture is not that clear any more:

> I am often asked if the furniture is art, since almost ten years ago some artists made art that was also furniture. The furniture is furniture and is only art in that architecture, ceramics, textiles and many things are art. We try to keep the furniture out of galleries to avoid this confusion. [...] I am often told that the furniture is not

22 Judd, 'It's Hard to Find a Good Lamp', p. 21.

> comfortable, and in that not functional. [...] The furniture is functional to me. Rather than making a chair to sleep in or a machine to live in, it is better to make a bed. A straight chair is best for eating and writing. The third position is standing.[22]

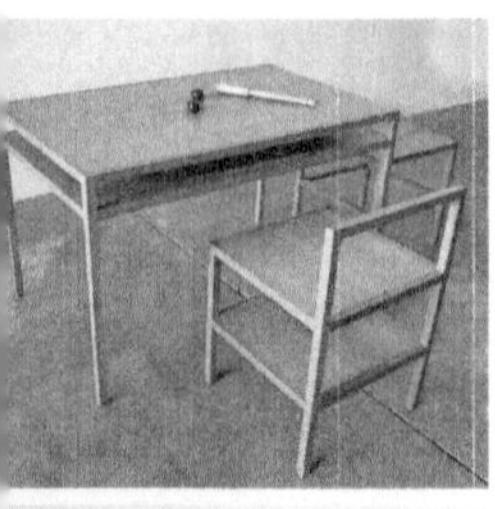

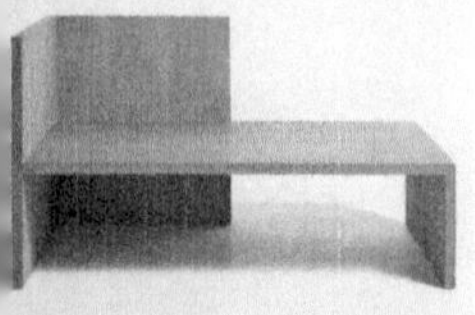

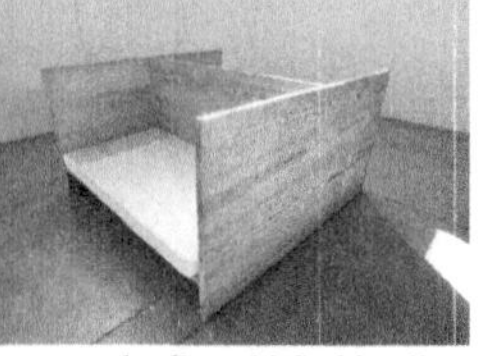

Furniture by Donald Judd, all wood

When Judd theorized the specific object, the difference between sculpture and painting was not relevant for him. In fact, he developed the notion of the specific object at first to open up a new vision on painting, although he was fully aware that it also had implications for sculpture. The fact that his artworks are now considered to be sculpture is due to their three-dimensionality and objecthood. One of the most important features of the logic of the specific object is that it is not medium-specific—one can see it as a new notion of painting, as well as sculpture.

In his writing on his own furniture, Judd does not refer to his own notion of the specific object; his framework is that of the medium-specific characteristics of furniture as functional and art as autonomous. But his conventional, modernist distinction between media is challenged when people criticize his furniture for not being comfortable. This criticism undermines his belief in the functionality of furniture. He can only defend the functionality of his chairs, tables, and benches by reducing it to the most rigid and elementary standards. I would like to argue that it is much more productive and relevant to consider Judd's furniture from the point of view of the specific object than that of functionality. When we do that, it is also no longer relevant to differentiate between the various media he works in, or sculpture versus furniture. All his works belong to the sculptural logic of the specific object, and all principles of the specific object can also be recognized in his furniture. Most importantly, the three-dimensionality of his pieces consist of real space; they are not illusional or representational. Second, they form a single whole, and third, their unity is 'one thing' rather than an arrangement of parts. One could object that his furniture does not comply with the third characteristic of the specific object, because the pieces usually consist of an arrangement of some planks and beams. But the same can be said for his sculptural works. The point is, however, that their wholeness is a single thing: a chair, a bench, a table.

Below I will discuss three Dutch artists whose works can be considered as specific objects. Their itinerary is, however, the opposite of Judd's. His specific objects were first limited to sculpture, and then began to include furniture. Because of their artistic training and background, the works of Maria van Kesteren, Geert Lap, and Aldo Bakker were initially considered to be design or applied art, but according to the logic of the specific object, their work could also be seen as sculpture. In the case of these three artists, the medium-specificity of design and sculpture is no longer relevant, or worse: it makes a good understanding and appreciation of their work impossible.

The Specific Forms of the Specific Objects of Maria van Kesteren

In the 2012 publication *Om de vorm: Leven en werk van Maria van Kesteren,* the artist tells of her sources of inspiration, which vary from the typical flat Dutch landscape, especially that of Friesland because of its emptiness; the work of Madeleine Boscher; the furniture of Dom van der Laan and Eileen Gray; the ceramic objects of Jan van der Vaart; the serial photography of Bernd and Hilla Becher; and last

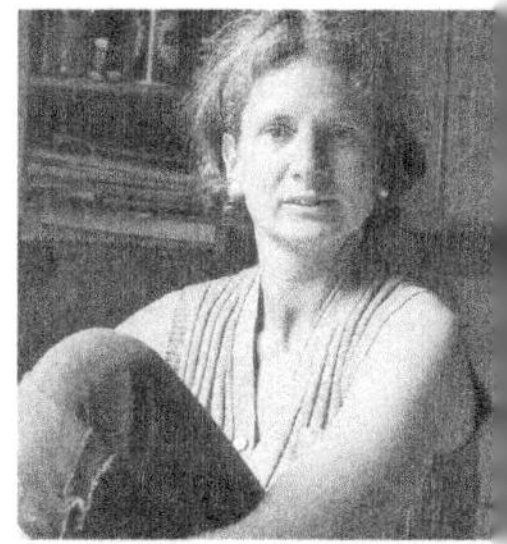

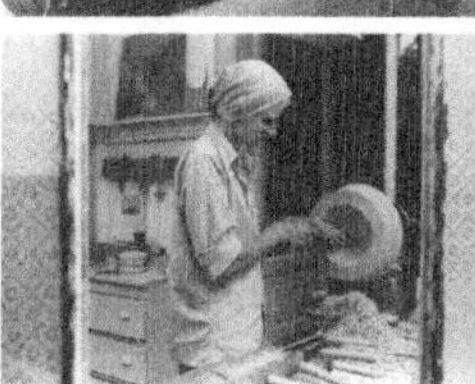

Maria van Kesteren (1933–2020)

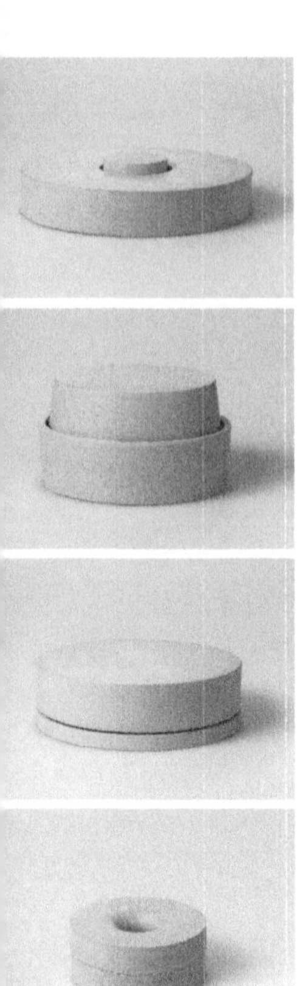

aria van Kesteren, *Box*, 1993; ox, 1992; *Box*, 1998; *Box*, 1994

but not least, the music of Simeon ten Holt. As diverse as all these examples of different media may be, one thing they have in common is that they share similarities with the aesthetics of Minimalism. Van Kesteren prefers forms that are reduced to utter simplicity and the work of these artists can be seen as endless variations on these simple forms. Due to this characteristic, most of her work and that of these artists is serial.

However, the reading of these artists' work as Minimalist is superficial, because it is only based on stylistic affinity. In what follows I will not approach Van Kesteren's work as a specific style, but rather as a specific working process and a very specific sculptural notion of art, namely that of the specific object. This means that her work is closer to that of Donald Judd and Sol LeWitt than contemporary design artists. It has often been argued that the Netherlands has a special affinity with Minimalism because of the Dutch *polder* landscape, in which serial lines and grids are recurrent features. Such a statement is, however, again based on stylistic affinity instead of a specific notion of art. In the Netherlands, Van Kesteren's work shows clear affinity with the work of Jan van der Vaart, although Van Kesteren works mainly in wood and Van der Vaart is a ceramicist. Another artist of a younger generation, and who claims his work is inspired by Van Kesteren, is the ceramicist Geert Lap. Whereas the work of both ceramicists differs in many respects to the turned, wooden forms of Van Kesteren, they have much in common in their working process.

Even though some of the turned forms of Van Kesteren are boxes or bowls, these categorizations focus on the possible function of these objects. But as objects, these functions are not really, or no longer, relevant. The turned forms result in the objects' *raison d'être*. However, this result does not rely on their function so much, but on their specific sculptural form. In the context of this chapter, 'specific' has a very specific meaning: it refers to the sculptural logic of the specific object as theorized and practised by Donald Judd. The objects of Van Kesteren can be called 'specific' in many respects. Although most of her work consists of turned forms in wood, a well-known statement of hers is that 'she cannot stand wood'. She also has a dislike of trees because they spoil the clear lines of the Dutch landscape. Like ceramics, wood tends to be seen as an expressive material, showing the hand of the artist in its processing. The turned forms in wood are thus supposed to demonstrate the sensibility of the artist. Van Kesteren loathes this notion of wood and ceramics. She is only concerned with the forms she turns. She does that in wood, nevertheless, but over the course of time she makes use of types of wood that have very little grain structure, and she started to make use of paints to cover the grains of the wood. It is only when we are no longer aware of the fact that these objects are made from wood that we can consider them as specific objects.

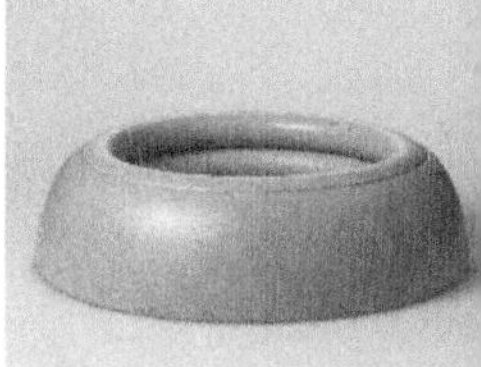
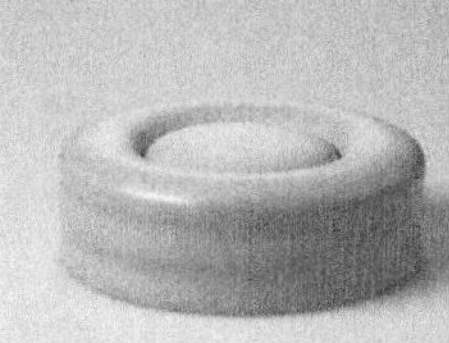
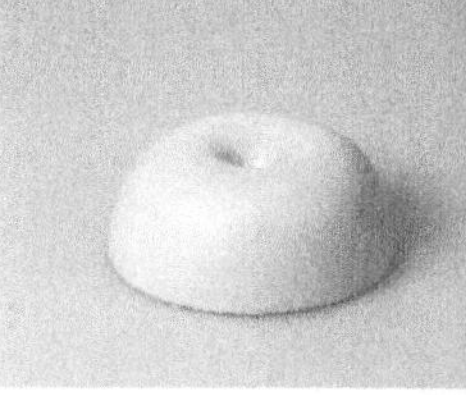
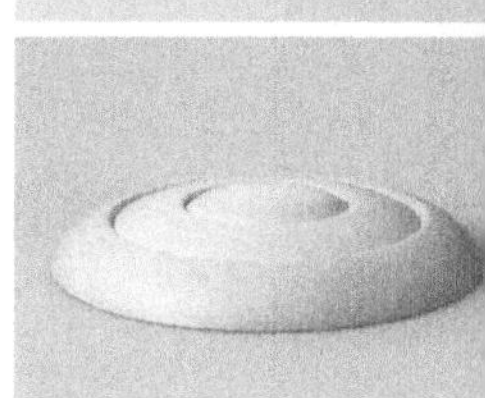

Maria van Kesteren, *Form*, 1984; *Box*, 1985; *Form*, 1974; *Box*, 1976

The technique employed by Van Kesteren belongs to traditional craftmanship; she turns the wooden objects on a wheel and shapes the form by keeping chisels against the turning wood. So, all her works are handmade, despite looking machine-made. The hand that has made these objects can never be read from them, her extreme perfectionism resulting in forms that suggest they have been industrially made. Her objects share that characteristic with the objects of Geert Lap, whose work I will discuss later in this chapter. But my earlier description of Judd's works is also appropriate for Van Kesteren's pieces: they are literal; they are what they are and do not express anything. The viewer should only focus on what she can see and what is there. Formally, Judd's and Van

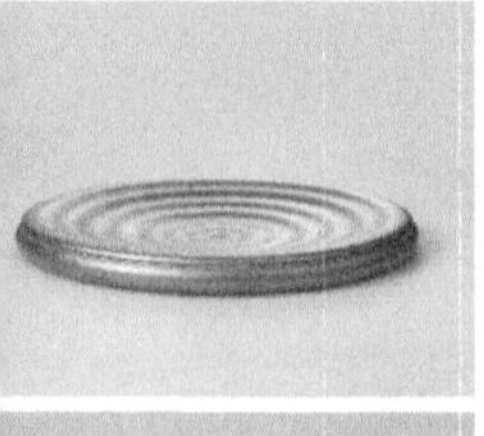

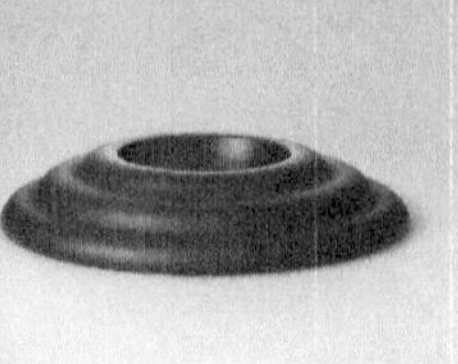

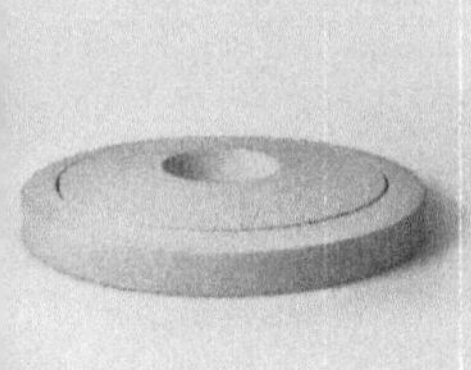

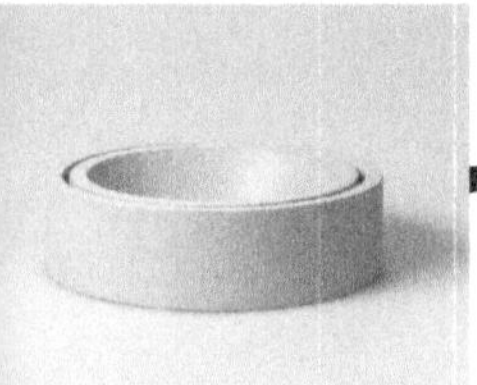

ıria van Kesteren, *Form*, 86; *Form*, 1987; *Form*, 1998; *rm*, 1995

Kesteren's work differs, but their working process, and the aesthetics that results from that, is very similar.

One of the most important characteristics of a specific object is that it counters relationships between parts of it. As a result, it is no longer a composed object, but rather a single object. At first sight, it is difficult to understand how we recognize this in the objects of Van Kesteren, especially when it concerns objects that can be seen as boxes—for they are composed of a container and a lid. Yet, I contend that her boxes also comply with the logic of the specific object and result in a single, unified whole. The lids are never designed from a functional point of view, but from an organic principle, as part of the rest of the object/form. Even more strongly, based on its form, the object being used as a box is not usually recognizable.

The Specific Objects of Geert Lap

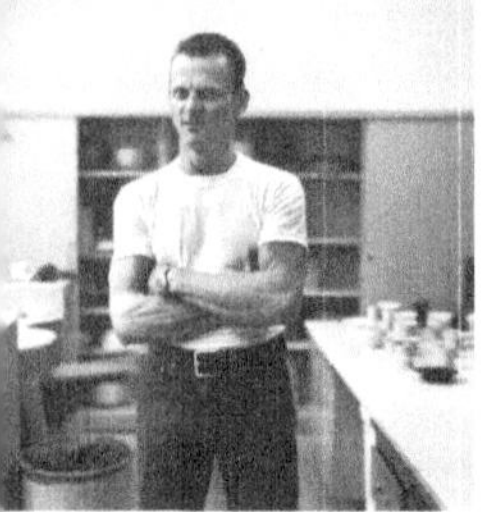

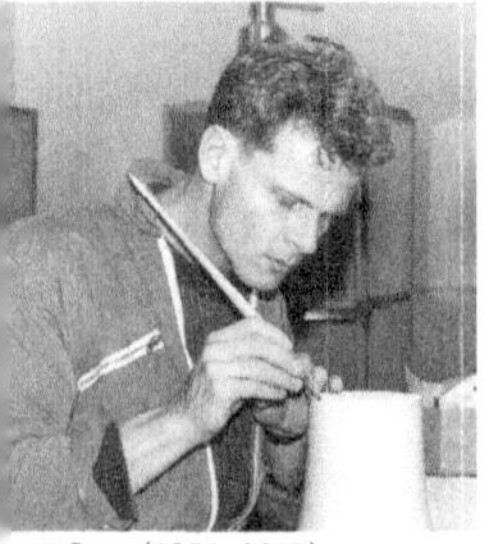

ert Lap (1951–2017)

In many languages the discourse one uses to describe vases is derived from the body. It deals with the container form of vases as bodies. Although not all vases have these body parts, the archetypical vase is supposed to have a *foot* on which it stands. It also has a *belly*, which contains most of the content; the belly narrows down into the *neck* of the vase; and the content of a vase is poured out through the *spout*. Although not literally derived from the body, but from the clothing with which bodies are covered, the *collar* is another possible body part of the archetypical vase. And in the case of a ceramic vase, the glaze that covers it is supposed to be its skin. All these different body parts explicitly express the anthropomorphized notion of the vase as body.

However, none of these parts can be recognized in the

container forms of ceramicist Geert Lap. While he has made an almost endless number of variations of the container form, it makes little sense to describe these variations with this bodily discourse. His vases never have a foot, a belly, a neck, a spout, or a collar. Although his vases have a bottom on which they stand, they never have a foot as an added element to the form.

In his work, one typically distinguishes three phases. In the first two, his vases still have a skin in the form of a glaze. The porcelain containers he made at the end of his studies at the Rietveld Academie and at the beginning of his career always have an unglazed strip along the edge. Some of the early porcelain objects have a kind of collar, but Geert Lap soon decided to omit these collars because he considered them as non-functional ornaments. The unglazed strips along the edge create a tension between the vase as body, with skin that is, and the container form that refuses to be imagined as body. For Lap, in the process of making these containers the fact that porcelain could not be fully controlled was problematic: during firing it shrinks and distorts its original form. Porcelain clay melts like glass in the kiln. During this melting process the originally thrown form dissolves a little and becomes 'weak'. This was the reason he switched to stoneware, a material that could be better controlled during the production process. Around 1984 he began to work in stoneware—stoneware vases still needed a glaze and he made many beautiful vases in this technique, pieces covered with a skin of frequently pastel-coloured glazes.

But although the choice to use stoneware instead of porcelain had solved a major problem, Lap was still not satisfied with the kind of vases he was making. The fact that the pure form of a piece had to be covered with a glaze disguising the original form and distracting from the shape as such

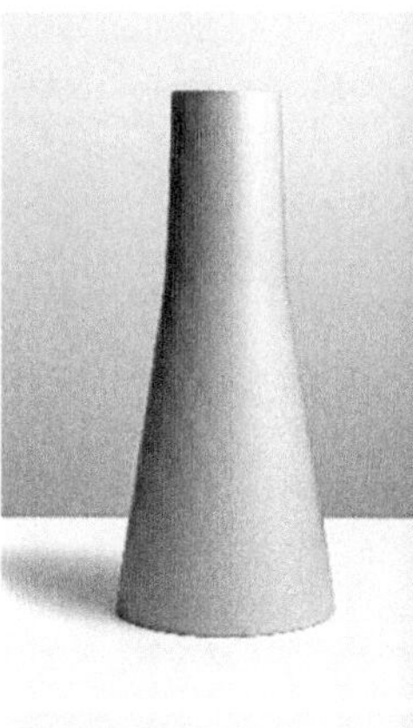

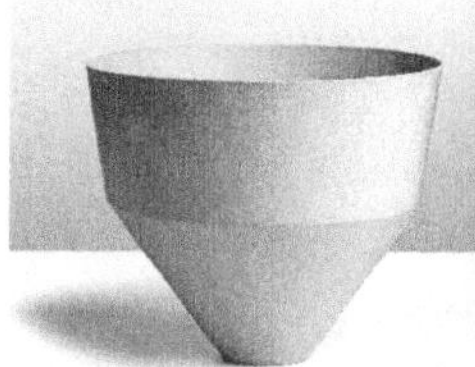

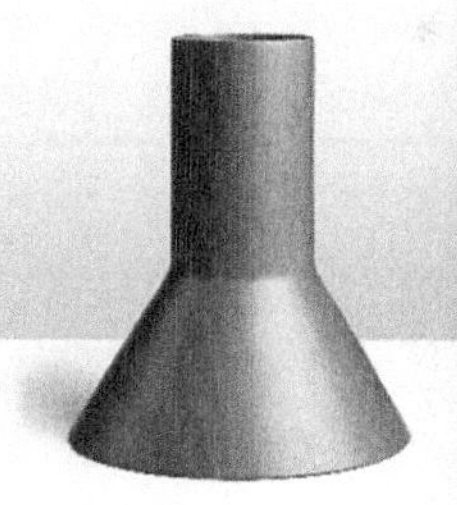

Geert Lap, ceramic forms, c. 1986; c. 1986; c. 1986

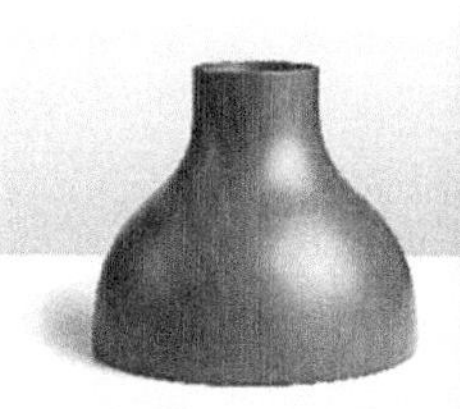

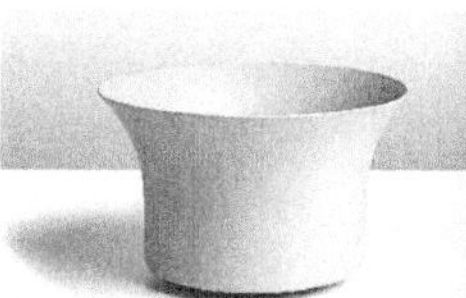

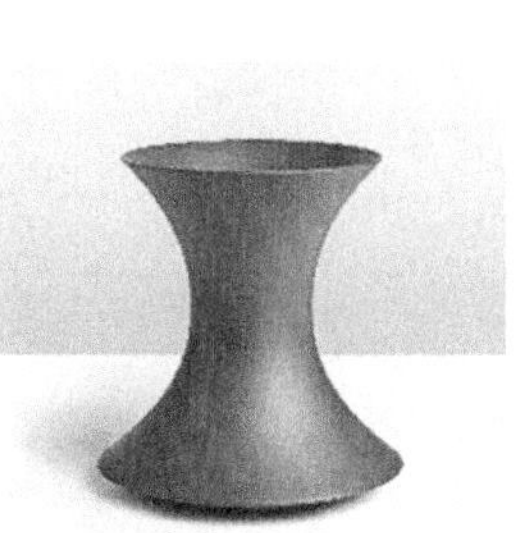

Geert Lap, ceramic forms, c. 1992; c. 1986; c. 1990

23 Beenker, 'Geert Lap', p. 49.
24 Beenker, 'Geert Lap', p. 49.

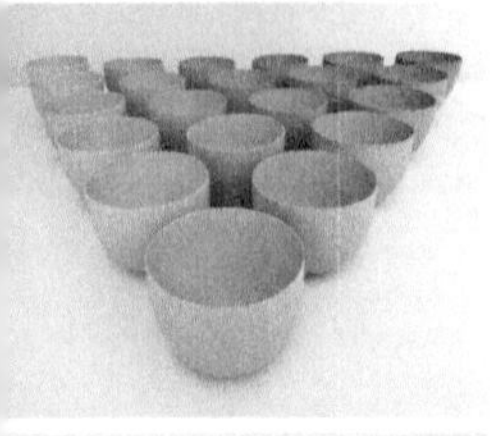

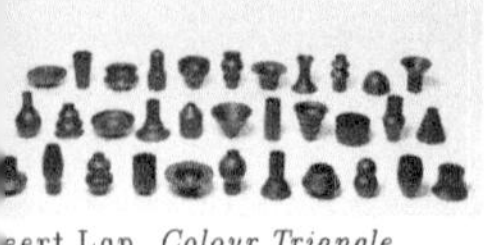

Geert Lap, *Colour Triangle*, 1988; *99 Variations*, 1993

constituted a problem for him. Therefore, around 1987 he started to work with the *terra sigillata* technique. In this technique, the stoneware body of the vase and the coating that is used to cover its surface are composed of the same kind of clay. The coating is made from the clay of which the form is made:

> With this technique the clay from which the form is made is thinned out with water to a milky mixture. After it has stood for a few days and the clay particles have settled, the top layer—containing the lightest clay particles—is skimmed off. The substance is mixed with color pigments and then painted onto the form. The flat, crystal-shaped particles fold over each other like scales and thus seal the earth (the clay), which after firing, is completely watertight and chemically inert.[23]

With the *terra sigillata* technique Geert Lap solved the problem of form and glaze (colour) being different substances—one covering the other as a skin—but not entirely because one cannot completely glaze the bottom of the form on which it stands. One can of course use a triangle when the bottom has also been glazed, but the three points of the triangle will still stick to the glaze and damage the 'skin'. The coating to which colour pigments have been added can be applied to the whole piece uniformly, including the bottom. Colour and form are of the same material and react to the firing in exactly the same way.[24] In terms of the bodily discourse used for the description of vases, one can also say that by using the *terra sigillata* technique Lap has banned the last body part from his forms as well. Considering his pieces as forms, instead of body-like vases, now becomes unavoidable.

The two elements that constitute his works are colour and form—it could be said that his work consists of nothing other than colour variations and form variations. Two groups of works concentrate on the kinds of variation: either colour or form. *Colour Triangle* (1988) is installed in the shape of a triangle, in the corners one yellow, one blue, and one pink ceramic form and consistently using the form of the bowl, all of which are exactly the same size.[25] This work repeats the same form but varies the colour. The work 99 *Variations* (1993) presents ninety-nine variations in form, all in black.[26] It repeats the same colour but varies the form.

His other works can be seen as combining the principle of the variation of colour as well as form. The most appropriate noun to describe these combined variations is 'object'. In contrast with 'vase', 'object' has no conventional meanings and traditions attached to it, but 'object' as a term is perhaps a little too general. It does not acknowledge the specificity at stake: a combination of a colour variation and form variation. Hence why I propose the use of the term explained above, introduced by Donald Judd for his own works and those of other Minimalist artists: 'specific object'.

In contrast with Donald Judd, Lap has never articulated and written down his ideas about his own work. But two interviews with him, one by Guus Beumer and another by Liesbeth den Besten, give a good impression of how Lap thought of his own artistic practice in relation to notions of art (and craft) in the nineteen-eighties and nineteen-nineties. However, that does not mean that Lap's poetics can be reconstructed on the basis of these interviews; one only gets a hint of them. When we pursue a deeper understanding and appreciation of Lap's work, we have to rely on the internal logic of his oeuvre and on comparisons with artists with whom he seems to have an affinity. And sometimes this can be supported by his own statements in interviews. Although working in a different medium, Judd seems to be the ideal fellow

25 Geert Lap, *21 Monochrome* is now in the collection of the Museum Boijmans Van Beuningen, Rotterdam.

26 This work is in the collection of three different museums: one third is in the collection of the Stedelijk Museum in Amsterdam, one third in the collection of the Keramiekmuseum Princessehof in Leeuwarden, and the other third in the Kunstmuseum in The Hague.

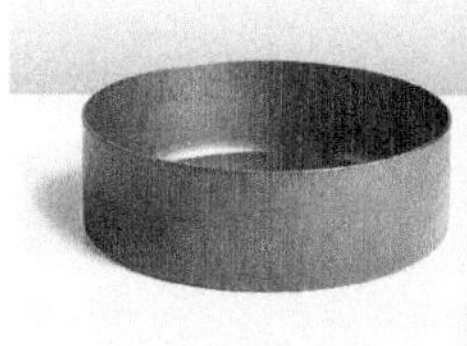

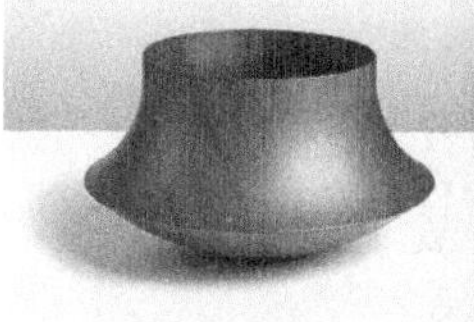

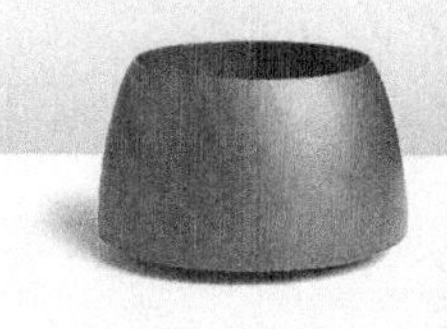

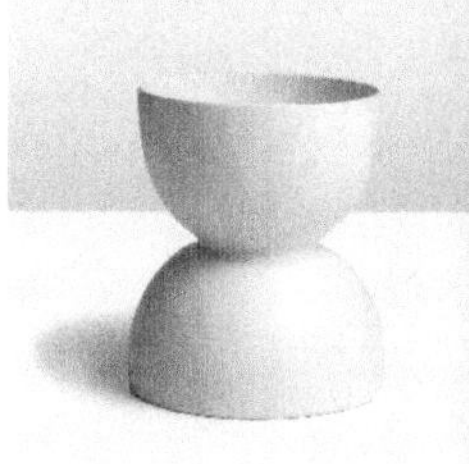

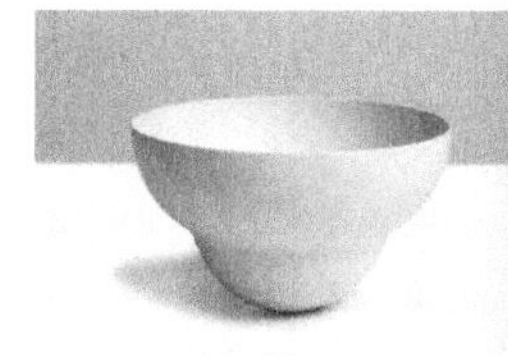

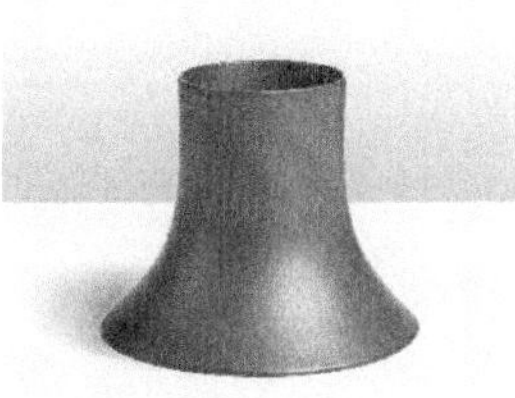

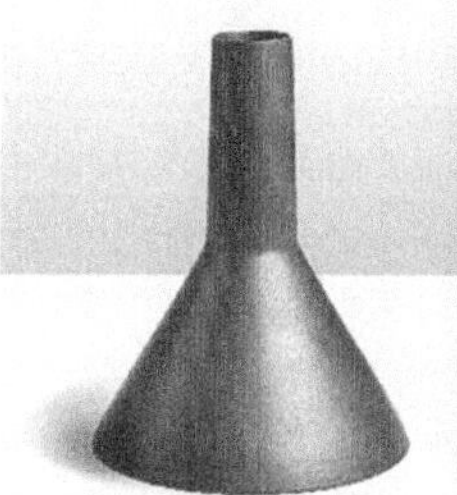

Geert Lap, ceramic forms, c. 1989; c. 1992; c. 1988; c. 1998; c. 1998; c. 1995, c. 1989

[27] Beenker, 'Geert Lap', p. 41.

artist to whom Lap can be compared. I will show how the internal logic of his oeuvre can be understood as a development from vase to specific object, in Judd's sense of that term.

Beenker's description of Geert Lap's work is very much to the point: 'It is pure cylindrical in form, functional by origin (mostly in vase form) and devoid of handles, spouts and decorations.'[27] This description places the emphasis on the cylindrical form instead of the vase as container, with a very specific tradition. Lap has departed and taken distance from the potter's conventional destination of making 'applied arts'. But at the same time, Geert Lap is a conventional potter and craftsman; he only uses traditional methods. All of his work is made by hand and is one of a kind, yet the fact that the whole process of making these cylindrical forms is fashioned by hand does not show in the result. His work gives the impression of having been produced industrially owing to its extreme perfection. It is never expressive and does not show the hand of the potter. My earlier description of Donald Judd's specific objects also applies to Lap's cylindrical forms: they are not expressive; that is, they do not express the inner subjectivity of the artist, but they are literal: they are what they are, and the viewer should focus on 'what's there'.

But how do his 'plastic objects' relate to Judd's notion of 'specific object'? An important characteristic of a specific object is that it opposes part-to-part relations, promoting instead the 'singleness' of the object. When Lap decided to use the *terra sigillata* technique, he mastered a problem that had greatly annoyed him when using glazes as skin for his objects. Glaze can never cover the whole form. If the bottom of an object were glazed it would stick to the bottom of the oven when being fired. The glaze would be damaged when removing it from the oven. In the words of Beenker: 'Lap tries to overcome this ugly transition between glazed and raw material by coloring the bottom with a similar engobe color, but this does not really solve the problem.'[28] Indeed, it does not really solve the problem, because although the colour appears to be uninterrupted, the material is not. I am not sure if ugliness is the problem here, because it concerns the bottom of the object, which one does not see. But the glazed object with the unglazed bottom disrupts the singleness of the object, because it forms a part-to-part relation. And this part-to-part relation is clearly hierarchical: the bottom is less important than the rest of the object because it is invisible. It only has a function because the object stands on the bottom. Lap got rid of this part-to-part relation by using the *terra sigillata* technique. The relation between glazed object and unglazed bottom and also between the body-like object and its skin are no longer at stake. His objects do not have parts anymore, they are no longer composed. They are single three-dimensional unities of form and colour. In other words, they are specific objects.

When Lap decided to make his works in stoneware instead of porcelain, his use of colour also changed. The porcelain objects always have an unglazed strip along the edge, creating a contrast in colour. The naked, white porcelain strip contrasts with the darker, coloured glaze that covers the rest of the object. When he began to work in stoneware, the whole object was glazed uniformly in one single colour, mostly bright pastel colours. Although the term monochrome is used to describe single-colour paintings, Geert Lap's stoneware objects are in fact also monochromes.

Monochromes in painting are commonly motivated negatively by what they refrain from. Monochrome is the extreme form of colour stripped of its illusionistic use and separated from its denotative of descriptive function.[29] Colours can have a spatial effect. Judd explains this effect of

28 Beenker, 'Geert Lap', p. 49.

29 Fer, 'Judd's Specific Objects', p. 140.

Fer, Judd's Specific Objects', 144.

Quoted in Fer, 'Judd's ecific Objects', p. 144.

colour in his text 'Specific Objects', commenting on the blue monochromes of Yves Klein, which were exhibited in New York in 1962. When two colours lie on a surface, they lie in different depths, as if one were always in front of another, or one recedes. When one colour is evenly applied over the whole canvas, this effect does not come about; the surface remains flat. Monochromes became such an important genre in the nineteen-fifties and nineteen-sixties because the genre cancelled illusionistic space and embodied the medium-specific ideal of (painting) flatness. In a review of Yves Klein's 1962 exhibition in New York, Donald Judd called him 'the biggest frog in a rather stagnant pond' that was Europe.[30] The blue monochromes are for Judd the most interesting paintings because they are 'unspatial'. Conventional paintings are not single objects because they are rectangles containing an illusionistic space, whether figurative or abstract. Klein's monochromes had much in common with recent American work and with Judd's own work: 'They are simple and broadly scaled; they tend to become objects.'[31] Judd could not have paid a more positive compliment.

The series of sculptures which Judd showed one year later, in December 1963, at the Green Gallery in New York was a monochrome series: all boxes were in cadmium red. His monochromes were completely even and smooth and did not create any pictorial effect or contain any gestural mark or brushstroke. The plywood out of which the boxes were made absorbed the colour. As a result, the cadmium red paint was not a substantial layer on top of the wooden objects, but it remained thinnish. The fact that he chose cadmium red (which has a slightly orangey tone) instead of primary red is also significant. Primary colours like red, yellow, and blue are considered to be the 'basic' colours within a system of colours. He avoided underlying, rational systems or *a priori* systems. Thus, he selected a colour which was not motivated by any rule or system —it 'is just there'.

Lap's use of colour, especially in the second phase of his career when he started to work in stoneware, has much in common with Judd's. Although Judd only made monochromes for a short period—and Lap did so for the rest of his life—the kinds of colours they selected for their works is never motivated by any *a priori* system. Within that similarity, Judd's palette of colours is very restricted, whereas Lap's palette is extremely diverse; he explored every possible tone of colour imaginable. In the work of both artists, primary colours are missing, although this is not true for Lap's first phase when he still worked in porcelain. During this period, he used black and white (colours with heavy idealistic connotations) and the three primary colours: red, yellow, and blue. The fact that he later started to explore all possible colour tones without the primary ones, however, shows that he expanded his palette in such a way that he began to avoid primary systems and embraced the phenomenological reception by viewers. His colours please, or frighten, the eye.

Common ground in the work of Lap and Judd is that both practices look very systematic. But, as I argued earlier, there are no underlying systems that produce their works as the origin from which they sprout. In the case of Lap, his works are the result of systematic research into form, size, and colour. To better understand the systematic nature of his work, it is important to return to the distinction between 'system' and 'method'. As I have said, a method is a means of obtaining an end and never an end in itself; a system is both a means and an end.[32] It implies that the systematic nature of Lap's work is the result of a specific method, not of a system, which makes it appropriate to consider his works as specific objects.

32 Chandler, 'Tony Smith and Sol LeWitt', p. 20.

Rethinking Form: Aldo Bakker

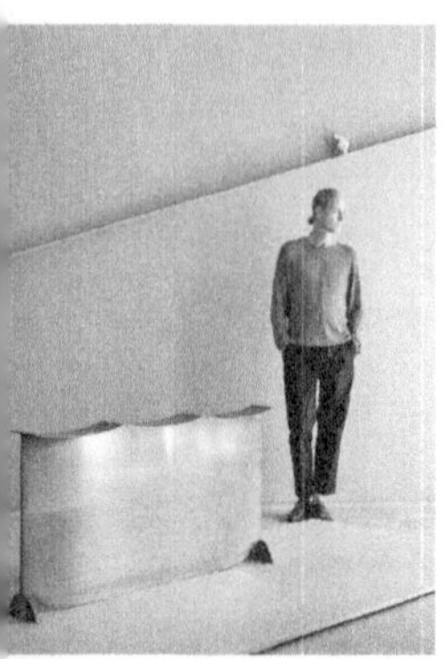

do Bakker (1971)

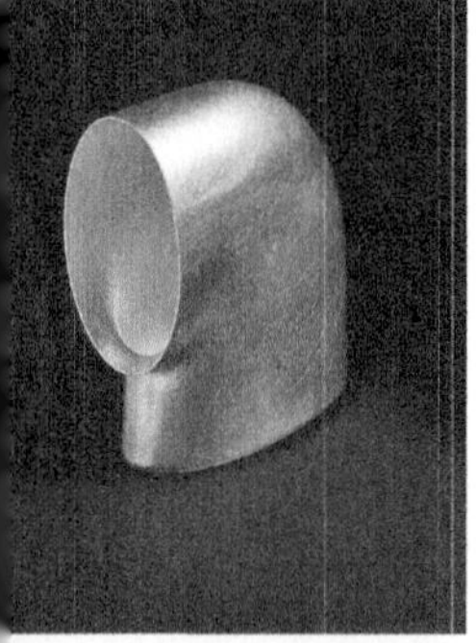

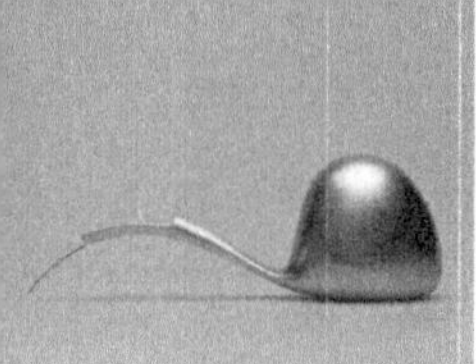

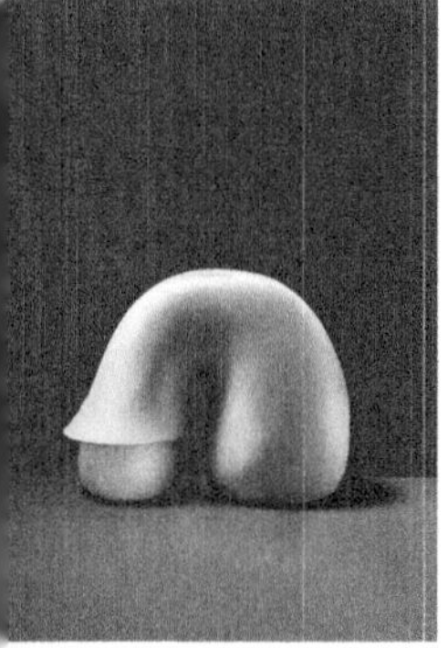

do Bakker, *Oil Can*, 2005; *Soy urer*, 2010; *Jug and Cup*, 2011, otos: Erik & Petra Hesmerg

As we saw in the cases of Judd, Van Kesteren, and Lap, the medium specificity of design and sculpture is seriously challenged; or to put it more bluntly, it makes a good understanding and appreciation of their work impossible. The principles of the specific object can be recognized in all their works: most importantly, the three-dimensionality of their pieces consists of real space; they are not illusional or representational. In addition, they form a single whole, and as a result their unity is 'one thing' rather than an arrangement of parts. As I argued, that is even the case with Judd's furniture or Van Kesteren's boxes with lids: their wholeness is one thing—a chair, a table, or a box. Or, to put it more clearly, although it is a chair or a box, the forms of these objects form one single unit.

At first, it is much more difficult to recognize the logic of the specific object in the works of Aldo Bakker. Although not necessarily a principle of the specific object, the works of the artists mentioned above can be seen as variations of simple, elementary forms. That is why their works often look serial. Bakker's works, however, never look serial; each object is unique and cannot be seen as a variation on other forms. His objects do not look minimalistic, as the works of Judd, LeWitt, Van Kesteren, and Lap do. They look baroque, though not in their entirety. Yet one of the most important characteristics of the specific object is that it counters relationships between parts of it. As a result, it is no longer a composed object, but a single object. That principle can always be recognized in the objects of Bakker. Even when the object consists of two parts, for instance a mug and a carafe, and a carafe and its stopper, the form is single, or forms a unity.

Over the course of the twentieth century, two dogmas became prevalent in the world of design: 'form follows function', and 'you get what you see', meaning that an object immediately discloses how it was made and for what it can or should be used. The first dogma concerns the maker or designer of objects, the second the viewer or user of them. The objects of Bakker violate these rules insistently. He always starts with a specific form that fascinates him. Through sketching and modelling, he tries to understand and develop the form. Having understood the logic that defines that specific form, he begins to reflect on the possible meanings of it. And it is very important in this respect that function should not be conflated with meaning; function is only one meaning among other possible meanings. This working process results in objects that can be called specific objects.

The signification of form happens in the interaction between the designed object and its user. With his objects, Bakker stages scenes in which the user is engaged in a seemingly ordinary act with possibilities and sensations that you rarely experience in everyday life. This engagement with form makes the user experience space, flow, time, and resistance. An affective awareness that can also result in the discovery of its function, but not necessarily so. As design curator Jan Boelen observed:

> For Aldo Bakker to function also implies making the user aware of the beauty, to astonish him or her. To sit, to lick, to function, to engage with a wide range of primal sensory experiences.[33]

As a result, the user gets much more than what s/he sees.

In Bakker's universe, fascinating forms are never complex. But their lack of complexity does not mean that his forms are simple. These qualities are not opposed in the

33 Quoted in Rawsthorn, 'Introduction', p. 9.

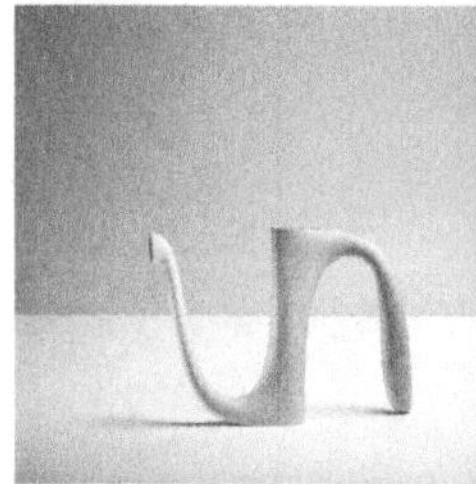

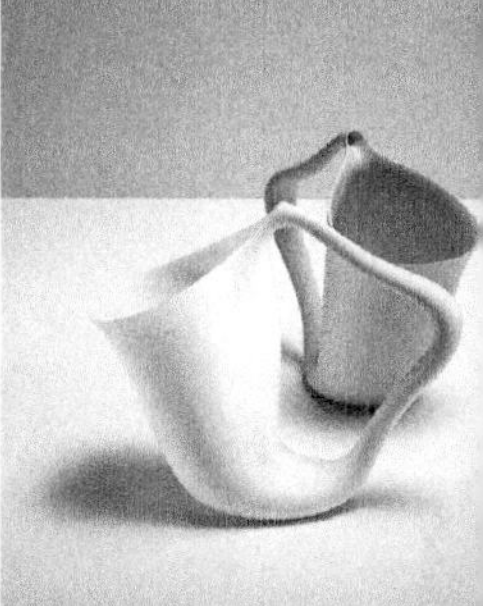

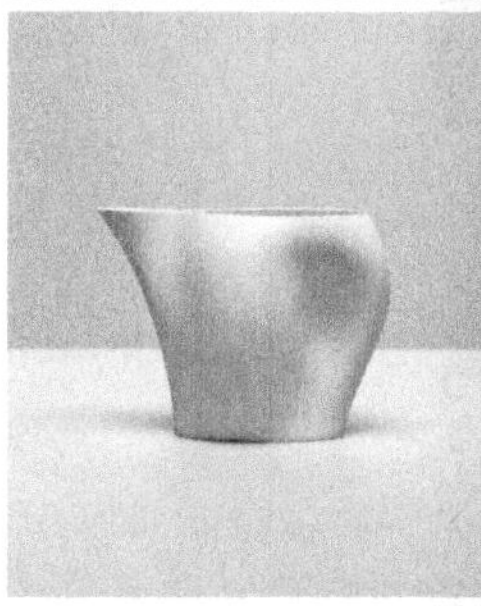

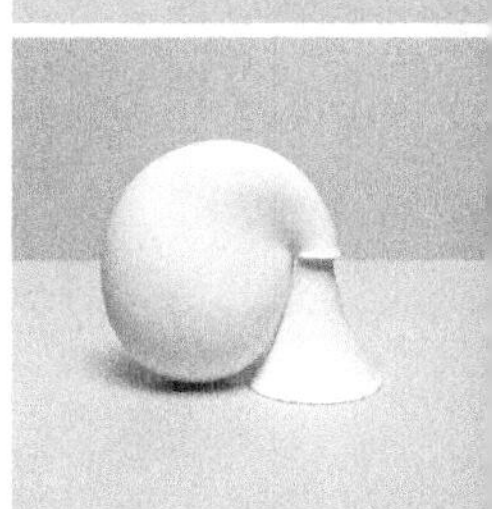

Aldo Bakker, *AlinetoB*, 2014; *Chalice*, 2014; *Pastis*, 2016; *Set*, 2018, photos: Erik & Petr[a] Hesmerg

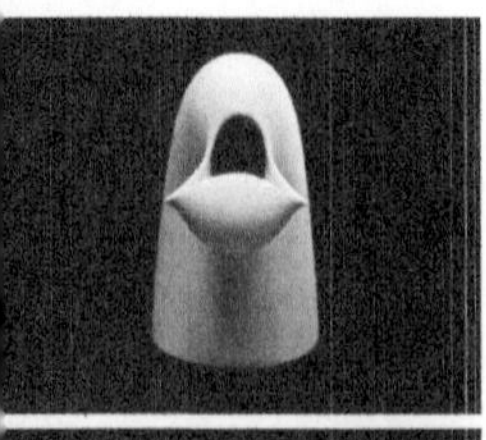

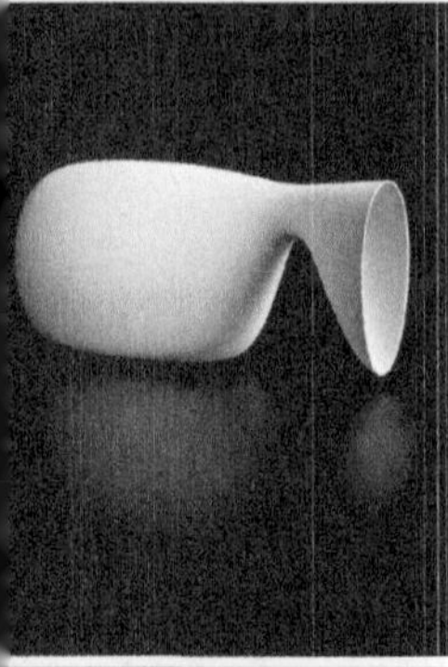

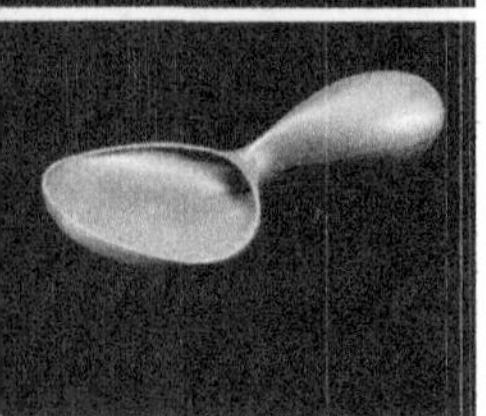

do Bakker, *Vinegar Flask*, 08; *Water Carafe*, 2007; *Salt llar*, 2007, photos: Erik & tra Hesmerg

objects of Bakker. Take the pouring vessel *AlinetoB* from 2014. This form is not complex in the sense that it is not composed; it consists of one fluent line. But as a line it is not at all simple, basic, or Minimalist. As a form it is highly unexpected because it completely differs from forms we know. We know this kind of form perhaps as part of handwriting, but not in a design object. It is unrecognizable, new, and original in the sense that it is without origins.

Bakker's designs have been compared to the sculptures of Constantin Brancusi and the paintings of Paul Cézanne because these artists' work can be understood as searches for 'primal form'. This primal form is supposed to be natural, with these artistic practices then becoming searches for lost origins. But in the case of Bakker's designs, there is no underlying form or system that generates his works as their origin. He is fascinated by specific forms, not by underlying, primal forms or systems. From this perspective, his designs can be better understood in terms of 'specific objects' à la Judd. The relation between a specific object and 'real space' is of great importance to Judd, with the latter being modified by the former. Real space is not the context of the specific object; real space is shaped by the form of a specific object. This means that space is the medium of the specific object. To reiterate: the specific object's silhouette outlines space as volume.

Although Judd proposed the term 'specific object' in the nineteen-sixties as an assessment of Minimalist painting and sculpture, it also provides a productive understanding of Bakker's design practice. At first glance, this comparison between Judd and Bakker makes little sense because as a designer Bakker works by definition in and with real space; painters and sculptors, by contrast, come from traditions in which space is not considered to be real, but illusionistic. But the fact that designers work in and with real space does

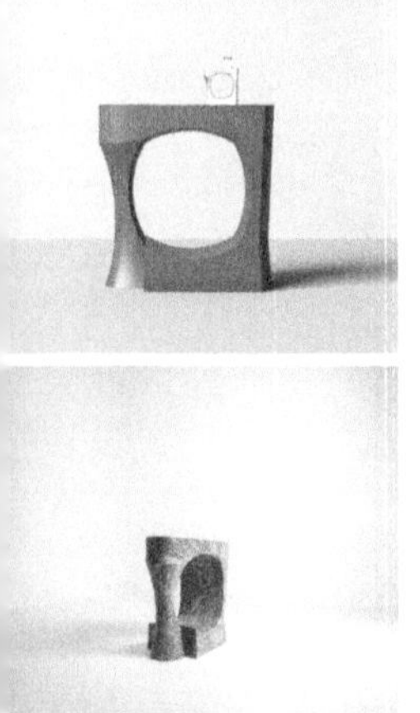

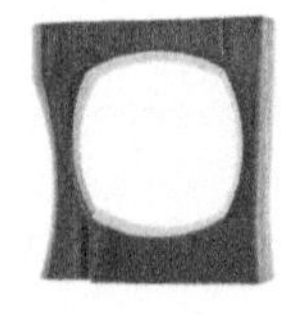

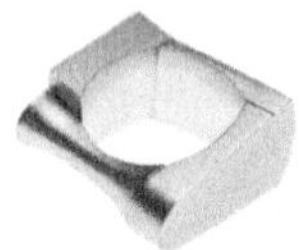

Aldo Bakker, *Ring Table*, 2021, console; bracelet; ring, photos: Erik & Petra Hesmerg

not mean that their objects make users aware of the dimensions in which design objects are handled: space and time. The wide range of sensory experiences invoked by Bakker's objects makes them exist in the dimension of 'real space' and 'real time'. This defines them as specific objects.

The objects Bakker designs can be categorized as sculpture, furniture—benches, stools, tables—and pouring vessels. For the last category, Bakker uses the neologism '*schenkers*'. The Dutch verb 'schenken' is an ambiguous word, meaning to pour but also to give. The noun 'schenker', however, normally only refers to a person who gives, not to a vessel that pours. But pouring is giving. It suggests that Bakker's neologism 'schenker' does not refer to the vessels that pour water, oil, vinegar, or salt, but to the objects that give new forms to the world.

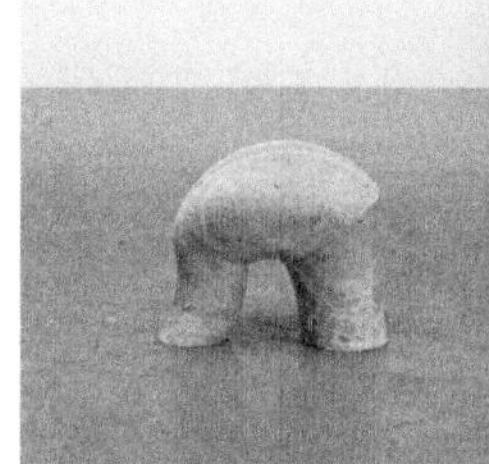

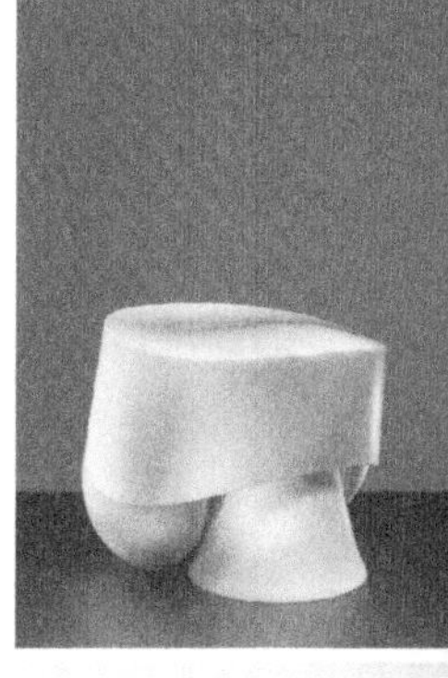

Not only do his pouring vessels give such new forms to the world, his furniture also does, as do his objects which have no function at all. With Bakker's working process and his ambition to make objects that can be called 'specific', in Judd's sense, it is completely logical that, although starting as a designer of functional objects, he began making objects that only classify as sculpture.

Bakker's bracketing of function is not the same as ignoring or cancelling function. His very recent work *Ring Table* (2021) is a good example of this. Depending on the size, it can be a ring, a bracelet, a stool, or a table. But it is one single form. One could also say that it is a sculpture that comes in three different sizes. It is constructed from circular fragments and straight lines. One sees the compilation, one sees the transitions between different forms, but rather paradoxically this compilation results in one single form that is completely new and unique. Although the logic of this work results in a unique form, it can also be recognized in some of his other

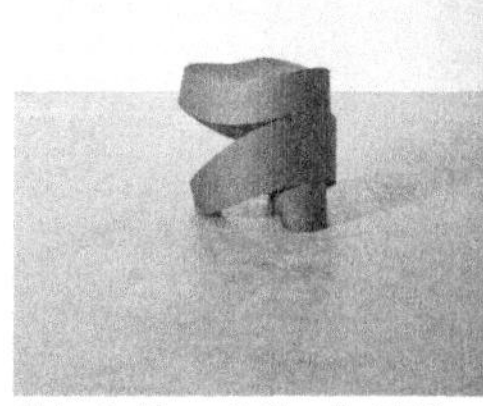

Aldo Bakker, *B (Azul)*, 2019; *Three Pair*, 2021; *Wait/Weight* (Basaltina), 2019, photos: Erik & Petra Hesmerg

works, such as *Stool* (2006), *Tonus* (2010), *Three Pair* (2013), and *B* (2019). But this does not mean that they are variations of one another. It means that *Ring Table* is not only a specific object, but also that the specificity of this object is based on a unique form.

The works of Judd, Lewitt, Van Kesteren, Lap, and Bakker discussed in this chapter are all examples of the logic of the specific object, but they differ in how they relate to it. The work of all of them cannot be appreciated in terms of the specificity of the media they work in; their objects belong to sculpture as well as to the world of design. But I contend that it is because they make specific objects that they transgress the boundaries of both media. At first, Judd and Bakker stand at opposite ends within this logic of the specific object: the first is known for his sculpture, the second for his position in the world of design. Judd ended up making sculptural furniture, while Bakker makes the notion of functionality more or less, but not completely, superfluous. Some of his objects are autonomous sculptures, and one could argue they all are. This conclusion is also telling about the logics of sculpture. Although this notion of logics suggests that sculpture has its own specificity, called medium specificity, the logic of the specific object indicates that this specificity can be transgressed, including objects that have so far been excluded from this medium of sculpture for being design.

Bibliography

Alberti, Leon Battista. *On Painting* (1435), translated by J.R. Spencer. New York: Yale University Press, 1966.

Alberto Giacometti. Exh. cat. New York: Museum of Modern Art, 1965.

Alberto Giacometti 1901–1966: Beelden, schilderijen, tekeningen, grafiek. Exh. cat. The Hague: Haags Gemeentemuseum, 1986.

Alphen, Ernst van. 'Sheer Skin: The Dissolution of Sculptural Skin and Sculpted Skin.' In *Alina Szapocznikow: Awkward* Objects, edited by Agata Jakubowska, p. 113–22. Warsaw: M books, 2011.

Anzieu, Didier. *The Skin Ego: A Psychoanalytic Approach of the Self*, translated from the French by Chris Turner. New Haven, CT: Yale University Press, 1989.

Bal, Mieke. *Louise Bourgeois' Spider: The Architecture of Art-Writing*. Chicago: University of Chicago Press, 2001.

—. *Fragments of Matter: Jeannette Christensen*. Bergen: Bergen National Academy of the Arts, 2009.

—. *Of What One Cannot Speak: Doris Salcedo's Political Art*. Chicago: University of Chicago Press, 2010.

—. *Endless Andness: The Politics of Abstraction According to Ann Veronica Janssens*. London: Bloomsbury, 2013.

—. *Narratology: Introduction to the Theory of Narrative*, fourth edition. Toronto: University of Toronto Press, 2017.

Barassi, Sebastiano. 'The Sculptor is a Blind Man: Constantin Brancusi's *Sculpture for the Blind*.' In *Sculpture and Touch*, edited by Peter Dent, pp. 169–80. London: Routledge, 2014.

Bataille, Georges. 'L'Informe.' *Documents* 7 (December 1929), p. 382.

Bauer, Douglas F. 'The Function of Pygmalion in the Metamorphoses of Ovid.' *Transactions and Proceedings of the American Philological Association* 93 (1962), pp. 1–21.

Beenker, Erik. 'Geert Lap.' In *Geert Lap: De gedraaide vorm/The Thrown Form*, pp. 41–50. Exh. cat. Rotterdam: Museum Boymans-van Beuningen, 1989.

Benjamin, Andrew. 'To Touch: Herder and Sculpture.' In *Sculpture and Touch*, edited by Peter Dent, pp. 79–90. London: Routledge, 2014.

Berkeley, George. *An Essay Towards a New Theory of Vision*. Dublin 1709.

Besten, Liesbeth den. 'Geert Lap: 'Not Finished by a Long Shot.' *Ceramics: Art and Perception* 29 (1997), pp. 69–73.

Beumer, Geert. 'Geert Lap.' *Bijvoorbeeld* 1988, no. 4, pp. 4–7.

Bishop, Claire. *Installation Art*. London: Tate Publishing, 2005.

Bodet, Frédéric. 'Details to the Point of Dizziness.' In *Elmar Trenkwalder: Angel above Light and Shadows: Of the Redemptive Silence of Form*, pp. 30–31. Vienna: Verlag für moderne Kunst, 2018.

Bois, Yve-Alain. 'Strzemiński and Kobro: In Search of Motivation.' In *Painting as Model*, pp. 123–56. Cambridge, MA: MIT Press, 1990.

—. 'A Picturesque Stroll around *Clara-Clara*.' In *Richard Serra* (October files; 1), edited by Hal Foster, pp. 59–97. Cambridge, MA: MIT Press, 2000.

—. 'Kobro and Strzemiński Revisited.' *October* 156 (Spring 2016), pp. 3–11.

—, and Rosalind E. Krauss. *Formless: A User's Guide*. New York: Zone Books, 1997.

—, et al. 'A Conversation with Hubert Damisch.' *October* 85 (1989), pp. 3–17.

Boogerd, Dominic van den. 'Caryatid by Moonlight.' In *Didier Vermeiren: Collection de Solides*, pp. 99–103. Exh. cat. Eindhoven: Van Abbemuseum, 2003.

Boot, Marjan. 'Preface.' In *Heringa/Van Kalsbeek: Controlled Accidents*. Amsterdam: Heringa/Van Kalsbeek, 2007, n.p.

Bourdon, David, 'The Razed Sites of Carl Andre: A Sculptor Laid Low by the Brancusi Syndrome.' *Artforum* 5, no. 2 (October 1966), p. 15. Reprinted in *About Carl Andre: Critical Texts Since 1965*, edited by Paula Feldman, Alistair Rider, and Karsten Huber, p. 25. London: Ridinghouse, 2006.

Bourgeois, Louise. *Spiral*. Bologna: Damiani, 2019.

Brillenburg Wurth, Kiene. 'Radical Indeterminacy: The Sublime Sculptures of Heringa/Van Kalsbeek.' In *Heringa/Van Kalsbeek: Controlled Accidents*. Amsterdam: Heringa/Van Kalsbeek, 2007, n.p.

Brown, Julia. 'Interview with James Turrell.' In *Occluded Front: James Turrell*, edited by Julia Brown, pp. 13–46. Los Angeles: Fellows of Contemporary Art; Larkspur Landing, CA: Lapis Press, 1985.

Cannon, Steve. 'David Hammons' New York: Twenty Years, Retro-Introspection.' In *David Hammons: Rousing the Rubble*, pp. 38–60. Cambridge, MA: MIT Press, 1991.

Chandler, John N. 'Tony Smith and Sol LeWitt: Mutations and Permutations.' In *Sol LeWitt*, pp. 18–20. The Hague: Haags Gemeentemuseum, 1970.

Clark, Garth. 'Geert Lap: Some Notes on Minimalism in Ceramic Art.' In *Geert Lap. De gedraaide vorm/The Thrown Form*, pp. 11–23. Rotterdam: Museum Boymans-van Beuningen, 1989.

Collins, Judith. *Sculpture Today*. London: Phaidon, 2014 (2007).

Criqui, Jean-Pierre. 'A Brief Tour of "Collections de Solides".' In Dominic van den Boogerd and Jean-Pierre Criqui, *Didier Vermeiren: Collections de Solides*, pp. 111–14. Exh. cat. Eindhoven: Van Abbemuseum, 2003

—. 'Charles Ray's Sculpture Fiction.' In Jean-Pierre Criqui and Caroline Bourgeois, *Charles Ray*, pp. 113–24. Exh. cat. Paris: Pinault Collection; Centre Pompidou, 2022.

Crone, Rainer, and Petrus Graf Schaesberg. *Louise Bourgeois: The Secret of the Cells*. Munich: Prestel, 1998.

Curtis, Penelope. *Sculpture: Vertical, Horizontal, Closed, Open*. New Haven, CT: Yale University Press, 2017.

Damisch, Hubert. *Le jugement de Pâris*. Paris: Flammarion, 1992.

—. *The Origin of Perspective*, translated by John Goodman. Chicago: University of Chicago Press, 1994 (1987).

Dent, Peter, ed. *Sculpture and Touch*. London: Routledge, 2014.

Diderot, Denis. *Letter on the Blind*. 1749.

Dubois, Philippe. 'Photography Mise-en-Film: Autobiographical (Hi)stories and Psychic Apparatuses.' In *Fugitive Images: From Photography to Video*, edited by Patrice Pedro, pp. 152–53. Bloomington, IN: Indiana University Press, 1965.

Eisenman, Peter. 'Interview by Eisenman.' In *Richard Serra/Writings Interviews*, pp. 141–56. Chicago: University of Chicago Press, 1994.

Ernst, Max. *Beyond Painting*. New York: Schulz, 1948.

Fer, Briony. 'Judd's Specific Objects.' In *On Abstract Art*, pp. 131–52. New Haven: Yale University Press, 1997.

—. 'The Work of Salvage: Eva Hesse's Latex Works.' In *Eva Hesse*, edited by Elisabeth Sussman, pp. 78–95. New Haven, CT: Yale University Press, 2002.

Finkelpearl, Tom. 'On the Ideology of Dirth.' In *David Hammons: Rousing the Rubble*, pp. 61–81. Cambridge, MA: MIT Press, 1991.

Foster, Hal. 'The Un/making of Sculpture' (1998). In *Richard Serra* (October files; 1), edited by Hal Foster; 1, pp. 175–200. Cambridge: MIT Press, 2000.

—. *Objets philosophiques: Une étude sur la sculpture de Charles Ray*. Paris: Bourse de Commerce – Pinault Collection, 2022.

—. 'Sculpture in a Sculptural Square: Charles Ray in Conversation with Hal Foster.' *Charles Ray: Figure Ground*, pp. 40–51. New York: The Metropolitan Museum of Art; Yale University Press, 2022.

Freud, Sigmund. *The Standard Edition of the Complete Psychological Works of Sigmund Freud: Vol. 21 (1927-1931): The Future of an Illusion: Civilization and its Discontents and Other Works*, edited by James Strachey. London: The Hogarth Press, 1966.

Fried, Michael. 'Art and Objecthood.' *Artforum* 5, no. 10 (June 1967), pp. 12–23. Reprinted in *Minimal Art: A Critical Anthology*, edited by Gregory Battock, p. 143. Ewing, NJ: University of California Press, 1995.

Fuchs, Rudi. 'Giotto's Circle.' In *Marien Schouten: 'Het vieze tafeltje.'* pp. 24–32. Exh. cat. Amsterdam: Stedelijk Museum, 1996.

Genet, Jean. 'The Studio of Alberto Giacometti.' In *Fragments of the Artwork*, translated by Charlotte Mandell. Redwood City, CA: Stanford University Press, 2003.

Giacometti, Alberto. *Ecrits*. Paris: Fondation Giacometti and Hermann, 2007.

Girardi, Anthony. 'I stood there trembling with anxiety – and I sensed an infinite scream passing through nature.' In Anne-Claire Schumacher, Marie-Émilie Fourneaux and Anthony Girardi, *Jonathan Tahon: Refuge/Silence*, pp. 56–63. Geneva: Musée Ariana, 2019.

Gorovoy, Jerry, and Pandora Tabatabai Asbaghi. *Louise Bourgeois: Blue Days and Pink Days*. Exh. cat. Milan: Fondazione Prada, 1997.

Greenberg, Clement. 'Towards a New Laocoon.' *Partisan Review* 7, no. 4 (July–August 1940), pp. 296–310.

Hammons, David. *David Hammons: Rousing the Rubble*. Cambridge, MA: MIT Press, 1991.

Hastings, Gail. 'The Power of Inclusion in Donald Judd's Art: Observations by an Artist.' *Art Journal* 77, no. 3 (Fall 2018), pp. 48–62.

Herder, Johann Gottfried, *Sculpture: Some Observations on Form and Shape from Pygmalion's Dream* (1778), edited and translated by Jason Gaiger. Chicago: The University of Chicago Press, 2002.

—. 'Über die schöne Kunst des Gefühls.' In *Sämtliche Werke* 8, edited by Bernard Suphan. Berlin: Weidmannsche Buchhandlung, 1878.

—. 'Von der Bildhauerkunst fürs Gefühl (Gedanken aus dem Garten zu Versailles).' *Sämtliche Werke* 8.

—. *Viertes Wäldchen*. In *Sämtliche Werke* 4, p. 64.

Hidding, Allaard. 'Geert Lap: 99 variaties.' *Geert Lap 99 Variaties/99 Variations*, pp. 4–13. Leeuwarden: Museum Het Princessehof, 1993.

Hlobil, Tomáš. 'Alexander Gottlieb Baumgarten: Ästhetik.' *Estetika* 46, no. 1 (2009), pp. 105–10.

Jędrzejczyk, Małgorzata. 'The Corporality of Form: Katarzyna Kobro and her Concept of Culture.' In *Katarzyna Kobro: The Movement of Space-Time*, edited by Katarzyna Słoboda and Małgorzata Jędrzejczyk, pp. 35–42. Łódź: Muzeum Sztuki; Cologne: Walther und Franz König, 2021.

Jones, Kellie. 'The Structure of Myth and the Potency of Magic.' In *David Hammons: Rousing the Rubble*, edited by Carole Kismaric, pp. 15–37. Exh. cat. New York: The Institute for Contemporary Art P.S. 1; Cambridge, MA: MIT Press, 1991.

Judd, Donald. 'It's Hard to Find a Good Lamp.' In *Donald Judd Furniture: Retrospective*, pp. 7–21. Rotterdam: Museum Boymans-van Beuningen, 1993.

—. '21 February 1993.' In *Writings*, pp. 810–18. New York: Donald Judd Foundation; David Zwirner Books, 2016.

—. 'Specific Objects.' In *Writings*, pp. 134–45. New York: Donald Judd Foundation; David Zwirner Books, 2016.

Kapfinger, Otto. 'The Art of Building in Brick.' In *Per Kirkeby: Brick Sculpture and Architecture. Catalogue Raisonné*, pp. 20–27. Cologne: Walther König, 1997.

Kenaan, Hagi. 'Touching Sculpture.' In *Sculpture and Touch*, edited by Peter Dent, pp. 45–60. London: Routledge, 2014.

Kobro, Katarzyna, and Wladyslaw Strzemiński. 'Composing the Space.' Translated by Ania Soliman. *October* 156 (Spring 2016), pp. 12–74.

Krauss, Rosalind. 'Allusion and Illusion in Donald Judd.' *Artforum* 4, no. 9 (May 1966), pp. 24–26.

—. 'LeWitt in Progress' (1976). In *Sol LeWitt: Critical Texts*, edited by Adachiara Zevi, pp. 239–49. Rome: I libri di AELUO, 1994.

—. 'Introduction.' In *Passages in Modern Sculpture*, pp. 1–6. New York: Viking Press, 1977.

—. 'The *Double Negative*: A New Syntax for Sculpture.' In *Passages in Modern Sculpture*, pp. 243–88. New York: Viking Press, 1977.

—. 'Grids' (1978). In *The Originality of Avant-Garde and Other Modernist Myths*, pp. 8–22. Cambridge, MA: MIT Press, 1985.

—. 'Sculpture in the Expanded Field' (1978). In *The Originality of the Avant-Garde and Other Modernist Myths*. Cambridge, MA: MIT Press, 1985, 276–90.

—. 'Sculpture in the Expanded Field.' *October 8* (Spring 1979), pp. 30–44.

—. 'Richard Serra: Sculpture' (1986). In *Richard Serra* (October files; 1), edited by Hal Foster, pp. 99–145. Cambridge, MA: MIT Press, 2000.

—. 'Portrait of the Artist as Filette.' In *Louise Bourgeois*, edited by Peter Weiermair, pp. 23–29. Exh. cat. Frankfurt: Frankfurter Kunstverein, 1989. English reprint: Zurich: Stemmle, 1995.

Krohn, Silke. 'Doubling and Pairing.' In *Hans Belmer—Louise Bourgeois: Double Sexus*, pp. 53–65. Exh. cat. The Hague: Gemeentemuseum, 2010.

—. 'Forme-Informe.' In *Hans Belmer—Louise Bourgeois: Double Sexus*, pp. 67–83. Exh. cat. The Hague: Gemeentemuseum, 2010.

—. 'Diana van Efeze.' In *Hans Belmer—Louise Bourgeois: Double Sexus*, pp. 85–97. Exh. cat. The Hague: Gemeentemuseum, 2010.

—. 'Histoire de l'oeil.' In *Hans Belmer—Louise Bourgeois: Double Sexus*, pp. 99–111. Exh. cat. The Hague: Gemeentemuseum, 2010.

Kumar, Brinda. 'Holding Space.' In Kelly Baum and Brinda Kumar, *Charles Ray: Figure Ground*. Exh. cat. New York: The Metropolitan Museum of Art; Yale University Press, 2022, pp. 30–39.

Kuspit, Donald. 'Sol LeWitt: The Look of Thought.' *Art in America* 63, no. 5 (September–October 1975), pp. 43–49.

Larsen, Ane Hejlskov. 'Between Minimalism and Romanticism: The Aesthetics and Iconography of Brick in Kirkeby's Painting and Sculpture.' In *Per Kirkeby: Brick Sculpture and Architecture: Catalogue Raisonné*, pp. 28–46. Cologne: Walther König, 1997.

LeWitt, Sol. 'Sentences on Conceptual Art.' In *Sol LeWitt Critical Texts*, edited by Adachiara Zevi, pp. 88–90. Rome: I libri di AELUO, 1994.

Lippard, Lucy. 'Eccentric Abstraction.' *Art International* 10 (November 1966), p. 28.

Maas, Sander van. 'Profound Obscenities.' In Heringa/Van Kalsbeek, *Controlled Accidents*. Amsterdam: Heringa/Van Kalsbeek, 2007, n.p.

Megged, Matti. *Dialogue in the Void: Beckett & Giacometti*. New York: Lumen Books, 1985.

Meyer-Thoss, Christiane. *Louise Bourgeois: Designing for Free Fall*, Zurich: Ammann, 1992.

Ovid. *Metamorphoses*, Book III, translated by Mary Innes. London: Penguin Books, 1955.

Paraskos, Michael. 'Bringing into Being: Vivifying Sculpture through Touch.' In *Sculpture and Touch*, edited by Peter Dent, pp. 61–70. Milton Park: Routledge, 2014.

Potts, Alex. *The Sculptural Imagination: Figurative, Modernist, Minimalist*. New Haven, CT: Yale University Press, 2000.

Rajchman, John. 'Fred Sandback's Line of Thought.' In *Fred Sandback*, pp. 8–24. Göttingen: Steidl/David Zwirner, 2009.

Rawsthorn, Alice. 'Introduction.' In *Aldo Bakker*, pp. 5–11. Rotterdam: nai010 publishers, 2016.

Ray, Charles, 'How Many Sculptures Can You Fit into a Room.' In *Charles Ray*, pp. 148–56. Exh. cat. Paris, Editions du Centre Pompidou; Bourse de Commerce—Pinault Collection, 2022.

Rider, Alistair. *Carl Andre: Things in Their Elements*. London: Phaidon, 2011.

Rousseau, Pascal. 'Ann Veronica Janssens: Light Games.' www.artpress.com/wp-content/uploads/2014/12/2583.pdf.

Sandback, Fred. 'Notes' (1973). Reprinted in *Fred Sandback*, edited by Christiane Meyer-Stoll and Friedemann Malsch, p. 120. Vaduz: Kunstmuseum Liechtenstein; Hatje Cantz, 2005.

—. 'Untitled' (1975). Reprinted in *Fred Sandback*, edited by Christiane Meyer-Stoll and Friedemann Malsch, p. 95. Vaduz: Kunstmuseum Liechtenstein; Hatje Cantz, 2005.

—. 'Pedestrian Sculptures: Ingrid Rein Interviews the Minimal Artist Fred Sandback' (1975). Reprinted in *Fred Sandback*, edited by Christiane Meyer-Stoll and Friedemann Malsch, p. 102. Vaduz: Kunstmuseum Liechtenstein; Hatje Cantz, 2005.

Schaardenburg, Lieneke van. 'Carl Andre: "Ik wil uit de tijd zijn."' *Vrij Nederland*, 27 April 1968.

Seitz, William C. *The Art of Assemblage*. Exh. cat. New York: Museum of Modern Art, 1961.

Sénéchal, Philippe. 'Animals in Silver and Stone: Materials and Presence in Charles Ray.' In *Charles Ray*, pp. 125–32. Paris: Pinault Collection; Centre Pompidou, 2022.

Serra, Richard. *Writings/Interviews*. Chicago: University of Chicago Press, 1994.

—. 'Donald Judd, 1928–1994.' *Parkett* 40–41 (1994), pp. 176–77.

—, and Friedrich Teja Bach. 'Interview.' In Richard Serra and Clara Weyergraf, *Serra: Interviews, Etc. 1970–1980*, pp. 48–49. Yonker, NY: Archer Fields; Hudson River Museum, 1980.

—, and Liz Béar. 'Sight Point '71–'75/ Delineator '74–'76.' In Richard Serra and Clara Weyergraf, *Serra: Interviews, Etc. 1970–1980*, pp. 58, 61–62. Yonker, NY: Archer Fields; Hudson River Museum, 1980.

—, and Peter Eisenman. 'Interview.' *Skyline* April 1989, pp. 14–17.

—, and Hal Foster. *Conversations about Sculpture*. New Haven and London: Yale University Press, 2018.

Shattuck, Roger. *The Banquet Years*. New York: Harcourt Brace, 1958.

Simmel, Georg. 'Michelangelo and the Metaphysics of Culture.' In: *Essays on Art and Aesthetics*, edited and with an introduction by Austin Harrington, pp. 279–97. Chicago: The University of Chicago Press, 2020.

Słoboda, Katarzyna. 'Katarzyna Kobro: The Movement of Space-Time.' In *Katarzyna Kobro: The Movement of Space-Time*, edited by Katarzyna Słoboda and Małgorzata Jędrzejczyk, pp. 9–33. Łódź, Muzeum Sztuki, 2021.

Smithson, Robert. 'A Thing is a Hole in a Thing It Is Not.' Reprinted in *Robert Smithson: The Collected Writings*, edited by Jack Flam, pp. 95–96. Berkeley, CA: University of California Press, 1994.

Stoichita, Victor. *The Pygmalion Effect: From Ovid to Hitchcock*, translated by Alison Anderson. Chicago: University of Chicago Press, 2008.

Strzemiński, Wladyslaw. 'Modern Art in Poland.' *L'Espace uniste*, edited and translated Antoine Baudin and Pierre-Maxime Jedryka. Lausanne: L'Age d'Homme, 1977.

—, and Katarzyna Kobro. 'The Composition of Space: Calculations of Spatio-Temporal Rhythm.' *L'Espace uniste*, edited and translated by Antoine Baudin and Pierre-Maxime Jedryka. Lausanne: L'Age d'Homme, 1977.

Sylvester, David. 'Interview.' In *Looking at Giacometti*, pp. 123–48. New York: Henry Holt and Company, 1994.

Teresa of Avila. *The Life of Saint Teresa of Ávila by Herself* (1565). London: Penguin Classics, 2002.

Tuchman, Phyllis. 'Interview with Carl Andre' (1970). *Artforum* 8, no. 10, pp. 55–61.

Verhagen, Erik. 'Endogenous/Exogenous Didier Vermeiren's Dangling Signs.' In *Didier Vermeiren: Solides Géométriques, Vues d'Atelier*, pp. 55–65. Paris: Musée Bourdelle, 2005.

Weiss, Jeffrey. 'Sense of Site.' In *Judd*, edited by Ann Temkin, pp. 188–204. New York: The Museum of Modern Art, 2020.

Zacharias, Kyllikki. 'Dolly and Prosthesis.' *Hans Belmer—Louise Bourgeois: Double Sexus*, pp. 33–51. Exh. cat. The Hague: Gemeentemuseum, 2010.

Index

About the Author

Ernst van Alphen (1958) is professor emeritus of Literary Studies at Leiden University. Before that he was Queen Beatrix Professor of Dutch Studies and Professor of Rhetoric at UC Berkeley. He is particularly interested in issues that are central in modern and post-modern literature and in the relation between literature and the visual arts. He published not only widely on literature, but also on art and photography. His most important publications on art are *Francis Bacon and the Loss of Self* (Harvard UP), *Armando: Shaping Memory* (NAi Publishers), *Caught By History: Holocaust Effects in Contemporary Art, Literature, and Theory* (Stanford UP), *Art In Mind: How Contemporary Images Shape Thought* (University of Chicago Press), *Staging The Archive: Art and Photography in the Age of New Media* (Reaktion Books), *Failed Images: Photography and Its Counter-Practices* (Valiz) and *Shame! And Masculinity* (ed., Valiz).

Author: Ernst van Alphen
Copy-editing: Neil Fawle
Proofreading: Els Brinkman
Index: Elke Stevens
Image editing: Ernst van Alphen, Simon Pillaud
Project editor: Simone Wegman
Design: Sam de Groot
Layout assistance: Jonathan Blaschke
Typefaces: Eldorado (William Addison Dwiggins, 1953), Computer Modern (Donald Knuth, 1984), SKI DATA (Tariq Heijboer, 2014)
Lithography: Mariska Bijl, Wilco Art Books
Paper: Munken Print White, 100 grs 1.5 (inside), Munken Lynx Rough, 300 grs (cover)
Printing and binding: Wilco Art Books, Amersfoort Scanlaser, Zaandam: POD
Publisher: Valiz, Amsterdam, 2023, www.valiz.nl Astrid Vorstermans & Pia Pol

This publication has been printed on FSC-certified paper by an FSC-certified printer. The FSC, Forest Stewardship Council promotes environmentally appropriate, socially beneficial, and economically viable management of the world's forests. fsc.org

Distribution
NL/LU: Centraal Boekhuis, www.cb.nl
BE: EPO, www.epo.be
Europe/Asia: Idea Books, www.ideabooks.nl
GB/IE: Central Books, www.centralbooks.com
USA */Canada/Latin America*: D.A.P., www.artbook.com
Australia: Perimeter Books, www.perimeterbooks.com
Individual orders: www.valiz.nl; info@valiz.nl

Amsterdam, 2023; POD 2024
ISBN 978-94-93246-15-7
Printed and bound in the EU